Lions' Commentary on UNIX 6th Edition with Source Code

COMPUTER CLASSICS REVISITED

Peter H. Salus, *Series Editor*

Other Books in the Series:

Packet Communication

Before the Internet Volume 1:
Planning the ARPANET

Before the Internet Volume 2:
Building the ARPANET

Lions' Commentary on UNIX 6th Edition with Source Code

Originally circulated as two restricted-release volumes:

UNIX OPERATING SYSTEM SOURCE CODE LEVEL SIX

and

A COMMENTARY ON THE UNIX OPERATING SYSTEM

John Lions

With Forewords by Dennis M. Ritchie and Ken Thompson;
Prefatory Notes by Peter H. Salus and Michael Tilson;
a Historical Note by Peter H. Salus; and Appreciations by Greg Rose,
Mike O'Dell, Berny Goodheart, Peter Collinson, and Peter Reintjes

PEER-TO-PEER
COMMUNICATIONS

Lions' Commentary on UNIX 6th Edition with Source Code

Computer Classics Revisited Series
Series Editor: Peter H. Salus

Published by:

Peer-to-Peer Communications LLC
PO Box 6970
Charlottesville, VA 22906-6970 U.S.A
Website: http://www.peerllc.com
Email: info@peerllc.com

Cover Design: Gordon Haber
Cover Illustration: Anne Wilkinson
Production: Bookwrights of Charlottesville, VA

Manufactured in the United States of America

3 4 5 6 7 8 9 10 11 12 13 14 15 16

ISBN 1-57398-013-7

The publisher offers discounts on this book when ordered in bulk quantities.

We are grateful to Addison-Wesley Publishing Company for permission to quote from Peter H. Salus' *A Quarter Century of UNIX* (1994).

DEDICATION

To Ken Thompson and Dennis Ritchie who created the UNIX software system and made the writing of this source code and commentary possible, to my former colleagues and students at the University of New South Wales for whom this book was originally prepared, and to my wife Marianne and daughters Katherine and Elizabeth who never tried to understand UNIX but always supported my work.

Lions Book /n./   The two parts of this book contained (1) the entire source listing of the UNIX Version 6 kernel, and (2) a commentary on the source discussing the algorithms. These were circulated internally at the University of New South Wales beginning 1976–77, and were, for years after, the *only* detailed kernel documentation available to anyone outside Bell Labs. Because Western Electric wished to maintain trade secret status on the kernel, the Lions book was never formally published and was only supposed to be distributed to affiliates of source licensees...In spite of this, it soon spread by *samizdat* to a good many of the early UNIX hackers.

— Eric S. Raymond, *New Hacker's Dictionary 2nd ed.*

CONTENTS

ACKNOWLEDGMENTS

My sincere thanks and appreciation go to everyone who helped get this book published even though it took 20 years to get there.

I would like to thank Dan Doernberg and the staff at Peer-to-Peer Communications, Inc. who have supported this publication. To SCO Inc. who followed the philosophy of UNIX and gave permission to publish these texts and arranged for the red tape to be overcome.

I am extremely grateful to Ken Thompson, Peter Collinson, Mike O'Dell, Peter Reintjes, Greg Rose and Michael Tilson who have contributed with their appreciations.

Finally, I am most indebted to Peter Salus and Dennis Ritchie who have both worked so hard producing this book and have battled through the legal barriers, and to Berny Goodheart whose unfailing persistence and invaluable friendship have helped me get this book out.

After producing the initial version of these booklets I was privileged to spend my sabbaticals in 1978, 1983 and 1989 at Bell Laboratories and work as part of the team. The support and friendship given by the many colleagues that I met there will never be forgotten. During that time, strong ties were formed between Bell Laboratories and my Australian colleagues, which resulted in several UNIX pioneers visiting Australia to work and speak at conferences. The Australian UNIX User Group appreciated this and greatly benefited from it.

John Lions

PREFATORY NOTES

When this book was first published, I was astonished by how much pleasure I got from reading what should have been a dry piece of technical documentation. John Lions had created a truly brilliant technical work. The UNIX operating system kernel code was itself an elegant work, and even today it remains worthy of study. John added a line-by-line analysis that was equally elegant. The source code and the annotations were perfectly suited to each other, and I haven't seen anything to equal this achievement since. A generation of operating system developers used this work as a key learning tool, and I wonder just how much it influenced the ultimate UNIX domination of technical workstations, internet servers, and business-critical computing. At the time, the circulation was limited, because it was an annotation of licensed proprietary source code. I'm very pleased that this work can now be made available to the public. It is part of our technical history, and we can still learn from it today.

Michael Tilson

Mike Tilson is President, UniForum Association and Chief Information Officer, The Santa Cruz Operation, Inc. (SCO).

In early 1993, I began preparing for the 25th birthday of the UNIX Operating System, created in the summer of 1969 by Dennis M. Ritchie, Ken Thompson, Doug McIlroy, and Rudd Canaday. One of the things I hoped to do by summer 1994 was to see legitimate publication of the material in this volume. John Lions was coming to the USENIX Association's celebration in Boston and would receive a Lifetime Achievement Award. Seeing this book would be a suitable tribute.

But that was not to be.

Thanks to the efforts of Dennis Ritchie, AT&T's lawyers stated that they had "no objection" to publication. Negotiations with Novell, purchasers of the UNIX system from AT&T, were sluggish. Then, late in 1995, came the announcement that The Santa Cruz Operation, Inc. ("SCO") had purchased UNIX from Novell. Dennis and I wrote to Mike Tilson and Doug Michels, executives at SCO we knew personally. Mike actually owned a copy of John Lions' work, treasured it, and within a short period of time had arranged with SCO's lawyers for permission.

John Lions' Code and Commentary volumes were the UNIX system's *samizdat* of the '70s and '80s. The code is now out of date. As most of the commentators note, the comments are not. To learn about operating systems one must read and understand code. John's work enabled many of us to do that.

In 1969 AT&T was an assemblage of telecommunications monopolies, including Bell Telephone Laboratories (a.k.a. BTL, Bell, Bell Labs, or The Labs) and the Western Electric Company. The former brought us a variety of research developments, including UNIX. The latter manufactured and marketed products. We have left the citations in the Code and Commentary as they appeared in 1977. The Labs are now part of Lucent; Western Electric is now AT&T Technologies.

I am proud to have been instrumental in finally bringing this to print. I can retire my many-generation photocopy now.

Peter H. Salus

Peter H. Salus, former Executive Director of USENIX and the Sun User Group, is Series Editor of "Computer Classics Revisited."

FOREWORDS

The appearance in open publication of John Lions' commentary on the code for the Sixth Edition UNIX operating system marks a satisfying culmination of a long story.

The propagation of UNIX has always showed a tense interplay between the interests of a changing commercial world and the research and academic communities. Remarkably liberal policies for distribution of the system's source code encouraged the seminal developments during the 1970s and 1980s; in particular, the widely available work on UNIX at the University of California at Berkeley was significant in building both today's Internet and the workstation industry. At the same time, the corporate guardians worried continually that they might be giving away all rights.

The tale of Lions' commentary illustrates the tensions. When Ken Thompson and I saw the two slim volumes containing the commentary and the code, we were both flattered by its very appearance, and also impressed by his depth of perception and by his skill in drawing lessons from the work. The UNIX Support Group was impressed too; in the course of time they reprinted it for Bell Labs training purposes. A couple of years later, John was invited to spend a year within that organization to consult and write further. This work and subsequent visits had effects that lasted for years: Bell Labs and the UNIX community have rejoiced in the talents of a crew of Australians raised under John's tutelage, some in his home institution of the University of New South Wales, some nearby at Sydney Uni, others elsewhere. Beyond Australia, the number of people throughout the world who learned about operating systems from John's book is large.

But still, the tension was evident: the very value and vividness of the Lions' commentary compelled caution, and so the license for the Seventh Edition of UNIX (1977) forbade using its source code as teaching material. Nevertheless, and despite official control, both Lions' work and the code for the Seventh Edition and its successors for the VAX architecture (32V from Bell Labs, the various BSD systems) remained sufficiently available, both internally and externally, for the important developments of the early 1980s.

The fundamental tension—how to publish software, comment on it, encourage learning from it, yet still retain commercial and technical control—still has not been resolved, and doubtless has no resolution. The Free Software Foundation wants all software available in source. Much of academia agrees in principle, but even there, important factions want to retain rights and make some money. The commercial world wants to guard rights carefully and make a lot of money. Over the years, UNIX has somehow steered a turbulent, sometimes crazily anarchic middle course.

Happily, SCO, the current leader in providing UNIX operating systems and applications, has agreed on the historical and educational value of republishing Lions's commentary and the source code on which it is based, and has consented to let it be published. I'm grateful to them.

The material in this monograph is indeed dated. You will not find here anything about graphics, about networks, about anything that's happened since 1975. You will find linear searches, primitive data structures, C code that wouldn't compile in 1979 let alone today, and an orientation towards a machine that's little more than a memory. You will see signs of sloppiness and naivete. But you will also see in the code an underlying structure that has lasted for a long time and has managed to accommodate vast changes in the computing environment. In Lions' commentary, you will see a fresh and questioning attitude, and the words and thoughts of someone deeply committed to education and learning. John clearly admired what he saw, but was quick to point out its inadequacies. He helped his students to understand the larger ideas and themes that were immanent in the code but not manifest, and also admitted where the code stumped him.

The document reproduced here educated a generation. It's notoriously one of the most-copied manuscripts of computerdom, and it's good to have it in the open record.

Dennis M. Ritchie

Finally—one of the most widely distributed underground computer science documents is freely available. I can still vividly remember the day in 1977 the first draft of these books came to me by mail. I took a casual look expecting very little. I ended up reading every word.

After 20 years, this is still the best exposition of the workings of a "real" operating system.

Ken Thompson

Ken Thompson and Dennis M. Ritchie shared the 1983 ACM Turing Award for the development and implementation of the UNIX operating system.

A HISTORICAL NOTE

In 1977, John Lions completed his *Commentary on the UNIX Operating System*, companion volume to his reproduction of the V6 source code. These two slim books may be the most important computer items never to be published. I asked him about the *Source Code* and the *Commentary*. He said:

> I was teaching Operating Systems; I was competing with a colleague who was teaching Compilers by getting students to write real compilers; so a code **reading** exercise seemed a good idea. Also **our** Unix license wasn't explicit enough to forbid the activity. Why Unix? There wasn't much choice. It was highly competent as you know, and it was much better than the competition (we had also acquired Brinch Hansen's SOLO system).

The March 1977 *UNIX NEWS* (vol. 2, no. 3) announced the availability of the book, to licensees, together with a note by Ferentz: "Ken Thompson has seen the first version of the book and reports that it is a good job." The price, including airmail, was $A17.70 (under $20 US, at that time). The UKUUG newsletter announced the availability of the code and commentary, but the next issue stated that future orders should be placed with Bell Laboratories and by 1978 the volumes were no longer available. They must be the most frequently photocopied books in the entire area of computer science. They carry the appropriate copyright notices and the restriction to licensees, but once again, there was no way that Western Electric could stem the circulation of something of such value. I confess to possessing both a many-generation photocopy and a copy, in the bright orange and red covers, inscribed to me by John Lions. ...

From Peter H. Salus, *A Quarter Century of UNIX* (Reading, MA: Addison-Wesley Publishing, 1994), 127-130; reprinted with the permission of the publisher.

UNIX OPERATING SYSTEM SOURCE CODE LEVEL SIX

This booklet has been produced for students at the University of New South Wales taking courses 6.602B and 6.657G.

It contains a specially edited selection of the UNIX Operating System source code, such as might be used on a typical PDP11/40 computer installation.

The UNIX Software System was written by K. Thompson and D. Ritchie of Bell Telephone Laboratories, Murray Hill, NJ. It has been made available to the University of New South Wales under a licence from the Western Electric Company.

J. Lions
Department of Computer Science
The University of New South Wales.
November 1977

Second Printing

6746 access	3472 getsid	2855 nosys	3439 setuid
6956 alloc	6181 getmdev	4999 notavail	8201 sgtty
0734 aretu:	3480 getpid	1771 nseg	3949 signal
1012 backup:	3413 getswit	6577 nulldev	2066 sleep
7040 badblock	3452 getuid	2864 nullsys	3595 smdate
4856 bawrite	4136 grow	5765 open	6086 smount
6585 bcopy	3420 gtime	5804 open1	1293 spl0:
4836 bdwrite	8165 gtty	6702 openi	1297 spl1:
5229 bflush	7067 ialloc	6791 owner	1302 spl4:
5055 binit	1284 idle:	2416 panic	1303 spl5:
6415 bmap	7134 ifree	6517 passc	1308 spl6:
4754 bread	7276 iget	8669 pcclose	1313 spl7:
4773 breada	6922 iinit	8763 pcleader	3614 ssig
4869 brelse	4899 incore	8648 pcopen	5979 sslep
4809 bwrite	0895 incupc:	8748 pcoutput	6028 stat
8274 canon	5018 iodone	8739 pcpint	6045 stat1
3538 chdir	6364 iomove	8682 pcread	3428 stime
3560 chmod	4982 iowait	8719 pcrint	4016 stop
3575 chown	7344 iput	8710 pcstart	8183 stty
8234 cinit	3991 issig	8701 pcwrite	0827 subyte:
0676 clearseg:	7414 itrunc	5259 physio	0826 suibyte:
3725 clock	7374 iupdat	7723 pipe	0860 suiword:
5846 close	3630 kill	7862 plock	6144 sumount
6643 closef	8055 klclose	2433 prdev	1739 sureg
6672 closei	8023 klopen	7882 prele	6811 suser
5038 clrbuf	3062 klread	2340 printf	0861 suword:
1244 copyin:	8078 klrint	2369 printn	5196 swap
1252 copyout:	8090 klsgtty	4204 procxmt	2178 swtch
0696 copyseg:	8066 klwrite	3667 profil	3486 sync
4094 core	8070 klxint	4043 psig	3845 timeout
6542 cpass	1393 ldiv:	3963 psignal	3656 times
5781 creat	5909 link	4164 ptrace	2693 trap
2447 deverror	8879 lpcanon	0967 putc:	2841 trap1
5096 devstart	8863 lpclose	2386 putchar	8535 ttread
0890 display:	8976 lpint	5731 rdwr	8486 ttrstrt
1319 dpadd:	8850 lpopen	5711 read	8505 ttstart
1327 dpcmp:	8986 lpoutput	6221 readi	8550 ttwrite
6069 dup	8967 lpstart	7758 readp	8333 ttyinput
1650 estabur	8870 lpwrite	0740 retu:	8373 ttyoutput
3020 exec	1401 lrem:	3205 rexit	8577 ttystty
3219 exit	1410 lshift:	5123 rhstart	7689 uchar
2268 expand	1550 main	5420 rkaddr	6824 ufalloc
6847 falloc	7455 maknode	5451 rkintr	3510 unlink
8252 flushtty	2528 malloc	5476 rkread	7201 update
3322 fork	5156 mapalloc	5440 rkstart	3270 wait
7000 free	5182 mapfree	5389 rkstrategy	2113 wakeup
6014 fstat	6326 max	5483 rkwrite	7477 wdir
0815 fubyte:	2556 mfree	0889 savfp:	8217 wflushtty
0814 fuibyte:	6339 min	0725 savu:	5720 write
0844 fuiword:	5952 mknod	3354 sbreak	6276 writei
0845 fuword:	9016 mmread	7679 schar	7805 writep
4921 getblk	9042 mmwrite	1940 sched	4433 xalloc
0930 getc:	7518 namei	5861 seek	4490 xccdec
5336 geterror	1826 newproc	3460 setsid	4398 xfree
6619 getf	3493 nice	2156 setpri	4368 xswap
7167 getfs	6566 nodev	2134 setrun	

File param.h	2369 printn	File text.c	6045 stat1	8023 klopen
File systm.h	2386 putchar	4368 xswap	6069 dup	8055 klclose
File seg.h	2416 panic	4398 xfree	6086 smount	8062 klread
File proc.h	2433 prdev	4433 xalloc	6144 sumount	8066 klwrite
File user.h	2447 deverror	4490 xccdec	6181 setmdev	8070 klxint
File low.s	File malloc.c	File buf.h	File rdwri.c	8078 klrint
File m40.s	2528 malloc	File conf.h	6221 readi	8090 klsstty
0676 _clearseg:	2556 mfree	File conf.c	6276 writei	File tty.c
0696 _copyseg:	File reg.h	File bio.c	6326 max	8165 stty
0725 _savu:	File trap.c	4754 bread	6339 min	8183 stty
0734 _aretu:	2693 trap	4773 breada	6364 iomove	8201 sstty
0740 _retu:	2841 trap1	4809 bwrite	File subr.c	8217 wflushtty
0814 _fuibyte:	2855 nosys	4836 bdwrite	6415 bmap	8234 cinit
0815 _fubyte:	2864 nullsys	4856 bawrite	6517 passc	8252 flushtty
0826 _suibyte:	File sysent.c	4869 brelse	6542 cpass	8274 canon
0827 _subyte:	File sys1.c	4899 incore	6566 nodev	8333 ttyinput
0844 _fuiword:	3020 exec	4921 getblk	6577 nulldev	8373 ttyoutput
0845 _fuword:	3205 rexit	4982 iowait	6585 bcopy	8486 ttrstrt
0860 _suiword:	3219 exit	4999 notavail	File fio.c	8505 ttstart
0861 _suword:	3270 wait	5018 iodone	6619 getf	8535 ttread
0889 _savfp:	3322 fork	5038 clrbuf	6643 closef	8550 ttwrite
0890 _display:	3354 sbreak	5055 binit	6672 closei	8577 ttystty
0895 _incupc:	File sys4.c	5096 devstart	6702 openi	File pc.c
0930 _setc:	3413 setswit	5123 rhstart	6746 access	8648 pcopen
0967 _putc:	3420 stime	5156 mapalloc	6791 owner	8669 pcclose
1012 _backup:	3428 stime	5182 mapfree	6811 suser	8682 pcread
1244 _copyin:	3439 setuid	5196 swap	6824 ufalloc	8701 pcwrite
1252 _copyout:	3452 setuid	5229 bflush	6847 falloc	8710 pcstart
1284 _idle:	3460 setgid	5259 physio	File alloc.c	8719 pcrint
1293 _sp10:	3472 setgid	5336 geterror	6922 iinit	8739 pcpint
1297 _sp11:	3480 getpid	File rk.c	6956 alloc	8748 pcoutput
1302 _sp14:	3486 sync	5389 rkstrategy	7000 free	8763 pcleader
1303 _sp15:	3493 nice	5420 rkaddr	7040 badblock	File lp.c
1308 _sp16:	3510 unlink	5440 rkstart	7067 ialloc	8850 lpopen
1313 _sp17:	3538 chdir	5451 rkintr	7134 ifree	8863 lpclose
1319 _dpadd:	3560 chmod	5476 rkread	7167 setfs	8870 lpwrite
1327 _dpcmp:	3575 chown	5483 rkwrite	7201 update	8879 lpcanon
1393 _ldiv:	3595 smdate	File file.h	File iget.c	8967 lpstart
1401 _lrem:	3614 ssig	File filsys.h	7276 iget	8976 lpint
1410 _lshift:	3630 kill	File ino.h	7344 iput	8986 lpoutput
File main.c	3656 times	File inode.h	7374 iupdat	File mem.c
1550 main	3667 profil	File sys2.c	7414 itrunc	9016 mmread
1650 estabur	File clock.c	5711 read	7455 maknode	9042 mmwrite
1739 sureg	3725 clock	5720 write	7477 wdir	
1771 nseg	3845 timeout	5731 rdwr	File nami.c	
File slp.c	File sig.c	5765 open	7518 namei	
1826 newproc	3949 signal	5781 creat	7679 schar	
1940 sched	3963 psignal	5804 open1	7689 uchar	
2066 sleep	3991 issig	5846 close	File pipe.c	
2113 wakeup	4016 stop	5861 seek	7723 pipe	
2134 setrun	4043 psig	5909 link	7758 readp	
2156 setpri	4094 core	5952 mknod	7805 writep	
2178 swtch	4136 grow	5979 sslep	7862 plock	
2268 expand	4164 ptrace	File sys3.c	7882 prele	
File prf.c	4204 procxmt	6014 fstat	File tty.h	
2340 printf	File text.h	6028 stat	File kl.c	

#	Symbol	Value	#	Symbol	Value	#	Symbol	Value	#	Symbol	Value	#	Symbol	Value
5372	ARDY	0100	0489	EMFILE	24	5696	IREAD	0400	0160	PUSER	100	7975	TBDELAY	006000
7993	ASLEEP	0100	0496	EMLINK	31	5627	ISGID	02000	0158	PWAIT	40	2615	TBIT	020
7992	BUSY	040	0488	ENFILE	23	5694	ISGID	02000	2605	R0	(0)	7984	TIMEOUT	01
8617	BUSY	04000	0484	ENODEV	19	7987	ISOPEN	04	2606	R1	(-2)	7961	TTHIWAT	50
4584	B_ASYNC	0400	0468	ENOENT	2	5626	ISUID	04000	2607	R2	(-9)	7951	TTIPRI	10
4576	B_BUSY	010	0474	ENOEXEC	8	5693	ISUID	04000	2608	R3	(-8)	7962	TTLOWAT	30
4586	B_DELWRI	01000	0478	ENOMEM	12	5628	ISVTX	01000	2609	R4	(-7)	7952	TTOPRI	20
4574	B_DONE	02	0493	ENOSPC	28	5695	ISVTX	01000	2610	R5	(-6)	7963	TTYHOG	256
4575	B_ERROR	04	0480	ENOTBLK	15	5684	ITEXT	040	2611	R6	(-3)	0311	UBMAP	0170200
4579	B_MAP	040	0485	ENOTDIR	20	5680	IUPD	02	2612	R7	(1)	0308	UDSA	0177660
4577	B_PHYS	020	0490	ENOTTY	25	5683	IWANT	020	7971	RAW	040	0306	UISA	0177640
4573	B_READ	01	0472	ENXIO	6	5630	IWRITE	0200	5094	RCOM	04	0304	UISD	0177600
4583	B_RELOC	0200	0612	EOF	3	5697	IWRITE	0200	8014	RDRENB	01	3706	UMODE	0170000
4581	B_WANTED	0100	0467	EPERM	1	0165	KL	0177560	8614	RDRENB	01	2659	UMODE	0170000
4572	B_WRITE	0	0497	EPIPE	32	8008	KLADDR	0177560	8611	READING	2	2662	USER	020
0140	CANBSIZ	256	0495	EROFS	30	8009	KLBASE	0176500	5367	RESET	0	0103	USIZE	16
8840	CAP	01	8618	ERROR	0100000	7968	LCASE	04	5121	RHRCOM	070	7977	VTDELAY	040000
7990	CARR_ON	020	0494	ESPIPE	29	8812	LPADDR	0177514	5120	RHWCOM	060	8610	WAITING	1
7955	CEOT	004	0469	ESRCH	3	8819	LPHWAT	100	5363	RKADDR	0177400	5093	WCOM	02
7954	CERASE	'#'	0491	ETXTBSY	26	8818	LPLWAT	50	0315	RO	02	5373	WLO	020000
7958	CINTR	0177	7973	EVENP	0200	8817	LPPRI	10	0106	ROOTINO	1	0316	WO	04
7956	CKILL	'@'	0483	EXDEV	18	8821	MAXCOL	80	2613	RPS	(2)	7985	WOPEN	02
1509	CLOCK1	0177546	3018	EXPRI	-1	0135	MAXMEM	(64*32)	0317	RW	06	7967	XTABS	02
1510	CLOCK2	0172540	8847	FORM	014	0130	NBUF	15	3707	SCHMAG	10			
8609	CLOSED	0	5519	FPIPE	04	0143	NCALL	20	2660	SETD	0170011			
0141	CMAPSIZ	100	5517	FREAD	01	0146	NCLIST	100	0385	SIDL	4			
7957	CQUIT	034	5518	FWRITE	02	8012	NDL11	0	0123	SIGBUS	10			
7976	CRDELAY	030000	5095	GO	01	0134	NEXEC	3	0120	SIGEMT	7			
7970	CRMOD	020	5368	GO	01	0132	NFILE	100	0121	SIGFPT	8			
5374	CTLRDY	0200	7966	HUPCL	01	0131	NINODE	100	0114	SIGHUP	1			
0107	DIRSIZ	14	0147	HZ	60	8011	NKL11	1	0117	SIGINS	4			
8010	DLBASE	0175610	5681	IACC	04	7974	NLDELAY	001400	0115	SIGINT	2			
7980	DONE	0200	5620	IALLOC	0100000	0133	NMOUNT	5	0119	SIGIOT	6			
8616	DONE	0200	5687	IALLOC	0100000	0105	NODEV	(-1)	0122	SIGKIL	9			
8815	DONE	0200	5092	IENABLE	0100	0139	NOFILE	15	0126	SIGPIPE	13			
5369	DRESET	014	5370	IENABLE	0100	0144	NPROC	50	0116	SIGQIT	3			
5371	DRY	0200	7981	IENABLE	0100	5364	NRK	4	0124	SIGSEG	11			
8013	DSRDY	02	8615	IENABLE	0100	5365	NRKBLK	4872	0125	SIGSYS	12			
0473	E2BIG	7	8814	IENABLE	0100	0113	NSIG	20	0118	SIGTRC	5			
0479	EACCES	13	5631	IEXEC	0100	0145	NTEXT	40	0138	SINCR	20			
0477	EAGAIN	11	5698	IEXEC	0100	0104	NULL	0	0391	SLOAD	01			
0475	EBADF	9	5624	IFBLK	060000	7972	ODDP	0100	0393	SLOCK	04			
2658	EBIT	1	5691	IFBLK	060000	8843	OPEN	04	0142	SMAPSIZ	100			
0481	EBUSY	16	5623	IFCHR	020000	8607	PCADDR	0177550	0384	SRUN	3			
0476	ECHILD	10	5690	IFCHR	020000	8624	PCIHWAT	250	0137	SSIZE	20			
7969	ECHO	010	5622	IFDIR	040000	8620	PCIPRI	30	0382	SSLEEP	1			
0318	ED	010	5689	IFDIR	040000	8623	PCOHWAT	100	7988	SSTART	010			
0482	EEXIST	17	5621	IFMT	060000	8622	PCOLWAT	50	0387	SSTOP	6			
0466	EFAULT	106	5688	IFMT	060000	8621	PCOPRI	40	0394	SSWAP	010			
0492	EFBIG	27	5625	ILARG	010000	0155	PINOD	-90	0392	SSYS	02			
0470	EINTR	4	5692	ILARG	010000	7715	PIPSIZ	4096	0395	STRC	020			
0487	EINVAL	22	5679	ILOCK	01	0157	PPIPE	1	0166	SW	0177570			
0471	EIO	5	5682	IMOUNT	010	0156	PRIBIO	-50	0383	SWAIT	2			
0486	EISDIR	21	8844	IND	010	0164	PS	0177776	0396	SWTED	040			
8842	EJECT	02	3914	IPCPRI	(-1)	0159	PSLEP	90	2661	SYS	0104400			
8820	EJLINE	60	5629	IREAD	0400	0154	PSWP	-100	0386	SZOMB	5			

```
aa         2556 2563
abae       5123 5125 5134
abn        7040 7046
abp        5156 5157 5171 5259
           5260 5268 5336 5337
           5341 5389 5390 5396
ac         8333 8340 8373 8382
access     3041 3552 4109 5815
           5817 6746 7563 7604
           7658
addr       8024 8039 8041 8043
           8044 8051 8052 8079
           8082 8083 8084 8086
           8508 8513 8515 8518
           8522
adev       4773 4778 4785 4795
           4899 4905 4906
adx        2344 2346 2355 2357
           2361
afp        7040 7045
aip        6221 6222 6229 6276
           6277 6284 6746 6747
           6751
alloc      6435 6448 6468 6480
           6497 6956
an         6364 6370
ARDY       5372
aretu      0724 0734 2106 2242
ars        3845 3871
ASLEEP     7993 8224 8562
atp        8217 8218 8221 8252
           8253 8257 8274 8275
           8282 8333 8334 8339
           8486 8490 8505 8506
           8512 8535 8536 8540
           8550 8551 8555 8577
           8578 8581
av         8577 8578 8582
av_back    4526 4884 4889 5008
           5009 5063
av_forw    4525 4888 4891 4953
           4960 5008 5009 5063
           5235 5236 5407 5412
           5470
backp      4872 4884 4888 4889
           4890
backup     1009 1012 1015 1047
           2812
badblock   6970 7008 7040
badtrap    1465 1468
bap        6419 6437 6439 6473
           6479 6484 6491 6497
           6499 6506
base       5264 5269 5273 5278
           5291 5305 5306 5307
           5308

bawrite    4845 4856 6310
bcopy      3238 6124 6585 6931
           6976 7019 7220 7636
bdevsw     4617 4622 4656 4763
           4785 4795 4819 4843
           4906 4934 5060 5076
           5212 6113 6166 6689
           6722 6926
bdp        5060 5076 5077
bdwrite    4836 6311 6443 6449
           6485 6500 6501
bfls       1049 1060 1094 1108
           1204 1238
bflush     5229 7230
bfreelis   4567 4878 4879 4880
           4884 4891 4932 4953
           4954 4955 4960 5062
           5063 5068 5069 5070
           5071 5235
bisger     3375 3386
binit      1614 5055
blkno      4754 4758 4773 4780
           4781 4799 4899 4908
           4921 4938 4974 5196
           5209
bmap       6248 6298 6415 7626
bno        6958 6967 6968 6970
           6973 6981 7000 7008
           7016 7025
bp1        8278 8319 8322
bread      3282 4754 4799 6051
           6116 6258 6305 6472
           6488 6927 6973 7097
           7319 7386 7426 7431
           7625
breada     4773 6256
brelse     3195 3298 4791 4822
           4848 4869 5028 5073
           6062 6118 6129 6172
           6261 6308 6481 6487
           6503 6932 6977 7112
           7324 7332 7436 7440
           7602 7624 7656
buf        4520 4523 4524 4525
           4526 4535 4555 4556
           4557 4558 4567 4721
           4756 4775 4810 4812
           4837 4839 4857 4859
           4870 4872 4902 4923
           4983 4985 5000 5002
           5019 5021 5057 5065
           5097 5101 5124 5128
           5157 5160 5183 5231
           5260 5263 5337 5339
           5387 5390 5392 5421
           5423 5442 5453 6365

buffers    4720 5067
BUSY       7992 8617 8691
bwrite     3239 4809 4863 4963
           5241 7021 7221 7400
b_addr     3049 3153 3238 3290
           4529 5044 5067 5107
           5136 5210 5305 5307
           6052 6124 6125 6371
           6437 6473 6491 6931
           6935 6974 7017 7098
           7174 7212 7220 7328
           7387 7427 7432 7433
           7636
B_ASYNC    4584 4793 4820 4862
           4887 4962 5027 5239
b_back     4524 4556 4967 4968
           4970 4971 5062 5068
           5070 5080
b_blkno    2454 4531 4908 4938
           4974 5209 5309 5402
           5428 6442 6450 6470
           6484 6498
B_BUSY     4576 4887 4941 4966
           5010 5072 5165 5169
           5202 5206 5219 5295
           5299 5321
B_DELWRI   4586 4817 4823 4847
           4961 5237
b_dev      2453 4527 4819 4843
           4883 4908 4938 4973
           5066 5207 5238 5300
           5399 5429 5431
B_DONE     4574 4759 4782 4790
           4817 4847 4989 5026
           5214 5315
b_error    4532
B_ERROR    4575 4817 4882 5220
b_error    5311
B_ERROR    5342
b_error    5343
B_ERROR    5403 5467 7323
b_flags    4522 4759 4761 4782
           4783 4790 4793 4816
           4817 4847 4862 4876
           4878 4879 4882 4887
           4941 4942 4954 4961
           4962 4966 4989 5010
           5024 5026 5027 5030
           5072 5111 5140 5172
           5186 5200 5237 5239
           5295 5296 5299 5315
           5318 5321 5342 5397
           5403 5467 7323
b_forw     4523 4555 4907 4937
           4967 4968 4969 4971
           4972 5062 5069 5070

           5071 5079
B_MAP      4579 5024 5172 5186
B_PHYS     4577 5206 5299 5397
B_READ     2034 2042 4573 4761
           4783 4793 4817 5111
           5140 5479 6260
B_RELOC    4583 4966
b_resid    4533 5322
B_WANTED   4581 4876 4878 4879
           4887 4942 4954 5030
           5166 5187 5203 5216
           5219 5296 5318 5321
b_wcount   4528 4762 4784 4794
           4818 5108 5137 5208
           5310
B_WRITE    4572 5486 6306 6373
           6386
b_xmem     4530 5110 5134 5139
           5173 5178 5211 5308
call       0555 0558 0561 0564
           0567 0570 0574 0577
           0752 0776 2669 2771
call1      0762 0771
callo      0260 3727 3847
callout    0265 3748 3750 3767
           3768 3773 3853
callp      2696 2754 2755 2761
           2762 2765 2771
CANBSIZ    0140 0202 8316
canon      8274 8543
canonb     0202 8291 8300 8316
           8320
CAP        8840 8884
CARR_ON    7990 8046 8285 8541
           8556
cblock     8140 8141 8146 8149
           8237
cc         8635 8731 8743 8754
           8830 8981 8988
ccc        8835 8910 8918 8935
           8937 8941 8942 8946
           8950 8954 8955 8962
ccp        8236 8239 8240 8244
           8246 8247
cdevsw     4635 4641 4669 6234
           6287 6685 6716 8213
           8238 8245
cdp        8238 8245
CEOT       7955 8306
CERASE     7954 8048
cf         8636 8831
cfree      8146 8239 8240
cfreeli    0928 0954 0955 0977
           0979 0986 0988
cfreelis   8149 8241 8242
chan       2066 2076 2089 2113
```

Symbol	References
	2118
chdir	2924 3538
chmod	2927 3560
chown	2928 3575
cinit	1613 8234
CINTR	7958 8344 8345
CKILL	7956 8049
cl	8637 8832
clearses	0675 0676 1566 3134 3395 4155
clist	7908 7928 7929 7930 8634 8643 8644
clock	0569 0570 3725
CLOCK1	1509 1601
CLOCK2	1510 1603
cloop	7542 7667
close	2918 5846
CLOSED	8609 8653 8675
closef	3230 5854 6643
closei	6656 6672
clrbuf	5038 6982
CMAPSIZ	0141 0203
colp	8378 8400 8401 8402 8404 8423 8429 8435 8436 8442 8443 8448 8454 8458 8459 8475
com	5102 5109 5112 5114 5115 5129 5138 5141 5142 5143
cont	7106 7110
copsu	1245 1253 1264
copyin	1243 1244 6374
copyout	1243 1252 1630 6376
copyses	0695 0696 1915 2292 3380 3392 4152
core	4076 4094
coreaddr	5196 5210 5211
coremap	0203 1568 1896 1982 2278 2282 2293 3241 4383 4497
count	2668 2762 2765 5196 5208 6585 6592
cp1	7480 7483 7485
cp2	7480 7484 7485
cpass	6388 6542 8558 8705 8874 9057
cputype	0208 1459 1461 1571 1655 1746 1756 5133 5162
CQUIT	7957 8344
CRDELAY	7976
creat	2920 5781
cret	1429 1430
CRMOD	7970 8047 8342 8412
csv	1419 1420
CTLRDY	5374 5462
ctype	8379 8424 8426 8440 8441 8445 8452 8453 8468 8469 8472
curpri	0222 2141 2165 2224
c_arg	0263 3770 3776 3866 3871
c_cc	7910 8074 8223 8349 8543 8544 8560
c_cf	7911
c_cl	7912
c_func	0264 3748 3751 3769 3770 3774 3855 3861 3865 3870
c_next	8141 8241
c_time	0262 3751 3753 3767 3769 3775 3855 3856 3859 3864 3869
dev	2433 2436 2693 2700 2702 2718 3725 4754 4758 4763 4776 4778 4780 4781 4788 4789 4799 4901 4905 4908 4921 4927 4931 4934 4938 4973 5229 5238 5259 5300 5476 5479 5483 5486 6676 6679 6685 6689 6706 6709 6716 6722 6956 6961 6970 6973 6981 6988 7000 7004 7008 7016 7040 7048 7067 7072 7078 7097 7104 7120 7134 7138 7167 7173 7178 7276 7286 7296 7314 7319 8023 8026 8030 8033 8039 8040 8042 8055 8057 8062 8063 8066 8067 8070 8072 8078 8081 8090 8093 8648 8669 8850 8863 9016 9021 9031 9042 9047 9064
devblk	5096 5106 5123 5135
deverror	2447 5460
devloc	5096 5098 5104 5123 5125 5131
devstart	5096 5447
devtab	4551 4840 4903 4924 5058 5386
DIRSIZ	0107 0429 0433 3524 3526 7484 7486 7572 7576 7589 7608 7637 7638 7645
display	0888 0890 3740
DLBASE	8010 8043
dn	6226 6243 6245 6247 6250 6252 6256 6258 6281 6300 6302 6304 6305
DONE	7980 8518 8616 8691 8714 8815 8971
dpadd	1318 1319 3292 3293 3295 3296 5756 5890 5895 5986 6382 9051
dpcmp	1326 1327 5988 5989 5990 6243 6312
DRESET	5369
DRY	5371
DSRDY	8013 8051
dump	0521 0523 1352 1353 1355
dup	2953 6069
d_actf	4557 5409 5410 5444 5457 5470
d_active	4553 5414 5446 5455 5458
d_actl	4558 5412 5413
d_close	4619 4637 6166 6685 6689
d_errcnt	4554 5463 5469
d_major	2436 4606 4763 4785 4795 4819 4843 4906 4927 4934 6113 6166 6192 6234 6287 6680 6710 6926 8213
d_minor	2436 4605 4883 5399 5429 5431 8026 8030 8039 8040 8042 8057 8063 8067 8072 8081 8093 9021 9031 9047 9064
d_open	4618 4636 5076 6113 6716 6722 6926 8245
d_read	4638 6234
d_sgtty	4640 8213
d_strate	4620 4763 4785 4795 4819 5212
d_tab	4621 4843 4906 4934 5077
d_write	4639 6287
E2BIG	0473 3064
EACCES	0479 6778
EAGAIN	0477 3330
EBADF	0475 5740 6630
EBIT	2658 2753 2776
EBUSY	0481 6135 6163
ECHILD	0476 3317
ECHO	7969 8047 8361
ED	0318 1711
edata	0611 0651
EEXIST	0482 5930 5960
EFAULT	0466 5326 6378 6524
	6551 7695
EFBIG	0492 6424
EINTR	0470 2773
EINVAL	0487 3620 6157
EIO	0471 4193 5344 8751 8854
EISDIR	0486 5819
EJECT	8842 8857 8923 8927
EJLINE	8820 8927
eloop	7592 7643 7647
EMFILE	0489 6833
EMLINK	0496 5918
end	0611 0632 0654
ENFILE	0488 6863 7311
ENODEV	0484 6569
ENOENT	0468 7538 7612
ENOEXEC	0474 3102
ENOMEM	0478 1728
ENOSPC	0493 6989 7121
ENOTBLK	0480 6190
ENOTDIR	0485 3547 7560
ENOTTY	0490 8210
ENXIO	0472 6193 6727 8027 8654
EOF	8612 8689 8728
ep	7418 7432 7433 7434 7435
EPERM	0467 6816
EPIPE	0497 7827
EROFS	0495 6755
err	0855 0872 0880 1656 1658 1661 1663 1727
error	4219 4226 4234 4241 4248 4260 4281
ERROR	8618 8691 8722 8727 8750
esc	8891 8895 8899 8903 8908
ESPIPE	0494 5870
ESRCH	0469 3652 4177
estabur	1629 1650 3118 3138 3152 3371 4120 4146 4460
ETXTBSY	0491 3106 6759
EVENP	7973
EXDEV	0483 5937
exec	2923 3020
execnt	0210 3037 3038 3039 3196 3197 3198
exit	3209 3219 4032 4080 4278
expand	1628 2268 3129 3132 3383 3387 4148 4459 4473
EXPRI	3018 3038
falloc	5827 6847 7731 7737

fetch	1051 1173 1180 1184	setblk	3040 3237 4758 4781	IFMT	3041 3522 3546 4110	ip_addr	3937 4185 4218 4220
	1222		4789 4921 6123 6304		5621 5688 5818 5921		4225 4227 4232 4240
ff	4368 4382		6928 6981 7016 7216		6189 6233 6242 6286		4242 4247 4249 4254
file	5507 5513 5807 6849	setc	0926 0930 8258 8259		6297 6682 6711 7559	ip_data	3938 4184 4191 4220
	6854 8204		8264 8292 8520 8544		8209		4227 4235 4242 4249
filsys	5561 7042		8673 8688 8714 8971	ifree	7134 7355		4264 4266 4268 4273
flag	4813 4816 4820 4823	seterror	4824 4992 5323 5336	iset	1616 1618 3519 7078	ip_lock	3935 4181 4183 4194
	6364 6373 6386 7518	setf	5736 5850 5866 6018		7276 7534 7664		4209
	7537 7603 7657 8023		6073 6619 8206	iinit	1615 6922	ip_reg	3936 4186 4189 4192
	8648 8652 8669 8671	ILARG	5625 5692 6427 6444				4211 4212 4282
	8833 8850 8853 8857	setfs	6754 6961 7004 7072		7425 7445	IREAD	5629 5696 5815 6651
	8863 8866 8884 8923		7138 7167 7383	ILOCK	1617 1619 5679 5926		7789 7850 7851
	8927 8936	setsid	2959 3472		7224 7225 7287 7303	ISGID	3176 5627 5694
flushtty	8227 8252 8346 8350	setmdev	6093 6151 6181		7316 7351 7868 7872	ISOPEN	7987 8045 8046
fmt	2340 2341 2348 2353	setpid	2932 3480		7888	issig	2073 2085 2821 3826
fork	2914 3322	setswit	2950 3413	IMOUNT	5682 6130 6168 7292		3991
FORM	8847 8859 8865 8921	setuid	2936 3452	incore	4780 4788 4899	ISUID	3171 5626 5693
	8928 8930	sid	3462 3464 3465 3466	incupc	0894 0895 3791	ISVTX	3568 4406 5628 5695
found	3329 3333 4176 4180		3467	IND	8844 8857 8936		5790
	6156 6160	GO	5095 5109 5138 5368	info	8142	ITEXT	3105 4410 4471 5684
found1	1994 2021		5461	ino	7070 7077 7078 7095		6758
found2	1983 2031	grow	2813 4056 4136		7100 7105 7107 7134	itrunc	4112 5825 7353 7414
FPIPE	5519 5746 5869 6649	stime	2925 3420		7143 7276 7286 7297	IUPD	3530 3570 3583 5680
	7746 7748	stty	2944 8165		7315 7319 7328		5942 6285 6318 6452
FREAD	5517 5713 5747 5753	sword	0818 0830 0848 0851	inode	5605 5659 5675 6147		6467 7382 7396 7448
	5814 5829 7748	hbcom	5096 5109		6161 6222 6227 6277		7462 7609 7751
free	7000 7435 7438 7442	hibyte	0180 3456 3476 3582		6282 6416 6793 7104	iupdat	6050 7226 7357 7374
from	6585 6586 6590		8585 8593		7105 7203 7225 7278	IWANT	5683 7288 7869 7889
fstat	2940 6014	httab	4728 4844		7285 7345 7521 8205		7890
fubyte	0807 0815 3058 4225	HUPCL	7966	inta	3921 4235 4254	IWRITE	4109 5630 5697 5817
	6550 7693	HZ	0147 3797 3800	intes	0175 2070 2095 2391		6651 6753 7604 7658
fuibyte	0809 0814 1564 4218	IACC	5681 6232 6285 7382		3416 3852 3872 4885		7776 7777 7836
	9034		7391 7462 7751		4892 5006 5011 8262	i_addr	5613 5672 5969 6191
fuiword	0813 0844 1602 1604	IALLOC	5620 5687		8266		6192 6234 6252 6287
	2734 2754 2756 2766	ialloc	7067 7459	IO	0641 1455		6302 6439 6440 6442
	4220	IALLOC	7463	iodone	5018 5404 5471		6447 6451 6456 6466
fun	3845 3870	ialloc	7728	iomove	6260 6306 6364		6470 6679 6680 6709
func	7518 7519 7532 7536	IALLOC	7752	iowait	4764 4800 4821 4982		6710 7082 7330 7389
	7574 7579 8510 8515	icode	1516 1630	ipc	3939 4181 4182 4183		7423 7430 8213
fuword	0811 0845 0847 2758	idle	1283 1284 2220 2423		4184 4185 4186 4189	i_atime	5614
	2763 3052 4227 8188	IENABLE	5092 5109 5138 5370		4190 4191 4192 4194	i_count	1883 3105 4472 5662
	8189 8190		7981 8051 8052 8615		4195 4209 4211 4212		6100 6681 7302 7306
FWRITE	5518 5722 5793 5795		8659 8663 8692 8732		4213 4218 4220 4225		7317 7350 7362 7750
	5816 5829 5832 6656		8814 8858		4227 4232 4235 4240		7787 7825
	7746	IEXEC	3041 3552 5631 5698		4242 4247 4249 4254	i_dev	3519 5663 5935 6051
f_count	1878 5510 5836 6079		6764 6765 7563		4264 4266 4268 4273		6053 6162 6260 6300
	6655 6657 6855 6857	IPCPRI	3914 4182 4190		4282		6422 6754 7104 7286
	7739	IFBLK	5624 5691 6100 6189	ipc	3939 4181 4182 4183		7314 7355 7383 7386
f_flag	5509 5739 5746 5829		6242 6297 6314 6688	iput	3194 3232 3533 3534		7426 7431 7435 7438
	5869 6649 6656 7746		6719 7421		3549 3554 3571 3584		7442 7459 7534 7625
	7748	IFCHR	5623 5690 6100 6233		4126 4411 5839 5931		7662
f_inode	5511 5754 5755 5830		6286 6314 6684 6713		5936 5945 5972 6037	i_flag	1617 1619 3105 3530
	5894 5895 6021 6650		7421 8209		6137 6169 6194 6691		3570 3583 4410 4471
	6656 7747 7749 7764	IFDIR	3522 3546 5622 5689		6802 7091 7325 7344		5661 5926 5942 6130
	7810 8208		5818 5921 7559		7490 7663 7670 7733		6168 6232 6285 6318
f_offset	5512 5751 5752 5756				7741		5452 6467 6758 7224

```
                7225 7287 7288 7292
                7303 7316 7351 7359
                7382 7391 7396 7448
                7462 7609 7751 7868
                7869 7872 7888 7889
                7890
i_sid           3177 3582 5610 5669
                6771 7466
i_lastr         5673 6255 6259 7318
i_mode          3041 3171 3176 3522
                3546 3566 3569 4110
                4406 5607 5666 5818
                5921 6100 6189 6233
                6242 6286 6297 6314
                6427 6444 6651 6682
                6711 6764 6774 7081
                7082 7329 7354 7388
                7421 7425 7445 7463
                7559 7752 7776 7777
                7789 7836 7850 7851
                8209
i_mtime         5615
i_nlink         3529 5608 5667 5917
                5941 7352 7464
i_number        5664 6051 6052 6162
                7105 7286 7315 7355
                7360 7385 7482 7534
i_size0         5611 5670 5894 6243
                6312 6315 7446
i_size1         5612 5671 5895 6243
                6312 6316 7447 7589
                7772 7775 7835 7845
i_uid           3173 3174 3581 5609
                5668 6769 6798 7465
j               7070 7099 7101
jfls            1018 1193 1239
k               7070 7103 7104 7105
ka6             0322 1459 1460 1560
                1589 1599 2716 9032
                9065
kill            2949 3630
KISA0           0619 1447
KISA6           0743 1368 1448 1460
KISD0           0620 1449
KL              0165 2393 2397 2398
                2399 2406
kl11            8015 8030 8057 8063
                8067 8072 8081 8093
KLADDR          8008 8039 8041
KLBASE          8009 8041 8043
klclose         4671 8055
klin            0526 0558
klopen          4671 8023
klou            0527 0561
klrbuf          8018 8083
klrcsr          8017 8051 8084

klread          4671 8062
klress          8016
klrint          0557 0558 8078
klsstty         4671 8090
kltbuf          8020 8086
kltcsr          8019 8052
klwrite         4671 8066
klxint          0560 0561 8070
kwlp            0534 0535 0570
large           6445 6462
lbn             6225 6239 6248 6255
                6259
lbolt           0212 3797 3800 3808
                4925 8650 8660
LCASE           7968 8047 8309 8353
                8399
ldiv            1392 1393 2373 4143
                5434 6051 7319 7386
                7589 7626
link            2921 5909
lks             0226 1601 1602 1603
                1604 1607 3734
lobyte          0180 3443 3444 3455
                3464 3465 3475 3581
                8584 8592
loop            1951 1957 1969 2025
                2048 2195 2221 2347
                2362 3245 3260 3276
                3315 4020 4030 4930
                4945 4957 4964 5233
                5242 7075 7092 7119
                7283 7290 7298 7765
                7791 7812 7839 7854
                8290 8305
lp11            8837 8853 8857 8866
                8884 8910 8918 8923
                8924 8925 8926 8927
                8931 8935 8936 8937
                8941 8942 8946 8950
                8952 8954 8955 8957
                8960 8962 8971 8981
                8982 8988 8989 8990
LPADDR          8812 8853 8858 8971
                8972
lpbuf           8825 8972
lpcanon         8859 8865 8875 8879
                8909
lpclose         4675 8863
LPHWAT          8819 8988
lpint           0573 0574 8976
LPLWAT          8818 8981
lpopen          4675 8858
lpou            0541 0574
lpoutput        8929 8951 8956 8959
                8986
LPPRI           8817 8989

lpsr            8824 8853 8858 8971
lpstart         8967 8980 8992
lpwrite         4675 8870
lrem            1400 1401 2375 5433
                6052 7328 7387
lshift          1409 1410 5309 6239
                6294 9024 9055
main            0611 0669 1550
maknode         4105 5790 5966 7455
malloc          1896 1982 2282 2528
                3234 4375 4457
map             2515 2529 2532 2557
                2559
mapalloc        5156 5398
mapfree         5025 5182
maplock         5155 5165 5166 5167
                5169 5187 5188 5189
maptab          8117 8309 8311
max             6326 8443
MAXCOL          8821 8954
MAXMEM          0135
maxmem          0224 1567 1576
MAXMEM          1582
maxmem          1582 1662
mcc             8834 8924 8925 8950
                8952 8955 8957 8960
mfree           1568 1583 2044 2278
                2293 2556 3241 3283
                4383 4408 4497
min             1582 6241 6247 6296
                6339 7846
mknod           2926 5952
mlc             8836 8924 8926 8927
                8931
mmread          4682 9016
mmwrite         4682 9042
mode            5731 5735 5804 5812
                6746 6752 7455 7463
mount           0272 0277 6090 6103
                6148 6154 6933 6934
                7169 7172 7204 7210
                7281 7293 7294
mpid            0216 1841 1842 1843
                1849 1867
MTC             1373 1450
m_addr          2518 2536 2537 2541
                2564 2565 2567 2571
                2576 2577 2580 2581
m_bufp          0275 6104 6123 6124
                6125 6155 6170 6171
                6933 7173 7174 7211
                7212
m_dev           0274 6105 6122 6155
                6934 7173 7216 7296
m_inodp         0276 6121 6167 7295
m_size          2517 2534 2535 2538

                2542 2564 2565 2566
                2568 2569 2572 2576
                2578 2583 2584
namei           3034 3515 3543 4101
                5770 5786 5914 5928
                5958 6033 6097 6186
                6796 7518
nblkdev         4631 4927 5084 6192
                6720
NBUF            0130 4535 4720 5064
NCALL           0143 0265
nchrdev         4647 6714 8247
NCLIST          0146 8146 8240
NDL11           8012 8015 8026
newproc         1627 1826 3334
newsize         2268 2275 2277 2278
                2282
NEXEC           0134 3037 3196
NFILE           0132 5513 6854
nice            2946 3493
NINODE          0131 5675 6161 7103
                7223 7285
NKL11           8011 8015 8026 8042
                8043
NLDELAY         7974
NMOUNT          0133 0277 6103 6154
                7172 7210 7294
NODEV           0105 3040
nodev           4659 4660 4661 4662
                4663 4664 4665 4673
                4675 4677 4678 4679
                4680 4681 4682 4684
                4686 4687 4688 4689
                4690 4691
NODEV           5238 6123
nodev           6566
NODEV           6928 7230
nofault         0757 0766 0854 0855
                0871 0872 0876 0881
                0909 0910 0918 1224
                1225 1228 1232 1259
                1267 1273 1277 1465
                1466
NOFILE          0139 0438 1876 3227
                6624 6828
nospace         6966 6969 6986
nosys           2855 2939 2941 2945
                2951 2952 2957 2961
                2962 2963 2964 2965
                2966 2967 2968 2969
                2970 2971 2972 2973
                2974 2975
notavail        4948 4960 4999 5240
NPROC           0144 0376 1846 1960
                1991 2006 2120 2203
                2206 3246 3250 3277
```

```
            3327 3639 3810 3953
            4023 4172
nps         2693 3725
NRK         5364
NRKBLK      5365 5402
nseg        1657 1660 1771 3366
NSIG        0113 0447 3183 3225
            3619 3968
nswap       0232 1583 4698
NTEXT       0145 4314 4441
nulldev     4658 4682 4684 6577
nullsys     2864 2912 2942
ODDP        7972
ok          4256 4259 4261
on          6225 6240 6241 6260
            6280 6295 6296 6306
            9018 9025 9034 9044
            9056 9067
open        2917 5765
OPEN        8843 8853 8857
open1       5774 5795 5795 5804
openi       5832 6702
out1        6119 6136
owner       3564 3579 6791
pad         5575
panic       1605 1853 2051 2416
            2719 3236 3521 4377
            4381 4451 4458 4928
            4936 6930 7184 7300
panicstr    2328 2419
partab      7947 8424 8522
passc       6394 6517 8544 8695
            9038
pc          2693 2734 2754 2756
            2757 2766 2767 3725
            3791
pc11        8641 8645 8653 8657
            8658 8673 8675 8688
            8689 8693 8714 8721
            8724 8726 8728 8730
            8731 8734 8743 8744
            8754 8755 8756
PCADDR      8607 8659 8663 8674
            8691 8692 8714 8715
            8722 8727 8730 8732
            8750
pcclose     4673 8669
PCIHWAT     8624 8731
pcin        0530 0564 8643 8673
            8688 8693 8730 8731
            8734
PCIPRI      8620 8660 8693
pcleader    8664 8678 8763
PCOHWAT     8623 8754
PCOLWAT     8622 8743
pcopen      4673 8648

PCOPRI      8621 8755
pcou        0531 0567
pcout       8644 8714 8743 8744
            8754 8755 8756
pcoutput    8706 8748 8769
pcpbuf      8630 8715
pcpcsr      8629 8663 8714 8750
pcpint      0566 0567 8739
pcrbuf      8628 8730
pcrcsr      8627 8659 8674 8691
            8692 8722 8727 8732
pcread      4673 8682
pcrint      0563 0564 8719
pcstart     8710 8742 8758
pcstate     8642 8653 8657 8658
            8675 8689 8721 8724
            8726 8728
pcwrite     4673 8701
physio      5259 5479 5486
PINOD       0155 6963 7007 7074
            7289
pipe        2954 7723
PIPSIZ      7715 7835 7846
plock       7768 7815 7862
PPIPE       0157 7790 7838 7870
prdev       2433 2453 6988 7048
            7120 7178
prele       3518 3556 5826 6131
            7227 7358 7363 7786
            7799 7817 7826 7837
            7849 7882
pri         2066 2072 2078 2091
PRIBIO      0156 4943 4955 4990
            5297 5316
printf      1576 1577 1578 1579
            1580 2340 2421 2436
            2454 2716 2717 2718
            6862 7310
printn      2355 2369 2374
proc        0358 0376 1589 1590
            1591 1592 1593 1829
            1830 1846 1942 1943
            1960 1991 2006 2115
            2119 2136 2180 2182
            2185 2193 2206 2207
            3222 3246 3248 3250
            3273 3277 3324 3327
            3632 3639 3644 3728
            3810 3951 3953 3994
            4018 4023 4166 4172
procxmt     4028 4204
profil      2956 3667
PS          0164 0668 0677 0679
            0691 0697 0700 0720
            0726 0731 0735 0741
            0748 0756 0773 0777

            0783 0787 0790 0798
            0852 0853 0869 0870
            0877 0882 0932 0934
            0935 0958 0964 0970
            0973 0974 0999 1005
            1285 1286 1288 1294
            1298 1299 1304 1305
            1309 1310 1314 1444
            2070 2095
PS          2693 2699 2717 2753
            2776 3725 3759 3788
            3798 3824
PS          3852 3872 4885 4892
            5006 5011 8262 8266
psig        2074 2086 2105 2822
            3827 4043
psignal     2793 2818 3649 3955
            3963 7828
PSLEP       0159 5994
PSWP        0154 1955 1968 5167
            5204 5215
ptrace      2938 4164
PUSER       0160 2162 3817 3973
            3974
putc        0926 0967 8323 8355
            8358 8414 8478 8730
            8756 8990
putchar     2351 2359 2375 2386
            2401 2402 2403 2405
PWAIT       0158 3314
pword       0840 0865 0868
p_addr      0371 1589 1743 1894
            1904 1913 2042 2044
            2045 2193 2228 2276
            2290 2294 3134 3241
            3242 3282 3376 3388
            4149 4380 4383 4384
            4467
p_cpu       0366 2161 3795 3796
            3814 3815 3816
p_flag      0361 1592 1862 1907
            1961 1992 2007 2023
            2046 2143 2208 2240
            2241 2286 3170 3224
            3289 3302 3303 3309
            3998 4028 4169 4187
            4379 4385 4466 4468
            4479 5312 5317
p_nice      0367 1865 2162 3502
p_pid       0369 1849 1867 1868
            3247 3251 3278 3281
            3285 3304 3335 3344
            3482 3642 4024 4174
            4175 4183 4209
p_ppid      0370 1868 3247 3251
            3252 3259 3278 3286

            4022 4024 4175
p_pri       0362 2078 2091 2141
            2167 2209 2211 3817
p_sig       0363 3287 3305 3625
            3626 3971 3972 3997
            4000 4049 4050 4273
p_size      0372 1590 1893 1895
            1978 2042 2044 2274
            2275 3241 4119 4148
            4149 4374 4375
p_stat      0360 1591 1847 1861
            1903 1908 1961 1993
            2008 2077 2090 2140
            2208 3243 3253 3280
            3284 3301 3328 3811
            3973 3974 3975 4026
            4173
p_textp     0374 1752 1866 1879
            1979 2032 4378 4401
            4402 4448 4469
p_time      0365 1869 1962 1964
            2009 2011 2047 3812
            3813 4386
p_ttyp      0368 1864 3288 3644
            3954 8031 8032
p_uid       0364 1863 3174 3446
            3646
p_wchan     0373 2076 2089 2122
            2139
q           3221 3225 3226 3227
            3228 3229 3240 3241
            3242 3243 3247 3251
            3259 3632 3638 3640
            3644
qc          5393
ql          5393
r           0185 1561 1563 1573
            1574 1599 1600 1745
            1750 1755 1760 5175
            5177 5306 7726 7736
            7740 7745 9026 9027
            9029 9030 9032 9035
            9036 9059 9060 9062
            9063 9065 9068 9069
R0          2605 2679
r0          2693 2701 2777
R0          3208 3281 3304 3335
            3344 3416 3423 3432
            3443 3455 3456 3464
            3475 3476 3482 3497
            3623 3637
r0          3725 3825
R0          4079 4184 4191 5736
            5758 5831 5850 5853
            5866 5986 6018 6073
            6830 7736 7744 7745
```

```
          8206                 rkread    4684 5476            SIGFPT    0121 2793 2797 4071   SRUN      0384 1591 1861 1908
R1        2606 2679            rkstart   5415 5440 5464 5472   SIGHUP    0114                            1961 2008 2140 2208
r1        2693                 rkstrate  4658 5389 5479 5486   SIGINS    0117 2734 2736 4053   ssig      2960 3614
R1        3297 3305 3424 3433  rktab     4658 5386 5409 5410             4067                  SSIZE     0137 3118 3131 3150
r1        3725                           5412 5413 5414 5444   SIGINT    0115 8345            SSLEEP    0382 2008 2090
R1        7744                           5446 5455 5457 5458   SIGIOT    0119 2744 4069        sslep     2947 5979
R2        2607 2679                      5463 5469 5470        SIGKIL    0122 3619 3971        ssr       0759 0760 1013 1016
R3        2608 2679            rkwc      5380                  signal    3949 8345                      1021 1023 1028 1050
R4        2609 2679            rkwrite   4684 5483             SIGPIPE   0126 7828                       1150 1171 1465 1467
R5        2610 2679            RO        0315 1668 1674        SIGQIT    0116 4066 8345        SSR0      0613 0647 0759 0761
R6        2611 2679 3155 4055  rootdev   0228 1616 1618 4695   SIGSEG    0124 2815 4073                  0765 1354 1445
          4059                           6926 6927 6934 7728   SIGSYS    0125 2781 4074        SSR2      0760 1446
R7        2612 2679 3188 3347  rootdir   0206 1616 1617 7533   SIGTRC    0118 2740 4053 4068   SSTART    7988 8514
          4058 4061            ROOTINO   0106 1616 1618 7297   SINCR     0138 4143             SSTOP     0387 1993 3253 3301
rablkno   4773 4788 4789       RPS       2613 2679 4057 4060   sleep     1955 1968 2066 3038             4026 4173
rablock   0235 6253 6256 6454            4262                            3314 4182 4190 4943   SSWAP     0394 1907 2240 2241
          6456 6504 6506       rrkbuf    5387 5479 5486                  4955 4990 5167 5204             2286 4479
rabp      4775 4789 4790 4791  rsr       2315                            5215 5297 5316 5994   SSYS      0392 1592 1992 2007
          4793 4794 4795       runin     0218 1954 1955 2080             6963 7007 7074 7289   start     0521 0522 0611 0612
RAW       7971 8297 8344 8356            2081 2082 3820 3821             7790 7838 7870 8225             0614
          8386                           3822                            8287 8563 8660 8693   stat      2930 6028
rbr       2316                 runout    0219 1967 1968 2143             8755 8989             stat1     6021 6036 6045
RCOM      5094 5112                      2144 2145 4387 4388   SLOAD     0391 1592 1862 1961   stime     2937 3428
rdfls     5196 5206                      4389                            1992 2007 2023 2046   stop      3999 4016
RDRENB    8014 8051 8084 8614  runrun    0220 0770 0788 2142             2143 2208 4385        str       2433 2436
          8659 8692 8732                 2166 2196 3807        SLOCK     0393 1992 2007 4379   strat     5259 5261 5313
rdwr      5713 5722 5731       RW        0317 1684 1690 1707             4385 4466 4468 5312   STRC      0395 3170 3224 3309
read      2915 5711                      1711                            5317                            3998 4028 4169
readi     3090 3142 4464 5754  rw        5259 5299 6672 6685   sloop     1953 2004 2014        stty      2943 8183
          6221 7797                      6689 6702 6716 6722   SMAPSIZ   0142 0204             subyte    0807 0827 3161 6523
READING   8611 8724 8726       savfp     0888 0889 2698        smount    2933 6086             suibyte   0809 0826 9067
readp     5748 7758            savu      0724 0725 1889 1905   smp       6090 6102 6108 6109   suiword   0813 0860 4240 4242
resloc    0237 1011 1025 1038            2189 2281 2284 2846             6111 6121 6122 6123   sumount   2934 6144
          1148 2677 3186 4258            4476 4477                       6124 6125 6126 6127   sures     1724 1739 2229 2295
RESET     5367 5461            sbreak    2929 3354                       6128                  suser     3431 3444 3465 3500
retry     1840 1844 1850       schar     1552 4097 4101 7679   SP        2693 2811 3725 4136             3522 3579 5921 5957
retu      0724 0740 2193 2228  sched     1637 1940                       4137 4141 4143                  6800 6811
          2294                 SCHMAG    3707 3814 3815        sp10      1292 1293 1976 2022   suword    0811 0861 0864 3156
rexit     2913 3205            seek      2931 5861                       2079 2092 4944 4947             3159 3164 3661 4057
rfp       6646 6648 6649 6650  sep       1650 1654 1677 1698             4956 4959 4991 5170             4058 4247 4249 6055
          6655 6656 6657                 1714 3023 3094 3100             5218 5245 5320 5416             6059 8175 8176 8177
RHRCOM    5121 5141                      3118 3151                       5996 8228 8289 8565   SW        0166 2391 3416
rhstart   5123                 SETD      2660 2734                       8676 8697 8759 8993   SWAIT     0383 1993 2077 3975
RHWCOM    5120 5142            setsid    2958 3460                       9037 9070             swap      2034 2042 4380 4467
RKADDR    5363                 setpri    2156 2823 3818 3828   sp11      1292 1297 3803                  5196
rkaddr    5420                 setres    1089 1099 1117 1120   sp14      1292 1302 8672 8686   swapdev   0229 3237 3282 4696
RKADDR    5447                           1196                            8757 8991                      5207 5212
rkaddr    5447                 setrun    2123 2134 3254 3310   sp15      1292 1303 3766 5408   swaper    2035 2043 2050
RKADDR    5459 5460 5461 5462            3976 4188                       8222 8263 8283 8559   swapmap   0204 1583 2044 3234
rkba      5381                 setuid    2935 3439             sp16      1292 1308 1958 1990             3283 4375 4408 4457
rkcs      5379 5459 5461 5462  sstty     8171 8191 8201                  2075 2088 4886 4940   swbuf     4721 5200 5207 5208
rkda      5382 5447            SIDL      0385 1903                       4952 4988 5007 5164             5209 5210 5211 5212
rkds      5377 5460            sig       3949 3955 3963 3968             5201 5213 5234 5294   swplo     0231 1583 4697
rker      5378 5460                      3972                            5314                  swtch     0770 0791 2084 2093
rkintr    0576 0577 5451       SIGBUS    0123 2722 4072        sp17      1292 1313 3854 5983             2178 2287 3256 4027
rkio      0544 0577            SIGEMT    0120 2748 4070                  9028 9061                       4480
```

Symbol	References
SWTED	0396 3302 3303 3309 4187
sync	2948 3486
SYS	2661 2759
sysent	2667 2670 2696 2754 2755 2761 2910
SZOMB	0386 3243 3280
s_flock	5570 6127 6936 6962 6963 6972 6978 6979 7006 7007 7015 7022 7023 7214
s_fmod	5572 6983 7005 7026 7084 7144 7213 7217
s_free	5567 6967 6976 7012 7019 7025
s_fsize	5564 7047
s_ilock	5571 6126 6937 7073 7074 7094 7116 7117 7139 7213
s_inode	5569 7077 7107 7143
s_isize	5563 7047 7096
s_nfree	5565 6965 6967 6971 6975 6987 7010 7011 7014 7018 7020 7025 7175 7179
s_ninode	5568 7076 7077 7107 7108 7113 7118 7141 7143 7176 7180
s_ronly	5573 6128 6754 6938 7214 7383
s_time	5574 6939 6940 7218 7219
t00	1056 1059
t01	1056 1079 1085 1101
t02	1056 1102
t03	1056 1103
t04	1056 1104
t05	1056 1105
t06	1056 1106
t07	1056 1093
t10	1057 1062
t11	1057 1110
t12	1057 1111
t13	1057 1112
t14	1057 1113
t15	1057 1114
t16	1057 1107
t17	1057 1140 1188
TBDELAY	7975
TBIT	2615 4060
text	4306 4314 4436 4441
tim	3845 3851
time	0213 3423 3424 3432 3433 3801 3802 3804 3806 5984 5985 5988 5989 6050 6939 6940
	7218 7219 7226 7357 7392 7393
timeout	3845
TIMEOUT	7984 8491 8518
timeout	8524
TIMEOUT	8525
times	2955 3656
tmtab	4727 4844
to	6585 6586 6591
tout	0214 3434 3804 3805 5989 5990 5991 5992 5994
trap	0512 0513 0514 0515 0516 0517 0518 0538 0547 0548 0549 0555 0752 0754 0755 0762 2693
trap1	2771 2841
trf	5804 5813 5824
TTHIWAT	7961 8560
TTIPRI	7951 8287
TTLOWAT	7962 8074
TTOPRI	7952 8225 8563
ttrbuf	8157
ttrcsr	8156
ttread	8063 8535
ttrstrt	8486 8524
ttstart	8073 8363 8492 8505 8561 8568
tttbuf	8159 8522
tttcsr	8158 8518
ttwrite	8067 8550
tty	7926 8015 8025 8056 8071 8080 8092 8218 8220 8253 8255 8275 8279 8334 8337 8374 8377 8488 8506 8509 8536 8538 8551 8553
TTYHOG	7963 8349
ttyinput	8087 8333
ttyoutpu	8362 8373 8392 8403 8413 8566
ttystty	8094 8577
t_addr	7932 8044 8082 8513
t_canq	7929 8258 8321 8543 8544
t_char	7940
t_col	7935 8393 8423
t_delct	7934 8265 8284 8294 8359
t_dev	7942 8033
t_erase	7936 8048 8299 8584 8592
t_flags	7931 8047 8297 830y 8336 8341 8342 8344 8353 8356 8361 8386
	8390 8399 8412 8440 8452 8463 8468 8586 8594
t_kill	7937 8049 8304 8585 8593
t_outq	7930 8074 8075 8223 8225 8259 8261 8414 8478 8520 8560 8563
t_rawq	7928 8260 8264 8287 8292 8349 8355 8357 8358
t_speeds	7941 8583 8591
t_state	7938 8045 8046 8059 8224 8285 8491 8514 8518 8525 8541 8556 8562
u	0646 0659 0662 0744 1440 1441
u0	1067 1096
u1	1067 1189
u2	1067 1190
u3	1067 1191
u4	1067 1087
u5	1067 1071 1075 1097
u6	1067 1069
u7	1067 1192
ub	6045 6055 6056 6059 6060
UBMAP	0311 1573 1574 5175 5177
uchar	3026 3034 3513 3515 3541 3543 5768 5770 5784 5786 5912 5914 5928 5955 5958 6031 6033 6091 6097 6184 6186 6794 6796 7689
UDSA	0308 5306
ufalloc	6076 6824 6852
uid	3441 3443 3444 3445 3446 3447
UISA	0306 1563 1599 1745 1750 1763 5306 9026 9029 9032 9035 9059 9062 9065 9068
UISA0	0678 0680 0690 0698 0701 0719 1451
UISA1	0699 0702 0718 1452
UISD	0304 1561 1600 1755 1760 1763 9027 9030 9036 9060 9063 9069
UISD0	0681 0682 0686 0703
UISD1	0704 0706 0716 1454
UMODE	2659 2699 3706 3788 3824
unlink	2922 3510
update	2420 3489 6150 7201
updlock	0234 1559 7207 7209 7229
user	0413
USER	2662 2700 2721 2733 2739 2743 2747 2751 2796 2810
USIZE	0103 0636 0646 0662 1442 1560 1590 1628 1662 1682 3129 3131 3133 3370 4116 4119 4233 4459 4467 4473
u_ar0	0452 2701 2812 3155 3187 3188 3208 3281 3297 3304 3305 3335 3344 3347 3416 3423 3424 3432 3433 3443 3455 3456 3464 3475 3476 3482 3497 3623 3637 3825 4055 4057 4058 4059 4060 4061 4079 4184 4191 4258 4262 5736 5758 5831 5850 5853 5866 5986 6018 6073 6830 7736 7744 7745 8206
u_arg	0440 2763 2766 2770 3052 3056 3085 3095 3096 3097 3099 3101 3105 3116 3117 3140 3141 3208 3297 3364 3568 3569 3581 3582 3618 3624 3649 3661 3662 3670 3671 3672 3673 4075 4079 4168 4174 4185 4186 4439 4455 4461 5743 5744 5756 5758 5773 5774 5790 5873 5875 5876 5880 5927 5966 5969 6021 6036 6096 6113 6128 8174 8187 8188 8189 8190 8590
u_base	0425 3085 3139 3525 4115 4121 4463 5269 5743 6372 6374 6376 6381 6522 6523 6530 6549 6550 6557 7488 9050
u_cdir	0428 1618 1619 1883 3232 3554 3555 7531
u_count	0426 3086 3141 3526 4116 4122 4461 5273 5291 5310 5322 5744 5756 5758 6230 6241 6262 6290 6296 6319

```
                   6383 6527 6531 6546    u_ofile   0438 1876 3227 5835              8580 8582 8583 8584
                   6554 7486 7589 7600              5853 6078 6626 6829              8585 8586 8590 8591
                   7639 7811 7818 7846              6856 7740                        8592 8593 8594
                   7847 9048 9049         u_pdir    0435 5935 5936 7459   VTDELAY    7977 8463
u_cstime   0451 3291 3292 3293                      7489 7490 7606       wait       2919 3270
           3336 3337                      u_procp   0424 1593 1743 1752   WAITING    8610 8657 8658 8721
u_cutime   0450 3294 3295 3296                      1859 1891 1917 2071   wakeup     2082 2113 2145 3197
           3339 3340                                2273 2793 2818 2823              3248 3249 3434 3805
u_dbuf     0429 7484 7570 7572                      3134 3170 3174 3224              3808 3822 4025 4195
           7576 7645 7646                           3240 3278 3314 3326              4213 4389 4877 4880
u_dent     0434 3519 3525 3527                      3376 3388 3446 3482              5031 5188 5217 5319
           7482 7483 7488 7636                      3502 3625 3626 3638              6652 6653 6979 7023
           7640 7646 7664                           3794 3828 3996 4021              7117 7778 7852 7891
u_dirp     0430 2770 4100 5927                      4048 4119 4148 4149              8075 8260 8261 8357
           6096 7682 7693                           4169 4175 4209 4273              8734 8744 8982
u_dsize    0442 3149 3152 3369                      4401 4402 4448 4465   WCOM       5093 5114
           3371 3373 4146 5291                      4478 4479 5312 5317   wdir       5940 7467 7477
u_error    0419 1728 2752 2773                      7828 8031 8032        wflushtt   8058 8217 8589
           2774 2775 2777 2857    u_prof    0453 3127 3670 3671   WLO        5373
           3064 3092 3102 3106              3672 3673 3790 3791   WO         0316 1762
           3317 3330 3547 3620    u_qsav    0445 2106 2846        WOPEN      7985
           3652 4052 4099 4103    u_rgid    0423 3465 3467 3475   write      2916 5720
           4127 4177 4193 5326    u_rsav    0415 1889 2189 2281   writei     3528 4118 4124 5755
           5343 5344 5740 5788              4476                             6276 7489 7848
           5819 5822 5833 5870    u_ruid    0422 3444 3447 3455   writep     5749 7805
           5918 5930 5933 5937              4111                  x1         2340 2346
           5960 5964 6094 6114    u_sesfls  0418 3089 3091 4117   x2         2340
           6117 6135 6152 6157              4123 5745 6372 6521   x3         2340
           6163 6190 6193 6262              6548 7487 7587        x4         2340
           6307 6319 6378 6424    u_sep     0444 3151 3152 3365   x5         2340
           6524 6551 6569 6630              3371 4146 5276 5306   x6         2340
           6727 6755 6759 6778    u_signal  0447 2734 3183 3225   x7         2340
           6816 6833 6863 6929              3623 3624 4003 4051   x8         2340
           6989 7121 7311 7538              4054                  x9         2340
           7548 7560 7571 7580    u_ssav    0446 1905 2242 2284   xa         2340
           7612 7695 7827 8027              4477                  xalloc     3130 4433
           8172 8210 8654 8751    u_ssize   0443 3150 3152 3370   xb         2340
           8854 9038 9057                   3371 3376 3378 3389   xbr        2318 2399
u_fsav     0416 3189 4255                   4141 4143 4146 4150   xc         2340
u_gid      0421 3177 3466 3476              4156 5292             xccdec     4378 4403 4490
           6771 7466              u_stime   0449 3293 3338 3793   xfree      3128 3233 4398
u_ino      0432 3519 3527 7482    u_tsize   0441 3148 3152 3366   xswap      1906 2024 2285 4368
           7640 7664                        3371 4146 5275                   4478
u_intfls   0454 2772 2845 2848    u_uid     0420 3172 3173 3445   XTABS      7967 8047 8390
u_name     0433 7483 7646                   3456 3567 3646 4111   x_caddr    1753 2036 4309 4497
u_offset   0427 3087 3088 3140              6763 6769 6798 6814   x_ccount   1881 1980 2033 2039
           3524 4113 4114 4462              7465                             4313 4453 4475 4483
           5309 5751 5752 6239    u_uisa    0436 1665 1678 1694              4495 4496
           6240 6244 6294 6295              1699 1715 1716 1717   x_count    1880 4312 4404 4447
           6309 6313 6315 6316              1744                             4452
           6382 6528 6529 6555    u_uisd    0437 1666 1719 1720   x_daddr    2034 4308 4409 4457
           6556 7585 7586 7608              1721 1754                        4467
           7622 7626 7636 7638    u_utime   0448 3296 3341 3660   x_iptr     4311 4405 4407 4442
           7642 7795 7796 7798              3789                             4446 4454
           7844 7845 7846 9024    v         8090 8091 8094 8167   x_size     1981 2034 2037 4310
           9025 9051 9055 9056              8170 8201 8202 8213              4408 4456 4497
```

1

Initialisation
Process Initiation

```
0100 /* fundamental constants: do not change */
0101
0102
0103 #define USIZE 16    /* size of user block (*64) */
0104 #define NULL 0
0105 #define NODEV (-1)
0106 #define ROOTINO 1  /* i number of all roots */
0107 #define DIRSIZ 14  /* max characters per directory */
0108
0109
0110 /* signals: do not change */
0111
0112
0113 #define   NSIG      20
0114 #define   SIGHUP     1        /* hangup */
0115 #define   SIGINT     2        /* interrupt (rubout) */
0116 #define   SIGQIT     3        /* quit (FS) */
0117 #define   SIGINS     4        /* illegal instruction */
0118 #define   SIGTRC     5        /* trace or breakpoint */
0119 #define   SIGIOT     6        /* iot */
0120 #define   SIGEMT     7        /* emt */
0121 #define   SIGFPT     8        /* floating exception */
0122 #define   SIGKIL     9        /* kill */
0123 #define   SIGBUS    10        /* bus error */
0124 #define   SIGSEG    11        /* segmentation violation */
0125 #define   SIGSYS    12        /* sys */
0126 #define   SIGPIPE   13        /* end of pipe */
0127
0128 /* tunable variables */
0129
0130 #define NBUF 15     /* size of buffer cache */
0131 #define NINODE 100 /* number of in core inodes */
0132 #define NFILE 100   /* number of in core file structures */
0133 #define NMOUNT 5    /* number of mountable file systems */
0134 #define NEXEC 3     /* number of simultaneous exec's */
0135 #define MAXMEM (64*32)  /* max core per process;
0136                          first number is kw */
0137 #define SSIZE 20    /* initial stack size (*64 bytes) */
0138 #define SINCR 20    /* increment of stack (*64 bytes) */
0139 #define NOFILE 15   /* max open files per process */
0140 #define CANBSIZ 256    /* max size of typewriter line */
0141 #define CMAPSIZ 100    /* size of core allocation area */
0142 #define SMAPSIZ 100    /* size of swap allocation area */
0143 #define NCALL 20    /* max simultaneous time callouts */
0144 #define NPROC 50    /* max number of processes */
0145 #define NTEXT 40    /* max number of pure texts */
0146 #define NCLIST 100 /* max total clist size */
0147 #define HZ 60       /* Ticks/second of the clock */
0148
0149
```

```
0150
0151 /* priorities: do not alter much */
0152
0153
0154 #define PSWP        -100
0155 #define PINOD       -90
0156 #define PRIBIO      -50
0157 #define PPIPE        1
0158 #define PWAIT        40
0159 #define PSLEP        90
0160 #define PUSER        100
0161
0162 /* Certain processor registers */
0163
0164 #define PS 0177776
0165 #define KL 0177560
0166 #define SW 0177570
0167
0168 /* -------------------------       */
0169
0170 /* structures to access integers : */
0171
0172
0173     /* single integer */
0174
0175 struct {   int    integ;   };
0176
0177
0178     /* in bytes  */
0179
0180 struct {   char lobyte;   char hibyte;   };
0181
0182
0183     /* as a sequence */
0184
0185 struct {   int    r[];   };
0186
0187
0188 /* -------------------------       */
0189
0190
0191
0192
0193
0194
0195
0196
0197
0198
0199
```

```
0200 /* various global variables */
0201
0202 char canonb[CANBSIZ];       /* buffer for erase and kill */
0203 int  coremap[CMAPSIZ];      /* space for core allocation */
0204 int  swapmap[SMAPSIZ];      /* space for swap allocation */
0205
0206 int  *rootdir;      /* pointer to inode of root directory */
0207
0208 int  cputype;       /* type of cpu =40, 45, or 70 */
0209
0210 int  execnt;        /* number of processes in exec */
0211
0212 int  lbolt;         /* time of day in 60th not in time */
0213 int  time[2];       /* time in sec from 1970 */
0214 int  tout[2];       /* time of day of next sleep */
0215
0216 int  mpid; /* generic for unique process id's */
0217
0218 char runin;         /* scheduling flag */
0219 char runout;        /* scheduling flag */
0220 char runrun;        /* scheduling flag */
0221
0222 char curpri;        /* more scheduling */
0223
0224 int  maxmem;        /* actual max memory per process */
0225
0226 int  *lks; /* pointer to clock device */
0227
0228 int  rootdev;       /* dev of root see conf.c */
0229 int  swapdev;       /* dev of swap see conf.c */
0230
0231 int  swplo;         /* block number of swap space */
0232 int  nswap;         /* size of swap space */
0233
0234 int  updlock;       /* lock for sync */
0235 int  rablock;       /* block to be read ahead */
0236
0237 char resloc[];      /* locs. of saved user registers
0238                            (see trap.c)  */
0239
0240
0241 /* ------------------------        */
0242
0243
0244
0245
0246
0247
0248
0249
0250
0251 /* ------------------------        */
0252
0253 /* The callout structure is for a routine
0254  * arranging to be called by the clock interrupt
0255  * (see clock.c), with a specified argument,
0256  * within a specified amount of time.
0257  * It is used, for example, to time tab delays
0258  * on teletypes. */
0259
0260 struct    callo
0261 {
0262     int  c_time;    /* incremental time */
0263     int  c_arg;     /* argument to routine */
0264     int  (*c_func)();        /* routine */
0265 } callout[NCALL];
0266 /* ------------------------        */
0267
0268 /* Mount structure:  used to locate
0269  * the super block of a mounted file.
0270  */
0271
0272 struct    mount
0273 {
0274     int  m_dev;     /* device mounted */
0275     int  *m_bufp;   /* pointer to superblock */
0276     int  *m_inodp;  /* pointer to mounted on inode */
0277 } mount[NMOUNT];
0278 /* ------------------------        */
0279
0280
0281
0282
0283
0284
0285
0286
0287
0288
0289
0290
0291
0292
0293
0294
0295
0296
0297
0298
0299
```

```
0300
0301 /* kt-11 addresses and bits */
0302
0303
0304 #define UISD  0177600 /* first user I-space descriptor
0305                          register */
0306 #define UISA  0177640 /* first user I-space address
0307                          register */
0308 #define UDSA  0177660 /* first user D-space address
0309                          register  */
0310
0311 #define UBMAP 0170200 /* access to 11/70 unibus map */
0312
0313
0314
0315 #define RO 02       /* access abilities */
0316 #define WO 04
0317 #define RW 06
0318 #define ED 010      /* expand segment downwards */
0319
0320 /* ------------------------         */
0321
0322 int       *ka6;    /* 11/40 KISA6; 11/45 KDSA6 */
0323
0324
0325
0326
0327
0328
0329
0330
0331
0332
0333
0334
0335
0336
0337
0338
0339
0340
0341
0342
0343
0344
0345
0346
0347
0348
0349
```

```
0350 /*
0351  * One structure allocated per active
0352  * process. It contains all data needed
0353  * about the process while the
0354  * process may be swapped out.
0355  * Other per process data (user.h)
0356  * is swapped with the process.
0357  */
0358 struct     proc
0359 {
0360   char     p_stat;
0361   char     p_flag;
0362   char     p_pri;  /* priority, negative is high */
0363   char     p_sig;  /* signal number sent to this process */
0364   char     p_uid;  /* user id, used to direct tty signals */
0365   char     p_time; /* resident time for scheduling */
0366   char     p_cpu;  /* cpu usage for scheduling */
0367   char     p_nice; /* nice for scheduling */
0368   int      p_ttyp; /* controlling tty */
0369   int      p_pid;  /* unique process id */
0370   int      p_ppid; /* process id of parent */
0371   int      p_addr; /* address of swappable image */
0372   int      p_size; /* size of swappable image (*64 bytes) */
0373   int      p_wchan;/* event process is awaiting */
0374   int      *p_textp;/* pointer to text structure */
0375
0376 } proc[NPROC];
0377 /* ------------------------         */
0378
0379 /* stat codes */
0380
0381 /*        null       0        not assigned */
0382 #define SSLEEP     1   /* sleeping on high priority */
0383 #define SWAIT      2   /* sleeping on low priority */
0384 #define SRUN       3   /* running */
0385 #define SIDL       4   /* process is being created */
0386 #define SZOMB      5   /* process is being terminated */
0387 #define SSTOP      6   /* process being traced */
0388
0389 /* flag codes */
0390
0391 #define SLOAD      01  /* in core */
0392 #define SSYS       02  /* scheduling process */
0393 #define SLOCK      04  /* process cannot be swapped */
0394 #define SSWAP      010 /* process is being swapped out */
0395 #define STRC       020 /* process is being traced */
0396 #define SWTED      040 /* another tracing flag */
0397
0398
0399
```

```
0400 /*
0401  * The user structure.
0402  * One allocated per process.
0403  * Contains all per process data
0404  * that doesn't need to be referenced
0405  * while the process is swapped.
0406  * The user block is USIZE*64 bytes
0407  * long; resides at virtual kernel
0408  * loc 140000; contains the system
0409  * stack per user; is cross referenced
0410  * with the proc structure for the
0411  * same process.
0412  */
0413 struct user
0414 {
0415   int u_rsav[2];     /* save r5,r6 when exchanging stacks */
0416   int u_fsav[25];    /* save fp registers */
0417                      /* rsav and fsav must be first in structure */
0418   char u_segfls;     /* flag for IO; user or kernel space */
0419   char u_error;      /* return error code */
0420   char u_uid;                /* effective user id */
0421   char u_gid;                /* effective group id */
0422   char u_ruid;               /* real user id */
0423   char u_rgid;               /* real group id */
0424   int u_procp;       /* pointer to proc structure */
0425   char *u_base;      /* base address for IO */
0426   char *u_count;     /* bytes remaining for IO */
0427   char *u_offset[2];         /* offset in file for IO */
0428   int *u_cdir;  /* pointer to inode of current directory */
0429   char u_dbuf[DIRSIZ];       /* current pathname component */
0430   char *u_dirp;      /* current pointer to inode */
0431   struct    {                /* current directory entry */
0432     int      u_ino;
0433     char     u_name[DIRSIZ];
0434   } u_dent;
0435   int *u_pdir;       /* inode of parent directory of dirp */
0436   int u_uisa[16];    /* prototype segmentation addresses */
0437   int u_uisd[16];    /* prototype segmentation descriptors */
0438   int u_ofile[NOFILE]; /* pointers to file structures of
0439                         open files */
0440   int u_arg[5];      /* arguments to current system call */
0441   int u_tsize;       /* text size (*64) */
0442   int u_dsize;       /* data size (*64) */
0443   int u_ssize;       /* stack size (*64) */
0444   int u_sep;         /* flag for I and D separation */
0445   int u_qsav[2];     /* label variable for quits & interrupts */
0446   int u_ssav[2];     /* label variable for swapping */
0447   int u_signal[NSIG];        /* disposition of signals */
0448   int u_utime;       /* this process user time */
0449   int u_stime;       /* this process system time */
```

```
0450   int u_cutime[2];   /* sum of childs' utimes */
0451   int u_cstime[2];   /* sum of childs' stimes */
0452   int *u_ar0;                /* address of users saved R0 */
0453   int u_prof[4];     /* profile arguments */
0454   char u_intfls;     /* catch intr from sys */
0455                      /* kernel stack per user
0456                       * extends from u + USIZE*64
0457                       * backward not to reach here
0458                       */
0459 } u;
0460 /* ------------------------           */
0461
0462 /* u_error codes */
0463                      /* See section "INTRO(II)" of
0464                       * the UNIX Programmer's manual
0465                       * for the meanings of these codes.  */
0466 #define    EFAULT    106
0467 #define    EPERM     1
0468 #define    ENOENT    2
0469 #define    ESRCH     3
0470 #define    EINTR     4
0471 #define    EIO       5
0472 #define    ENXIO     6
0473 #define    E2BIG     7
0474 #define    ENOEXEC   8
0475 #define    EBADF     9
0476 #define    ECHILD    10
0477 #define    EAGAIN    11
0478 #define    ENOMEM    12
0479 #define    EACCES    13
0480 #define    ENOTBLK   15
0481 #define    EBUSY     16
0482 #define    EEXIST    17
0483 #define    EXDEV     18
0484 #define    ENODEV    19
0485 #define    ENOTDIR   20
0486 #define    EISDIR    21
0487 #define    EINVAL    22
0488 #define    ENFILE    23
0489 #define    EMFILE    24
0490 #define    ENOTTY    25
0491 #define    ETXTBSY   26
0492 #define    EFBIG     27
0493 #define    ENOSPC    28
0494 #define    ESPIPE    29
0495 #define    EROFS     30
0496 #define    EMLINK    31
0497 #define    EPIPE     32
0498
0499
```

```
0500 / low core
0501
0502 br4 = 200
0503 br5 = 240
0504 br6 = 300
0505 br7 = 340
0506
0507 . = 0^.
0508     br      1f
0509     4
0510
0511 / trap vectors
0512     trap; br7+0.          / bus error
0513     trap; br7+1.          / illegal instruction
0514     trap; br7+2.          / bpt-trace trap
0515     trap; br7+3.          / iot trap
0516     trap; br7+4.          / power fail
0517     trap; br7+5.          / emulator trap
0518     trap; br7+6.          / system entry
0519
0520 . = 40^.
0521 .globl     start, dump
0522 1: jmp     start
0523    jmp     dump
0524
0525 . = 60^.
0526    klin; br4
0527    klou; br4
0528
0529 . = 70^.
0530    pcin; br4
0531    pcou; br4
0532
0533 . = 100^.
0534    kwlp; br6
0535    kwlp; br6
0536
0537 . = 114^.
0538    trap; br7+7.          / 11/70 parity
0539
0540 . = 200^.
0541    lpou; br4
0542
0543 . = 220^.
0544    rkio; br5
0545
0546 . = 240^.
0547    trap; br7+7.          / programmed interrupt
0548    trap; br7+8.          / floating point
0549    trap; br7+9.          / segmentation violation
```

```
0550
0551 ////////////////////////////////////////////////
0552 /           interface code to C
0553 ////////////////////////////////////////////////
0554
0555 .globl     call, trap
0556
0557 .globl     _klrint
0558 klin:       jsr      r0,call; _klrint
0559
0560 .globl     _klxint
0561 klou:       jsr      r0,call; _klxint
0562
0563 .globl     _pcrint
0564 pcin:       jsr      r0,call; _pcrint
0565
0566 .globl     _pcpint
0567 pcou:       jsr      r0,call; _pcpint
0568
0569 .globl     _clock
0570 kwlp:       jsr      r0,call; _clock
0571
0572
0573 .globl     _lpint
0574 lpou:       jsr      r0,call; _lpint
0575
0576 .globl     _rkintr
0577 rkio:       jsr      r0,call; _rkintr
0578
0579
0580
0581
0582
0583
0584
0585
0586
0587
0588
0589
0590
0591
0592
0593
0594
0595
0596
0597
0598
0599
```

```
0600 / machine language assist
0601 / for 11/40
0602
0603 / non-UNIX instructions
0604 mfpi      = 6500^tst
0605 mtpi      = 6600^tst
0606 wait      = 1
0607 rtt       = 6
0608 reset     = 5
0609
0610 /* -------------------------      */
0611 .globl    start, _end, _edata, _main
0612 start:
0613    bit     $1,SSR0
0614    bne     start                  / loop if restart
0615    reset
0616
0617 / initialize systems segments
0618
0619    mov     $KISA0,r0
0620    mov     $KISD0,r1
0621    mov     $200,r4
0622    clr     r2
0623    mov     $6,r3
0624 1:
0625    mov     r2,(r0)+
0626    mov     $77406,(r1)+           / 4k rw
0627    add     r4,r2
0628    sob     r3,1b
0629
0630 / initialize user segment
0631
0632    mov     $_end+63.,r2
0633    ash     $-6,r2
0634    bic     $!1777,r2
0635    mov     r2,(r0)+               / ksr6 = sysu
0636    mov     $USIZE-1\<8!6,(r1)+
0637
0638 / initialize io segment
0639 / set up counts on supervisor segments
0640
0641    mov     $IO,(r0)+
0642    mov     $77406,(r1)+           / rw 4k
0643
0644 / set a sp and start segmentation
0645
0646    mov     $_u+[USIZE*64.],sp
0647    inc     SSR0
0648
0649 / clear bss
```

```
0650
0651    mov     $_edata,r0
0652 1:
0653    clr     (r0)+
0654    cmp     r0,$_end
0655    blo     1b
0656
0657 / clear user block
0658
0659    mov     $_u,r0
0660 1:
0661    clr     (r0)+
0662    cmp     r0,$_u+[USIZE*64.]
0663    blo     1b
0664
0665 / set up previous mode and call main
0666 / on return, enter user mode at 0R
0667
0668    mov     $30000,PS
0669    jsr     pc,_main
0670    mov     $170000,-(sp)
0671    clr     -(sp)
0672    rtt
0673
0674 /* -------------------------      */
0675 .globl    _clearseg
0676 _clearseg:
0677    mov     PS,-(sp)
0678    mov     UISA0,-(sp)
0679    mov     $30340,PS
0680    mov     6(sp),UISA0
0681    mov     UISD0,-(sp)
0682    mov     $6,UISD0
0683    clr     r0
0684    mov     $32.,r1
0685 1:
0686    clr     -(sp)
0687    mtpi    (r0)+
0688    sob     r1,1b
0689    mov     (sp)+,UISD0
0690    mov     (sp)+,UISA0
0691    mov     (sp)+,PS
0692    rts     pc
0693
0694 /* -------------------------      */
0695 .globl    _copyseg
0696 _copyseg:
0697    mov     PS,-(sp)
0698    mov     UISA0,-(sp)
0699    mov     UISA1,-(sp)
```

```
0700     mov     $30340,PS
0701     mov     10(sp),UISA0
0702     mov     12(sp),UISA1
0703     mov     UISD0,-(sp)
0704     mov     UISD1,-(sp)
0705     mov     $6,UISD0
0706     mov     $6,UISD1
0707     mov     r2,-(sp)
0708     clr     r0
0709     mov     $8192.,r1
0710     mov     $32.,r2
0711 1:
0712     mfpi    (r0)+
0713     mtpi    (r1)+
0714     sob     r2,1b
0715     mov     (sp)+,r2
0716     mov     (sp)+,UISD1
0717     mov     (sp)+,UISD0
0718     mov     (sp)+,UISA1
0719     mov     (sp)+,UISA0
0720     mov     (sp)+,PS
0721     rts     pc
0722
0723 /* ---------------------------  */
0724 .globl    _savu, _retu, _aretu
0725 _savu:
0726     bis     $340,PS
0727     mov     (sp)+,r1
0728     mov     (sp),r0
0729     mov     sp,(r0)+
0730     mov     r5,(r0)+
0731     bic     $340,PS
0732     jmp     (r1)
0733
0734 _aretu:
0735     bis     $340,PS
0736     mov     (sp)+,r1
0737     mov     (sp),r0
0738     br      1f
0739
0740 _retu:
0741     bis     $340,PS
0742     mov     (sp)+,r1
0743     mov     (sp),KISA6
0744     mov     $_u,r0
0745 1:
0746     mov     (r0)+,sp
0747     mov     (r0)+,r5
0748     bic     $340,PS
0749     jmp     (r1)
```

```
0750
0751 /* ---------------------------  */
0752 .globl    trap, call
0753 /* ---------------------------  */
0754 .globl    _trap
0755 trap:
0756     mov     PS,-4(sp)
0757     tst     nofault
0758     bne     1f
0759     mov     SSR0,ssr
0760     mov     SSR2,ssr+4
0761     mov     $1,SSR0
0762     jsr     r0,call1; _trap
0763     / no return
0764 1:
0765     mov     $1,SSR0
0766     mov     nofault,(sp)
0767     rtt
0768
0769 /* ---------------------------  */
0770 .globl    _runrun, _swtch
0771 call1:
0772     tst     -(sp)
0773     bic     $340,PS
0774     br      1f
0775
0776 call:
0777     mov     PS,-(sp)
0778 1:
0779     mov     r1,-(sp)
0780     mfpi    sp
0781     mov     4(sp),-(sp)
0782     bic     $!37,(sp)
0783     bit     $30000,PS
0784     beq     1f
0785     jsr     pc,*(r0)+
0786 2:
0787     bis     $340,PS
0788     tstb    _runrun
0789     beq     2f
0790     bic     $340,PS
0791     jsr     pc,_swtch
0792     br      2b
0793 2:
0794     tst     (sp)+
0795     mtpi    sp
0796     br      2f
0797 1:
0798     bis     $30000,PS
0799     jsr     pc,*(r0)+
```

Sheet 07

Sheet 07

```
0800     cmp      (sp)+,(sp)+
0801 2:
0802     mov      (sp)+,r1
0803     tst      (sp)+
0804     mov      (sp)+,r0
0805     rtt
0806 /* -------------------------------- */
0807 .globl     _fubyte, _subyte
0808 /* -------------------------------- */
0809 .globl     _fuibyte, _suibyte
0810 /* -------------------------------- */
0811 .globl     _fuword, _suword
0812 /* -------------------------------- */
0813 .globl     _fuiword, _suiword
0814 _fuibyte:
0815 _fubyte:
0816     mov      2(sp),r1
0817     bic      $1,r1
0818     jsr      pc,sword
0819     cmp      r1,2(sp)
0820     beq      1f
0821     swab     r0
0822 1:
0823     bic      $!377,r0
0824     rts      pc
0825
0826 _suibyte:
0827 _subyte:
0828     mov      2(sp),r1
0829     bic      $1,r1
0830     jsr      pc,sword
0831     mov      r0,-(sp)
0832     cmp      r1,4(sp)
0833     beq      1f
0834     movb     6(sp),1(sp)
0835     br       2f
0836 1:
0837     movb     6(sp),(sp)
0838 2:
0839     mov      (sp)+,r0
0840     jsr      pc,pword
0841     clr      r0
0842     rts      pc
0843
0844 _fuiword:
0845 _fuword:
0846     mov      2(sp),r1
0847 fuword:
0848     jsr      pc,sword
0849     rts      pc
```

```
0850
0851 sword:
0852     mov      PS,-(sp)
0853     bis      $340,PS
0854     mov      nofault,-(sp)
0855     mov      $err,nofault
0856     mfpi     (r1)
0857     mov      (sp)+,r0
0858     br       1f
0859
0860 _suiword:
0861 _suword:
0862     mov      2(sp),r1
0863     mov      4(sp),r0
0864 suword:
0865     jsr      pc,pword
0866     rts      pc
0867
0868 pword:
0869     mov      PS,-(sp)
0870     bis      $340,PS
0871     mov      nofault,-(sp)
0872     mov      $err,nofault
0873     mov      r0,-(sp)
0874     mtpi     (r1)
0875 1:
0876     mov      (sp)+,nofault
0877     mov      (sp)+,PS
0878     rts      pc
0879
0880 err:
0881     mov      (sp)+,nofault
0882     mov      (sp)+,PS
0883     tst      (sp)+
0884     mov      $-1,r0
0885     rts      pc
0886
0887 /* -------------------------- */
0888 .globl     _savfp, _display
0889 _savfp:
0890 _display:
0891     rts      pc
0892
0893 /* -------------------------- */
0894 .globl     _incupc
0895 _incupc:
0896     mov      r2,-(sp)
0897     mov      6(sp),r2   / base of prof with base,lens,off,scale
0898     mov      4(sp),r0          / pc
0899     sub      4(r2),r0          / offset
```

```
0900        clc
0901        ror        r0
0902        mul        6(r2),r0          / scale
0903        ashc       $-14.,r0
0904        inc        r1
0905        bic        $1,r1
0906        cmp        r1,2(r2)          / length
0907        bhis       1f
0908        add        (r2),r1           / base
0909        mov        nofault,-(sp)
0910        mov        $2f,nofault
0911        mfpi       (r1)
0912        inc        (sp)
0913        mtpi       (r1)
0914        br         3f
0915 2:
0916        clr        6(r2)
0917 3:
0918        mov        (sp)+,nofault
0919 1:
0920        mov        (sp)+,r2
0921        rts        pc
0922
0923 / Character list set/put
0924
0925 /* --------------------------        */
0926 .globl     _setc, _putc
0927 /* --------------------------        */
0928 .globl     _cfreelist
0929
0930 _setc:
0931        mov        2(sp),r1
0932        mov        PS,-(sp)
0933        mov        r2,-(sp)
0934        bis        $340,PS
0935        bic        $100,PS           / spl 5
0936        mov        2(r1),r2          / first ptr
0937        beq        9f                / empty
0938        movb       (r2)+,r0          / character
0939        bic        $!377,r0
0940        mov        r2,2(r1)
0941        dec        (r1)+             / count
0942        bne        1f
0943        clr        (r1)+
0944        clr        (r1)+             / last block
0945        br         2f
0946 1:
0947        bit        $7,r2
0948        bne        3f
0949        mov        -10(r2),(r1)      / next block
```

```
0950        add        $2,(r1)
0951 2:
0952        dec        r2
0953        bic        $7,r2
0954        mov        _cfreelist,(r2)
0955        mov        r2,_cfreelist
0956 3:
0957        mov        (sp)+,r2
0958        mov        (sp)+,PS
0959        rts        pc
0960 9:
0961        clr        4(r1)
0962        mov        $-1,r0
0963        mov        (sp)+,r2
0964        mov        (sp)+,PS
0965        rts        pc
0966
0967 _putc:
0968        mov        2(sp),r0
0969        mov        4(sp),r1
0970        mov        PS,-(sp)
0971        mov        r2,-(sp)
0972        mov        r3,-(sp)
0973        bis        $340,PS
0974        bic        $100,PS           / spl 5
0975        mov        4(r1),r2          / last ptr
0976        bne        1f
0977        mov        _cfreelist,r2
0978        beq        9f
0979        mov        (r2),_cfreelist
0980        clr        (r2)+
0981        mov        r2,2(r1)          / first ptr
0982        br         2f
0983 1:
0984        bit        $7,r2
0985        bne        2f
0986        mov        _cfreelist,r3
0987        beq        9f
0988        mov        (r3),_cfreelist
0989        mov        r3,-10(r2)
0990        mov        r3,r2
0991        clr        (r2)+
0992 2:
0993        movb       r0,(r2)+
0994        mov        r2,4(r1)
0995        inc        (r1)              / count
0996        clr        r0
0997        mov        (sp)+,r3
0998        mov        (sp)+,r2
0999        mov        (sp)+,PS
```

```
1000    rts     PC
1001 9:
1002    mov     PC,r0
1003    mov     (SP)+,r3
1004    mov     (SP)+,r2
1005    mov     (SP)+,PS
1006    rts     PC
1007
1008 /* --------------------------       */
1009 .globl      _backup
1010 /* --------------------------       */
1011 .globl      _resloc
1012 _backup:
1013    mov     2(SP),ssr+2
1014    mov     r2,-(SP)
1015    jsr     PC,backup
1016    mov     r2,ssr+2
1017    mov     (SP)+,r2
1018    movb    jfls,r0
1019    bne     2f
1020    mov     2(SP),r0
1021    movb    ssr+2,r1
1022    jsr     PC,1f
1023    movb    ssr+3,r1
1024    jsr     PC,1f
1025    movb    _resloc+7,r1
1026    asl     r1
1027    add     r0,r1
1028    mov     ssr+4,(r1)
1029    clr     r0
1030 2:
1031    rts     PC
1032 1:
1033    mov     r1,-(SP)
1034    asr     (SP)
1035    asr     (SP)
1036    asr     (SP)
1037    bic     $!7,r1
1038    movb    _resloc(r1),r1
1039    asl     r1
1040    add     r0,r1
1041    sub     (SP)+,(r1)
1042    rts     PC
1043
1044 / hard part
1045 / simulate the ssr2 register missing on 11/40
1046
1047 backup:
1048    clr     r2              / backup register ssr1
1049    mov     $1,bfls         / clrs jfls
```

```
1050    mov     ssr+4,r0
1051    jsr     PC,fetch
1052    mov     r0,r1
1053    ash     $-11.,r0
1054    bic     $!36,r0
1055    jmp     *0f(r0)
1056 0:     t00; t01; t02; t03; t04; t05; t06; t07
1057        t10; t11; t12; t13; t14; t15; t16; t17
1058
1059 t00:
1060    clrb    bfls
1061
1062 t10:
1063    mov     r1,r0
1064    swab    r0
1065    bic     $!16,r0
1066    jmp     *0f(r0)
1067 0:     u0; u1; u2; u3; u4; u5; u6; u7
1068
1069 u6:        / single op, m[tf]pi, sxt, illegal
1070    bit     $400,r1
1071    beq     u5              / all but m[tf], sxt
1072    bit     $200,r1
1073    beq     1f              / mfpi
1074    bit     $100,r1
1075    bne     u5              / sxt
1076
1077 / simulate mtpi with double (sp)+,dd
1078    bic     $4000,r1        / turn instr into (sp)+
1079    br      t01
1080
1081 / simulate mfpi with double ss,-(sp)
1082 1:
1083    ash     $6,r1
1084    bis     $46,r1          / -(sp)
1085    br      t01
1086
1087 u4:        / jsr
1088    mov     r1,r0
1089    jsr     PC,setres       / assume no fault
1090    bis     $173000,r2      / -2 from sp
1091    rts     PC
1092
1093 t07:       / EIS
1094    clrb    bfls
1095
1096 u0:        / jmp, swab
1097 u5:        / single op
1098    mov     r1,r0
1099    br      setres
```

```
1100
1101 t01:         / mov
1102 t02:         / cmp
1103 t03:         / bit
1104 t04:         / bic
1105 t05:         / bis
1106 t06:         / add
1107 t16:         / sub
1108    clrb     bfls
1109
1110 t11:         / movb
1111 t12:         / cmpb
1112 t13:         / bitb
1113 t14:         / bicb
1114 t15:         / bisb
1115    mov      r1,r0
1116    ash      $-6,r0
1117    jsr      pc,setres
1118    swab     r2
1119    mov      r1,r0
1120    jsr      pc,setres
1121
1122 / if delta(dest) is zero,
1123 / no need to fetch source
1124
1125    bit      $370,r2
1126    beq      1f
1127
1128 / if mode(source) is R,
1129 / no fault is possible
1130
1131    bit      $7000,r1
1132    beq      1f
1133
1134 / if res(source) is res(dest),
1135 / too bad.
1136
1137    mov      r2,-(sp)
1138    bic      $174370,(sp)
1139    cmpb     1(sp),(sp)+
1140    beq      t17
1141
1142 / start source cycle
1143 / pick up value of res
1144
1145    mov      r1,r0
1146    ash      $-6,r0
1147    bic      $!7,r0
1148    movb     _resloc(r0),r0
1149    asl      r0
```

```
1150    add      ssr+2,r0
1151    mov      (r0),r0
1152
1153 / if res has been incremented,
1154 / must decrement it before fetch
1155
1156    bit      $174000,r2
1157    ble      2f
1158    dec      r0
1159    bit      $10000,r2
1160    beq      2f
1161    dec      r0
1162 2:
1163
1164 / if mode is 6,7 fetch and add X(R) to R
1165
1166    bit      $4000,r1
1167    beq      2f
1168    bit      $2000,r1
1169    beq      2f
1170    mov      r0,-(sp)
1171    mov      ssr+4,r0
1172    add      $2,r0
1173    jsr      pc,fetch
1174    add      (sp)+,r0
1175 2:
1176
1177 / fetch operand
1178 / if mode is 3,5,7 fetch *
1179
1180    jsr      pc,fetch
1181    bit      $1000,r1
1182    beq      1f
1183    bit      $6000,r1
1184    bne      fetch
1185 1:
1186    rts      pc
1187
1188 t17:         / illegal
1189 u1:          / br
1190 u2:          / br
1191 u3:          / br
1192 u7:          / illegal
1193    incb     jfls
1194    rts      pc
1195
1196 setres:
1197    mov      r0,-(sp)
1198    bic      $!7,r0
1199    bis      r0,r2
```

```
1200      mov      (sp)+,r0
1201      ash      $-3,r0
1202      bic      $!7,r0
1203      movb     0f(r0),r0
1204      tstb     bfls
1205      beq      1f
1206      bit      $2,r2
1207      beq      2f
1208      bit      $4,r2
1209      beq      2f
1210 1:
1211      cmp      r0,$20
1212      beq      2f
1213      cmp      r0,$-20
1214      beq      2f
1215      asl      r0
1216 2:
1217      bisb     r0,r2
1218      rts      pc
1219
1220 0:   .byte    0,0,10,20,-10,-20,0,0
1221
1222 fetch:
1223      bic      $1,r0
1224      mov      nofault,-(sp)
1225      mov      $1f,nofault
1226      mfpi     (r0)
1227      mov      (sp)+,r0
1228      mov      (sp)+,nofault
1229      rts      pc
1230
1231 1:
1232      mov      (sp)+,nofault
1233      clrb     r2                     / clear out dest on fault
1234      mov      $-1,r0
1235      rts      pc
1236
1237 .bss
1238 bfls:    .=.+1
1239 jfls:    .=.+1
1240 .text
1241
1242 /* ---------------------------      */
1243 .globl    _copyin, _copyout
1244 _copyin:
1245      jsr      pc,copsu
1246 1:
1247      mfpi     (r0)+
1248      mov      (sp)+,(r1)+
1249      sob      r2,1b
```

```
1250      br       2f
1251
1252 _copyout:
1253      jsr      pc,copsu
1254 1:
1255      mov      (r0)+,-(sp)
1256      mtpi     (r1)+
1257      sob      r2,1b
1258 2:
1259      mov      (sp)+,nofault
1260      mov      (sp)+,r2
1261      clr      r0
1262      rts      pc
1263
1264 copsu:
1265      mov      (sp)+,r0
1266      mov      r2,-(sp)
1267      mov      nofault,-(sp)
1268      mov      r0,-(sp)
1269      mov      10(sp),r0
1270      mov      12(sp),r1
1271      mov      14(sp),r2
1272      asr      r2
1273      mov      $1f,nofault
1274      rts      pc
1275
1276 1:
1277      mov      (sp)+,nofault
1278      mov      (sp)+,r2
1279      mov      $-1,r0
1280      rts      pc
1281
1282 /* ---------------------------      */
1283 .globl    _idle
1284 _idle:
1285      mov      PS,-(sp)
1286      bic      $340,PS
1287      wait
1288      mov      (sp)+,PS
1289      rts      pc
1290
1291 /* ---------------------------      */
1292 .globl    _sp10, _sp11, _sp14, _sp15, _sp16, _sp17
1293 _sp10:
1294      bic      $340,PS
1295      rts      pc
1296
1297 _sp11:
1298      bis      $40,PS
1299      bic      $300,PS
```

```
1300     rts     pc
1301
1302 _spl4:
1303 _spl5:
1304     bis     $340,PS
1305     bic     $100,PS
1306     rts     pc
1307
1308 _spl6:
1309     bis     $340,PS
1310     bic     $40,PS
1311     rts     pc
1312
1313 _spl7:
1314     bis     $340,PS
1315     rts     pc
1316
1317 /* -------------------------       */
1318 .globl    _dpadd
1319 _dpadd:
1320     mov     2(sp),r0
1321     add     4(sp),2(r0)
1322     adc     (r0)
1323     rts     pc
1324
1325 /* -------------------------       */
1326 .globl    _dpcmp
1327 _dpcmp:
1328     mov     2(sp),r0
1329     mov     4(sp),r1
1330     sub     6(sp),r0
1331     sub     8(sp),r1
1332     sbc     r0
1333     bge     1f
1334     cmp     r0,$-1
1335     bne     2f
1336     cmp     r1,$-512.
1337     bhi     3f
1338 2:
1339     mov     $-512.,r0
1340     rts     pc
1341 1:
1342     bne     2f
1343     cmp     r1,$512.
1344     blo     3f
1345 2:
1346     mov     $512.,r1
1347 3:
1348     mov     r1,r0
1349     rts     pc
```

```
1350
1351 /* -------------------------       */
1352 .globl    dump
1353 dump:
1354     bit     $1,SSR0
1355     bne     dump
1356
1357 / save regs r0,r1,r2,r3,r4,r5,r6,KIA6
1358 / starting at abs location 4
1359
1360     mov     r0,4
1361     mov     $6,r0
1362     mov     r1,(r0)+
1363     mov     r2,(r0)+
1364     mov     r3,(r0)+
1365     mov     r4,(r0)+
1366     mov     r5,(r0)+
1367     mov     sp,(r0)+
1368     mov     KISA6,(r0)+
1369
1370 / dump all of core (ie to first mt error)
1371 / onto mag tape. (9 track or 7 track 'binary')
1372
1373     mov     $MTC,r0
1374     mov     $60004,(r0)+
1375     clr     2(r0)
1376 1:
1377     mov     $-512.,(r0)
1378     inc     -(r0)
1379 2:
1380     tstb    (r0)
1381     bge     2b
1382     tst     (r0)+
1383     bge     1b
1384     reset
1385
1386 / end of file and loop
1387
1388     mov     $60007,-(r0)
1389     br      .
1390
1391 /* -------------------------       */
1392 .globl    _ldiv
1393 _ldiv:
1394     clr     r0
1395     mov     2(sp),r1
1396     div     4(sp),r0
1397     rts     pc
1398
1399 /* -------------------------       */
```

```
1400 .globl     _lrem
1401 _lrem:
1402    clr     r0
1403    mov     2(sp),r1
1404    div     4(sp),r0
1405    mov     r1,r0
1406    rts     pc
1407
1408 /* ------------------------- */
1409 .globl     _lshift
1410 _lshift:
1411    mov     2(sp),r1
1412    mov     (r1)+,r0
1413    mov     (r1),r1
1414    ashc    4(sp),r0
1415    mov     r1,r0
1416    rts     pc
1417
1418 /* ------------------------- */
1419 .globl     csv
1420 csv:
1421    mov     r5,r0
1422    mov     sp,r5
1423    mov     r4,-(sp)
1424    mov     r3,-(sp)
1425    mov     r2,-(sp)
1426    jsr     pc,(r0)
1427
1428 /* ------------------------- */
1429 .globl cret
1430 cret:
1431    mov     r5,r1
1432    mov     -(r1),r4
1433    mov     -(r1),r3
1434    mov     -(r1),r2
1435    mov     r5,sp
1436    mov     (sp)+,r5
1437    rts     pc
1438
1439 /* ------------------------- */
1440 .globl     _u
1441 _u = 140000
1442 USIZE      = 16.
1443
1444 PS         = 177776
1445 SSR0       = 177572
1446 SSR2       = 177576
1447 KISA0      = 172340
1448 KISA6      = 172354
1449 KISD0      = 172300
```

```
1450 MTC        = 172522
1451 UISA0      = 177640
1452 UISA1      = 177642
1453 UISD0      = 177600
1454 UISD1      = 177602
1455 IO = 7600
1456
1457 .data
1458 /* ------------------------- */
1459 .globl     _ka6, _cputype
1460 _ka6:      KISA6
1461 _cputype:40.
1462
1463 .bss
1464 /* ------------------------- */
1465 .globl     nofault, ssr, badtrap
1466 nofault:.=.+2
1467 ssr:       .=.+6
1468 badtrap:.=.+2
1469
1470
1471
1472
1473
1474
1475
1476
1477
1478
1479
1480
1481
1482
1483
1484
1485
1486
1487
1488
1489
1490
1491
1492
1493
1494
1495
1496
1497
1498
1499
```

```
1500 #
1501 #include "../param.h"
1502 #include "../user.h"
1503 #include "../systm.h"
1504 #include "../proc.h"
1505 #include "../text.h"
1506 #include "../inode.h"
1507 #include "../seg.h"
1508
1509 #define    CLOCK1   0177546
1510 #define    CLOCK2   0172540
1511 /*
1512  * Icode is the octal bootstrap
1513  * program executed in user mode
1514  * to bring up the system.
1515  */
1516 int        icode[]
1517 {
1518    0104413,          /* sys exec; init; initp */
1519    0000014,
1520    0000010,
1521    0000777,          /* br . */
1522    0000014,          /* initp: init; 0 */
1523    0000000,
1524    0062457,          /* init: </etc/init\0> */
1525    0061564,
1526    0064457,
1527    0064556,
1528    0000164,
1529 };
1530 /* ------------------------       */
1531
1532 /*
1533  * Initialization code.
1534  * Called from m40.s or m45.s as
1535  * soon as a stack and segmentation
1536  * have been established.
1537  * Functions:
1538  * clear and free user core
1539  * find which clock is configured
1540  * hand craft 0th process
1541  * call all initialization routines
1542  * fork - process 0 to schedule
1543  *      - process 1 execute bootstrap
1544  *
1545  * panic: no clock -- neither clock responds
1546  * loop at loc 6 in user mode -- /etc/init
1547  * cannot be executed.
1548  */
1549
```

```
1550 main()
1551 {
1552    extern schar;
1553    register i, *p;
1554
1555    /*
1556     * zero and free all of core
1557     */
1558
1559    updlock = 0;
1560    i = *ka6 + USIZE;
1561    UISD->r[0] = 077406;
1562    for(;;) {
1563        UISA->r[0] = i;
1564        if(fuibyte(0) < 0)
1565            break;
1566        clearseg(i);
1567        maxmem++;
1568        mfree(coremap, 1, i);
1569        i++;
1570    }
1571    if(cputype == 70)
1572    for(i=0; i<62; i=+2) {
1573        UBMAP->r[i] = i<<12;
1574        UBMAP->r[i+1] = 0;
1575    }
1576    printf("mem = %l\n", maxmem*5/16);
1577    printf("RESTRICTED RIGHTS\n\n");
1578    printf("Use, duplication or disclosure is subject to\n");
1579    printf("restrictions stated in Contract with Western\n");
1580    printf("Electric Company, Inc.\n");
1581
1582    maxmem = min(maxmem, MAXMEM);
1583    mfree(swapmap, nswap, swplo);
1584
1585    /*
1586     * set up system process
1587     */
1588
1589    proc[0].p_addr = *ka6;
1590    proc[0].p_size = USIZE;
1591    proc[0].p_stat = SRUN;
1592    proc[0].p_flag =! SLOAD!SSYS;
1593    u.u_procp = &proc[0];
1594
1595    /*
1596     * determine clock
1597     */
1598
1599    UISA->r[7] = ka6[1]; /* io segment */
```

```
1600      UISD->r[7] = 077406;
1601      lks = CLOCK1;
1602      if(fuiword(lks) == -1) {
1603              lks = CLOCK2;
1604              if(fuiword(lks) == -1)
1605                      panic("no clock");
1606      }
1607      *lks = 0115;
1608
1609      /*
1610       * set up 'known' i-nodes
1611       */
1612
1613      cinit();
1614      binit();
1615      iinit();
1616      rootdir = iget(rootdev, ROOTINO);
1617      rootdir->i_flag =& ~ILOCK;
1618      u.u_cdir = iget(rootdev, ROOTINO);
1619      u.u_cdir->i_flag =& ~ILOCK;
1620
1621      /*
1622       * make init process
1623       * enter scheduling loop
1624       * with system process
1625       */
1626
1627      if(newproc()) {
1628              expand(USIZE+1);
1629              estabur(0, 1, 0, 0);
1630              copyout(icode, 0, sizeof icode);
1631              /*
1632               * Return goes to loc. 0 of user init
1633               * code just copied out.
1634               */
1635              return;
1636      }
1637      sched();
1638 }
1639 /* ------------------------       */
1640
1641 /*
1642  * Set up software prototype segmentation
1643  * registers to implement the 3 pseudo
1644  * text,data,stack segment sizes passed
1645  * as arguments.
1646  * The argument sep specifies if the
1647  * text and data+stack segments are to
1648  * be separated.
1649  */
```

```
1650 estabur(nt, nd, ns, sep)
1651 {
1652      register a, *ap, *dp;
1653
1654      if(sep) {
1655              if(cputype == 40)
1656                      goto err;
1657              if(nseg(nt) > 8 || nseg(nd)+nseg(ns) > 8)
1658                      goto err;
1659      } else
1660              if(nseg(nt)+nseg(nd)+nseg(ns) > 8)
1661                      goto err;
1662      if(nt+nd+ns+USIZE > maxmem)
1663              goto err;
1664      a = 0;
1665      ap = &u.u_uisa[0];
1666      dp = &u.u_uisd[0];
1667      while(nt >= 128) {
1668              *dp++ = (127<<8) | RO;
1669              *ap++ = a;
1670              a =+ 128;
1671              nt =- 128;
1672      }
1673      if(nt) {
1674              *dp++ = ((nt-1)<<8) | RO;
1675              *ap++ = a;
1676      }
1677      if(sep)
1678      while(ap < &u.u_uisa[8]) {
1679              *ap++ = 0;
1680              *dp++ = 0;
1681      }
1682      a = USIZE;
1683      while(nd >= 128) {
1684              *dp++ = (127<<8) | RW;
1685              *ap++ = a;
1686              a =+ 128;
1687              nd =- 128;
1688      }
1689      if(nd) {
1690              *dp++ = ((nd-1)<<8) | RW;
1691              *ap++ = a;
1692              a =+ nd;
1693      }
1694      while(ap < &u.u_uisa[8]) {
1695              *dp++ = 0;
1696              *ap++ = 0;
1697      }
1698      if(sep)
1699      while(ap < &u.u_uisa[16]) {
```

```
1700               *dp++ = 0;
1701               *ap++ = 0;
1702        }
1703        a =+ ns;
1704        while(ns >= 128) {
1705               a =- 128;
1706               ns =- 128;
1707               *--dp = (127<<8) | RW;
1708               *--ap = a;
1709        }
1710        if(ns) {
1711               *--dp = ((128-ns)<<8) | RW | ED;
1712               *--ap = a-128;
1713        }
1714        if(!sep) {
1715               ap = &u.u_uisa[0];
1716               dp = &u.u_uisa[8];
1717               while(ap < &u.u_uisa[8])
1718                       *dp++ = *ap++;
1719               ap = &u.u_uisd[0];
1720               dp = &u.u_uisd[8];
1721               while(ap < &u.u_uisd[8])
1722                       *dp++ = *ap++;
1723        }
1724        sureg();
1725        return(0);
1726
1727 err:
1728        u.u_error = ENOMEM;
1729        return(-1);
1730 }
1731 /* ------------------------       */
1732
1733 /*
1734  * Load the user hardware segmentation
1735  * registers from the software prototype.
1736  * The software registers must have
1737  * been setup prior by estabur.
1738  */
1739 sureg()
1740 {
1741        register *up, *rp, a;
1742
1743        a = u.u_procp->p_addr;
1744        up = &u.u_uisa[16];
1745        rp = &UISA->r[16];
1746        if(cputype == 40) {
1747               up =- 8;
1748               rp =- 8;
1749        }
```

```
1750        while(rp > &UISA->r[0])
1751               *--rp = *--up + a;
1752        if((up=u.u_procp->p_textp) != NULL)
1753               a =- up->x_caddr;
1754        up = &u.u_uisd[16];
1755        rp = &UISD->r[16];
1756        if(cputype == 40) {
1757               up =- 8;
1758               rp =- 8;
1759        }
1760        while(rp > &UISD->r[0]) {
1761               *--rp = *--up;
1762               if((*rp & WO) == 0)
1763                       rp[(UISA-UISD)/2] =- a;
1764        }
1765 }
1766 /* ------------------------       */
1767
1768 /*
1769  * Return the arg/128 rounded up.
1770  */
1771 nseg(n)
1772 {
1773
1774        return((n+127)>>7);
1775 }
1776 /* ------------------------       */
1777
1778
1779
1780
1781
1782
1783
1784
1785
1786
1787
1788
1789
1790
1791
1792
1793
1794
1795
1796
1797
1798
1799
```

```
1800 #
1801 /*
1802 */
1803
1804 #include "../param.h"
1805 #include "../user.h"
1806 #include "../proc.h"
1807 #include "../text.h"
1808 #include "../systm.h"
1809 #include "../file.h"
1810 #include "../inode.h"
1811 #include "../buf.h"
1812 /* --------------------------      */
1813 /*
1814  * Create a new process-- the internal version of
1815  * sys fork.
1816  * It returns 1 in the new process.
1817  * How this happens is rather hard to understand.
1818  * The essential fact is that the new process is created
1819  * in such a way that it appears to have started executing
1820  * in the same call to newproc as the parent;
1821  * but in fact the code that runs is that of swtch.
1822  * The subtle implication of the returned value of swtch
1823  * (see above) is that this is the value that newproc's
1824  * caller in the new process sees.
1825  */
1826 newproc()
1827 {
1828     int a1, a2;
1829     struct proc *p, *up;
1830     register struct proc *rpp;
1831     register *rip, n;
1832
1833     p = NULL;
1834     /*
1835      * First, Just locate a slot for a process
1836      * and copy the useful info from this process into it.
1837      * The panic "cannot happen" because fork has already
1838      * checked for the existence of a slot.
1839      */
1840 retry:
1841     mpid++;
1842     if(mpid < 0) {
1843         mpid = 0;
1844         goto retry;
1845     }
1846     for(rpp = &proc[0]; rpp < &proc[NPROC]; rpp++) {
1847         if(rpp->p_stat == NULL && p==NULL)
1848             p = rpp;
1849         if (rpp->p_pid==mpid)
```

```
1850                 goto retry;
1851     }
1852     if ((rpp = p)==NULL)
1853         panic("no procs");
1854
1855     /*
1856      * make proc entry for new proc
1857      */
1858
1859     rip = u.u_procp;
1860     up = rip;
1861     rpp->p_stat = SRUN;
1862     rpp->p_flag = SLOAD;
1863     rpp->p_uid = rip->p_uid;
1864     rpp->p_ttyp = rip->p_ttyp;
1865     rpp->p_nice = rip->p_nice;
1866     rpp->p_textp = rip->p_textp;
1867     rpp->p_pid = mpid;
1868     rpp->p_ppid = rip->p_pid;
1869     rpp->p_time = 0;
1870
1871     /*
1872      * make duplicate entries
1873      * where needed
1874      */
1875
1876     for(rip = &u.u_ofile[0]; rip < &u.u_ofile[NOFILE];)
1877         if((rpp = *rip++) != NULL)
1878             rpp->f_count++;
1879     if((rpp=up->p_textp) != NULL) {
1880         rpp->x_count++;
1881         rpp->x_ccount++;
1882     }
1883     u.u_cdir->i_count++;
1884     /*
1885      * Partially simulate the environment
1886      * of the new process so that when it is actually
1887      * created (by copying) it will look right.
1888      */
1889     savu(u.u_rsav);
1890     rpp = p;
1891     u.u_procp = rpp;
1892     rip = up;
1893     n = rip->p_size;
1894     a1 = rip->p_addr;
1895     rpp->p_size = n;
1896     a2 = malloc(coremap, n);
1897     /*
1898      * If there is not enough core for the
1899      * new process, swap out the current process to
```

```
1900        * generate the copy.
1901        */
1902    if(a2 == NULL) {
1903            rip->p_stat = SIDL;
1904            rpp->p_addr = a1;
1905            savu(u.u_ssav);
1906            xswap(rpp, 0, 0);
1907            rpp->p_flag =| SSWAP;
1908            rip->p_stat = SRUN;
1909    } else {
1910        /*
1911         * There is core, so just copy.
1912         */
1913            rpp->p_addr = a2;
1914            while(n--)
1915                    copyseg(a1++, a2++);
1916    }
1917    u.u_procp = rip;
1918    return(0);
1919 }
1920 /* ---------------------------       */
1921
1922 /*
1923  * The main loop of the scheduling (swapping)
1924  * process.
1925  * The basic idea is:
1926  *   see if anyone wants to be swapped in;
1927  *   swap out processes until there is room;
1928  *   swap him in;
1929  *   repeat.
1930  * Although it is not remarkably evident, the basic
1931  * synchronization here is on the runin flag, which is
1932  * slept on and is set once per second by the clock routine.
1933  * Core shuffling therefore takes place once per second.
1934  *
1935  * panic: swap error -- IO error while swapping.
1936  * this is the one panic that should be
1937  * handled in a less drastic way. Its
1938  * very hard.
1939  */
1940 sched()
1941 {
1942    struct proc *p1;
1943    register struct proc *rp;
1944    register a, n;
1945
1946    /*
1947     * find user to swap in
1948     * of users ready, select one out longest
1949     */
```

```
1950
1951    goto loop;
1952
1953 sloop:
1954    runin++;
1955    sleep(&runin, PSWP);
1956
1957 loop:
1958    spl6();
1959    n = -1;
1960    for(rp = &proc[0]; rp < &proc[NPROC]; rp++)
1961    if(rp->p_stat==SRUN && (rp->p_flag&SLOAD)==0 &&
1962        rp->p_time > n) {
1963            p1 = rp;
1964            n = rp->p_time;
1965    }
1966    if(n == -1) {
1967            runout++;
1968            sleep(&runout, PSWP);
1969            goto loop;
1970    }
1971
1972    /*
1973     * see if there is core for that process
1974     */
1975
1976    spl0();
1977    rp = p1;
1978    a = rp->p_size;
1979    if((rp=rp->p_textp) != NULL)
1980            if(rp->x_ccount == 0)
1981                    a =+ rp->x_size;
1982    if((a=malloc(coremap, a)) != NULL)
1983            goto found2;
1984
1985    /*
1986     * none found,
1987     * look around for easy core
1988     */
1989
1990    spl6();
1991    for(rp = &proc[0]; rp < &proc[NPROC]; rp++)
1992    if((rp->p_flag&(SSYS|SLOCK|SLOAD))==SLOAD &&
1993        (rp->p_stat == SWAIT || rp->p_stat==SSTOP))
1994            goto found1;
1995
1996    /*
1997     * no easy core,
1998     * if this process is deserving,
1999     * look around for
```

Sheet 19

Sheet 19

```
2000         * oldest process in core
2001         */
2002
2003         if(n < 3)
2004                 goto sloop;
2005         n = -1;
2006         for(rp = &proc[0]; rp < &proc[NPROC]; rp++)
2007         if((rp->p_flag&(SSYS|SLOCK|SLOAD))==SLOAD &&
2008            (rp->p_stat==SRUN !! rp->p_stat==SSLEEP) &&
2009            rp->p_time > n) {
2010                 p1 = rp;
2011                 n = rp->p_time;
2012         }
2013         if(n < 2)
2014                 goto sloop;
2015         rp = p1;
2016
2017         /*
2018          * swap user out
2019          */
2020
2021 found1:
2022         spl0();
2023         rp->p_flag =& ~SLOAD;
2024         xswap(rp, 1, 0);
2025         goto loop;
2026
2027         /*
2028          * swap user in
2029          */
2030
2031 found2:
2032         if((rp=p1->p_textp) != NULL) {
2033                 if(rp->x_ccount == 0) {
2034                         if(swap(rp->x_daddr, a, rp->x_size, B_READ))
2035                                 goto swaper;
2036                         rp->x_caddr = a;
2037                         a =+ rp->x_size;
2038                 }
2039                 rp->x_ccount++;
2040         }
2041         rp = p1;
2042         if(swap(rp->p_addr, a, rp->p_size, B_READ))
2043                 goto swaper;
2044         mfree(swapmap, (rp->p_size+7)/8, rp->p_addr);
2045         rp->p_addr = a;
2046         rp->p_flag =| SLOAD;
2047         rp->p_time = 0;
2048         goto loop;
2049
```

```
2050 swaper:
2051         panic("swap error");
2052 }
2053 /* -------------------------        */
2054
2055 /*
2056  * Give up the processor till a wakeup occurs
2057  * on chan, at which time the process
2058  * enters the scheduling queue at priority pri.
2059  * The most important effect of pri is that when
2060  * pri<0 a signal cannot disturb the sleep;
2061  * if pri>=0 signals will be processed.
2062  * Callers of this routine must be prepared for
2063  * premature return, and check that the reason for
2064  * sleeping has gone away.
2065  */
2066 sleep(chan, pri)
2067 {
2068         register *rp, s;
2069
2070         s = PS->integ;
2071         rp = u.u_procp;
2072         if(pri >= 0) {
2073                 if(issig())
2074                         goto psig;
2075                 spl6();
2076                 rp->p_wchan = chan;
2077                 rp->p_stat = SWAIT;
2078                 rp->p_pri = pri;
2079                 spl0();
2080                 if(runin != 0) {
2081                         runin = 0;
2082                         wakeup(&runin);
2083                 }
2084                 swtch();
2085                 if(issig())
2086                         goto psig;
2087         } else {
2088                 spl6();
2089                 rp->p_wchan = chan;
2090                 rp->p_stat = SSLEEP;
2091                 rp->p_pri = pri;
2092                 spl0();
2093                 swtch();
2094         }
2095         PS->integ = s;
2096         return;
2097
2098         /*
2099          * If priority was low (>=0) and
```

```
2100        * there has been a signal,
2101        * execute non-local goto to
2102        * the asav location.
2103        * (see trap1/trap.c)
2104        */
2105 psig:
2106        aretu(u.u_qsav);
2107 }
2108 /* ------------------------        */
2109
2110 /*
2111  * Wake up all processes sleeping on chan.
2112  */
2113 wakeup(chan)
2114 {
2115    register struct proc *p;
2116    register c, i;
2117
2118    c = chan;
2119    p = &proc[0];
2120    i = NPROC;
2121    do {
2122            if(p->p_wchan == c) {
2123                    setrun(p);
2124            }
2125            p++;
2126    } while(--i);
2127 }
2128 /* ------------------------        */
2129
2130 /*
2131  * Set the process running;
2132  * arrange for it to be swapped in if necessary.
2133  */
2134 setrun(p)
2135 {
2136    register struct proc *rp;
2137
2138    rp = p;
2139    rp->p_wchan = 0;
2140    rp->p_stat = SRUN;
2141    if(rp->p_pri < curpri)
2142            runrun++;
2143    if(runout != 0 && (rp->p_flag&SLOAD) == 0) {
2144            runout = 0;
2145            wakeup(&runout);
2146    }
2147 }
2148 /* ------------------------        */
2149
```

```
2150 /*
2151  * Set user priority.
2152  * The rescheduling flag (runrun)
2153  * is set if the priority is higher
2154  * than the currently running process.
2155  */
2156 setpri(up)
2157 {
2158    register *pp, p;
2159
2160    pp = up;
2161    p = (pp->p_cpu & 0377)/16;
2162    p =+ PUSER + pp->p_nice;
2163    if(p > 127)
2164            p = 127;
2165    if(p > curpri)
2166            runrun++;
2167    pp->p_pri = p;
2168 }
2169 /* ------------------------        */
2170
2171
2172 /*
2173  * This routine is called to reschedule the CPU.
2174  * if the calling process is not in RUN state,
2175  * arrangements for it to restart must have
2176  * been made elsewhere, usually by calling via sleep.
2177  */
2178 swtch()
2179 {
2180    static struct proc *p;
2181    register i, n;
2182    register struct proc *rp;
2183
2184    if(p == NULL)
2185            p = &proc[0];
2186    /*
2187     * Remember stack of caller
2188     */
2189    savu(u.u_rsav);
2190    /*
2191     * Switch to scheduler's stack
2192     */
2193    retu(proc[0].p_addr);
2194
2195 loop:
2196    runrun = 0;
2197    rp = p;
2198    p = NULL;
2199    n = 128;
```

```
2200     /*
2201      * Search for highest-priority runnable process
2202      */
2203     i = NPROC;
2204     do {
2205             rp++;
2206             if(rp >= &proc[NPROC])
2207                     rp = &proc[0];
2208             if(rp->p_stat==SRUN && (rp->p_flag&SLOAD)!=0) {
2209                     if(rp->p_pri < n) {
2210                             p = rp;
2211                             n = rp->p_pri;
2212                     }
2213             }
2214     } while(--i);
2215     /*
2216      * If no process is runnable, idle.
2217      */
2218     if(p == NULL) {
2219             p = rp;
2220             idle();
2221             goto loop;
2222     }
2223     rp = p;
2224     curpri = n;
2225     /* Switch to stack of the new process and set up
2226      * his segmentation registers.
2227      */
2228     retu(rp->p_addr);
2229     sureg();
2230     /*
2231      * If the new process paused because it was
2232      * swapped out, set the stack level to the last call
2233      * to savu(u_ssav).  This means that the return
2234      * which is executed immediately after the call to aretu
2235      * actually returns from the last routine which did
2236      * the savu.
2237      *
2238      * You are not expected to understand this.
2239      */
2240     if(rp->p_flag&SSWAP) {
2241             rp->p_flag =& ~SSWAP;
2242             aretu(u.u_ssav);
2243     }
2244     /* The value returned here has many subtle implications.
2245      * See the newproc comments.
2246      */
2247     return(1);
2248 }
2249 /* ------------------------------          */
```

```
2250
2251 /*
2252  * Change the size of the data+stack regions of the process.
2253  * If the size is shrinking, it's easy-- just release the
2254  * extra core. If it's growing, and there is core, just
2255  * allocate it and copy the image, taking care to reset
2256  * registers to account for the fact that the system's
2257  * stack has moved.
2258  * If there is no core, arrange for the process to be
2259  * swapped out after adjusting the size requirement--
2260  * when it comes in, enough core will be allocated.
2261  * Because of the ssave and SSWAP flags, control will
2262  * resume after the swap in swtch, which executes the return
2263  * from this stack level.
2264  *
2265  * After the expansion, the caller will take care of copying
2266  * the user's stack towards or away from the data area.
2267  */
2268 expand(newsize)
2269 {
2270     int i, n;
2271     register *p, a1, a2;
2272
2273     p = u.u_procp;
2274     n = p->p_size;
2275     p->p_size = newsize;
2276     a1 = p->p_addr;
2277     if(n >= newsize) {
2278             mfree(coremap, n-newsize, a1+newsize);
2279             return;
2280     }
2281     savu(u.u_rsav);
2282     a2 = malloc(coremap, newsize);
2283     if(a2 == NULL) {
2284             savu(u.u_ssav);
2285             xswap(p, 1, n);
2286             p->p_flag =! SSWAP;
2287             swtch();
2288             /* no return */
2289     }
2290     p->p_addr = a2;
2291     for(i=0; i<n; i++)
2292             copyseg(a1+i, a2++);
2293     mfree(coremap, n, a1);
2294     retu(p->p_addr);
2295     sureg();
2296 }
2297 /* ------------------------          */
2298
2299
```

```
2300 #
2301 /*
2302  */
2303
2304 #include "../param.h"
2305 #include "../seg.h"
2306 #include "../buf.h"
2307 #include "../conf.h"
2308
2309 /*
2310  * Address and structure of the
2311  * KL-11 console device registers.
2312  */
2313 struct
2314 {
2315     int     rsr;
2316     int     rbr;
2317     int     xsr;
2318     int     xbr;
2319 };
2320 /* ------------------------        */
2321
2322 /*
2323  * In case console is off,
2324  * panicstr contains argument to last
2325  * call to panic.
2326  */
2327
2328 char        *panicstr;
2329
2330 /*
2331  * Scaled down version of C Library printf.
2332  * Only %s %l %d (==%l) %o are recognized.
2333  * Used to print diagnostic information
2334  * directly on console tty.
2335  * Since it is not interrupt driven,
2336  * all system activities are pretty much
2337  * suspended.
2338  * Printf should not be used for chit-chat.
2339  */
2340 printf(fmt,x1,x2,x3,x4,x5,x6,x7,x8,x9,xa,xb,xc)
2341 char fmt[];
2342 {
2343     register char *s;
2344     register *adx, c;
2345
2346     adx = &x1;
2347 loop:
2348     while((c = *fmt++) != '%') {
2349         if(c == '\0')
```

```
2350             return;
2351         putchar(c);
2352     }
2353     c = *fmt++;
2354     if(c == 'd' || c == 'l' || c == 'o')
2355         printn(*adx, c=='o'? 8: 10);
2356     if(c == 's') {
2357         s = *adx;
2358         while(c = *s++)
2359             putchar(c);
2360     }
2361     adx++;
2362     goto loop;
2363 }
2364 /* ------------------------        */
2365
2366 /*
2367  * Print an unsigned integer in base b.
2368  */
2369 printn(n, b)
2370 {
2371     register a;
2372
2373     if(a = ldiv(n, b))
2374         printn(a, b);
2375     putchar(lrem(n, b) + '0');
2376 }
2377 /* ------------------------        */
2378
2379 /*
2380  * Print a character on console.
2381  * Attempts to save and restore device
2382  * status.
2383  * If the switches are 0, all
2384  * printing is inhibited.
2385  */
2386 putchar(c)
2387 {
2388     register rc, s;
2389
2390     rc = c;
2391     if(SW->integ == 0)
2392         return;
2393     while((KL->xsr&0200) == 0)
2394         ;
2395     if(rc == 0)
2396         return;
2397     s = KL->xsr;
2398     KL->xsr = 0;
2399     KL->xbr = rc;
```

```
2400     if(rc == '\n') {
2401             putchar('\r');
2402             putchar(0177);
2403             putchar(0177);
2404     }
2405     putchar(0);
2406     KL->xsr = s;
2407 }
2408 /* -------------------------         */
2409
2410 /*
2411  * Panic is called on unresolvable
2412  * fatal errors.
2413  * It syncs, prints "panic: mess" and
2414  * then loops.
2415  */
2416 panic(s)
2417 char *s;
2418 {
2419     panicstr = s;
2420     update();
2421     printf("panic: %s\n", s);
2422     for(;;)
2423             idle();
2424 }
2425 /* -------------------------         */
2426
2427 /*
2428  * prdev prints a warning message of the
2429  * form "mess on dev x/y".
2430  * x and y are the major and minor parts of
2431  * the device argument.
2432  */
2433 prdev(str, dev)
2434 {
2435
2436     printf("%s on dev %l/%l\n", str, dev.d_major, dev.d_minor);
2437 }
2438 /* -------------------------         */
2439
2440 /*
2441  * deverr prints a diagnostic from
2442  * a device driver.
2443  * It prints the device, block number,
2444  * and an octal word (usually some error
2445  * status register) passed as argument.
2446  */
2447 deverror(bp, o1, o2)
2448 int *bp;
2449 {
```

```
2450     register *rbp;
2451
2452     rbp = bp;
2453     prdev("err", rbp->b_dev);
2454     printf("bn%l er%o %o\n", rbp->b_blkno, o1, o2);
2455 }
2456 /* -------------------------         */
2457
2458
2459
2460
2461
2462
2463
2464
2465
2466
2467
2468
2469
2470
2471
2472
2473
2474
2475
2476
2477
2478
2479
2480
2481
2482
2483
2484
2485
2486
2487
2488
2489
2490
2491
2492
2493
2494
2495
2496
2497
2498
2499
```

```
2500 #
2501 /*
2502  */
2503
2504 /*
2505  * Structure of the coremap and swapmap
2506  * arrays. Consists of non-zero count
2507  * and base address of that many
2508  * contiguous units.
2509  * (The coremap unit is 64 bytes,
2510  * the swapmap unit is 512 bytes)
2511  * The addresses are increasing and
2512  * the list is terminated with the
2513  * first zero count.
2514  */
2515 struct map
2516 {
2517     char *m_size;
2518     char *m_addr;
2519 };
2520 /* ------------------------        */
2521
2522 /*
2523  * Allocate size units from the given
2524  * map. Return the base of the allocated
2525  * space.
2526  * Algorithm is first fit.
2527  */
2528 malloc(mp, size)
2529 struct map *mp;
2530 {
2531     register int a;
2532     register struct map *bp;
2533
2534     for (bp = mp; bp->m_size; bp++) {
2535             if (bp->m_size >= size) {
2536                     a = bp->m_addr;
2537                     bp->m_addr =+ size;
2538                     if ((bp->m_size =- size) == 0)
2539                             do {
2540                                     bp++;
2541                                     (bp-1)->m_addr = bp->m_addr;
2542                             } while((bp-1)->m_size = bp->m_size);
2543                     return(a);
2544             }
2545     }
2546     return(0);
2547 }
2548 /* ------------------------        */
2549
```

```
2550 /*
2551  * Free the previously allocated space aa
2552  * of size units into the specified map.
2553  * Sort aa into map and combine on
2554  * one or both ends if possible.
2555  */
2556 mfree(mp, size, aa)
2557 struct map *mp;
2558 {
2559     register struct map *bp;
2560     register int t;
2561     register int a;
2562
2563     a = aa;
2564     for (bp = mp; bp->m_addr<=a && bp->m_size!=0; bp++);
2565     if (bp>mp && (bp-1)->m_addr+(bp-1)->m_size == a) {
2566             (bp-1)->m_size =+ size;
2567             if (a+size == bp->m_addr) {
2568                     (bp-1)->m_size =+ bp->m_size;
2569                     while (bp->m_size) {
2570                             bp++;
2571                             (bp-1)->m_addr = bp->m_addr;
2572                             (bp-1)->m_size = bp->m_size;
2573                     }
2574             }
2575     } else {
2576             if (a+size == bp->m_addr && bp->m_size) {
2577                     bp->m_addr =- size;
2578                     bp->m_size =+ size;
2579             } else if (size) do {
2580                     t = bp->m_addr;
2581                     bp->m_addr = a;
2582                     a = t;
2583                     t = bp->m_size;
2584                     bp->m_size = size;
2585                     bp++;
2586             } while (size = t);
2587     }
2588 }
2589 /* ------------------------        */
2590
2591
2592
2593
2594
2595
2596
2597
2598
2599
```

2

**Traps, Interrupts
and System Calls
Process Management**

```
2600 /*
2601  * Location of the users' stored
2602  * registers relative to R0.
2603  * Usage is u.u_ar0[XX].
2604  */
2605 #define    R0        (0)
2606 #define    R1        (-2)
2607 #define    R2        (-9)
2608 #define    R3        (-8)
2609 #define    R4        (-7)
2610 #define    R5        (-6)
2611 #define    R6        (-3)
2612 #define    R7        (1)
2613 #define    RPS       (2)
2614
2615 #define    TBIT      020              /* PS trace bit */
2616
2617
2618
2619
2620
2621
2622
2623
2624
2625
2626
2627
2628
2629
2630
2631
2632
2633
2634
2635
2636
2637
2638
2639
2640
2641
2642
2643
2644
2645
2646
2647
2648
2649
```

```
2650 #
2651 #include "../param.h"
2652 #include "../systm.h"
2653 #include "../user.h"
2654 #include "../proc.h"
2655 #include "../reg.h"
2656 #include "../seg.h"
2657
2658 #define    EBIT      1        /* user error bit in PS: C-bit */
2659 #define    UMODE     0170000  /* user-mode bits in PS word */
2660 #define    SETD      0170011  /* SETD instruction */
2661 #define    SYS       0104400  /* sys (trap) instruction */
2662 #define    USER      020      /* user-mode flag added to dev */
2663
2664 /*
2665  * structure of the system entry table (sysent.c)
2666  */
2667 struct sysent       {
2668     int     count;              /* argument count */
2669     int     (*call)();          /* name of handler */
2670 } sysent[64];
2671 /* ------------------------        */
2672
2673 /*
2674  * Offsets of the user's registers relative to
2675  * the saved r0. See reg.h
2676  */
2677 char        resloc[9]
2678 {
2679     R0, R1, R2, R3, R4, R5, R6, R7, RPS
2680 };
2681 /* ------------------------        */
2682
2683 /*
2684  * Called from 140.s or 145.s when a processor trap occurs.
2685  * The arguments are the words saved on the system stack
2686  * by the hardware and software during the trap processing.
2687  * Their order is dictated by the hardware and the details
2688  * of C's calling sequence. They are peculiar in that
2689  * this call is not 'by value' and changed user registers
2690  * get copied back on return.
2691  * dev is the kind of trap that occurred.
2692  */
2693 trap(dev, sp, r1, nps, r0, pc, ps)
2694 {
2695     register i, a;
2696     register struct sysent *callp;
2697
2698     savfp();
2699     if ((ps&UMODE) == UMODE)
```

```
2700            dev =! USER;
2701    u.u_ar0 = &r0;
2702    switch(dev) {
2703
2704    /*
2705     * Trap not expected.
2706     * Usually a kernel mode bus error.
2707     * The numbers printed are used to
2708     * find the hardware PS/PC as follows.
2709     * (all numbers in octal 18 bits)
2710     *       address_of_saved_ps =
2711     *              (ka6*0100) + aps - 0140000;
2712     *       address_of_saved_pc =
2713     *              address_of_saved_ps - 2;
2714    */
2715    default:
2716            printf("ka6 = %o\n", *ka6);
2717            printf("aps = %o\n", &ps);
2718            printf("trap type %o\n", dev);
2719            panic("trap");
2720
2721    case 0+USER: /* bus error */
2722            i = SIGBUS;
2723            break;
2724
2725    /*
2726     * If illegal instructions are not
2727     * being caught and the offending instruction
2728     * is a SETD, the trap is ignored.
2729     * This is because C produces a SETD at
2730     * the beginning of every program which
2731     * will trap on CPUs without 11/45 FPU.
2732    */
2733    case 1+USER: /* illegal instruction */
2734            if(fuiword(pc-2)==SETD && u.u_signal[SIGINS]==0)
2735                    goto out;
2736            i = SIGINS;
2737            break;
2738
2739    case 2+USER: /* bpt or trace */
2740            i = SIGTRC;
2741            break;
2742
2743    case 3+USER: /* iot */
2744            i = SIGIOT;
2745            break;
2746
2747    case 5+USER: /* emt */
2748            i = SIGEMT;
2749            break;
```

```
2750
2751    case 6+USER: /* sys call */
2752            u.u_error = 0;
2753            ps =& ~EBIT;
2754            callp = &sysent[fuiword(pc-2)&077];
2755            if (callp == sysent) { /* indirect */
2756                    a = fuiword(pc);
2757                    pc =+ 2;
2758                    i = fuword(a);
2759                    if ((i & ~077) != SYS)
2760                            i = 077;           /* illegal */
2761                    callp = &sysent[i&077];
2762                    for(i=0; i<callp->count; i++)
2763                            u.u_arg[i] = fuword(a =+ 2);
2764            } else {
2765                    for(i=0; i<callp->count; i++) {
2766                            u.u_arg[i] = fuiword(pc);
2767                            pc =+ 2;
2768                    }
2769            }
2770            u.u_dirp = u.u_arg[0];
2771            trap1(callp->call);
2772            if(u.u_intflg)
2773                    u.u_error = EINTR;
2774            if(u.u_error < 100) {
2775                    if(u.u_error) {
2776                            ps =! EBIT;
2777                            r0 = u.u_error;
2778                    }
2779                    goto out;
2780            }
2781            i = SIGSYS;
2782            break;
2783
2784    /*
2785     * Since the floating exception is an
2786     * imprecise trap, a user generated
2787     * trap may actually come from kernel
2788     * mode. In this case, a signal is sent
2789     * to the current process to be picked
2790     * up later.
2791    */
2792    case 8: /* floating exception */
2793            psignal(u.u_procp, SIGFPT);
2794            return;
2795
2796    case 8+USER:
2797            i = SIGFPT;
2798            break;
2799
```

```
2800     /*
2801      * If the user SP is below the stack segment,
2802      * grow the stack automatically.
2803      * This relies on the ability of the hardware
2804      * to restart a half executed instruction.
2805      * On the 11/40 this is not the case and
2806      * the routine backup/140.s may fail.
2807      * The classic example is on the instruction
2808      *       cmp      -(SP),-(SP)
2809      */
2810     case 9+USER: /* segmentation exception */
2811             a = SP;
2812             if(backup(u.u_ar0) == 0)
2813             if(grow(a))
2814                     goto out;
2815             i = SIGSEG;
2816             break;
2817     }
2818     psignal(u.u_procp, i);
2819
2820 out:
2821     if(issig())
2822             psig();
2823     setpri(u.u_procp);
2824 }
2825 /* ------------------------       */
2826
2827 /*
2828  * Call the system-entry routine f (out of the
2829  * sysent table). This is a subroutine for trap, and
2830  * not in-line, because if a signal occurs
2831  * during processing, an (abnormal) return is simulated from
2832  * the last caller to savu(qsav); if this took place
2833  * inside of trap, it wouldn't have a chance to clean up.
2834  *
2835  * If this occurs, the return takes place without
2836  * clearing u_intfls; if it's still set, trap
2837  * marks an error which means that a system
2838  * call (like read on a typewriter) got interrupted
2839  * by a signal.
2840  */
2841 trap1(f)
2842 int (*f)();
2843 {
2844
2845     u.u_intfls = 1;
2846     savu(u.u_qsav);
2847     (*f)();
2848     u.u_intfls = 0;
2849 }
```

```
2850 /* ------------------------       */
2851
2852 /*
2853  * nonexistent system call-- set fatal error code.
2854  */
2855 nosys()
2856 {
2857     u.u_error = 100;
2858 }
2859 /* ------------------------       */
2860
2861 /*
2862  * Ignored system call
2863  */
2864 nullsys()
2865 {
2866 }
2867 /* ------------------------       */
2868
2869
2870
2871
2872
2873
2874
2875
2876
2877
2878
2879
2880
2881
2882
2883
2884
2885
2886
2887
2888
2889
2890
2891
2892
2893
2894
2895
2896
2897
2898
2899
```

```
2900 #
2901 /*
2902  */
2903
2904 /*
2905  * This table is the switch used to transfer
2906  * to the appropriate routine for processing a system call.
2907  * Each row contains the number of arguments expected
2908  * and a pointer to the routine.
2909  */
2910 int        sysent[]
2911 {
2912    0, &nullsys,              /*  0 = indir */
2913    0, &rexit,               /*  1 = exit */
2914    0, &fork,                /*  2 = fork */
2915    2, &read,                /*  3 = read */
2916    2, &write,               /*  4 = write */
2917    2, &open,                /*  5 = open */
2918    0, &close,               /*  6 = close */
2919    0, &wait,                /*  7 = wait */
2920    2, &creat,               /*  8 = creat */
2921    2, &link,                /*  9 = link */
2922    1, &unlink,              /* 10 = unlink */
2923    2, &exec,                /* 11 = exec */
2924    1, &chdir,               /* 12 = chdir */
2925    0, &stime,               /* 13 = time */
2926    3, &mknod,               /* 14 = mknod */
2927    2, &chmod,               /* 15 = chmod */
2928    2, &chown,               /* 16 = chown */
2929    1, &sbreak,              /* 17 = break */
2930    2, &stat,                /* 18 = stat */
2931    2, &seek,                /* 19 = seek */
2932    0, &getpid,              /* 20 = getpid */
2933    3, &smount,              /* 21 = mount */
2934    1, &sumount,             /* 22 = umount */
2935    0, &setuid,              /* 23 = setuid */
2936    0, &getuid,              /* 24 = getuid */
2937    0, &stime,               /* 25 = stime */
2938    3, &ptrace,              /* 26 = ptrace */
2939    0, &nosys,               /* 27 = x */
2940    1, &fstat,               /* 28 = fstat */
2941    0, &nosys,               /* 29 = x */
2942    1, &nullsys,    /* inoperative  /* 30 = smdate */
2943    1, &stty,                /* 31 = stty */
2944    1, &gtty,                /* 32 = gtty */
2945    0, &nosys,               /* 33 = x */
2946    0, &nice,                /* 34 = nice */
2947    0, &sslep,               /* 35 = sleep */
2948    0, &sync,                /* 36 = sync */
2949    1, &kill,                /* 37 = kill */
```

```
2950    0, &setswit,             /* 38 = switch */
2951    0, &nosys,               /* 39 = x */
2952    0, &nosys,               /* 40 = x */
2953    0, &dup,                 /* 41 = dup */
2954    0, &pipe,                /* 42 = pipe */
2955    1, &times,               /* 43 = times */
2956    4, &profil,              /* 44 = prof */
2957    0, &nosys,               /* 45 = tiu */
2958    0, &setgid,              /* 46 = setgid */
2959    0, &getgid,              /* 47 = getgid */
2960    2, &ssig,                /* 48 = sig */
2961    0, &nosys,               /* 49 = x */
2962    0, &nosys,               /* 50 = x */
2963    0, &nosys,               /* 51 = x */
2964    0, &nosys,               /* 52 = x */
2965    0, &nosys,               /* 53 = x */
2966    0, &nosys,               /* 54 = x */
2967    0, &nosys,               /* 55 = x */
2968    0, &nosys,               /* 56 = x */
2969    0, &nosys,               /* 57 = x */
2970    0, &nosys,               /* 58 = x */
2971    0, &nosys,               /* 59 = x */
2972    0, &nosys,               /* 60 = x */
2973    0, &nosys,               /* 61 = x */
2974    0, &nosys,               /* 62 = x */
2975    0, &nosys                /* 63 = x */
2976 };
2977 /* --------------------------- */
2978
2979
2980
2981
2982
2983
2984
2985
2986
2987
2988
2989
2990
2991
2992
2993
2994
2995
2996
2997
2998
2999
```

```
3000 #
3001 #include "../param.h"
3002 #include "../systm.h"
3003 #include "../user.h"
3004 #include "../proc.h"
3005 #include "../buf.h"
3006 #include "../reg.h"
3007 #include "../inode.h"
3008
3009 /*
3010  * exec system call.
3011  * Because of the fact that an I/O buffer is used
3012  * to store the caller's arguments during exec,
3013  * and more buffers are needed to read in the text file,
3014  * deadly embraces waiting for free buffers are possible.
3015  * Therefore the number of processes simultaneously
3016  * running in exec has to be limited to NEXEC.
3017  */
3018 #define EXPRI      -1
3019
3020 exec()
3021 {
3022     int ap, na, nc, *bp;
3023     int ts, ds, sep;
3024     register c, *ip;
3025     register char *cp;
3026     extern uchar;
3027
3028     /*
3029      * pick up file names
3030      * and check various modes
3031      * for execute permission
3032      */
3033
3034     ip = namei(&uchar, 0);
3035     if(ip == NULL)
3036             return;
3037     while(execnt >= NEXEC)
3038             sleep(&execnt, EXPRI);
3039     execnt++;
3040     bp = getblk(NODEV);
3041     if(access(ip, IEXEC) || (ip->i_mode&IFMT)!=0)
3042             goto bad;
3043
3044     /*
3045      * pack up arguments into
3046      * allocated disk buffer
3047      */
3048
3049     cp = bp->b_addr;
```

```
3050     na = 0;
3051     nc = 0;
3052     while(ap = fuword(u.u_arg[1])) {
3053             na++;
3054             if(ap == -1)
3055                     goto bad;
3056             u.u_arg[1] =+ 2;
3057             for(;;) {
3058                     c = fubyte(ap++);
3059                     if(c == -1)
3060                             goto bad;
3061                     *cp++ = c;
3062                     nc++;
3063                     if(nc > 510) {
3064                             u.u_error = E2BIG;
3065                             goto bad;
3066                     }
3067                     if(c == 0)
3068                             break;
3069             }
3070     }
3071     if((nc&1) != 0) {
3072             *cp++ = 0;
3073             nc++;
3074     }
3075
3076     /* read in first 8 bytes
3077      * of file for segment
3078      * sizes:
3079      * w0 = 407/410/411 (410 -> RO text) (411 -> sep ID)
3080      * w1 = text size
3081      * w2 = data size
3082      * w3 = bss size
3083      */
3084
3085     u.u_base = &u.u_arg[0];
3086     u.u_count = 8;
3087     u.u_offset[1] = 0;
3088     u.u_offset[0] = 0;
3089     u.u_segfls = 1;
3090     readi(ip);
3091     u.u_segfls = 0;
3092     if(u.u_error)
3093             goto bad;
3094     sep = 0;
3095     if(u.u_arg[0] == 0407) {
3096             u.u_arg[2] =+ u.u_arg[1];
3097             u.u_arg[1] = 0;
3098     } else
3099     if(u.u_arg[0] == 0411)
```

```
3100            sep++; else
3101        if(u.u_arg[0] != 0410) {
3102                u.u_error = ENOEXEC;
3103                goto bad;
3104        }
3105        if(u.u_arg[1]!=0&&(ip->i_flag&ITEXT)==0&&ip->i_count!=1){
3106                u.u_error = ETXTBSY;
3107                goto bad;
3108        }
3109
3110        /*
3111         * find text and data sizes
3112         * try them out for possible
3113         * exceed of max sizes
3114         */
3115
3116        ts = ((u.u_arg[1]+63)>>6) & 01777;
3117        ds = ((u.u_arg[2]+u.u_arg[3]+63)>>6) & 01777;
3118        if(estabur(ts, ds, SSIZE, sep))
3119                goto bad;
3120
3121        /*
3122         * allocate and clear core
3123         * at this point, committed
3124         * to the new image
3125         */
3126
3127        u.u_prof[3] = 0;
3128        xfree();
3129        expand(USIZE);
3130        xalloc(ip);
3131        c = USIZE+ds+SSIZE;
3132        expand(c);
3133        while(--c >= USIZE)
3134                clearseg(u.u_procp->p_addr+c);
3135
3136        /* read in data segment */
3137
3138        estabur(0, ds, 0, 0);
3139        u.u_base = 0;
3140        u.u_offset[1] = 020+u.u_arg[1];
3141        u.u_count = u.u_arg[2];
3142        readi(ip);
3143
3144        /*
3145         * initialize stack segment
3146         */
3147
3148        u.u_tsize = ts;
3149        u.u_dsize = ds;
```

```
3150        u.u_ssize = SSIZE;
3151        u.u_sep = sep;
3152        estabur(u.u_tsize, u.u_dsize, u.u_ssize, u.u_sep);
3153        cp = bp->b_addr;
3154        ap = -nc - na*2 - 4;
3155        u.u_ar0[R6] = ap;
3156        suword(ap, na);
3157        c = -nc;
3158        while(na--) {
3159                suword(ap=+2, c);
3160                do
3161                        subyte(c++, *cp);
3162                while(*cp++);
3163        }
3164        suword(ap+2, -1);
3165
3166        /*
3167         * set SUID/SGID protections, if no tracing
3168         */
3169
3170        if ((u.u_procp->p_flag&STRC)==0) {
3171                if(ip->i_mode&ISUID)
3172                        if(u.u_uid != 0) {
3173                                u.u_uid = ip->i_uid;
3174                                u.u_procp->p_uid = ip->i_uid;
3175                        }
3176                if(ip->i_mode&ISGID)
3177                        u.u_gid = ip->i_gid;
3178        }
3179
3180        /* clear sigs, regs and return */
3181
3182        c = ip;
3183        for(ip = &u.u_signal[0]; ip < &u.u_signal[NSIG]; ip++)
3184                if((*ip & 1) == 0)
3185                        *ip = 0;
3186        for(cp = &regloc[0]; cp < &regloc[6];)
3187                u.u_ar0[*cp++] = 0;
3188        u.u_ar0[R7] = 0;
3189        for(ip = &u.u_fsav[0]; ip < &u.u_fsav[25];)
3190                *ip++ = 0;
3191        ip = c;
3192
3193 bad:
3194        iput(ip);
3195        brelse(bp);
3196        if(execnt >= NEXEC)
3197                wakeup(&execnt);
3198        execnt--;
3199 }
```

```
3200 /* ------------------------           */
3201
3202 /* exit system call:
3203  * pass back caller's r0
3204  */
3205 rexit()
3206 {
3207
3208     u.u_ar5[0] = u.u_ar0[R0] << 8;
3209     exit();
3210 }
3211 /* ------------------------           */
3212
3213 /* Release resources.
3214  * Save u. area for parent to look at.
3215  * Enter zombie state.
3216  * Wake up parent and init processes,
3217  * and dispose of children.
3218  */
3219 exit()
3220 {
3221     register int *q, a;
3222     register struct proc *p;
3223
3224     u.u_procp->p_flag =& ~STRC;
3225     for(q = &u.u_signal[0]; q < &u.u_signal[NSIG];)
3226             *q++ = 1;
3227     for(q = &u.u_ofile[0]; q < &u.u_ofile[NOFILE]; q++)
3228             if(a = *q) {
3229                     *q = NULL;
3230                     closef(a);
3231             }
3232     iput(u.u_cdir);
3233     xfree();
3234     a = malloc(swapmap, 1);
3235     if(a == NULL)
3236             panic("out of swap");
3237     p = getblk(swapdev, a);
3238     bcopy(&u, p->b_addr, 256);
3239     bwrite(p);
3240     q = u.u_procp;
3241     mfree(coremap, q->p_size, q->p_addr);
3242     q->p_addr = a;
3243     q->p_stat = SZOMB;
3244 loop:
3245
3246     for(p = &proc[0]; p < &proc[NPROC]; p++)
3247     if(q->p_ppid == p->p_pid) {
3248             wakeup(&proc[1]);
3249             wakeup(p);
```

```
3250             for(p = &proc[0]; p < &proc[NPROC]; p++)
3251             if(q->p_pid == p->p_ppid) {
3252                     p->p_ppid  = 1;
3253                     if (p->p_stat == SSTOP)
3254                             setrun(p);
3255             }
3256             swtch();
3257             /* no return */
3258     }
3259     q->p_ppid = 1;
3260     goto loop;
3261 }
3262 /* ------------------------           */
3263
3264 /* Wait system call.
3265  * Search for a terminated (zombie) child,
3266  * finally lay it to rest, and collect its status.
3267  * Look also for stopped (traced) children,
3268  * and pass back status from them.
3269  */
3270 wait()
3271 {
3272     register f, *bp;
3273     register struct proc *p;
3274
3275     f = 0;
3276 loop:
3277     for(p = &proc[0]; p < &proc[NPROC]; p++)
3278     if(p->p_ppid == u.u_procp->p_pid) {
3279             f++;
3280             if(p->p_stat == SZOMB) {
3281                     u.u_ar0[R0] = p->p_pid;
3282                     bp = bread(swapdev, f=p->p_addr);
3283                     mfree(swapmap, 1, f);
3284                     p->p_stat = NULL;
3285                     p->p_pid = 0;
3286                     p->p_ppid = 0;
3287                     p->p_sig = 0;
3288                     p->p_ttyp = 0;
3289                     p->p_flag = 0;
3290                     p = bp->b_addr;
3291                     u.u_cstime[0] =+ p->u_cstime[0];
3292                     dpadd(u.u_cstime, p->u_cstime[1]);
3293                     dpadd(u.u_cstime, p->u_stime);
3294                     u.u_cutime[0] =+ p->u_cutime[0];
3295                     dpadd(u.u_cutime, p->u_cutime[1]);
3296                     dpadd(u.u_cutime, p->u_utime);
3297                     u.u_ar0[R1] = p->u_ar5[0];
3298                     brelse(bp);
3299                     return;
```

```
3300                 }
3301                 if(p->p_stat == SSTOP) {
3302                         if((p->p_flag&SWTED) == 0) {
3303                                 p->p_flag =| SWTED;
3304                                 u.u_ar0[R0] = p->p_pid;
3305                                 u.u_ar0[R1] = (p->p_sig<<8) |
3306                                                 0177;
3307                                 return;
3308                         }
3309                         p->p_flag =& ~(STRC|SWTED);
3310                         setrun(p);
3311                 }
3312         }
3313         if(f) {
3314                 sleep(u.u_procp, PWAIT);
3315                 goto loop;
3316         }
3317         u.u_error = ECHILD;
3318 }
3319 /* -------------------------          */
3320
3321 /* fork system call. */
3322 fork()
3323 {
3324         register struct proc *p1, *p2;
3325
3326         p1 = u.u_procp;
3327         for(p2 = &proc[0]; p2 < &proc[NPROC]; p2++)
3328                 if(p2->p_stat == NULL)
3329                         goto found;
3330         u.u_error = EAGAIN;
3331         goto out;
3332
3333 found:
3334         if(newproc()) {
3335                 u.u_ar0[R0] = p1->p_pid;
3336                 u.u_cstime[0] = 0;
3337                 u.u_cstime[1] = 0;
3338                 u.u_stime = 0;
3339                 u.u_cutime[0] = 0;
3340                 u.u_cutime[1] = 0;
3341                 u.u_utime = 0;
3342                 return;
3343         }
3344         u.u_ar0[R0] = p2->p_pid;
3345
3346 out:
3347         u.u_ar0[R7] =+ 2;
3348 }
3349 /* -------------------------          */
```

```
3350
3351 /* break system call.
3352  *   -- bad planning: "break" is a dirty word in C.
3353  */
3354 sbreak()
3355 {
3356         register a, n, d;
3357         int i;
3358
3359         /* set n to new data size
3360          * set d to new-old
3361          * set n to new total size
3362          */
3363
3364         n = (((u.u_arg[0]+63)>>6) & 01777);
3365         if(!u.u_sep)
3366                 n =- nseg(u.u_tsize) * 128;
3367         if(n < 0)
3368                 n = 0;
3369         d = n - u.u_dsize;
3370         n =+ USIZE+u.u_ssize;
3371         if(estabur(u.u_tsize, u.u_dsize+d, u.u_ssize, u.u_sep))
3372                 return;
3373         u.u_dsize =+ d;
3374         if(d > 0)
3375                 goto bigger;
3376         a = u.u_procp->p_addr + n - u.u_ssize;
3377         i = n;
3378         n = u.u_ssize;
3379         while(n--) {
3380                 copyseg(a-d, a);
3381                 a++;
3382         }
3383         expand(i);
3384         return;
3385
3386 bigger:
3387         expand(n);
3388         a = u.u_procp->p_addr + n;
3389         n = u.u_ssize;
3390         while(n--) {
3391                 a--;
3392                 copyseg(a-d, a);
3393         }
3394         while(d--)
3395                 clearseg(--a);
3396 }
3397 /* -------------------------          */
3398
3399
```

```
3400 #
3401 /*
3402  * Everything in this file is
3403  * a routine implementing a system call.
3404  */
3405
3406 #include "../param.h"
3407 #include "../user.h"
3408 #include "../reg.h"
3409 #include "../inode.h"
3410 #include "../systm.h"
3411 #include "../proc.h"
3412
3413 setswit()
3414 {
3415
3416     u.u_ar0[R0] = SW->integ;
3417 }
3418 /* ------------------------- */
3419
3420 stime()
3421 {
3422
3423     u.u_ar0[R0] = time[0];
3424     u.u_ar0[R1] = time[1];
3425 }
3426 /* ------------------------- */
3427
3428 stime()
3429 {
3430
3431     if(suser()) {
3432             time[0] = u.u_ar0[R0];
3433             time[1] = u.u_ar0[R1];
3434             wakeup(tout);
3435     }
3436 }
3437 /* ------------------------- */
3438
3439 setuid()
3440 {
3441     register uid;
3442
3443     uid = u.u_ar0[R0].lobyte;
3444     if(u.u_ruid == uid.lobyte || suser()) {
3445             u.u_uid = uid;
3446             u.u_procp->p_uid = uid;
3447             u.u_ruid = uid;
3448     }
3449 }
```

```
3450 /* ------------------------- */
3451
3452 setuid()
3453 {
3454
3455     u.u_ar0[R0].lobyte = u.u_ruid;
3456     u.u_ar0[R0].hibyte = u.u_uid;
3457 }
3458 /* ------------------------- */
3459
3460 setgid()
3461 {
3462     register gid;
3463
3464     gid = u.u_ar0[R0].lobyte;
3465     if(u.u_rgid == gid.lobyte || suser()) {
3466             u.u_gid = gid;
3467             u.u_rgid = gid;
3468     }
3469 }
3470 /* ------------------------- */
3471
3472 setgid()
3473 {
3474
3475     u.u_ar0[R0].lobyte = u.u_rgid;
3476     u.u_ar0[R0].hibyte = u.u_gid;
3477 }
3478 /* ------------------------- */
3479
3480 getpid()
3481 {
3482     u.u_ar0[R0] = u.u_procp->p_pid;
3483 }
3484 /* ------------------------- */
3485
3486 sync()
3487 {
3488
3489     update();
3490 }
3491 /* ------------------------- */
3492
3493 nice()
3494 {
3495     register n;
3496
3497     n = u.u_ar0[R0];
3498     if(n > 20)
3499             n = 20;
```

```
3500     if(n < 0 && !suser())
3501             n = 0;
3502     u.u_procp->p_nice = n;
3503 }
3504 /* ------------------------        */
3505
3506 /*
3507  * Unlink system call.
3508  * panic: unlink -- 'cannot happen'
3509  */
3510 unlink()
3511 {
3512     register *ip, *pp;
3513     extern uchar;
3514
3515     pp = namei(&uchar, 2);
3516     if(pp == NULL)
3517             return;
3518     prele(pp);
3519     ip = iget(pp->i_dev, u.u_dent.u_ino);
3520     if(ip == NULL)
3521             panic("unlink -- iget");
3522     if((ip->i_mode&IFMT)==IFDIR && !suser())
3523             goto out;
3524     u.u_offset[1] =- DIRSIZ+2;
3525     u.u_base = &u.u_dent;
3526     u.u_count = DIRSIZ+2;
3527     u.u_dent.u_ino = 0;
3528     writei(pp);
3529     ip->i_nlink--;
3530     ip->i_flag =| IUPD;
3531
3532 out:
3533     iput(pp);
3534     iput(ip);
3535 }
3536 /* ------------------------        */
3537
3538 chdir()
3539 {
3540     register *ip;
3541     extern uchar;
3542
3543     ip = namei(&uchar, 0);
3544     if(ip == NULL)
3545             return;
3546     if((ip->i_mode&IFMT) != IFDIR) {
3547             u.u_error = ENOTDIR;
3548     bad:
3549             iput(ip);
```

```
3550             return;
3551     }
3552     if(access(ip, IEXEC))
3553             goto bad;
3554     iput(u.u_cdir);
3555     u.u_cdir = ip;
3556     prele(ip);
3557 }
3558 /* ------------------------        */
3559
3560 chmod()
3561 {
3562     register *ip;
3563
3564     if ((ip = owner()) == NULL)
3565             return;
3566     ip->i_mode =& ~07777;
3567     if (u.u_uid)
3568             u.u_arg[1] =& ~ISVTX;
3569     ip->i_mode =| u.u_arg[1]&07777;
3570     ip->i_flag =| IUPD;
3571     iput(ip);
3572 }
3573 /* ------------------------        */
3574
3575 chown()
3576 {
3577     register *ip;
3578
3579     if (!suser() || (ip = owner()) == NULL)
3580             return;
3581     ip->i_uid = u.u_arg[1].lobyte;
3582     ip->i_gid = u.u_arg[1].hibyte;
3583     ip->i_flag =| IUPD;
3584     iput(ip);
3585 }
3586 /* ------------------------        */
3587
3588 /*
3589  * Change modified date of file:
3590  * time to r0-r1; sys smdate; file
3591  * This call has been withdrawn because it messes up
3592  * incremental dumps (pseudo-old files aren't dumped).
3593  * It works though and you can uncomment it if you like.
3594
3595 smdate()
3596 {
3597     register struct inode *ip;
3598     register int *tp;
3599     int tbuf[2];
```

```
3600
3601     if ((ip = owner()) == NULL)
3602             return;
3603     ip->i_flag =| IUPD;
3604     tp = &tbuf[2];
3605     *--tp = u.u_ar0[R1];
3606     *--tp = u.u_ar0[R0];
3607     iupdat(ip, tp);
3608     ip->i_flag =& ~IUPD;
3609     iput(ip);
3610 }
3611 */
3612 /* -------------------------        */
3613
3614 ssig()
3615 {
3616     register a;
3617
3618     a = u.u_ar[0];
3619     if(a<=0 || a>=NSIG || a ==SIGKIL) {
3620             u.u_error = EINVAL;
3621             return;
3622     }
3623     u.u_ar0[R0] = u.u_signal[a];
3624     u.u_signal[a] = u.u_ar[1];
3625     if(u.u_procp->p_sig == a)
3626             u.u_procp->p_sig = 0;
3627 }
3628 /* -------------------------        */
3629
3630 kill()
3631 {
3632     register struct proc *p, *q;
3633     register a;
3634     int f;
3635
3636     f = 0;
3637     a = u.u_ar0[R0];
3638     q = u.u_procp;
3639     for(p = &proc[0]; p < &proc[NPROC]; p++) {
3640             if(p == q)
3641                     continue;
3642             if(a != 0 && p->p_pid != a)
3643                     continue;
3644             if(a==0&&(p->p_ttyp!=q->p_ttyp||p<=&proc[1]))
3645                     continue;
3646             if(u.u_uid != 0 && u.u_uid != p->p_uid)
3647                     continue;
3648             f++;
3649             psignal(p, u.u_ar[0]);
```

```
3650     }
3651     if(f == 0)
3652             u.u_error = ESRCH;
3653 }
3654 /* -------------------------        */
3655
3656 times()
3657 {
3658     register *p;
3659
3660     for(p = &u.u_utime; p  < &u.u_utime+6;) {
3661             suword(u.u_ar[0], *p++);
3662             u.u_ar[0] =+ 2;
3663     }
3664 }
3665 /* -------------------------        */
3666
3667 profil()
3668 {
3669
3670     u.u_prof[0] = u.u_ar[0] & ~1;  /* base of sample buf */
3671     u.u_prof[1] = u.u_ar[1];       /* size of same */
3672     u.u_prof[2] = u.u_ar[2];       /* pc offset */
3673     u.u_prof[3] = (u.u_ar[3]>>1) & 077777; /* pc scale */
3674 }
3675 /* -------------------------        */
3676
3677
3678
3679
3680
3681
3682
3683
3684
3685
3686
3687
3688
3689
3690
3691
3692
3693
3694
3695
3696
3697
3698
3699
```

```
3700 #
3701 #include "../param.h"
3702 #include "../systm.h"
3703 #include "../user.h"
3704 #include "../proc.h"
3705
3706 #define    UMODE   0170000
3707 #define    SCHMAG  10
3708
3709 /*
3710  * clock is called straight from
3711  * the real time clock interrupt.
3712  *
3713  * Functions:
3714  * reprime clock
3715  * copy *switches to display
3716  * implement callouts
3717  * maintain user/system times
3718  * maintain date
3719  * profile
3720  * tout wakeup (sys sleep)
3721  * lightning bolt wakeup (every 4 sec)
3722  * alarm clock signals
3723  * jab the scheduler
3724  */
3725 clock(dev, sp, r1, nps, r0, pc, ps)
3726 {
3727     register struct callo *p1, *p2;
3728     register struct proc *pp;
3729
3730     /*
3731      * restart clock
3732      */
3733
3734     *lks = 0115;
3735
3736     /*
3737      * display register
3738      */
3739
3740     display();
3741
3742     /*
3743      * callouts
3744      * if none, just return
3745      * else update first non-zero time
3746      */
3747
3748     if(callout[0].c_func == 0)
3749         goto out;
```

```
3750     p2 = &callout[0];
3751     while(p2->c_time<=0 && p2->c_func!=0)
3752         p2++;
3753     p2->c_time--;
3754
3755     /*
3756      * if ps is high, just return
3757      */
3758
3759     if((ps&0340) != 0)
3760         goto out;
3761
3762     /*
3763      * callout
3764      */
3765
3766     sp15();
3767     if(callout[0].c_time <= 0) {
3768         p1 = &callout[0];
3769         while(p1->c_func != 0 && p1->c_time <= 0) {
3770             (*p1->c_func)(p1->c_arg);
3771             p1++;
3772         }
3773         p2 = &callout[0];
3774         while(p2->c_func = p1->c_func) {
3775             p2->c_time = p1->c_time;
3776             p2->c_arg = p1->c_arg;
3777             p1++;
3778             p2++;
3779         }
3780     }
3781
3782     /*
3783      * lightning bolt time-out
3784      * and time of day
3785      */
3786
3787 out:
3788     if((ps&UMODE) == UMODE) {
3789         u.u_utime++;
3790         if(u.u_prof[3])
3791             incupc(pc, u.u_prof);
3792     } else
3793         u.u_stime++;
3794     pp = u.u_procp;
3795     if(++pp->p_cpu == 0)
3796         pp->p_cpu--;
3797     if(++lbolt >= HZ) {
3798         if((ps&0340) != 0)
3799             return;
```

```
3800              lbolt =- HZ;
3801              if(++time[1] == 0)
3802                      ++time[0];
3803              spl1();
3804              if(time[1]==tout[1] && time[0]==tout[0])
3805                      wakeup(tout);
3806              if((time[1]&03) == 0) {
3807                      runrun++;
3808                      wakeup(&lbolt);
3809              }
3810              for(pp = &proc[0]; pp < &proc[NPROC]; pp++)
3811              if (pp->p_stat) {
3812                      if(pp->p_time != 127)
3813                              pp->p_time++;
3814                      if((pp->p_cpu & 0377) > SCHMAG)
3815                              pp->p_cpu =- SCHMAG; else
3816                              pp->p_cpu = 0;
3817                      if(pp->p_pri > PUSER)
3818                              setpri(pp);
3819              }
3820              if(runin!=0) {
3821                      runin = 0;
3822                      wakeup(&runin);
3823              }
3824              if((ps&UMODE) == UMODE) {
3825                      u.u_ar0 = &r0;
3826                      if(issig())
3827                              psig();
3828                      setpri(u.u_procp);
3829              }
3830      }
3831 }
3832 /* --------------------------       */
3833
3834 /*
3835  * timeout is called to arrange that
3836  * fun(arg) is called in tim/HZ seconds.
3837  * An entry is sorted into the callout
3838  * structure. The time in each structure
3839  * entry is the number of HZ's more
3840  * than the previous entry.
3841  * In this way, decrementing the
3842  * first entry has the effect of
3843  * updating all entries.
3844  */
3845 timeout(fun, arg, tim)
3846 {
3847      register struct callo *p1, *p2;
3848      register t;
3849      int s;
```

```
3850
3851      t = tim;
3852      s = PS->integ;
3853      p1 = &callout[0];
3854      spl7();
3855      while(p1->c_func != 0 && p1->c_time <= t) {
3856              t =- p1->c_time;
3857              p1++;
3858      }
3859      p1->c_time =- t;
3860      p2 = p1;
3861      while(p2->c_func != 0)
3862              p2++;
3863      while(p2 >= p1) {
3864              (p2+1)->c_time = p2->c_time;
3865              (p2+1)->c_func = p2->c_func;
3866              (p2+1)->c_arg = p2->c_arg;
3867              p2--;
3868      }
3869      p1->c_time = t;
3870      p1->c_func = fun;
3871      p1->c_arg = arg;
3872      PS->integ = s;
3873 }
3874 /* --------------------------       */
3875
3876
3877
3878
3879
3880
3881
3882
3883
3884
3885
3886
3887
3888
3889
3890
3891
3892
3893
3894
3895
3896
3897
3898
3899
```

```
3900 #
3901 /*
3902  */
3903
3904 #include "../param.h"
3905 #include "../systm.h"
3906 #include "../user.h"
3907 #include "../proc.h"
3908 #include "../inode.h"
3909 #include "../reg.h"
3910
3911 /*
3912  * Priority for tracing
3913  */
3914 #define    IPCPRI  (-1)
3915
3916 /*
3917  * Structure to access an array of integers.
3918  */
3919 struct
3920 {
3921     int      inta[];
3922 };
3923 /* ------------------------        */
3924
3925 /*
3926  * Tracing variables.
3927  * Used to pass trace command from
3928  * parent to child being traced.
3929  * This data base cannot be
3930  * shared and is locked
3931  * per user.
3932  */
3933 struct
3934 {
3935     int      ip_lock;
3936     int      ip_req;
3937     int      ip_addr;
3938     int      ip_data;
3939 } ipc;
3940 /* ------------------------        */
3941
3942 /*
3943  * Send the specified signal to
3944  * all processes with 'tp' as its
3945  * controlling teletype.
3946  * Called by tty.c for quits and
3947  * interrupts.
3948  */
3949 signal(tp, sig)
```

```
3950 {
3951     register struct proc *p;
3952
3953     for(p = &proc[0]; p < &proc[NPROC]; p++)
3954         if(p->p_ttyp == tp)
3955             psignal(p, sig);
3956 }
3957 /* ------------------------        */
3958
3959 /*
3960  * Send the specified signal to
3961  * the specified process.
3962  */
3963 psignal(p, sig)
3964 int *p;
3965 {
3966     register *rp;
3967
3968     if(sig >= NSIG)
3969         return;
3970     rp = p;
3971     if(rp->p_sig != SIGKIL)
3972         rp->p_sig = sig;
3973     if(rp->p_stat > PUSER)
3974         rp->p_stat = PUSER;
3975     if(rp->p_stat == SWAIT)
3976         setrun(rp);
3977 }
3978 /* ------------------------        */
3979
3980 /*
3981  * Returns true if the current
3982  * process has a signal to process.
3983  * This is asked at least once
3984  * each time a process enters the
3985  * system.
3986  * A signal does not do anything
3987  * directly to a process; it sets
3988  * a flag that asks the process to
3989  * do something to itself.
3990  */
3991 issig()
3992 {
3993     register n;
3994     register struct proc *p;
3995
3996     p = u.u_procp;
3997     if(n = p->p_sig) {
3998         if (p->p_flag&STRC) {
3999             stop();
```

```
4000                   if ((n = p->p_sis) == 0)
4001                           return(0);
4002               }
4003           if((u.u_signal[n]&1) == 0)
4004                   return(n);
4005       }
4006    return(0);
4007 }
4008 /* ----------------------         */
4009
4010 /*
4011  * Enter the tracins STOP state.
4012  * In this state, the parent is
4013  * informed and the process is able to
4014  * receive commands from the parent.
4015  */
4016 stop()
4017 {
4018    resister struct proc *pp, *cp;
4019
4020 loop:
4021    cp = u.u_procp;
4022    if(cp->p_ppid != 1)
4023    for (pp = &proc[0]; pp < &proc[NPROC]; pp++)
4024            if (pp->p_pid == cp->p_ppid) {
4025                    wakeup(pp);
4026                    cp->p_stat = SSTOP;
4027                    swtch();
4028                    if ((cp->p_flas&STRC)==0 || procxmt())
4029                            return;
4030                    soto loop;
4031            }
4032    exit();
4033 }
4034 /* ----------------------         */
4035
4036 /*
4037  * Perform the action specified by
4038  * the current signal.
4039  * The usual sequence is:
4040  * if(issis())
4041  *          psis();
4042  */
4043 psis()
4044 {
4045    resister n, p;
4046    resister *rp;
4047
4048    rp = u.u_procp;
4049    n = rp->p_sis;
```

```
4050    rp->p_sis = 0;
4051    if((p=u.u_signal[n]) != 0) {
4052            u.u_error = 0;
4053            if(n != SIGINS && n != SIGTRC)
4054                    u.u_signal[n] = 0;
4055            n = u.u_ar0[R6] - 4;
4056            srow(n);
4057            suword(n+2, u.u_ar0[RPS]);
4058            suword(n, u.u_ar0[R7]);
4059            u.u_ar0[R6] = n;
4060            u.u_ar0[RPS] =& ~TBIT;
4061            u.u_ar0[R7] = p;
4062            return;
4063    }
4064    switch(n) {
4065
4066    case SIGQIT:
4067    case SIGINS:
4068    case SIGTRC:
4069    case SIGIOT:
4070    case SIGEMT:
4071    case SIGFPT:
4072    case SIGBUS:
4073    case SIGSEG:
4074    case SIGSYS:
4075            u.u_ars[0] = n;
4076            if(core())
4077                    n =+ 0200;
4078    }
4079    u.u_ars[0] = (u.u_ar0[R0]<<8) | n;
4080    exit();
4081 }
4082 /* ----------------------         */
4083
4084 /*
4085  * Create a core image on the file "core"
4086  * If you are lookins for protection slitches,
4087  * there are probably a wealth of them here
4088  * when this occurs to a suid command.
4089  *
4090  * It writes USIZE block of the
4091  * user.h area followed by the entire
4092  * data+stack segments.
4093  */
4094 core()
4095 {
4096    resister s, *ip;
4097    extern schar;
4098
4099    u.u_error = 0;
```

```
4100        u.u_dirp = "core";
4101        ip = namei(&schar, 1);
4102        if(ip == NULL) {
4103                if(u.u_error)
4104                        return(0);
4105                ip = maknode(0666);
4106                if(ip == NULL)
4107                        return(0);
4108        }
4109        if(!access(ip, IWRITE) &&
4110           (ip->i_mode&IFMT) == 0 &&
4111           u.u_uid == u.u_ruid) {
4112                itrunc(ip);
4113                u.u_offset[0] = 0;
4114                u.u_offset[1] = 0;
4115                u.u_base = &u;
4116                u.u_count = USIZE*64;
4117                u.u_segfls = 1;
4118                writei(ip);
4119                s = u.u_procp->p_size - USIZE;
4120                estabur(0, s, 0, 0);
4121                u.u_base = 0;
4122                u.u_count = s*64;
4123                u.u_segfls = 0;
4124                writei(ip);
4125        }
4126        iput(ip);
4127        return(u.u_error==0);
4128 }
4129 /* ------------------------          */
4130
4131 /*
4132  * grow the stack to include the SP
4133  * true return if successful.
4134  */
4135
4136 grow(sp)
4137 char *sp;
4138 {
4139     register a, si, i;
4140
4141     if(sp >= -u.u_ssize*64)
4142             return(0);
4143     si = ldiv(-sp, 64) - u.u_ssize + SINCR;
4144     if(si <= 0)
4145             return(0);
4146     if(estabur(u.u_tsize, u.u_dsize, u.u_ssize+si, u.u_sep))
4147             return(0);
4148     expand(u.u_procp->p_size+si);
4149     a = u.u_procp->p_addr + u.u_procp->p_size;
```

```
4150     for(i=u.u_ssize; i; i--) {
4151             a--;
4152             copyses(a-si, a);
4153     }
4154     for(i=si; i; i--)
4155             clearses(--a);
4156     u.u_ssize =+ si;
4157     return(1);
4158 }
4159 /* ------------------------          */
4160
4161 /*
4162  * sys-trace system call.
4163  */
4164 ptrace()
4165 {
4166     register struct proc *p;
4167
4168     if (u.u_arg[2] <= 0) {
4169             u.u_procp->p_flag =: STRC;
4170             return;
4171     }
4172     for (p=proc; p < &proc[NPROC]; p++)
4173             if (p->p_stat==SSTOP
4174              && p->p_pid==u.u_arg[0]
4175              && p->p_ppid==u.u_procp->p_pid)
4176                     goto found;
4177     u.u_error = ESRCH;
4178     return;
4179
4180     found:
4181     while (ipc.ip_lock)
4182             sleep(&ipc, IPCPRI);
4183     ipc.ip_lock = p->p_pid;
4184     ipc.ip_data = u.u_ar0[R0];
4185     ipc.ip_addr = u.u_arg[1] & ~01;
4186     ipc.ip_req = u.u_arg[2];
4187     p->p_flag =& ~SWTED;
4188     setrun(p);
4189     while (ipc.ip_req > 0)
4190             sleep(&ipc, IPCPRI);
4191     u.u_ar0[R0] = ipc.ip_data;
4192     if (ipc.ip_req < 0)
4193             u.u_error = EIO;
4194     ipc.ip_lock = 0;
4195     wakeup(&ipc);
4196 }
4197 /* ------------------------          */
4198
4199 /*
```

```
4200     * Code that the child process
4201     * executes to implement the command
4202     * of the parent process in tracing.
4203     */
4204   procxmt()
4205   {
4206      register int i;
4207      register int *p;
4208
4209      if (ipc.ip_lock != u.u_procp->p_pid)
4210           return(0);
4211      i = ipc.ip_req;
4212      ipc.ip_req = 0;
4213      wakeup(&ipc);
4214      switch (i) {
4215
4216      /* read user I */
4217      case 1:
4218           if (fuibyte(ipc.ip_addr) == -1)
4219                goto error;
4220           ipc.ip_data = fuiword(ipc.ip_addr);
4221           break;
4222
4223      /* read user D */
4224      case 2:
4225           if (fubyte(ipc.ip_addr) == -1)
4226                goto error;
4227           ipc.ip_data = fuword(ipc.ip_addr);
4228           break;
4229
4230      /* read u */
4231      case 3:
4232           i = ipc.ip_addr;
4233           if (i<0 || i >= (USIZE<<6))
4234                goto error;
4235           ipc.ip_data = u.int[i>>1];
4236           break;
4237
4238      /* write user I (for now, always an error) */
4239      case 4:
4240           if (suiword(ipc.ip_addr, 0) < 0)
4241                goto error;
4242           suiword(ipc.ip_addr, ipc.ip_data);
4243           break;
4244
4245      /* write user D */
4246      case 5:
4247           if (suword(ipc.ip_addr, 0) < 0)
4248                goto error;
4249           suword(ipc.ip_addr, ipc.ip_data);
```

```
4250           break;
4251
4252      /* write u */
4253      case 6:
4254           p = &u.int[ipc.ip_addr>>1];
4255           if (p >= u.u_fsav && p < &u.u_fsav[25])
4256                goto ok;
4257           for (i=0; i<9; i++)
4258                if (p == &u.u_ar0[resloc[i]])
4259                     goto ok;
4260           goto error;
4261      ok:
4262           if (p == &u.u_ar0[RPS]) {
4263                     /* assure user space */
4264                ipc.ip_data =| 0170000;
4265                     /* priority 0  */
4266                ipc.ip_data =& ~0340;
4267           }
4268           *p = ipc.ip_data;
4269           break;
4270
4271      /* set signal and continue */
4272      case 7:
4273           u.u_procp->p_sig = ipc.ip_data;
4274           return(1);
4275
4276      /* force exit */
4277      case 8:
4278           exit();
4279
4280      default:
4281      error:
4282           ipc.ip_req = -1;
4283      }
4284      return(0);
4285   }
4286   /* ----------------------         */
4287
4288
4289
4290
4291
4292
4293
4294
4295
4296
4297
4298
4299
```

3

Program Swapping
Basic Input/Output
Block Devices

```
4300 /*
4301  * Text structure.
4302  * One allocated per pure
4303  * procedure on swap device.
4304  * Manipulated by text.c
4305  */
4306 struct text
4307 {
4308   int      x_daddr;        /* disk address of segment */
4309   int      x_caddr;        /* core address, if loaded */
4310   int      x_size; /* size (*64) */
4311   int      *x_iptr;        /* inode of prototype */
4312   char     x_count;        /* reference count */
4313   char     x_ccount;       /* number of loaded references */
4314 } text[NTEXT];
4315 /* ------------------------          */
4316
4317
4318
4319
4320
4321
4322
4323
4324
4325
4326
4327
4328
4329
4330
4331
4332
4333
4334
4335
4336
4337
4338
4339
4340
4341
4342
4343
4344
4345
4346
4347
4348
4349
```

```
4350 #
4351 #include "../param.h"
4352 #include "../systm.h"
4353 #include "../user.h"
4354 #include "../proc.h"
4355 #include "../text.h"
4356 #include "../inode.h"
4357
4358 /* Swap out process p.
4359  * The ff flag causes its core to be freed--
4360  * it may be off when called to create an image for a
4361  * child process in newproc.
4362  * Os is the old size of the data area of the process,
4363  * and is supplied during core expansion swaps.
4364  *
4365  * panic: out of swap space
4366  * panic: swap error -- IO error
4367  */
4368 xswap(p, ff, os)
4369 int *p;
4370 {   register *rp, a;
4371
4372     rp = p;
4373     if(os == 0)
4374             os = rp->p_size;
4375     a = malloc(swapmap, (rp->p_size+7)/8);
4376     if(a == NULL)
4377             panic("out of swap space");
4378     xccdec(rp->p_textp);
4379     rp->p_flag =| SLOCK;
4380     if(swap(a, rp->p_addr, os, 0))
4381             panic("swap error");
4382     if(ff)
4383             mfree(coremap, os, rp->p_addr);
4384     rp->p_addr = a;
4385     rp->p_flag =& ~(SLOAD|SLOCK);
4386     rp->p_time = 0;
4387     if(runout) {
4388             runout = 0;
4389             wakeup(&runout);
4390     }
4391 }
4392 /* ------------------------          */
4393
4394 /*
4395  * relinquish use of the shared text segment
4396  * of a process.
4397  */
4398 xfree()
4399 {   register *xp, *ip;
```

```
4400
4401        if((xp=u.u_procp->p_textp) != NULL) {
4402                u.u_procp->p_textp = NULL;
4403                xccdec(xp);
4404                if(--xp->x_count == 0) {
4405                        ip = xp->x_iptr;
4406                        if((ip->i_mode&ISVTX) == 0) {
4407                                xp->x_iptr = NULL;
4408                                mfree(swapmap, (xp->x_size+7)/8,
4409                                        xp->x_daddr);
4410                                ip->i_flag =& ~ITEXT;
4411                                iput(ip);
4412                        }
4413                }
4414        }
4415 }
4416 /* -------------------------         */
4417
4418 /* Attach to a shared text segment.
4419  * If there is no shared text, just return.
4420  * If there is, hook up to it:
4421  * if it is not currently being used, it has to be read
4422  * in from the inode (ip) and established in the swap space.
4423  * If it is being used, but is not currently in core,
4424  * a swap has to be done to get it back.
4425  * The full coroutine glory has to be invoked--
4426  * see slp.c-- because if the calling process
4427  * is misplaced in core the text image might not fit.
4428  * Quite possibly the code after 'out:' could check to
4429  * see if the text does fit and simply swap it in.
4430  *
4431  * panic: out of swap space
4432  */
4433 xalloc(ip)
4434 int *ip;
4435 {
4436     register struct text *xp;
4437     register *rp, ts;
4438
4439     if(u.u_arg[1] == 0) return;
4440     rp = NULL;
4441     for(xp = &text[0]; xp < &text[NTEXT]; xp++)
4442             if(xp->x_iptr == NULL) {
4443                     if(rp == NULL)
4444                             rp = xp;
4445             } else
4446                     if(xp->x_iptr == ip) {
4447                             xp->x_count++;
4448                             u.u_procp->p_textp = xp;
4449                             goto out;
4450                     }
4451     if((xp=rp) == NULL) panic("out of text");
4452     xp->x_count = 1;
4453     xp->x_ccount = 0;
4454     xp->x_iptr = ip;
4455     ts = ((u.u_arg[1]+63)>>6) & 01777;
4456     xp->x_size = ts;
4457     if((xp->x_daddr = malloc(swapmap, (ts+7)/8)) == NULL)
4458             panic("out of swap space");
4459     expand(USIZE+ts);
4460     estabur(0, ts, 0, 0);
4461     u.u_count = u.u_arg[1];
4462     u.u_offset[1] = 020;
4463     u.u_base = 0;
4464     readi(ip);
4465     rp = u.u_procp;
4466     rp->p_flag =! SLOCK;
4467     swap(xp->x_daddr, rp->p_addr+USIZE, ts, 0);
4468     rp->p_flag =& ~SLOCK;
4469     rp->p_textp = xp;
4470     rp = ip;
4471     rp->i_flag =! ITEXT;
4472     rp->i_count++;
4473     expand(USIZE);
4474 out:
4475     if(xp->x_ccount == 0) {
4476             savu(u.u_rsav);
4477             savu(u.u_ssav);
4478             xswap(u.u_procp, 1, 0);
4479             u.u_procp->p_flag =! SSWAP;
4480             swtch();
4481             /* no return */
4482     }
4483     xp->x_ccount++;
4484 }
4485 /* -------------------------         */
4486
4487 /* Decrement the in-core usage count of a shared text
4488  * segment. When it drops to zero, free the core space.
4489  */
4490 xccdec(xp)
4491 int *xp;
4492 {
4493     register *rp;
4494
4495     if((rp=xp)!=NULL && rp->x_ccount!=0)
4496             if(--rp->x_ccount == 0)
4497                     mfree(coremap, rp->x_size, rp->x_caddr);
4498 }
4499
```

```
4500  /*
4501   * Each buffer in the pool is usually doubly linked into two
4502   * lists: for the device with which it is currently associat-
4503   * ed (always) and also for a list of blocks available for
4504   * allocation for other use (usually).
4505   * The latter list is kept in last-used order, and the two
4506   * lists are doubly linked to make it easy to remove
4507   * a buffer from one list when it was found by
4508   * looking through the other.
4509   * A buffer is on the available list, and is liable
4510   * to be reassigned to another disk block, if and only
4511   * if it is not marked BUSY.  When a buffer is busy, the
4512   * available-list pointers can be used for other purposes.
4513   * Most drivers use the forward ptr as a link in their I/O
4514   * active queue.
4515   * A buffer header contains all the information required
4516   * to perform I/O.
4517   * Most of the routines which manipulate these things
4518   * are in bio.c.
4519   */
4520  struct buf
4521  {
4522      int    b_flags;        /* see defines below */
4523      struct buf *b_forw;    /* headed by devtab of b_dev */
4524      struct buf *b_back;    /* "   */
4525      struct buf *av_forw;   /* position on free list, */
4526      struct buf *av_back;   /*    if not BUSY*/
4527      int    b_dev;          /* major+minor device name */
4528      int    b_wcount;       /* transfer count (usu. words) */
4529      char   *b_addr;        /* low order core address */
4530      char   *b_xmem;        /* high order core address */
4531      char   *b_blkno;       /* block # on device */
4532      char   b_error;        /* returned after I/O */
4533      char   *b_resid;       /* words not transferred after
4534                                              error */
4535  } buf[NBUF];
4536  /* ------------------------       */
4537
4538  /*
4539   * Each block device has a devtab, which contains private
4540   * state stuff and 2 list heads: the b_forw/b_back list,
4541   * which is doubly linked and has all the buffers currently
4542   * associated with that major device;
4543   * and the d_actf/d_actl list, which is private to the
4544   * device but in fact is always used for the head and tail
4545   * of the I/O queue for the device.
4546   * Various routines in bio.c look at b_forw/b_back
4547   * (notice they are the same as in the buf structure)
4548   * but the rest is private to each device driver.
4549   */
```

```
4550
4551  struct devtab
4552  {
4553      char   d_active;       /* busy flag */
4554      char   d_errcnt;       /* error count (for recovery)*/
4555      struct buf *b_forw;    /* first buffer for this dev */
4556      struct buf *b_back;    /* last buffer for this dev */
4557      struct buf *d_actf;    /* head of I/O queue */
4558      struct buf *d_actl;    /* tail of I/O queue */
4559  };
4560  /* ------------------------       */
4561
4562  /*
4563   * This is the head of the queue of available
4564   * buffers-- all unused except for the 2 list heads.
4565   */
4566
4567  struct      buf bfreelist;
4568
4569  /*
4570   * These flags are kept in b_flags.
4571   */
4572  #define   B_WRITE    0       /* non-read pseudo-flag */
4573  #define   B_READ     01      /* read when I/O occurs */
4574  #define   B_DONE     02      /* transaction finished */
4575  #define   B_ERROR    04      /* transaction aborted */
4576  #define   B_BUSY     010     /* not on av_forw/back list */
4577  #define   B_PHYS     020     /* Physical IO potentially
4578                                  using the Unibus map */
4579  #define   B_MAP      040     /* This block has the UNIBUS
4580                                  map allocated */
4581  #define   B_WANTED   0100    /* issue wakeup when
4582                                  BUSY goes off */
4583  #define   B_RELOC    0200    /* no longer used */
4584  #define   B_ASYNC    0400    /* don't wait for I/O
4585                                          completion */
4586  #define   B_DELWRI   01000   /* don't write till block
4587                                  leaves available list */
4588
4589
4590
4591
4592
4593
4594
4595
4596
4597
4598
4599
```

```
4600 /* Used to dissect integer device code
4601  * into major (driver designation) and
4602  * minor (driver parameter) parts.
4603  */
4604 struct      {
4605             char    d_minor;
4606             char    d_major;
4607 };
4608 /* -------------------------      */
4609 /* Declaration of block device
4610  * switch. Each entry (row) is
4611  * the only link between the
4612  * main unix code and the driver.
4613  * The initialization of the
4614  * device switches is in the
4615  * file conf.c.
4616  */
4617 struct      bdevsw  {
4618     int     (*d_open)();
4619     int     (*d_close)();
4620     int     (*d_strategy)();
4621     int     *d_tab;
4622 } bdevsw[];
4623 /* -------------------------      */
4624 /* Nblkdev is the number of entries
4625  * (rows) in the block switch. It is
4626  * set in binit/bio.c by making
4627  * a pass over the switch.
4628  * Used in bounds checking on major
4629  * device numbers.
4630  */
4631 int         nblkdev;
4632
4633 /* Character device switch.
4634  */
4635 struct      cdevsw  {
4636     int     (*d_open)();
4637     int     (*d_close)();
4638     int     (*d_read)();
4639     int     (*d_write)();
4640     int     (*d_sgtty)();
4641 } cdevsw[];
4642 /* -------------------------      */
4643
4644 /* Number of character switch entries.
4645  * Set by cinit/tty.c
4646  */
4647 int         nchrdev;
4648
4649
```

```
4650 /*
4651  * this file is created, along with the file "low.s",
4652  * by the program "mkconf.c", to reflect the actual
4653  * configuration of peripheral devices on a system.
4654  */
4655
4656 int (*bdevsw[])()
4657 {
4658     &nulldev, &nulldev, &rkstrategy, &rktab, /* rk */
4659     &nodev, &nodev, &nodev, 0, /* rp */
4660     &nodev, &nodev, &nodev, 0, /* rf */
4661     &nodev, &nodev, &nodev, 0, /* tm */
4662     &nodev, &nodev, &nodev, 0, /* tc */
4663     &nodev, &nodev, &nodev, 0, /* hs */
4664     &nodev, &nodev, &nodev, 0, /* hp */
4665     &nodev, &nodev, &nodev, 0, /* ht */
4666     0
4667 };
4668
4669 int (*cdevsw[])()
4670 {
4671     &klopen, &klclose, &klread, &klwrite, &klsgtty,
4672                                 /* console */
4673     &pcopen, &pcclose, &pcread, &pcwrite, &nodev,
4674                                 /* pc */
4675     &lpopen, &lpclose, &nodev, &lpwrite, &nodev,
4676                                 /* lp */
4677     &nodev, &nodev, &nodev,  &nodev,  &nodev, /* dc */
4678     &nodev, &nodev, &nodev,  &nodev,  &nodev, /* dh */
4679     &nodev, &nodev, &nodev,  &nodev,  &nodev, /* dp */
4680     &nodev, &nodev, &nodev,  &nodev,  &nodev, /* dj */
4681     &nodev, &nodev, &nodev,  &nodev,  &nodev, /* dn */
4682     &nulldev, &nulldev, &mmread, &mmwrite, &nodev,
4683                                 /* mem */
4684     &nulldev, &nulldev, &rkread, &rkwrite, &nodev,
4685                                 /* rk */
4686     &nodev, &nodev, &nodev,  &nodev,  &nodev, /* rf */
4687     &nodev, &nodev, &nodev,  &nodev,  &nodev, /* rp */
4688     &nodev, &nodev, &nodev,  &nodev,  &nodev, /* tm */
4689     &nodev, &nodev, &nodev,  &nodev,  &nodev, /* hs */
4690     &nodev, &nodev, &nodev,  &nodev,  &nodev, /* hp */
4691     &nodev, &nodev, &nodev,  &nodev,  &nodev, /* ht */
4692     0
4693 };
4694
4695 int rootdev {(0<<8)|0};
4696 int swapdev {(0<<8)|0};
4697 int swplo 4000; /* cannot be zero */
4698 int nswap 872;
4699
```

```
4700 #
4701 /*
4702  */
4703
4704 #include "../param.h"
4705 #include "../user.h"
4706 #include "../buf.h"
4707 #include "../conf.h"
4708 #include "../systm.h"
4709 #include "../proc.h"
4710 #include "../seg.h"
4711
4712 /*
4713  * This is the set of buffers proper, whose heads
4714  * were declared in buf.h.  There can exist buffer
4715  * headers not pointing here that are used purely
4716  * as arguments to the I/O routines to describe
4717  * I/O to be done-- e.g. swbuf, just below, for
4718  * swapping.
4719  */
4720 char        buffers[NBUF][514];
4721 struct      buf       swbuf;
4722
4723 /*
4724  * Declarations of the tables for the magtape devices;
4725  * see bdwrite.
4726  */
4727 int         tmtab;
4728 int         httab;
4729
4730 /*
4731  * The following several routines allocate and free
4732  * buffers with various side effects.  In general the
4733  * arguments to an allocate routine are a device and
4734  * a block number, and the value is a pointer to
4735  * to the buffer header; the buffer is marked "busy"
4736  * so that no on else can touch it.  If the block was
4737  * already in core, no I/O need be done; if it is
4738  * already busy, the process waits until it becomes free.
4739  * The following routines allocate a buffer:
4740  * setblk
4741  * bread
4742  * breada
4743  * Eventually the buffer must be released, possibly with the
4744  * side effect of writing it out, by using one of
4745  * bwrite
4746  * bdwrite
4747  * bawrite
4748  * brelse
4749  */
```

```
4750
4751 /* Read in (if necessary) the block and
4752  * return a buffer pointer.
4753  */
4754 bread(dev, blkno)
4755 {
4756     register struct buf *rbp;
4757
4758     rbp = setblk(dev, blkno);
4759     if (rbp->b_flags&B_DONE)
4760         return(rbp);
4761     rbp->b_flags =! B_READ;
4762     rbp->b_wcount = -256;
4763     (*bdevsw[dev.d_major].d_strategy)(rbp);
4764     iowait(rbp);
4765     return(rbp);
4766 }
4767 /* ------------------------         */
4768
4769 /*
4770  * Read in the block, like bread, but also start I/O on the
4771  * read-ahead block (which is not allocated to the caller)
4772  */
4773 breada(adev, blkno, rablkno)
4774 {
4775     register struct buf *rbp, *rabp;
4776     register int dev;
4777
4778     dev = adev;
4779     rbp = 0;
4780     if (!incore(dev, blkno)) {
4781         rbp = setblk(dev, blkno);
4782         if ((rbp->b_flags&B_DONE) == 0) {
4783             rbp->b_flags =! B_READ;
4784             rbp->b_wcount = -256;
4785             (*bdevsw[adev.d_major].d_strategy)(rbp);
4786         }
4787     }
4788     if (rablkno && !incore(dev, rablkno)) {
4789         rabp = setblk(dev, rablkno);
4790         if (rabp->b_flags & B_DONE)
4791             brelse(rabp);
4792         else {
4793             rabp->b_flags =! B_READ!B_ASYNC;
4794             rabp->b_wcount = -256;
4795             (*bdevsw[adev.d_major].d_strategy)(rabp);
4796         }
4797     }
4798     if (rbp==0)
4799         return(bread(dev, blkno));
```

```
4800       iowait(rbp);
4801       return(rbp);
4802 }
4803 /* ------------------------             */
4804
4805 /*
4806  * Write the buffer, waiting for completion.
4807  * Then release the buffer.
4808  */
4809 bwrite(bp)
4810 struct buf *bp;
4811 {
4812       register struct buf *rbp;
4813       register flag;
4814
4815       rbp = bp;
4816       flag = rbp->b_flags;
4817       rbp->b_flags =& ~(B_READ | B_DONE | B_ERROR | B_DELWRI);
4818       rbp->b_wcount = -256;
4819       (*bdevsw[rbp->b_dev.d_major].d_strategy)(rbp);
4820       if ((flag&B_ASYNC) == 0) {
4821               iowait(rbp);
4822               brelse(rbp);
4823       } else if ((flag&B_DELWRI)==0)
4824               geterror(rbp);
4825 }
4826 /* ---------------------------          */
4827
4828 /*
4829  * Release the buffer, marking it so that if it is grabbed
4830  * for another purpose it will be written out before being
4831  * given up (e.g. when writing a partial block where it is
4832  * assumed that another write for the same block will soon
4833  * follow). This can't  be done for magtape, since writes
4834  * must be done in the same order as requested.
4835  */
4836 bdwrite(bp)
4837 struct buf *bp;
4838 {
4839       register struct buf *rbp;
4840       register struct devtab *dp;
4841
4842       rbp = bp;
4843       dp = bdevsw[rbp->b_dev.d_major].d_tab;
4844       if (dp == &tmtab || dp == &httab)
4845               bawrite(rbp);
4846       else {
4847               rbp->b_flags =| B_DELWRI | B_DONE;
4848               brelse(rbp);
4849       }
```

```
4850 }
4851 /* ------------------------             */
4852
4853 /* Release the buffer, start I/O on it, but don't wait
4854  *                      for completion */
4855
4856 bawrite(bp)
4857 struct buf *bp;
4858 {
4859       register struct buf *rbp;
4860
4861       rbp = bp;
4862       rbp->b_flags =| B_ASYNC;
4863       bwrite(rbp);
4864 }
4865 /* -----------------------             */
4866
4867 /* release the buffer, with no I/O implied.
4868  */
4869 brelse(bp)
4870 struct buf *bp;
4871 {
4872       register struct buf *rbp, **backp;
4873       register int sps;
4874
4875       rbp = bp;
4876       if (rbp->b_flags&B_WANTED)
4877               wakeup(rbp);
4878       if (bfreelist.b_flags&B_WANTED) {
4879               bfreelist.b_flags =& ~B_WANTED;
4880               wakeup(&bfreelist);
4881       }
4882       if (rbp->b_flags&B_ERROR)
4883               rbp->b_dev.d_minor = -1;   /* no assoc. on error */
4884       backp = &bfreelist.av_back;
4885       sps = PS->integ;
4886       sp16();
4887       rbp->b_flags =& ~(B_WANTED|B_BUSY|B_ASYNC);
4888       (*backp)->av_forw = rbp;
4889       rbp->av_back = *backp;
4890       *backp = rbp;
4891       rbp->av_forw = &bfreelist;
4892       PS->integ = sps;
4893 }
4894 /* ---------------------------          */
4895
4896 /* See if the block is associated with some buffer
4897  * (mainly to avoid getting hung up on a wait in breada)
4898  */
4899 incore(adev, blkno)
```

```
4900 {
4901     register int dev;
4902     register struct buf *bp;
4903     register struct devtab *dp;
4904
4905     dev = adev;
4906     dp = bdevsw[adev.d_major].d_tab;
4907     for (bp=dp->b_forw; bp != dp; bp = bp->b_forw)
4908             if (bp->b_blkno==blkno && bp->b_dev==dev)
4909                     return(bp);
4910     return(0);
4911 }
4912 /* ------------------------       */
4913
4914 /* Assign a buffer for the given block.  If the appropriate
4915  * block is already associated, return it; otherwise search
4916  * for the oldest non-busy buffer and reassign it.
4917  * When a 512-byte area is wanted for some random reason
4918  * (e.g. during exec, for the user arglist) getblk can be
4919  * called with device NODEV to avoid unwanted associativity.
4920  */
4921 getblk(dev, blkno)
4922 {
4923     register struct buf *bp;
4924     register struct devtab *dp;
4925     extern lbolt;
4926
4927     if(dev.d_major >= nblkdev)
4928             panic('blkdev');
4929
4930      loop:
4931     if (dev < 0)
4932             dp = &bfreelist;
4933     else {
4934             dp = bdevsw[dev.d_major].d_tab;
4935             if(dp == NULL)
4936                     panic('devtab');
4937             for (bp=dp->b_forw; bp != dp; bp = bp->b_forw) {
4938                     if (bp->b_blkno!=blkno || bp->b_dev!=dev)
4939                             continue;
4940                     sp16();
4941                     if (bp->b_flags&B_BUSY) {
4942                             bp->b_flags =| B_WANTED;
4943                             sleep(bp, PRIBIO);
4944                             spl0();
4945                             goto loop;
4946                     }
4947                     spl0();
4948                     notavail(bp);
4949                     return(bp);
```

```
4950                     }
4951             }
4952     spl6();
4953     if (bfreelist.av_forw == &bfreelist) {
4954             bfreelist.b_flags =| B_WANTED;
4955             sleep(&bfreelist, PRIBIO);
4956             spl0();
4957             goto loop;
4958     }
4959     spl0();
4960     notavail(bp = bfreelist.av_forw);
4961     if (bp->b_flags & B_DELWRI) {
4962             bp->b_flags =| B_ASYNC;
4963             bwrite(bp);
4964             goto loop;
4965     }
4966     bp->b_flags = B_BUSY | B_RELOC;
4967     bp->b_back->b_forw = bp->b_forw;
4968     bp->b_forw->b_back = bp->b_back;
4969     bp->b_forw = dp->b_forw;
4970     bp->b_back = dp;
4971     dp->b_forw->b_back = bp;
4972     dp->b_forw = bp;
4973     bp->b_dev = dev;
4974     bp->b_blkno = blkno;
4975     return(bp);
4976 }
4977 /* ------------------------       */
4978
4979 /* Wait for I/O completion on the buffer; return errors
4980  * to the user.
4981  */
4982 iowait(bp)
4983 struct buf *bp;
4984 {
4985     register struct buf *rbp;
4986
4987     rbp = bp;
4988     spl6();
4989     while ((rbp->b_flags&B_DONE)==0)
4990             sleep(rbp, PRIBIO);
4991     spl0();
4992     geterror(rbp);
4993 }
4994 /* ------------------------       */
4995
4996 /* Unlink a buffer from the available list and mark it busy.
4997  * (internal interface)
4998  */
4999 notavail(bp)
```

```
5000 struct buf *bP;
5001 {
5002     register struct buf *rbP;
5003     register int sps;
5004
5005     rbP = bP;
5006     sps = PS->integ;
5007     spl6();
5008     rbP->av_back->av_forw = rbP->av_forw;
5009     rbP->av_forw->av_back = rbP->av_back;
5010     rbP->b_flags =! B_BUSY;
5011     PS->integ = sps;
5012 }
5013 /* ------------------------- */
5014
5015 /* Mark I/O complete on a buffer, release it if i/o is
5016  * asynchronous, and wake up anyone waiting for it.
5017  */
5018 iodone(bP)
5019 struct buf *bP;
5020 {
5021     register struct buf *rbP;
5022
5023     rbP = bP;
5024     if(rbP->b_flags&B_MAP)
5025             mapfree(rbP);
5026     rbP->b_flags =! B_DONE;
5027     if (rbP->b_flags&B_ASYNC)
5028             brelse(rbP);
5029     else {
5030             rbP->b_flags =& ~B_WANTED;
5031             wakeup(rbP);
5032     }
5033 }
5034 /* ------------------------- */
5035
5036 /* Zero the core associated with a buffer.
5037  */
5038 clrbuf(bP)
5039 int *bP;
5040 {
5041     register *P;
5042     register c;
5043
5044     P = bP->b_addr;
5045     c = 256;
5046     do
5047             *P++ = 0;
5048     while (--c);
5049 }
```

```
5050 /* ------------------------- */
5051
5052 /* Initialize the buffer I/O system by freeing
5053  * all buffers and setting all device buffer lists to empty.
5054  */
5055 binit()
5056 {
5057     register struct buf *bP;
5058     register struct devtab *dP;
5059     register int i;
5060     struct bdevsw *bdP;
5061
5062     bfreelist.b_forw = bfreelist.b_back =
5063         bfreelist.av_forw = bfreelist.av_back = &bfreelist;
5064     for (i=0; i<NBUF; i++) {
5065             bP = &buf[i];
5066             bP->b_dev = -1;
5067             bP->b_addr = buffers[i];
5068             bP->b_back = &bfreelist;
5069             bP->b_forw = bfreelist.b_forw;
5070             bfreelist.b_forw->b_back = bP;
5071             bfreelist.b_forw = bP;
5072             bP->b_flags = B_BUSY;
5073             brelse(bP);
5074     }
5075     i = 0;
5076     for (bdP = bdevsw; bdP->d_open; bdP++) {
5077             dP = bdP->d_tab;
5078             if(dP) {
5079                     dP->b_forw = dP;
5080                     dP->b_back = dP;
5081             }
5082             i++;
5083     }
5084     nblkdev = i;
5085 }
5086 /* ------------------------- */
5087
5088 /* Device start routine for disks
5089  * and other devices that have the register
5090  * layout of the older DEC controllers (RF, RK, RP, TM)
5091  */
5092 #define     IENABLE 0100
5093 #define     WCOM    02
5094 #define     RCOM    04
5095 #define     GO      01
5096 devstart(bP, devloc, devblk, hbcom)
5097 struct buf *bP;
5098 int *devloc;
5099 {
```

```
5100     register int *dp;
5101     register struct buf *rbp;
5102     register int com;
5103
5104     dp = devloc;
5105     rbp = bp;
5106     *dp = devblk;                        /* block address */
5107     *--dp = rbp->b_addr;                 /* buffer address */
5108     *--dp = rbp->b_wcount;               /* word count */
5109     com = (hbcom<<8) | IENABLE | GO |
5110             ((rbp->b_xmem & 03) << 4);
5111     if (rbp->b_flags&B_READ)             /* command + x-mem */
5112             com =| RCOM;
5113     else
5114             com =| WCOM;
5115     *--dp = com;
5116 }
5117 /* ------------------------- */
5118
5119 /* startup routine for RH controllers. */
5120 #define    RHWCOM    060
5121 #define    RHRCOM    070
5122
5123 rhstart(bp, devloc, devblk, abae)
5124 struct buf *bp;
5125 int *devloc, *abae;
5126 {
5127     register int *dp;
5128     register struct buf *rbp;
5129     register int com;
5130
5131     dp = devloc;
5132     rbp = bp;
5133     if(cputype == 70)
5134             *abae = rbp->b_xmem;
5135     *dp = devblk;                        /* block address */
5136     *--dp = rbp->b_addr;                 /* buffer address */
5137     *--dp = rbp->b_wcount;               /* word count */
5138     com = IENABLE | GO |
5139             ((rbp->b_xmem & 03) << 8);
5140     if (rbp->b_flags&B_READ)             /* command + x-mem */
5141             com =| RHRCOM; else
5142             com =| RHWCOM;
5143     *--dp = com;
5144 }
5145 /* ------------------------- */
5146
5147 /*
5148  * 11/70 routine to allocate the
5149  * UNIBUS map and initialize for
```

```
5150  * a unibus device.
5151  * The code here and in
5152  * rhstart assumes that an rh on an 11/70
5153  * is an rh70 and contains 22 bit addressing.
5154  */
5155 int    maplock;
5156 mapalloc(abp)
5157 struct buf *abp;
5158 {
5159     register i, a;
5160     register struct buf *bp;
5161
5162     if(cputype != 70)
5163             return;
5164     sp16();
5165     while(maplock&B_BUSY) {
5166             maplock =| B_WANTED;
5167             sleep(&maplock, PSWP);
5168     }
5169     maplock =| B_BUSY;
5170     sp10();
5171     bp = abp;
5172     bp->b_flags =| B_MAP;
5173     a = bp->b_xmem;
5174     for(i=16; i<32; i=+2)
5175             UBMAP->r[i+1] = a;
5176     for(a++; i<48; i=+2)
5177             UBMAP->r[i+1] = a;
5178     bp->b_xmem = 1;
5179 }
5180 /* ------------------------- */
5181
5182 mapfree(bp)
5183 struct buf *bp;
5184 {
5185
5186     bp->b_flags =& ~B_MAP;
5187     if(maplock&B_WANTED)
5188             wakeup(&maplock);
5189     maplock = 0;
5190 }
5191 /* ------------------------- */
5192
5193 /*
5194  * swap I/O
5195  */
5196 swap(blkno, coreaddr, count, rdflg)
5197 {
5198     register int *fp;
5199
```

```
5200    fp = &swbuf.b_flags;
5201    spl6();
5202    while (*fp&B_BUSY) {
5203            *fp =| B_WANTED;
5204            sleep(fp, PSWP);
5205    }
5206    *fp = B_BUSY | B_PHYS | rdfls;
5207    swbuf.b_dev = swapdev;
5208    swbuf.b_wcount = - (count<<5);   /* 32 w/block */
5209    swbuf.b_blkno = blkno;
5210    swbuf.b_addr = coreaddr<<6;       /* 64 b/block */
5211    swbuf.b_xmem = (coreaddr>>10) & 077;
5212    (*bdevsw[swapdev>>8].d_strategy)(&swbuf);
5213    spl6();
5214    while((*fp&B_DONE)==0)
5215            sleep(fp, PSWP);
5216    if (*fp&B_WANTED)
5217            wakeup(fp);
5218    spl0();
5219    *fp =& ~(B_BUSY|B_WANTED);
5220    return(*fp&B_ERROR);
5221 }
5222 /* -------------------------       */
5223
5224 /* make sure all write-behind blocks
5225  * on dev (or NODEV for all)
5226  * are flushed out.
5227  * (from umount and update)
5228  */
5229 bflush(dev)
5230 {
5231    register struct buf *bp;
5232
5233 loop:
5234    spl6();
5235    for (bp = bfreelist.av_forw; bp != &bfreelist;
5236                            bp = bp->av_forw) {
5237            if (bp->b_flags&B_DELWRI &&
5238                    (dev == NODEV||dev == bp->b_dev)) {
5239                    bp->b_flags =| B_ASYNC;
5240                    notavail(bp);
5241                    bwrite(bp);
5242                    goto loop;
5243            }
5244    }
5245    spl0();
5246 }
5247 /* -------------------------       */
5248
5249 /*
```

```
5250  * Raw I/O. The arguments are
5251  * The strategy routine for the device
5252  * A buffer, which will always be a special buffer
5253  *    header owned exclusively by the device for this purpose
5254  * The device number
5255  * Read/write flag
5256  * Essentially all the work is computing physical addresses
5257  * and validating them.
5258  */
5259 physio(strat, abp, dev, rw)
5260 struct buf *abp;
5261 int (*strat)();
5262 {
5263    register struct buf *bp;
5264    register char *base;
5265    register int nb;
5266    int ts;
5267
5268    bp = abp;
5269    base = u.u_base;
5270    /*
5271     * Check odd base, odd count, and address wraparound
5272     */
5273    if (base&01 || u.u_count&01 || base>=base+u.u_count)
5274            goto bad;
5275    ts = (u.u_tsize+127) & ~0177;
5276    if (u.u_sep)
5277            ts = 0;
5278    nb = (base>>6) & 01777;
5279    /*
5280     * Check overlap with text. (ts and nb now
5281     * in 64-byte clicks)
5282     */
5283    if (nb < ts)
5284            goto bad;
5285    /*
5286     * Check that transfer is either entirely in the
5287     * data or in the stack: that is, either
5288     * the end is in the data or the start is in the stack
5289     * (remember wraparound was already checked).
5290     */
5291    if (((((base+u.u_count)>>6)&01777) >= ts+u.u_dsize
5292        && nb < 1024-u.u_ssize)
5293            goto bad;
5294    spl6();
5295    while (bp->b_flags&B_BUSY) {
5296            bp->b_flags =| B_WANTED;
5297            sleep(bp, PRIBIO);
5298    }
5299    bp->b_flags = B_BUSY | B_PHYS | rw;
```

```
5300     bp->b_dev = dev;
5301     /*
5302      * Compute physical address by simulating
5303      * the segmentation hardware.
5304      */
5305     bp->b_addr = base&077;
5306     base = (u.u_sep? UDSA: UISA)->r[nb>>7] + (nb&0177);
5307     bp->b_addr =+ base<<6;
5308     bp->b_xmem = (base>>10) & 077;
5309     bp->b_blkno = lshift(u.u_offset, -9);
5310     bp->b_wcount = -((u.u_count>>1) & 077777);
5311     bp->b_error = 0;
5312     u.u_procp->p_flag =| SLOCK;
5313     (*strat)(bp);
5314     spl6();
5315     while ((bp->b_flags&B_DONE) == 0)
5316             sleep(bp, PRIBIO);
5317     u.u_procp->p_flag =& ~SLOCK;
5318     if (bp->b_flags&B_WANTED)
5319             wakeup(bp);
5320     spl0();
5321     bp->b_flags =& ~(B_BUSY!B_WANTED);
5322     u.u_count = (-bp->b_resid)<<1;
5323     geterror(bp);
5324     return;
5325 bad:
5326     u.u_error = EFAULT;
5327 }
5328 /* ------------------------       */
5329
5330 /*
5331  * Pick up the device's error number and pass it to the
5332  * user; if there is an error but the number is 0 set a
5333  * generalised code.  Actually the latter is always true
5334  * because devices don't yet return specific errors.
5335  */
5336 geterror(abp)
5337 struct buf *abp;
5338 {
5339     register struct buf *bp;
5340
5341     bp = abp;
5342     if (bp->b_flags&B_ERROR)
5343             if ((u.u_error = bp->b_error)==0)
5344                     u.u_error = EIO;
5345 }
5346 /* ------------------------       */
5347
5348
5349
```

```
5350 #
5351 /*
5352  */
5353
5354 /*
5355  * RK disk driver
5356  */
5357
5358 #include "../param.h"
5359 #include "../buf.h"
5360 #include "../conf.h"
5361 #include "../user.h"
5362
5363 #define     RKADDR   0177400
5364 #define     NRK      4
5365 #define     NRKBLK   4872
5366
5367 #define     RESET    0
5368 #define     GO       01
5369 #define     DRESET   014
5370 #define     IENABLE  0100
5371 #define     DRY      0200
5372 #define     ARDY     0100
5373 #define     WLO      020000
5374 #define     CTLRDY   0200
5375
5376 struct {
5377     int rkds;
5378     int rker;
5379     int rkcs;
5380     int rkwc;
5381     int rkba;
5382     int rkda;
5383 };
5384 /* ------------------------       */
5385
5386 struct     devtab   rktab;
5387 struct     buf      rrkbuf;
5388
5389 rkstrategy(abp)
5390 struct buf *abp;
5391 {
5392     register struct buf *bp;
5393     register *ac, *al;
5394     int d;
5395
5396     bp = abp;
5397     if(bp->b_flags&B_PHYS)
5398             mapalloc(bp);
5399     d = bp->b_dev.d_minor-7;
```

```
5400     if(d <= 0)
5401             d = 1;
5402     if (bp->b_blkno >= NRKBLK*d) {
5403             bp->b_flags =! B_ERROR;
5404             iodone(bp);
5405             return;
5406     }
5407     bp->av_forw = 0;
5408     sp15();
5409     if (rktab.d_actf==0)
5410             rktab.d_actf = bp;
5411     else
5412             rktab.d_actl->av_forw = bp;
5413     rktab.d_actl = bp;
5414     if (rktab.d_active==0)
5415             rkstart();
5416     sp10();
5417 }
5418 /* ------------------------         */
5419
5420 rkaddr(bp)
5421 struct buf *bp;
5422 {
5423     register struct buf *p;
5424     register int b;
5425     int d, m;
5426
5427     p = bp;
5428     b = p->b_blkno;
5429     m = p->b_dev.d_minor - 7;
5430     if(m <= 0)
5431             d = p->b_dev.d_minor;
5432     else {
5433             d = lrem(b, m);
5434             b = ldiv(b, m);
5435     }
5436     return(d<<13 | (b/12)<<4 | b%12);
5437 }
5438 /* ------------------------         */
5439
5440 rkstart()
5441 {
5442     register struct buf *bp;
5443
5444     if ((bp = rktab.d_actf) == 0)
5445             return;
5446     rktab.d_active++;
5447     devstart(bp, &RKADDR->rkda, rkaddr(bp), 0);
5448 }
5449 /* ------------------------         */
```

```
5450
5451 rkintr()
5452 {
5453     register struct buf *bp;
5454
5455     if (rktab.d_active == 0)
5456             return;
5457     bp = rktab.d_actf;
5458     rktab.d_active = 0;
5459     if (RKADDR->rkcs < 0) {          /* error bit */
5460             deverror(bp, RKADDR->rker, RKADDR->rkds);
5461             RKADDR->rkcs = RESET|GO;
5462             while((RKADDR->rkcs&CTLRDY) == 0) ;
5463             if (++rktab.d_errcnt <= 10) {
5464                     rkstart();
5465                     return;
5466             }
5467             bp->b_flags =! B_ERROR;
5468     }
5469     rktab.d_errcnt = 0;
5470     rktab.d_actf = bp->av_forw;
5471     iodone(bp);
5472     rkstart();
5473 }
5474 /* ------------------------         */
5475
5476 rkread(dev)
5477 {
5478
5479     physio(rkstrategy, &rrkbuf, dev, B_READ);
5480 }
5481 /* ------------------------         */
5482
5483 rkwrite(dev)
5484 {
5485
5486     physio(rkstrategy, &rrkbuf, dev, B_WRITE);
5487 }
5488 /* ------------------------         */
5489
5490
5491
5492
5493
5494
5495
5496
5497
5498
5499
```

4

Files and Directories
File Systems
Pipes

```
5500 /*
5501  * One file structure is allocated
5502  * for each open/creat/pipe call.
5503  * Main use is to hold the read/write
5504  * pointer associated with each open
5505  * file.
5506  */
5507 struct      file
5508 {
5509     char    f_flag;
5510     char    f_count;        /* reference count */
5511     int     f_inode;        /* pointer to inode structure */
5512     char    *f_offset[2];   /* read/write character pointer */
5513 } file[NFILE];
5514 /* ---------------------------        */
5515
5516 /* flags */
5517 #define    FREAD    01
5518 #define    FWRITE   02
5519 #define    FPIPE    04
5520
5521
5522
5523
5524
5525
5526
5527
5528
5529
5530
5531
5532
5533
5534
5535
5536
5537
5538
5539
5540
5541
5542
5543
5544
5545
5546
5547
5548
5549
```

```
5550 /*
5551  * Definition of the unix super block.
5552  * The root super block is allocated and
5553  * read in iinit/alloc.c. Subsequently
5554  * a super block is allocated and read
5555  * with each mount (smount/sys3.c) and
5556  * released with unmount (sumount/sys3.c).
5557  * A disk block is ripped off for storage.
5558  * See alloc.c for general alloc/free
5559  * routines for free list and I list.
5560  */
5561 struct filsys
5562 {
5563     int  s_isize;       /* size in blocks of I list */
5564     int  s_fsize;       /* size in blocks of entire volume */
5565     int  s_nfree;       /* number of in core free blocks
5566                            (between 0 and 100) */
5567     int  s_free[100];   /* in core free blocks */
5568     int  s_ninode;      /* number of in core I nodes (0-100) */
5569     int  s_inode[100];  /* in core free I nodes */
5570     char s_flock;       /* lock during free list manipulation */
5571     char s_ilock;       /* lock during I list manipulation */
5572     char s_fmod;        /* super block modified flag */
5573     char s_ronly;       /* mounted read-only flag */
5574     int  s_time[2];     /* current date of last update */
5575     int  pad[50];
5576 };
5577 /* ---------------------------        */
5578
5579
5580
5581
5582
5583
5584
5585
5586
5587
5588
5589
5590
5591
5592
5593
5594
5595
5596
5597
5598
5599
```

```
5600 /*
5601  * Inode structure as it appears on
5602  * the disk. Not used by the system,
5603  * but by things like check, df, dump.
5604  */
5605 struct      inode
5606 {
5607     int     i_mode;
5608     char    i_nlink;
5609     char    i_uid;
5610     char    i_gid;
5611     char    i_size0;
5612     char    *i_size1;
5613     int     i_addr[8];
5614     int     i_atime[2];
5615     int     i_mtime[2];
5616 };
5617 /* --------------------------- */
5618
5619 /* modes */
5620 #define     IALLOC  0100000
5621 #define     IFMT    060000
5622 #define     IFDIR   040000
5623 #define     IFCHR   020000
5624 #define     IFBLK   060000
5625 #define     ILARG   010000
5626 #define     ISUID   04000
5627 #define     ISGID   02000
5628 #define     ISVTX   01000
5629 #define     IREAD   0400
5630 #define     IWRITE  0200
5631 #define     IEXEC   0100
5632
5633
5634
5635
5636
5637
5638
5639
5640
5641
5642
5643
5644
5645
5646
5647
5648
5649
```

```
5650 /* The I node is the focus of all
5651  * file activity in unix. There is a unique
5652  * inode allocated for each active file,
5653  * each current directory, each mounted-on
5654  * file, text file, and the root. An inode is 'named'
5655  * by its dev/inumber pair. (iget/iget.c)
5656  * Data, from mode on, is read in
5657  * from permanent inode on volume.
5658  */
5659 struct      inode
5660 {
5661     char    i_flag;
5662     char    i_count;  /* reference count */
5663     int     i_dev;    /* device where inode resides */
5664     int     i_number; /* i number, 1-to-1 with device
5665                                         address */
5666     int     i_mode;
5667     char    i_nlink;  /* directory entries */
5668     char    i_uid;    /* owner */
5669     char    i_gid;    /* group of owner */
5670     char    i_size0;  /* most significant of size */
5671     char    *i_size1; /* least sig */
5672     int     i_addr[8];/* device addresses constituting file */
5673     int     i_lastr;  /* last logical block read (for
5674                                         read-ahead) */
5675 } inode[NINODE];
5676 /* --------------------------- */
5677
5678 /* flags */
5679 #define ILOCK   01   /* inode is locked */
5680 #define IUPD    02   /* inode has been modified */
5681 #define IACC    04   /* inode access time to be updated */
5682 #define IMOUNT  010  /* inode is mounted on */
5683 #define IWANT   020  /* some process waiting on lock */
5684 #define ITEXT   040  /* inode is pure text prototype */
5685
5686 /* modes */
5687 #define IALLOC 0100000 /* file is used */
5688 #define IFMT    060000  /* type of file */
5689 #define IFDIR   040000  /* directory */
5690 #define IFCHR   020000  /* character special */
5691 #define IFBLK   060000  /* block special, 0 is regular */
5692 #define ILARG   010000  /* large addressing algorithm */
5693 #define ISUID   04000   /* set user id on execution */
5694 #define ISGID   02000   /* set group id on execution */
5695 #define ISVTX   01000   /* save swapped text even after use */
5696 #define IREAD   0400    /* read, write, execute permissions */
5697 #define IWRITE  0200
5698 #define IEXEC   0100
5699
```

```
5700 #
5701 #include "../param.h"
5702 #include "../systm.h"
5703 #include "../user.h"
5704 #include "../reg.h"
5705 #include "../file.h"
5706 #include "../inode.h"
5707
5708 /*
5709  * read system call
5710  */
5711 read()
5712 {
5713     rdwr(FREAD);
5714 }
5715 /* ------------------------        */
5716
5717 /*
5718  * write system call
5719  */
5720 write()
5721 {
5722     rdwr(FWRITE);
5723 }
5724 /* ------------------------        */
5725
5726 /*
5727  * common code for read and write calls:
5728  * check permissions, set base, count, and offset,
5729  * and switch out to readi, writei, or pipe code.
5730  */
5731 rdwr(mode)
5732 {
5733     register *fp, m;
5734
5735     m = mode;
5736     fp = getf(u.u_ar0[R0]);
5737     if(fp == NULL)
5738             return;
5739     if((fp->f_flag&m) == 0) {
5740             u.u_error = EBADF;
5741             return;
5742     }
5743     u.u_base = u.u_arg[0];
5744     u.u_count = u.u_arg[1];
5745     u.u_segfls = 0;
5746     if(fp->f_flag&FPIPE) {
5747             if(m==FREAD)
5748                     readp(fp); else
5749                     writep(fp);
```

```
5750     } else {
5751             u.u_offset[1] = fp->f_offset[1];
5752             u.u_offset[0] = fp->f_offset[0];
5753             if(m==FREAD)
5754                     readi(fp->f_inode); else
5755                     writei(fp->f_inode);
5756             dpadd(fp->f_offset, u.u_arg[1]-u.u_count);
5757     }
5758     u.u_ar0[R0] = u.u_arg[1]-u.u_count;
5759 }
5760 /* ------------------------        */
5761
5762 /*
5763  * open system call
5764  */
5765 open()
5766 {
5767     register *ip;
5768     extern uchar;
5769
5770     ip = namei(&uchar, 0);
5771     if(ip == NULL)
5772             return;
5773     u.u_arg[1]++;
5774     open1(ip, u.u_arg[1], 0);
5775 }
5776 /* ------------------------        */
5777
5778 /*
5779  * creat system call
5780  */
5781 creat()
5782 {
5783     register *ip;
5784     extern uchar;
5785
5786     ip = namei(&uchar, 1);
5787     if(ip == NULL) {
5788             if(u.u_error)
5789                     return;
5790             ip = maknode(u.u_arg[1]&07777&(~ISVTX));
5791             if (ip==NULL)
5792                     return;
5793             open1(ip, FWRITE, 2);
5794     } else
5795             open1(ip, FWRITE, 1);
5796 }
5797 /* ------------------------        */
5798
5799 /*
```

```
5800   * common code for open and creat.
5801   * Check permissions, allocate an open file structure,
5802   * and call the device open routine if any.
5803   */
5804 open1(ip, mode, trf)
5805 int *ip;
5806 {
5807    register struct file *fp;
5808    register *rip, m;
5809    int i;
5810
5811    rip = ip;
5812    m = mode;
5813    if(trf != 2) {
5814            if(m&FREAD)
5815                    access(rip, IREAD);
5816            if(m&FWRITE) {
5817                    access(rip, IWRITE);
5818                    if((rip->i_mode&IFMT) == IFDIR)
5819                            u.u_error = EISDIR;
5820            }
5821    }
5822    if(u.u_error)
5823            goto out;
5824    if(trf)
5825            itrunc(rip);
5826    prele(rip);
5827    if ((fp = falloc()) == NULL)
5828            goto out;
5829    fp->f_flag = m&(FREAD!FWRITE);
5830    fp->f_inode = rip;
5831    i = u.u_ar0[R0];
5832    openi(rip, m&FWRITE);
5833    if(u.u_error == 0)
5834            return;
5835    u.u_ofile[i] = NULL;
5836    fp->f_count--;
5837
5838 out:
5839    iput(rip);
5840 }
5841 /* --------------------------        */
5842
5843 /*
5844  * close system call
5845  */
5846 close()
5847 {
5848    register *fp;
5849
```

```
5850    fp = getf(u.u_ar0[R0]);
5851    if(fp == NULL)
5852            return;
5853    u.u_ofile[u.u_ar0[R0]] = NULL;
5854    closef(fp);
5855 }
5856 /* --------------------------        */
5857
5858 /*
5859  * seek system call
5860  */
5861 seek()
5862 {
5863    int n[2];
5864    register *fp, t;
5865
5866    fp = getf(u.u_ar0[R0]);
5867    if(fp == NULL)
5868            return;
5869    if(fp->f_flag&FPIPE) {
5870            u.u_error = ESPIPE;
5871            return;
5872    }
5873    t = u.u_arg[1];
5874    if(t > 2) {
5875            n[1] = u.u_arg[0]<<9;
5876            n[0] = u.u_arg[0]>>7;
5877            if(t == 3)
5878                    n[0] =& 0777;
5879    } else {
5880            n[1] = u.u_arg[0];
5881            n[0] = 0;
5882            if(t!=0 && n[1]<0)
5883                    n[0] = -1;
5884    }
5885    switch(t) {
5886
5887    case 1:
5888    case 4:
5889            n[0] =+ fp->f_offset[0];
5890            dpadd(n, fp->f_offset[1]);
5891            break;
5892
5893    default:
5894            n[0] =+ fp->f_inode->i_size0&0377;
5895            dpadd(n, fp->f_inode->i_size1);
5896
5897    case 0:
5898    case 3:
5899            ;
```

```
5900      }
5901      fp->f_offset[1] = n[1];
5902      fp->f_offset[0] = n[0];
5903 }
5904 /* ----------------------        */
5905
5906
5907 /* link system call
5908  */
5909 link()
5910 {
5911      register *ip, *xp;
5912      extern uchar;
5913
5914      ip = namei(&uchar, 0);
5915      if(ip == NULL)
5916              return;
5917      if(ip->i_nlink >= 127) {
5918              u.u_error = EMLINK;
5919              goto out;
5920      }
5921      if((ip->i_mode&IFMT)==IFDIR && !suser())
5922              goto out;
5923      /*
5924       * unlock to avoid possibly hanging the namei
5925       */
5926      ip->i_flag =& ~ILOCK;
5927      u.u_dirp = u.u_arg[1];
5928      xp = namei(&uchar, 1);
5929      if(xp != NULL) {
5930              u.u_error = EEXIST;
5931              iput(xp);
5932      }
5933      if(u.u_error)
5934              goto out;
5935      if(u.u_pdir->i_dev != ip->i_dev) {
5936              iput(u.u_pdir);
5937              u.u_error = EXDEV;
5938              goto out;
5939      }
5940      wdir(ip);
5941      ip->i_nlink++;
5942      ip->i_flag =! IUPD;
5943
5944 out:
5945      iput(ip);
5946 }
5947 /* ----------------------        */
5948
5949 /*
```

```
5950  * mknod system call
5951  */
5952 mknod()
5953 {
5954      register *ip;
5955      extern uchar;
5956
5957      if(suser()) {
5958              ip = namei(&uchar, 1);
5959              if(ip != NULL) {
5960                      u.u_error = EEXIST;
5961                      goto out;
5962              }
5963      }
5964      if(u.u_error)
5965              return;
5966      ip = maknode(u.u_arg[1]);
5967      if (ip==NULL)
5968              return;
5969      ip->i_addr[0] = u.u_arg[2];
5970
5971 out:
5972      iput(ip);
5973 }
5974 /* ----------------------        */
5975
5976 /* sleep system call
5977  * not to be confused with the sleep internal routine.
5978  */
5979 sslep()
5980 {
5981      char *d[2];
5982
5983      spl7();
5984      d[0] = time[0];
5985      d[1] = time[1];
5986      dpadd(d, u.u_ar0[R0]);
5987
5988      while(dpcmp(d[0], d[1], time[0], time[1]) > 0) {
5989          if(dpcmp(tout[0], tout[1], time[0], time[1]) <= 0 ||
5990              dpcmp(tout[0], tout[1], d[0], d[1]) > 0) {
5991                  tout[0] = d[0];
5992                  tout[1] = d[1];
5993          }
5994          sleep(tout, PSLEP);
5995      }
5996      spl0();
5997 }
5998 /* ----------------------        */
5999
```

```
6000 #
6001 #include "../param.h"
6002 #include "../systm.h"
6003 #include "../reg.h"
6004 #include "../buf.h"
6005 #include "../filsys.h"
6006 #include "../user.h"
6007 #include "../inode.h"
6008 #include "../file.h"
6009 #include "../conf.h"
6010
6011 /*
6012  * the fstat system call.
6013  */
6014 fstat()
6015 {
6016     register *fp;
6017
6018     fp = getf(u.u_ar0[R0]);
6019     if(fp == NULL)
6020             return;
6021     stat1(fp->f_inode, u.u_arg[0]);
6022 }
6023 /* ------------------------          */
6024
6025 /*
6026  * the stat system call.
6027  */
6028 stat()
6029 {
6030     register ip;
6031     extern uchar;
6032
6033     ip = namei(&uchar, 0);
6034     if(ip == NULL)
6035             return;
6036     stat1(ip, u.u_arg[1]);
6037     iput(ip);
6038 }
6039 /* ------------------------          */
6040
6041 /*
6042  * The basic routine for fstat and stat:
6043  * get the inode and pass appropriate parts back.
6044  */
6045 stat1(ip, ub)
6046 int *ip;
6047 {
6048     register i, *bp, *cp;
6049
```

```
6050     iupdat(ip, time);
6051     bp = bread(ip->i_dev, ldiv(ip->i_number+31, 16));
6052     cp = bp->b_addr + 32*lrem(ip->i_number+31, 16) + 24;
6053     ip = &(ip->i_dev);
6054     for(i=0; i<14; i++) {
6055             suword(ub, *ip++);
6056             ub =+ 2;
6057     }
6058     for(i=0; i<4; i++) {
6059             suword(ub, *cp++);
6060             ub =+ 2;
6061     }
6062     brelse(bp);
6063 }
6064 /* ------------------------          */
6065
6066 /*
6067  * the dup system call.
6068  */
6069 dup()
6070 {
6071     register i, *fp;
6072
6073     fp = getf(u.u_ar0[R0]);
6074     if(fp == NULL)
6075             return;
6076     if ((i = ufalloc()) < 0)
6077             return;
6078     u.u_ofile[i] = fp;
6079     fp->f_count++;
6080 }
6081 /* ------------------------          */
6082
6083 /*
6084  * the mount system call.
6085  */
6086 smount()
6087 {
6088     int d;
6089     register *ip;
6090     register struct mount *mp, *smp;
6091     extern uchar;
6092
6093     d = getmdev();
6094     if(u.u_error)
6095             return;
6096     u.u_dirp = u.u_arg[1];
6097     ip = namei(&uchar, 0);
6098     if(ip == NULL)
6099             return;
```

```
6100     if(ip->i_count!=1 || (ip->i_mode&(IFBLK&IFCHR))!=0)
6101             goto out;
6102     smp = NULL;
6103     for(mp = &mount[0]; mp < &mount[NMOUNT]; mp++) {
6104             if(mp->m_bufp != NULL) {
6105                     if(d == mp->m_dev)
6106                             goto out;
6107             } else
6108                     if(smp == NULL)
6109                             smp = mp;
6110     }
6111     if(smp == NULL)
6112             goto out;
6113     (*bdevsw[d.d_major].d_open)(d, !u.u_arg[2]);
6114     if(u.u_error)
6115             goto out;
6116     mp = bread(d, 1);
6117     if(u.u_error) {
6118             brelse(mp);
6119             goto out1;
6120     }
6121     smp->m_inodp = ip;
6122     smp->m_dev = d;
6123     smp->m_bufp = getblk(NODEV);
6124     bcopy(mp->b_addr, smp->m_bufp->b_addr, 256);
6125     smp = smp->m_bufp->b_addr;
6126     smp->s_ilock = 0;
6127     smp->s_flock = 0;
6128     smp->s_ronly = u.u_arg[2] & 1;
6129     brelse(mp);
6130     ip->i_flag =| IMOUNT;
6131     prele(ip);
6132     return;
6133
6134 out:
6135     u.u_error = EBUSY;
6136 out1:
6137     iput(ip);
6138 }
6139 /* -------------------------        */
6140
6141 /*
6142  * the umount system call.
6143  */
6144 sumount()
6145 {
6146     int d;
6147     register struct inode *ip;
6148     register struct mount *mp;
6149
```

```
6150     update();
6151     d = getmdev();
6152     if(u.u_error)
6153             return;
6154     for(mp = &mount[0]; mp < &mount[NMOUNT]; mp++)
6155             if(mp->m_bufp!=NULL && d==mp->m_dev)
6156                     goto found;
6157     u.u_error = EINVAL;
6158     return;
6159
6160 found:
6161     for(ip = &inode[0]; ip < &inode[NINODE]; ip++)
6162             if(ip->i_number!=0 && d==ip->i_dev) {
6163                     u.u_error = EBUSY;
6164                     return;
6165             }
6166     (*bdevsw[d.d_major].d_close)(d, 0);
6167     ip = mp->m_inodp;
6168     ip->i_flag =& ~IMOUNT;
6169     iput(ip);
6170     ip = mp->m_bufp;
6171     mp->m_bufp = NULL;
6172     brelse(ip);
6173 }
6174 /* -------------------------        */
6175
6176 /*
6177  * Common code for mount and umount.
6178  * Check that the user's argument is a reasonable thing
6179  *  on which to mount, and return the device number if so.
6180  */
6181 getmdev()
6182 {
6183     register d, *ip;
6184     extern uchar;
6185
6186     ip = namei(&uchar, 0);
6187     if(ip == NULL)
6188             return;
6189     if((ip->i_mode&IFMT) != IFBLK)
6190             u.u_error = ENOTBLK;
6191     d = ip->i_addr[0];
6192     if(ip->i_addr[0].d_major >= nblkdev)
6193             u.u_error = ENXIO;
6194     iput(ip);
6195     return(d);
6196 }
6197 /* -------------------------        */
6198
6199
```

```
6200  #
6201  /*
6202  */
6203
6204  #include "../param.h"
6205  #include "../inode.h"
6206  #include "../user.h"
6207  #include "../buf.h"
6208  #include "../conf.h"
6209  #include "../systm.h"
6210
6211  /*
6212   * Read the file corresponding to
6213   * the inode pointed at by the argument.
6214   * The actual read arguments are found
6215   * in the variables:
6216   *      u_base          core address for destination
6217   *      u_offset        byte offset in file
6218   *      u_count         number of bytes to read
6219   *      u_segflg        read to kernel/user
6220   */
6221  readi(aip)
6222  struct inode *aip;
6223  {
6224      int *bp;
6225      int lbn, bn, on;
6226      register dn, n;
6227      register struct inode *ip;
6228
6229      ip = aip;
6230      if(u.u_count == 0)
6231              return;
6232      ip->i_flag =| IACC;
6233      if((ip->i_mode&IFMT) == IFCHR) {
6234          (*cdevsw[ip->i_addr[0].d_major].d_read)(ip->i_addr[0]);
6235              return;
6236      }
6237
6238      do {
6239              lbn = bn = lshift(u.u_offset, -9);
6240              on = u.u_offset[1] & 0777;
6241              n = min(512-on, u.u_count);
6242              if((ip->i_mode&IFMT) != IFBLK) {
6243                      dn = dpcmp(ip->i_size0&0377, ip->i_size1,
6244                          u.u_offset[0], u.u_offset[1]);
6245                      if(dn <= 0)
6246                              return;
6247                      n = min(n, dn);
6248                      if ((bn = bmap(ip, lbn)) == 0)
6249                              return;
```

```
6250                      dn = ip->i_dev;
6251              } else {
6252                      dn = ip->i_addr[0];
6253                      rablock = bn+1;
6254              }
6255              if (ip->i_lastr+1 == lbn)
6256                      bp = breada(dn, bn, rablock);
6257              else
6258                      bp = bread(dn, bn);
6259              ip->i_lastr = lbn;
6260              iomove(bp, on, n, B_READ);
6261              brelse(bp);
6262      } while(u.u_error==0 && u.u_count!=0);
6263  }
6264  /* ------------------------         */
6265
6266  /*
6267   * Write the file corresponding to
6268   * the inode pointed at by the argument.
6269   * The actual write arguments are found
6270   * in the variables:
6271   *      u_base          core address for source
6272   *      u_offset        byte offset in file
6273   *      u_count         number of bytes to write
6274   *      u_segflg        write to kernel/user
6275   */
6276  writei(aip)
6277  struct inode *aip;
6278  {
6279      int *bp;
6280      int n, on;
6281      register dn, bn;
6282      register struct inode *ip;
6283
6284      ip = aip;
6285      ip->i_flag =| IACC|IUPD;
6286      if((ip->i_mode&IFMT) == IFCHR) {
6287          (*cdevsw[ip->i_addr[0].d_major].d_write)(ip->i_addr[0]);
6288              return;
6289      }
6290      if (u.u_count == 0)
6291              return;
6292
6293      do {
6294              bn = lshift(u.u_offset, -9);
6295              on = u.u_offset[1] & 0777;
6296              n = min(512-on, u.u_count);
6297              if((ip->i_mode&IFMT) != IFBLK) {
6298                      if ((bn = bmap(ip, bn)) == 0)
6299                              return;
```

```
6300                    dn = ip->i_dev;
6301            } else
6302                    dn = ip->i_addr[0];
6303            if(n == 512)
6304                    bp = getblk(dn, bn); else
6305                    bp = bread(dn, bn);
6306            iomove(bp, on, n, B_WRITE);
6307            if(u.u_error != 0)
6308                    brelse(bp); else
6309            if ((u.u_offset[1]&0777)==0)
6310                    bawrite(bp); else
6311                    bdwrite(bp);
6312            if(dpcmp(ip->i_size0&0377, ip->i_size1,
6313                u.u_offset[0], u.u_offset[1]) < 0 &&
6314                (ip->i_mode&(IFBLK&IFCHR)) == 0) {
6315                    ip->i_size0 = u.u_offset[0];
6316                    ip->i_size1 = u.u_offset[1];
6317            }
6318            ip->i_flag =| IUPD;
6319        } while(u.u_error==0 && u.u_count!=0);
6320 }
6321 /* ----------------------------             */
6322
6323 /* Return the logical maximum
6324  * of the 2 arguments.
6325  */
6326 max(a, b)
6327 char *a, *b;
6328 {
6329
6330    if(a > b)
6331            return(a);
6332    return(b);
6333 }
6334 /* ----------------------------             */
6335
6336 /* Return the logical minimum
6337  * of the 2 arguments.
6338  */
6339 min(a, b)
6340 char *a, *b;
6341 {
6342
6343    if(a < b)
6344            return(a);
6345    return(b);
6346 }
6347 /* ----------------------------             */
6348
6349
```

```
6350 /* Move 'an' bytes at byte location
6351  * &bp->b_addr[o] to/from (flag) the
6352  * user/kernel (u.segfls) area starting at u.base.
6353  * Update all the arguments by the number
6354  * of bytes moved.
6355  *
6356  * There are 2 algorithms,
6357  * if source address, dest address and count
6358  * are all even in a user copy,
6359  * then the machine language copyin/copyout
6360  * is called.
6361  * If not, its done byte-by-byte with
6362  * cpass and passc.
6363  */
6364 iomove(bp, o, an, flag)
6365 struct buf *bp;
6366 {
6367    register char *cp;
6368    register int n, t;
6369
6370    n = an;
6371    cp = bp->b_addr + o;
6372    if(u.u_segfls==0 && ((n | cp | u.u_base)&01)==0) {
6373            if (flag==B_WRITE)
6374                    cp = copyin(u.u_base, cp, n);
6375            else
6376                    cp = copyout(cp, u.u_base, n);
6377            if (cp) {
6378                    u.u_error = EFAULT;
6379                    return;
6380            }
6381            u.u_base =+ n;
6382            dpadd(u.u_offset, n);
6383            u.u_count =- n;
6384            return;
6385    }
6386    if (flag==B_WRITE) {
6387            while(n--) {
6388                    if ((t = cpass()) < 0)
6389                            return;
6390                    *cp++ = t;
6391            }
6392    } else
6393            while (n--)
6394                    if(passc(*cp++) < 0)
6395                            return;
6396 }
6397 /* ----------------------------             */
6398
6399
```

Sheet 63

Sheet 63

```
6400 #
6401 #include "../param.h"
6402 #include "../conf.h"
6403 #include "../inode.h"
6404 #include "../user.h"
6405 #include "../buf.h"
6406 #include "../systm.h"
6407
6408 /* Bmap defines the structure of file system storage
6409  * by returning the physical block number on a device given
6410  * the inode and the logical block number in a file.
6411  * When convenient, it also leaves the physical
6412  * block number of the next block of the file in rablock
6413  * for use in read-ahead.
6414  */
6415 bmap(ip, bn)
6416 struct inode *ip;
6417 int bn;
6418 {
6419     register *bp, *bap, nb;
6420     int *nbp, d, i;
6421
6422     d = ip->i_dev;
6423     if(bn & ~077777) {
6424             u.u_error = EFBIG;
6425             return(0);
6426     }
6427     if((ip->i_mode&ILARG) == 0) {
6428
6429             /* small file algorithm */
6430
6431             if((bn & ~7) != 0) {
6432
6433                     /* convert small to large */
6434
6435                     if ((bp = alloc(d)) == NULL)
6436                             return(NULL);
6437                     bap = bp->b_addr;
6438                     for(i=0; i<8; i++) {
6439                             *bap++ = ip->i_addr[i];
6440                             ip->i_addr[i] = 0;
6441                     }
6442                     ip->i_addr[0] = bp->b_blkno;
6443                     bdwrite(bp);
6444                     ip->i_mode =| ILARG;
6445                     goto large;
6446             }
6447             nb = ip->i_addr[bn];
6448             if(nb == 0 && (bp = alloc(d)) != NULL) {
6449                     bdwrite(bp);
```

```
6450                     nb = bp->b_blkno;
6451                     ip->i_addr[bn] = nb;
6452                     ip->i_flag =| IUPD;
6453             }
6454             rablock = 0;
6455             if (bn<7)
6456                     rablock = ip->i_addr[bn+1];
6457             return(nb);
6458     }
6459
6460     /* large file algorithm */
6461
6462     large:
6463     i = bn>>8;
6464     if(bn & 0174000)
6465             i = 7;
6466     if((nb=ip->i_addr[i]) == 0) {
6467             ip->i_flag =| IUPD;
6468             if ((bp = alloc(d)) == NULL)
6469                     return(NULL);
6470             ip->i_addr[i] = bp->b_blkno;
6471     } else
6472             bp = bread(d, nb);
6473     bap = bp->b_addr;
6474
6475     /* "huge" fetch of double indirect block */
6476
6477     if(i == 7) {
6478             i = ((bn>>8) & 0377) - 7;
6479             if((nb=bap[i]) == 0) {
6480                     if((nbp = alloc(d)) == NULL) {
6481                             brelse(bp);
6482                             return(NULL);
6483                     }
6484                     bap[i] = nbp->b_blkno;
6485                     bdwrite(bp);
6486             } else {
6487                     brelse(bp);
6488                     nbp = bread(d, nb);
6489             }
6490             bp = nbp;
6491             bap = bp->b_addr;
6492     }
6493
6494     /* normal indirect fetch */
6495
6496     i = bn & 0377;
6497     if((nb=bap[i]) == 0 && (nbp = alloc(d)) != NULL) {
6498             nb = nbp->b_blkno;
6499             bap[i] = nb;
```

```
6500                 bdwrite(nbp);
6501                 bdwrite(bp);
6502        } else
6503                 brelse(bp);
6504        rablock = 0;
6505        if(i < 255)
6506                 rablock = bap[i+1];
6507        return(nb);
6508 }
6509 /* ------------------------       */
6510
6511 /* Pass back  c  to the user at his location u_base;
6512  * update u_base, u_count, and u_offset.  Return -1
6513  * on the last character of the user's read.
6514  * u_base is in the user address space unless u_segfls
6515  * is set.
6516  */
6517 passc(c)
6518 char c;
6519 {
6520
6521     if(u.u_segfls)
6522                 *u.u_base = c; else
6523                 if(subyte(u.u_base, c) < 0) {
6524                         u.u_error = EFAULT;
6525                         return(-1);
6526                 }
6527     u.u_count--;
6528     if(++u.u_offset[1] == 0)
6529                 u.u_offset[0]++;
6530     u.u_base++;
6531     return(u.u_count == 0? -1: 0);
6532 }
6533 /* ------------------------       */
6534
6535 /*
6536  * Pick up and return the next character from the user's
6537  * write call at location u_base;
6538  * update u_base, u_count, and u_offset.  Return -1
6539  * when u_count is exhausted.  u_base is in the user's
6540  * address space unless u_segfls is set.
6541  */
6542 cpass()
6543 {
6544     register c;
6545
6546     if(u.u_count == 0)
6547                 return(-1);
6548     if(u.u_segfls)
6549                 c = *u.u_base; else
```

```
6550                 if((c=fubyte(u.u_base)) < 0) {
6551                         u.u_error = EFAULT;
6552                         return(-1);
6553                 }
6554     u.u_count--;
6555     if(++u.u_offset[1] == 0)
6556                 u.u_offset[0]++;
6557     u.u_base++;
6558     return(c&0377);
6559 }
6560 /* ------------------------       */
6561
6562 /*
6563  * Routine which sets a user error; placed in
6564  * illegal entries in the bdevsw and cdevsw tables.
6565  */
6566 nodev()
6567 {
6568
6569     u.u_error = ENODEV;
6570 }
6571 /* ------------------------       */
6572
6573 /*
6574  * Null routine; placed in insignificant entries
6575  * in the bdevsw and cdevsw tables.
6576  */
6577 nulldev()
6578 {
6579 }
6580 /* ------------------------       */
6581
6582 /*
6583  * copy count words from from to to.
6584  */
6585 bcopy(from, to, count)
6586 int *from, *to;
6587 {
6588     register *a, *b, c;
6589
6590     a = from;
6591     b = to;
6592     c = count;
6593     do
6594                 *b++ = *a++;
6595     while(--c);
6596 }
6597 /* ------------------------       */
6598
6599
```

```
6600 #
6601 /*
6602  */
6603
6604 #include "../param.h"
6605 #include "../user.h"
6606 #include "../filsys.h"
6607 #include "../file.h"
6608 #include "../conf.h"
6609 #include "../inode.h"
6610 #include "../reg.h"
6611
6612 /*
6613  * Convert a user supplied
6614  * file descriptor into a pointer
6615  * to a file structure.
6616  * Only task is to check range
6617  * of the descriptor.
6618  */
6619 getf(f)
6620 {
6621     register *fp, rf;
6622
6623     rf = f;
6624     if(rf<0 || rf>=NOFILE)
6625             goto bad;
6626     fp = u.u_ofile[rf];
6627     if(fp != NULL)
6628             return(fp);
6629 bad:
6630     u.u_error = EBADF;
6631     return(NULL);
6632 }
6633 /* --------------------------     */
6634
6635 /*
6636  * Internal form of close.
6637  * Decrement reference count on
6638  * file structure and call closei
6639  * on last close.
6640  * Also make sure the pipe protocol
6641  * does not constipate.
6642  */
6643 closef(fp)
6644 int *fp;
6645 {
6646     register *rfp, *ip;
6647
6648     rfp = fp;
6649     if(rfp->f_flag&FPIPE) {
```

```
6650             ip = rfp->f_inode;
6651             ip->i_mode =& ~(IREAD|IWRITE);
6652             wakeup(ip+1);
6653             wakeup(ip+2);
6654     }
6655     if(rfp->f_count <= 1)
6656             closei(rfp->f_inode, rfp->f_flag&FWRITE);
6657     rfp->f_count--;
6658 }
6659 /* --------------------------     */
6660
6661 /*
6662  * Decrement reference count on an
6663  * inode due to the removal of a
6664  * referencing file structure.
6665  * On the last closei, switchout
6666  * to the close entry point of special
6667  * device handler.
6668  * Note that the handler gets called
6669  * on every open and only on the last
6670  * close.
6671  */
6672 closei(ip, rw)
6673 int *ip;
6674 {
6675     register *rip;
6676     register dev, maj;
6677
6678     rip = ip;
6679     dev = rip->i_addr[0];
6680     maj = rip->i_addr[0].d_major;
6681     if(rip->i_count <= 1)
6682     switch(rip->i_mode&IFMT) {
6683
6684     case IFCHR:
6685             (*cdevsw[maj].d_close)(dev, rw);
6686             break;
6687
6688     case IFBLK:
6689             (*bdevsw[maj].d_close)(dev, rw);
6690     }
6691     iput(rip);
6692 }
6693 /* --------------------------     */
6694
6695 /*
6696  * openi called to allow handler
6697  * of special files to initialize and
6698  * validate before actual IO.
6699  * Called on all sorts of opens
```

```
6700  * and also on mount.
6701  */
6702 openi(ip, rw)
6703 int *ip;
6704 {
6705     register *rip;
6706     register dev, maj;
6707
6708     rip = ip;
6709     dev = rip->i_addr[0];
6710     maj = rip->i_addr[0].d_major;
6711     switch(rip->i_mode&IFMT) {
6712
6713     case IFCHR:
6714             if(maj >= nchrdev)
6715                     goto bad;
6716             (*cdevsw[maj].d_open)(dev, rw);
6717             break;
6718
6719     case IFBLK:
6720             if(maj >= nblkdev)
6721                     goto bad;
6722             (*bdevsw[maj].d_open)(dev, rw);
6723     }
6724     return;
6725
6726 bad:
6727     u.u_error = ENXIO;
6728 }
6729 /* --------------------------      */
6730
6731 /*
6732  * Check mode permission on inode pointer.
6733  * Mode is READ, WRITE or EXEC.
6734  * In the case of WRITE, the
6735  * read-only status of the file
6736  * system is checked.
6737  * Also in WRITE, prototype text
6738  * segments cannot be written.
6739  * The mode is shifted to select
6740  * the owner/group/other fields.
6741  * The super user is granted all
6742  * permissions except for EXEC where
6743  * at least one of the EXEC bits must
6744  * be on.
6745  */
6746 access(aip, mode)
6747 int *aip;
6748 {
6749     register *ip, m;
```

```
6750
6751     ip = aip;
6752     m = mode;
6753     if(m == IWRITE) {
6754             if(getfs(ip->i_dev)->s_ronly != 0) {
6755                     u.u_error = EROFS;
6756                     return(1);
6757             }
6758             if(ip->i_flag & ITEXT) {
6759                     u.u_error = ETXTBSY;
6760                     return(1);
6761             }
6762     }
6763     if(u.u_uid == 0) {
6764             if(m == IEXEC && (ip->i_mode &
6765               (IEXEC | (IEXEC>>3) | (IEXEC>>6))) == 0)
6766                     goto bad;
6767             return(0);
6768     }
6769     if(u.u_uid != ip->i_uid) {
6770             m =>> 3;
6771             if(u.u_gid != ip->i_gid)
6772                     m =>> 3;
6773     }
6774     if((ip->i_mode&m) != 0)
6775             return(0);
6776
6777 bad:
6778     u.u_error = EACCES;
6779     return(1);
6780 }
6781 /* --------------------------      */
6782
6783 /*
6784  * Look up a pathname and test if
6785  * the resultant inode is owned by the
6786  * current user.
6787  * If not, try for super-user.
6788  * If permission is granted,
6789  * return inode pointer.
6790  */
6791 owner()
6792 {
6793     register struct inode *ip;
6794     extern uchar();
6795
6796     if ((ip = namei(uchar, 0)) == NULL)
6797             return(NULL);
6798     if(u.u_uid == ip->i_uid)
6799             return(ip);
```

Sheet 67

Sheet 67

```
6800     if (suser())
6801             return(ip);
6802     iput(ip);
6803     return(NULL);
6804 }
6805 /* -------------------------     */
6806
6807 /*
6808  * Test if the current user is the
6809  * super user.
6810  */
6811 suser()
6812 {
6813
6814     if(u.u_uid == 0)
6815             return(1);
6816     u.u_error = EPERM;
6817     return(0);
6818 }
6819 /* -------------------------     */
6820
6821 /*
6822  * Allocate a user file descriptor.
6823  */
6824 ufalloc()
6825 {
6826     register i;
6827
6828     for (i=0; i<NOFILE; i++)
6829             if (u.u_ofile[i] == NULL) {
6830                     u.u_ar0[R0] = i;
6831                     return(i);
6832             }
6833     u.u_error = EMFILE;
6834     return(-1);
6835 }
6836 /* -------------------------     */
6837
6838 /*
6839  * Allocate a user file descriptor
6840  * and a file structure.
6841  * Initialize the descriptor
6842  * to point at the file structure.
6843  *
6844  * no file -- if there are no available
6845  *      file structures.
6846  */
6847 falloc()
6848 {
6849     register struct file *fp;
```

```
6850     register i;
6851
6852     if ((i = ufalloc()) < 0)
6853             return(NULL);
6854     for (fp = &file[0]; fp < &file[NFILE]; fp++)
6855             if (fp->f_count==0) {
6856                     u.u_ofile[i] = fp;
6857                     fp->f_count++;
6858                     fp->f_offset[0] = 0;
6859                     fp->f_offset[1] = 0;
6860                     return(fp);
6861             }
6862     printf("no file\n");
6863     u.u_error = ENFILE;
6864     return(NULL);
6865 }
6866 /* -------------------------     */
6867
6868
6869
6870
6871
6872
6873
6874
6875
6876
6877
6878
6879
6880
6881
6882
6883
6884
6885
6886
6887
6888
6889
6890
6891
6892
6893
6894
6895
6896
6897
6898
6899
```

```
6900 #
6901 /*
6902  */
6903
6904 #include "../param.h"
6905 #include "../systm.h"
6906 #include "../filsys.h"
6907 #include "../conf.h"
6908 #include "../buf.h"
6909 #include "../inode.h"
6910 #include "../user.h"
6911
6912 /*
6913  * iinit is called once (from main)
6914  * very early in initialization.
6915  * It reads the root's super block
6916  * and initializes the current date
6917  * from the last modified date.
6918  *
6919  * panic: iinit -- cannot read the super
6920  * block. Usually because of an IO error.
6921  */
6922 iinit()
6923 {
6924     register *cp, *bp;
6925
6926     (*bdevsw[rootdev.d_major].d_open)(rootdev, 1);
6927     bp = bread(rootdev, 1);
6928     cp = getblk(NODEV);
6929     if(u.u_error)
6930             panic("iinit");
6931     bcopy(bp->b_addr, cp->b_addr, 256);
6932     brelse(bp);
6933     mount[0].m_bufp = cp;
6934     mount[0].m_dev = rootdev;
6935     cp = cp->b_addr;
6936     cp->s_flock = 0;
6937     cp->s_ilock = 0;
6938     cp->s_ronly = 0;
6939     time[0] = cp->s_time[0];
6940     time[1] = cp->s_time[1];
6941 }
6942 /* ------------------------      */
6943 /* ------------------------      */
6944
6945 /*
6946  * alloc will obtain the next available
6947  * free disk block from the free list of
6948  * the specified device.
6949  * The super block has up to 100 remembered
```

```
6950  * free blocks; the last of these is read to
6951  * obtain 100 more . . .
6952  *
6953  * no space on dev x/y -- when
6954  * the free list is exhausted.
6955  */
6956 alloc(dev)
6957 {
6958     int bno;
6959     register *bp, *ip, *fp;
6960
6961     fp = getfs(dev);
6962     while(fp->s_flock)
6963             sleep(&fp->s_flock, PINOD);
6964     do {
6965             if(fp->s_nfree <= 0)
6966                     goto nospace;
6967             bno = fp->s_free[--fp->s_nfree];
6968             if(bno == 0)
6969                     goto nospace;
6970     } while (badblock(fp, bno, dev));
6971     if(fp->s_nfree <= 0) {
6972             fp->s_flock++;
6973             bp = bread(dev, bno);
6974             ip = bp->b_addr;
6975             fp->s_nfree = *ip++;
6976             bcopy(ip, fp->s_free, 100);
6977             brelse(bp);
6978             fp->s_flock = 0;
6979             wakeup(&fp->s_flock);
6980     }
6981     bp = getblk(dev, bno);
6982     clrbuf(bp);
6983     fp->s_fmod = 1;
6984     return(bp);
6985
6986 nospace:
6987     fp->s_nfree = 0;
6988     prdev("no space", dev);
6989     u.u_error = ENOSPC;
6990     return(NULL);
6991 }
6992 /* ------------------------      */
6993 /* ------------------------      */
6994
6995 /*
6996  * place the specified disk block
6997  * back on the free list of the
6998  * specified device.
6999  */
```

Sheet 69

Sheet 69

```
7000 free(dev, bno)
7001 {
7002     register *fp, *bp, *ip;
7003
7004     fp = getfs(dev);
7005     fp->s_fmod = 1;
7006     while(fp->s_flock)
7007             sleep(&fp->s_flock, PINOD);
7008     if (badblock(fp, bno, dev))
7009             return;
7010     if(fp->s_nfree <= 0) {
7011             fp->s_nfree = 1;
7012             fp->s_free[0] = 0;
7013     }
7014     if(fp->s_nfree >= 100) {
7015             fp->s_flock++;
7016             bp = getblk(dev, bno);
7017             ip = bp->b_addr;
7018             *ip++ = fp->s_nfree;
7019             bcopy(fp->s_free, ip, 100);
7020             fp->s_nfree = 0;
7021             bwrite(bp);
7022             fp->s_flock = 0;
7023             wakeup(&fp->s_flock);
7024     }
7025     fp->s_free[fp->s_nfree++] = bno;
7026     fp->s_fmod = 1;
7027 }
7028 /* ------------------------        */
7029 /* ------------------------        */
7030
7031 /*
7032  * Check that a block number is in the
7033  * range between the I list and the size
7034  * of the device.
7035  * This is used mainly to check that a
7036  * garbage file system has not been mounted.
7037  *
7038  * bad block on dev x/y -- not in range
7039  */
7040 badblock(afp, abn, dev)
7041 {
7042     register struct filsys *fp;
7043     register char *bn;
7044
7045     fp = afp;
7046     bn = abn;
7047     if (bn < fp->s_isize+2 || bn >= fp->s_fsize) {
7048             prdev("bad block", dev);
7049             return(1);
```

```
7050     }
7051     return(0);
7052 }
7053 /* ------------------------        */
7054 /* ------------------------        */
7055
7056 /*
7057  * Allocate an unused I node
7058  * on the specified device.
7059  * Used with file creation.
7060  * The algorithm keeps up to
7061  * 100 spare I nodes in the
7062  * super block. When this runs out,
7063  * a linear search through the
7064  * I list is instituted to pick
7065  * up 100 more.
7066  */
7067 ialloc(dev)
7068 {
7069     register *fp, *bp, *ip;
7070     int i, j, k, ino;
7071
7072     fp = getfs(dev);
7073     while(fp->s_ilock)
7074             sleep(&fp->s_ilock, PINOD);
7075 loop:
7076     if(fp->s_ninode > 0) {
7077             ino = fp->s_inode[--fp->s_ninode];
7078             ip = iget(dev, ino);
7079             if (ip==NULL)
7080                     return(NULL);
7081             if(ip->i_mode == 0) {
7082                     for(bp = &ip->i_mode; bp < &ip->i_addr[8];)
7083                             *bp++ = 0;
7084                     fp->s_fmod = 1;
7085                     return(ip);
7086             }
7087             /*
7088              * Inode was allocated after all.
7089              * Look some more.
7090              */
7091             iput(ip);
7092             goto loop;
7093     }
7094     fp->s_ilock++;
7095     ino = 0;
7096     for(i=0; i<fp->s_isize; i++) {
7097             bp = bread(dev, i+2);
7098             ip = bp->b_addr;
7099             for(j=0; j<256; j+=16) {
```

```
7100                    ino++;                         7150  * setfs maps a device number into
7101                    if(ip[j] != 0)                  7151  * a pointer to the incore super
7102                            continue;               7152  * block.
7103                    for(k=0; k<NINODE; k++)         7153  * The algorithm is a linear
7104                    if(dev == inode[k].i_dev &&     7154  * search through the mount table.
7105                            ino == inode[k].i_number) 7155 * A consistency check of the
7106                            goto cont;              7156  * in core free-block and i-node
7107                    fp->s_inode[fp->s_ninode++] = ino; 7157 * counts.
7108                    if(fp->s_ninode >= 100)         7158  *
7109                            break;                  7159  * bad count on dev x/y -- the count
7110            cont:;                                  7160  * check failed. At this point, all
7111            }                                       7161  * the counts are zeroed which will
7112            brelse(bp);                             7162  * almost certainly lead to "no space"
7113            if(fp->s_ninode >= 100)                 7163  * diagnostic
7114                    break;                          7164  * panic: no fs -- the device is not mounted.
7115    }                                               7165  * this "cannot happen"
7116    fp->s_ilock = 0;                                7166  */
7117    wakeup(&fp->s_ilock);                           7167  setfs(dev)
7118    if (fp->s_ninode > 0)                           7168  {
7119            goto loop;                              7169      register struct mount *p;
7120    prdev("Out of inodes", dev);                    7170      register char *n1, *n2;
7121    u.u_error = ENOSPC;                             7171
7122    return(NULL);                                   7172      for(p = &mount[0]; p < &mount[NMOUNT]; p++)
7123  }                                                 7173      if(p->m_bufp != NULL && p->m_dev == dev) {
7124  /* --------------------------     */              7174              p = p->m_bufp->b_addr;
7125  /* --------------------------     */              7175              n1 = p->s_nfree;
7126                                                    7176              n2 = p->s_ninode;
7127  /*                                                7177              if(n1 > 100 || n2 > 100) {
7128   * Free the specified I node                      7178                      prdev("bad count", dev);
7129   * on the specified device.                       7179                      p->s_nfree = 0;
7130   * The algorithm stores up                        7180                      p->s_ninode = 0;
7131   * to 100 I nodes in the super                    7181              }
7132   * block and throws away any more.                7182              return(p);
7133   */                                               7183      }
7134  ifree(dev, ino)                                   7184      panic("no fs");
7135  {                                                 7185  }
7136      register *fp;                                 7186  /* --------------------------     */
7137                                                    7187  /* --------------------------     */
7138      fp = setfs(dev);                              7188
7139      if(fp->s_ilock)                               7189  /*
7140              return;                               7190   * update is the internal name of
7141      if(fp->s_ninode >= 100)                       7191   * 'sync'. It goes through the disk
7142              return;                               7192   * queues to initiate sandbagged IO;
7143      fp->s_inode[fp->s_ninode++] = ino;            7193   * goes through the I nodes to write
7144      fp->s_fmod = 1;                               7194   * modified nodes; and it goes through
7145  }                                                 7195   * the mount table to initiate modified
7146  /* --------------------------     */              7196   * super blocks.
7147  /* --------------------------     */              7197   */
7148                                                    7198
7149  /*                                                7199
```

```
7200
7201 update()
7202 {
7203     register struct inode *ip;
7204     register struct mount *mp;
7205     register *bp;
7206
7207     if(updlock)
7208             return;
7209     updlock++;
7210     for(mp = &mount[0]; mp < &mount[NMOUNT]; mp++)
7211             if(mp->m_bufp != NULL) {
7212                     ip = mp->m_bufp->b_addr;
7213                     if(ip->s_fmod==0 || ip->s_ilock!=0 ||
7214                        ip->s_flock!=0 || ip->s_ronly!=0)
7215                             continue;
7216                     bp = getblk(mp->m_dev, 1);
7217                     ip->s_fmod = 0;
7218                     ip->s_time[0] = time[0];
7219                     ip->s_time[1] = time[1];
7220                     bcopy(ip, bp->b_addr, 256);
7221                     bwrite(bp);
7222             }
7223     for(ip = &inode[0]; ip < &inode[NINODE]; ip++)
7224             if((ip->i_flag&ILOCK) == 0) {
7225                     ip->i_flag =| ILOCK;
7226                     iupdat(ip, time);
7227                     prele(ip);
7228             }
7229     updlock = 0;
7230     bflush(NODEV);
7231 }
7232 /* ------------------------- */
7233 /* ------------------------- */
7234
7235
7236
7237
7238
7239
7240
7241
7242
7243
7244
7245
7246
7247
7248
7249
```

```
7250 #
7251 #include "../param.h"
7252 #include "../systm.h"
7253 #include "../user.h"
7254 #include "../inode.h"
7255 #include "../filsys.h"
7256 #include "../conf.h"
7257 #include "../buf.h"
7258
7259 /*
7260  * Look up an inode by device,inumber.
7261  * If it is in core (in the inode structure),
7262  * honor the locking protocol.
7263  * If it is not in core, read it in from the
7264  * specified device.
7265  * If the inode is mounted on, perform
7266  * the indicated indirection.
7267  * In all cases, a pointer to a locked
7268  * inode structure is returned.
7269  *
7270  * printf warning: no inodes -- if the inode
7271  * structure is full
7272  * panic: no imt -- if the mounted file
7273  * system is not in the mount table.
7274  * 'cannot happen'
7275  */
7276 iget(dev, ino)
7277 {
7278     register struct inode *p;
7279     register *ip2;
7280     int *ip1;
7281     register struct mount *ip;
7282
7283 loop:
7284     ip = NULL;
7285     for(p = &inode[0]; p < &inode[NINODE]; p++) {
7286             if(dev==p->i_dev && ino==p->i_number) {
7287                     if((p->i_flag&ILOCK) != 0) {
7288                             p->i_flag =| IWANT;
7289                             sleep(p, PINOD);
7290                             goto loop;
7291                     }
7292                     if((p->i_flag&IMOUNT) != 0) {
7293                             for (ip = &mount[0];
7294                                 ip < &mount[NMOUNT]; ip++)
7295                                     if (ip->m_inodp == p) {
7296                                             dev = ip->m_dev;
7297                                             ino = ROOTINO;
7298                                             goto loop;
7299
```

```
7300                                panic("no imt");
7301                        }
7302                        p->i_count++;
7303                        p->i_flag =: ILOCK;
7304                        return(p);
7305                }
7306                if(ip==NULL && p->i_count==0)
7307                        ip = p;
7308        }
7309        if((p=ip) == NULL) {
7310                printf("Inode table overflow\n");
7311                u.u_error = ENFILE;
7312                return(NULL);
7313        }
7314        p->i_dev = dev;
7315        p->i_number = ino;
7316        p->i_flag = ILOCK;
7317        p->i_count++;
7318        p->i_lastr = -1;
7319        ip = bread(dev, ldiv(ino+31,16));
7320        /*
7321         * Check I/O errors
7322         */
7323        if (ip->b_flags&B_ERROR) {
7324                brelse(ip);
7325                iput(p);
7326                return(NULL);
7327        }
7328        ip1 = ip->b_addr + 32*lrem(ino+31, 16);
7329        ip2 = &p->i_mode;
7330        while(ip2 < &p->i_addr[8])
7331                *ip2++ = *ip1++;
7332        brelse(ip);
7333        return(p);
7334 }
7335 /* ------------------------          */
7336
7337 /*
7338  * Decrement reference count of
7339  * an inode structure.
7340  * On the last reference,
7341  * write the inode out and if necessary,
7342  * truncate and deallocate the file.
7343  */
7344 iput(p)
7345 struct inode *p;
7346 {
7347     register *rp;
7348
7349     rp = p;
```

```
7350     if(rp->i_count == 1) {
7351             rp->i_flag =: ILOCK;
7352             if(rp->i_nlink <= 0) {
7353                     itrunc(rp);
7354                     rp->i_mode = 0;
7355                     ifree(rp->i_dev, rp->i_number);
7356             }
7357             iupdat(rp, time);
7358             prele(rp);
7359             rp->i_flag = 0;
7360             rp->i_number = 0;
7361     }
7362     rp->i_count--;
7363     prele(rp);
7364 }
7365 /* ------------------------          */
7366
7367 /*
7368  * Check accessed and update flags on
7369  * an inode structure.
7370  * If either is on, update the inode
7371  * with the corresponding dates
7372  * set to the argument tm.
7373  */
7374 iupdat(p, tm)
7375 int *p;
7376 int *tm;
7377 {
7378     register *ip1, *ip2, *rp;
7379     int *bp, i;
7380
7381     rp = p;
7382     if((rp->i_flag&(IUPD|IACC)) != 0) {
7383             if(getfs(rp->i_dev)->s_ronly)
7384                     return;
7385             i = rp->i_number+31;
7386             bp = bread(rp->i_dev, ldiv(i,16));
7387             ip1 = bp->b_addr + 32*lrem(i, 16);
7388             ip2 = &rp->i_mode;
7389             while(ip2 < &rp->i_addr[8])
7390                     *ip1++ = *ip2++;
7391             if(rp->i_flag&IACC) {
7392                     *ip1++ = time[0];
7393                     *ip1++ = time[1];
7394             } else
7395                     ip1 =+ 2;
7396             if(rp->i_flag&IUPD) {
7397                     *ip1++ = *tm++;
7398                     *ip1++ = *tm;
7399             }
```

Sheet 73

Sheet 73

```
7400               bwrite(bp);
7401     }
7402 }
7403 /* --------------------------       */
7404
7405 /*
7406  * Free all the disk blocks associated
7407  * with the specified inode structure.
7408  * The blocks of the file are removed
7409  * in reverse order. This FILO
7410  * algorithm will tend to maintain
7411  * a contiguous free list much longer
7412  * than FIFO.
7413  */
7414 itrunc(ip)
7415 int *ip;
7416 {
7417     register *rp, *bp, *cp;
7418     int *dp, *ep;
7419
7420     rp = ip;
7421     if((rp->i_mode&(IFCHR&IFBLK)) != 0)
7422               return;
7423     for(ip = &rp->i_addr[7]; ip >= &rp->i_addr[0]; ip--)
7424     if(*ip) {
7425               if((rp->i_mode&ILARG) != 0) {
7426                         bp = bread(rp->i_dev, *ip);
7427                         for(cp = bp->b_addr+512; cp >= bp->b_addr;
7428                                              cp--)
7429                         if(*cp) {
7430                                   if(ip == &rp->i_addr[7]) {
7431                                             dp = bread(rp->i_dev, *cp);
7432                                             for(ep = dp->b_addr+512;
7433                                                     ep >= dp->b_addr; ep--)
7434                                             if(*ep)
7435                                                     free(rp->i_dev, *ep);
7436                                             brelse(dp);
7437                                   }
7438                                   free(rp->i_dev, *cp);
7439                         }
7440                         brelse(bp);
7441               }
7442               free(rp->i_dev, *ip);
7443               *ip = 0;
7444     }
7445     rp->i_mode =& ~ILARG;
7446     rp->i_size0 = 0;
7447     rp->i_size1 = 0;
7448     rp->i_flag =| IUPD;
7449 }
```

```
7450 /* --------------------------       */
7451
7452 /*
7453  * Make a new file.
7454  */
7455 maknode(mode)
7456 {
7457     register *ip;
7458
7459     ip = ialloc(u.u_pdir->i_dev);
7460     if (ip==NULL)
7461               return(NULL);
7462     ip->i_flag =| IACC|IUPD;
7463     ip->i_mode = mode|IALLOC;
7464     ip->i_nlink = 1;
7465     ip->i_uid = u.u_uid;
7466     ip->i_gid = u.u_gid;
7467     wdir(ip);
7468     return(ip);
7469 }
7470 /* --------------------------       */
7471
7472 /*
7473  * Write a directory entry with
7474  * parameters left as side effects
7475  * to a call to namei.
7476  */
7477 wdir(ip)
7478 int *ip;
7479 {
7480     register char *cp1, *cp2;
7481
7482     u.u_dent.u_ino = ip->i_number;
7483     cp1 = &u.u_dent.u_name[0];
7484     for(cp2 = &u.u_dbuf[0]; cp2 < &u.u_dbuf[DIRSIZ];)
7485               *cp1++ = *cp2++;
7486     u.u_count = DIRSIZ+2;
7487     u.u_segfls = 1;
7488     u.u_base = &u.u_dent;
7489     writei(u.u_pdir);
7490     iput(u.u_pdir);
7491 }
7492 /* --------------------------       */
7493
7494
7495
7496
7497
7498
7499
```

```
7500 #
7501 #include "../param.h"
7502 #include "../inode.h"
7503 #include "../user.h"
7504 #include "../systm.h"
7505 #include "../buf.h"
7506
7507 /*
7508  * Convert a pathname into a pointer to
7509  * an inode. Note that the inode is locked.
7510  *
7511  * func = function called to get next char of name
7512  * &uchar if name is in user space
7513  * &schar if name is in system space
7514  * flag = 0 if name is sought
7515  * 1 if name is to be created
7516  * 2 if name is to be deleted
7517  */
7518 namei(func, flag)
7519 int (*func)();
7520 {
7521     register struct inode *dp;
7522     register c;
7523     register char *cp;
7524     int eo, *bp;
7525
7526     /*
7527      * If name starts with '/' start from
7528      * root; otherwise start from current dir.
7529      */
7530
7531     dp = u.u_cdir;
7532     if((c=(*func)()) == '/')
7533             dp = rootdir;
7534     iget(dp->i_dev, dp->i_number);
7535     while(c == '/')
7536             c = (*func)();
7537     if(c == '\0' && flag != 0) {
7538             u.u_error = ENOENT;
7539             goto out;
7540     }
7541
7542 cloop:
7543     /*
7544      * Here dp contains pointer
7545      * to last component matched.
7546      */
7547
7548     if(u.u_error)
7549             goto out;
```

```
7550     if(c == '\0')
7551             return(dp);
7552
7553     /*
7554      * If there is another component,
7555      * dp must be a directory and
7556      * must have x permission.
7557      */
7558
7559     if((dp->i_mode&IFMT) != IFDIR) {
7560             u.u_error = ENOTDIR;
7561             goto out;
7562     }
7563     if(access(dp, IEXEC))
7564             goto out;
7565
7566     /* Gather up name into
7567      * users' dir buffer.
7568      */
7569
7570     cp = &u.u_dbuf[0];
7571     while(c!='/' && c!='\0' && u.u_error==0) {
7572             if(cp < &u.u_dbuf[DIRSIZ])
7573                     *cp++ = c;
7574             c = (*func)();
7575     }
7576     while(cp < &u.u_dbuf[DIRSIZ])
7577             *cp++ = '\0';
7578     while(c == '/')
7579             c = (*func)();
7580     if(u.u_error)
7581             goto out;
7582
7583     /* Set up to search a directory. */
7584
7585     u.u_offset[1] = 0;
7586     u.u_offset[0] = 0;
7587     u.u_segflg = 1;
7588     eo = 0;
7589     u.u_count = ldiv(dp->i_size1, DIRSIZ+2);
7590     bp = NULL;
7591
7592 eloop:
7593
7594     /*
7595      * If at the end of the directory,
7596      * the search failed. Report what
7597      * is appropriate as per flag.
7598      */
7599
```

Sheet 75

Sheet 75

```
7600    if(u.u_count == 0) {                          7650        /* Here a component matched in a directory.
7601            if(bp != NULL)                         7651         * If there is more pathname, go back to
7602                    brelse(bp);                    7652         * cloop, otherwise return.
7603            if(flag==1 && c=='\0') {               7653         */
7604                    if(access(dp, IWRITE))         7654
7605                            goto out;              7655        if(bp != NULL)
7606                    u.u_pdir = dp;                 7656                brelse(bp);
7607                    if(eo)                         7657        if(flag==2 && c=='\0') {
7608                            u.u_offset[1] = eo-DIRSIZ-2; else  7658                if(access(dp, IWRITE))
7609                            dp->i_flag =| IUPD;    7659                        goto out;
7610                    return(NULL);                  7660                return(dp);
7611            }                                      7661        }
7612            u.u_error = ENOENT;                    7662        bp = dp->i_dev;
7613            goto out;                              7663        iput(dp);
7614    }                                              7664        dp = iget(bp, u.u_dent.u_ino);
7615                                                   7665        if(dp == NULL)
7616    /*                                             7666                return(NULL);
7617     * If offset is on a block boundary,           7667        goto cloop;
7618     * read the next directory block.              7668
7619     * Release previous if it exists.             7669 out:
7620     */                                            7670    iput(dp);
7621                                                   7671    return(NULL);
7622    if((u.u_offset[1]&0777) == 0) {               7672 }
7623            if(bp != NULL)                         7673 /* ------------------------       */
7624                    brelse(bp);                    7674
7625            bp = bread(dp->i_dev,                  7675 /*
7626                    bmap(dp, ldiv(u.u_offset[1], 512)));  7676  * Return the next character from the
7627    }                                              7677  * kernel string pointed at by dirp.
7628                                                   7678  */
7629    /* Note first empty directory slot             7679 schar()
7630     * in eo for possible creat.                  7680 {
7631     * String compare the directory entry          7681
7632     * and the current component.                 7682    return(*u.u_dirp++ & 0377);
7633     * If they do not match, go back to eloop.     7683 }
7634     */                                            7684 /* ------------------------       */
7635                                                   7685
7636    bcopy(bp->b_addr+(u.u_offset[1]&0777), &u.u_dent,  7686 /* Return the next character from the
7637                            (DIRSIZ+2)/2);         7687  * user string pointed at by dirp.
7638    u.u_offset[1] =+ DIRSIZ+2;                     7688  */
7639    u.u_count--;                                   7689 uchar()
7640    if(u.u_dent.u_ino == 0) {                      7690 {
7641            if(eo == 0)                            7691    register c;
7642                    eo = u.u_offset[1];            7692
7643            goto eloop;                            7693    c = fubyte(u.u_dirp++);
7644    }                                              7694    if(c == -1)
7645    for(cp = &u.u_dbuf[0]; cp < &u.u_dbuf[DIRSIZ]; cp++)  7695            u.u_error = EFAULT;
7646            if(*cp != cp[u.u_dent.u_name - u.u_dbuf])  7696    return(c);
7647                    goto eloop;                    7697 }
7648                                                   7698 /* ------------------------       */
7649                                                   7699
```

```
7700 #include "../param.h"
7701 #include "../systm.h"
7702 #include "../user.h"
7703 #include "../inode.h"
7704 #include "../file.h"
7705 #include "../reg.h"
7706
7707 /* Max allowable buffering per pipe.
7708  * This is also the max size of the
7709  * file created to implement the pipe.
7710  * If this size is bigger than 4096,
7711  * pipes will be implemented in LARGe
7712  * files, which is probably not good.
7713  */
7714
7715 #define    PIPSIZ   4096
7716
7717 /* The sys-pipe entry.
7718  * Allocate an inode on the root device.
7719  * Allocate 2 file structures.
7720  * Put it all together with flags.
7721  */
7722
7723 pipe()
7724 {
7725     register *ip, *rf, *wf;
7726     int r;
7727
7728     ip = ialloc(rootdev);
7729     if(ip == NULL)
7730             return;
7731     rf = falloc();
7732     if(rf == NULL) {
7733             iput(ip);
7734             return;
7735     }
7736     r = u.u_ar0[R0];
7737     wf = falloc();
7738     if(wf == NULL) {
7739             rf->f_count = 0;
7740             u.u_ofile[r] = NULL;
7741             iput(ip);
7742             return;
7743     }
7744     u.u_ar0[R1] = u.u_ar0[R0];
7745     u.u_ar0[R0] = r;
7746     wf->f_flag = FWRITE|FPIPE;
7747     wf->f_inode = ip;
7748     rf->f_flag = FREAD|FPIPE;
7749     rf->f_inode = ip;
```

```
7750     ip->i_count = 2;
7751     ip->i_flag = IACC|IUPD;
7752     ip->i_mode = IALLOC;
7753 }
7754 /* ------------------------        */
7755
7756 /* Read call directed to a pipe.
7757  */
7758 readp(fp)
7759 int *fp;
7760 {
7761     register *rp, *ip;
7762
7763     rp = fp;
7764     ip = rp->f_inode;
7765 loop:
7766     /* Very conservative locking.
7767      */
7768     plock(ip);
7769     /* If the head (read) has caught up with
7770      * the tail (write), reset both to 0.
7771      */
7772     if(rp->f_offset[1] == ip->i_size1) {
7773             if(rp->f_offset[1] != 0) {
7774                     rp->f_offset[1] = 0;
7775                     ip->i_size1 = 0;
7776                     if(ip->i_mode&IWRITE) {
7777                             ip->i_mode =& ~IWRITE;
7778                             wakeup(ip+1);
7779                     }
7780             }
7781
7782             /* If there are not both reader and
7783              * writer active, return without
7784              * satisfying read.
7785              */
7786             prele(ip);
7787             if(ip->i_count < 2)
7788                     return;
7789             ip->i_mode =| IREAD;
7790             sleep(ip+2, PPIPE);
7791             goto loop;
7792     }
7793     /* Read and return
7794      */
7795     u.u_offset[0] = 0;
7796     u.u_offset[1] = rp->f_offset[1];
7797     readi(ip);
7798     rp->f_offset[1] = u.u_offset[1];
7799     prele(ip);
```

```
7800 }
7801 /* --------------------------        */
7802
7803 /* Write call directed to a pipe.
7804  */
7805 writep(fp)
7806 {
7807     register *rp, *ip, c;
7808
7809     rp = fp;
7810     ip = rp->f_inode;
7811     c = u.u_count;
7812 loop:
7813     /* If all done, return.
7814      */
7815     plock(ip);
7816     if(c == 0) {
7817             prele(ip);
7818             u.u_count = 0;
7819             return;
7820     }
7821     /* If there are not both read and
7822      * write sides of the pipe active,
7823      * return error and signal too.
7824      */
7825     if(ip->i_count < 2) {
7826             prele(ip);
7827             u.u_error = EPIPE;
7828             psignal(u.u_procp, SIGPIPE);
7829             return;
7830     }
7831     /* If the pipe is full,
7832      * wait for reads to deplete
7833      * and truncate it.
7834      */
7835     if(ip->i_size1 == PIPSIZ) {
7836             ip->i_mode =| IWRITE;
7837             prele(ip);
7838             sleep(ip+1, PPIPE);
7839             goto loop;
7840     }
7841     /* Write what is possible and
7842      * loop back.
7843      */
7844     u.u_offset[0] = 0;
7845     u.u_offset[1] = ip->i_size1;
7846     u.u_count = min(c, PIPSIZ-u.u_offset[1]);
7847     c =- u.u_count;
7848     writei(ip);
7849     prele(ip);
```

```
7850     if(ip->i_mode&IREAD) {
7851             ip->i_mode =& ~IREAD;
7852             wakeup(ip+2);
7853     }
7854     goto loop;
7855 }
7856 /* --------------------------        */
7857
7858 /* Lock a pipe.
7859  * If its already locked,
7860  * set the WANT bit and sleep.
7861  */
7862 plock(ip)
7863 int *ip;
7864 {
7865     register *rp;
7866
7867     rp = ip;
7868     while(rp->i_flag&ILOCK) {
7869             rp->i_flag =| IWANT;
7870             sleep(rp, PPIPE);
7871     }
7872     rp->i_flag =| ILOCK;
7873 }
7874 /* --------------------------        */
7875
7876 /* Unlock a pipe.
7877  * If WANT bit is on,
7878  * wakeup.
7879  * This routine is also used
7880  * to unlock inodes in general.
7881  */
7882 prele(ip)
7883 int *ip;
7884 {
7885     register *rp;
7886
7887     rp = ip;
7888     rp->i_flag =& ~ILOCK;
7889     if(rp->i_flag&IWANT) {
7890             rp->i_flag =& ~IWANT;
7891             wakeup(rp);
7892     }
7893 }
7894 /* --------------------------        */
7895
7896
7897
7898
7899
```

5

**Character Oriented
Special Files**

```
7900 /*
7901  * A clist structure is the head
7902  * of a linked list queue of characters.
7903  * The characters are stored in 4-word
7904  * blocks containing a link and 6 characters.
7905  * The routines getc and putc (m45.s or m40.s)
7906  * manipulate these structures.
7907  */
7908 struct clist
7909 {
7910     int     c_cc;           /* character count */
7911     int     c_cf;           /* pointer to first block */
7912     int     c_cl;           /* pointer to last block */
7913 };
7914 /* -------------------------      */
7915
7916 /*
7917  * A tty structure is needed for
7918  * each UNIX character device that
7919  * is used for normal terminal IO.
7920  * The routines in tty.c handle the
7921  * common code associated with
7922  * these structures.
7923  * The definition and device dependent
7924  * code is in each driver. (kl.c dc.c dh.c)
7925  */
7926 struct tty
7927 {
7928   struct clist t_rawq; /* input chars right off device */
7929   struct clist t_canq; /* input chars after erase and kill */
7930   struct clist t_outq; /* output list to device */
7931   int     t_flags;     /* mode, settable by stty call */
7932   int     *t_addr;     /* device address (register or
7933                                  startup fcn) */
7934   char    t_delct;     /* number of delimiters in raw q */
7935   char    t_col;       /* printing column of device */
7936   char    t_erase;     /* erase character */
7937   char    t_kill;      /* kill character */
7938   char    t_state;     /* internal state, not visible
7939                                  externally */
7940   char    t_char;      /* character temporary */
7941   int     t_speeds;    /* output+input line speed */
7942   int     t_dev;       /* device name */
7943 };
7944 /* -------------------------      */
7945
7946
7947 char partab[];   /* ASCII table: parity, character class */
7948
7949
```

```
7950
7951 #define    TTIPRI    10
7952 #define    TTOPRI    20
7953
7954 #define    CERASE    '#'   /* default special characters */
7955 #define    CEOT      004
7956 #define    CKILL     '@'
7957 #define    CQUIT     034   /* FS, cntl shift L */
7958 #define    CINTR     0177  /* DEL */
7959
7960 /* limits */
7961 #define    TTHIWAT 50
7962 #define    TTLOWAT 30
7963 #define    TTYHOG  256
7964
7965 /* modes */
7966 #define    HUPCL     01
7967 #define    XTABS     02
7968 #define    LCASE     04
7969 #define    ECHO      010
7970 #define    CRMOD     020
7971 #define    RAW       040
7972 #define    ODDP      0100
7973 #define    EVENP     0200
7974 #define    NLDELAY   001400
7975 #define    TBDELAY   006000
7976 #define    CRDELAY   030000
7977 #define    VTDELAY   040000
7978
7979 /* Hardware bits */
7980 #define    DONE      0200
7981 #define    IENABLE   0100
7982
7983 /* Internal state bits */
7984 #define TIMEOUT    01        /* Delay timeout in progress */
7985 #define WOPEN      02        /* Waiting for open to
7986                                 complete */
7987 #define ISOPEN     04        /* Device is open */
7988 #define SSTART     010       /* Has special start routine
7989                                 at addr */
7990 #define CARR_ON    020       /* Software copy of
7991                                 carrier-present */
7992 #define BUSY       040       /* Output in progress */
7993 #define ASLEEP     0100      /* Wakeup when output done */
7994
7995
7996
7997
7998
7999
```

```
8000 #
8001 /*    KL/DL-11 driver */
8002 #include "../param.h"
8003 #include "../conf.h"
8004 #include "../user.h"
8005 #include "../tty.h"
8006 #include "../proc.h"
8007              /* base address */
8008 #define     KLADDR   0177560 /* console */
8009 #define     KLBASE   0176500 /* kl and dl11-a */
8010 #define     DLBASE   0175610 /* dl-e */
8011 #define     NKL11    1
8012 #define     NDL11    0
8013 #define     DSRDY    02
8014 #define     RDRENB   01
8015 struct      tty kl11[NKL11+NDL11];
8016 struct klregs {
8017     int klrcsr;
8018     int klrbuf;
8019     int kltcsr;
8020     int kltbuf;
8021 }
8022 /* -------------------------       */
8023 klopen(dev, flag)
8024 {  register char *addr;
8025    register struct tty *tp;
8026    if(dev.d_minor >= NKL11+NDL11) {
8027          u.u_error = ENXIO;
8028          return;
8029    }
8030    tp = &kl11[dev.d_minor];
8031    if (u.u_procp->p_ttyp == 0) {
8032          u.u_procp->p_ttyp = tp;
8033          tp->t_dev = dev;
8034    }
8035    /* set up minor 0 to address KLADDR
8036     * set up minor 1 thru NKL11-1 to address from KLBASE
8037     * set up minor NKL11 on to address from DLBASE
8038     */
8039    addr = KLADDR + 8*dev.d_minor;
8040    if(dev.d_minor)
8041          addr =+ KLBASE-KLADDR-8;
8042    if(dev.d_minor >= NKL11)
8043          addr =+ DLBASE-KLBASE-8*NKL11+8;
8044    tp->t_addr = addr;
8045    if ((tp->t_state&ISOPEN) == 0) {
8046          tp->t_state = ISOPEN|CARR_ON;
8047          tp->t_flags = XTABS|LCASE|ECHO|CRMOD;
8048          tp->t_erase = CERASE;
8049          tp->t_kill = CKILL;
```

```
8050    }
8051    addr->klrcsr =| IENABLE|DSRDY|RDRENB;
8052    addr->kltcsr =| IENABLE;
8053 }
8054 /* -------------------------       */
8055 klclose(dev)
8056 {  register struct tty *tp;
8057    tp = &kl11[dev.d_minor];
8058    wflushtty(tp);
8059    tp->t_state = 0;
8060 }
8061 /* -------------------------       */
8062 klread(dev)
8063 {  ttread(&kl11[dev.d_minor]);
8064 }
8065 /* -------------------------       */
8066 klwrite(dev)
8067 {  ttwrite(&kl11[dev.d_minor]);
8068 }
8069 /* -------------------------       */
8070 klxint(dev)
8071 {  register struct tty *tp;
8072    tp = &kl11[dev.d_minor];
8073    ttstart(tp);
8074    if (tp->t_outq.c_cc == 0 || tp->t_outq.c_cc == TTLOWAT)
8075          wakeup(&tp->t_outq);
8076 }
8077 /* -------------------------       */
8078 klrint(dev)
8079 {  register int c, *addr;
8080    register struct tty *tp;
8081    tp = &kl11[dev.d_minor];
8082    addr = tp->t_addr;
8083    c = addr->klrbuf;
8084    addr->klrcsr =| RDRENB;
8085    if ((c&0177)==0)
8086          addr->kltbuf = c;        /* hardware botch */
8087    ttyinput(c, tp);
8088 }
8089 /* -------------------------       */
8090 klsgtty(dev, v)
8091 int *v;
8092 {  register struct tty *tp;
8093    tp = &kl11[dev.d_minor];
8094    ttystty(tp, v);
8095 }
8096 /* -------------------------       */
8097
8098
8099
```

```
8100 #   /* general TTY subroutines */
8101
8102 #include "../param.h"
8103 #include "../systm.h"
8104 #include "../user.h"
8105 #include "../tty.h"
8106 #include "../proc.h"
8107 #include "../inode.h"
8108 #include "../file.h"
8109 #include "../reg.h"
8110 #include "../conf.h"
8111
8112 /* Input mapping table-- if an entry is non-zero, when the
8113  * corresponding character is typed preceded by "\" the
8114  * escape sequence is replaced by the table value.
8115  * Mostly used for upper-case only terminals.
8116  */
8117 char        maptab[]
8118 {
8119     000,000,000,000,004,000,000,000,
8120     000,000,000,000,000,000,000,000,
8121     000,000,000,000,000,000,000,000,
8122     000,000,000,000,000,000,000,000,
8123     000,'!',000,'#',000,000,000,'`',
8124     '{','}',000,000,000,000,000,000,
8125     000,000,000,000,000,000,000,000,
8126     000,000,000,000,000,000,000,000,
8127     '@',000,000,000,000,000,000,000,
8128     000,000,000,000,000,000,000,000,
8129     000,000,000,000,000,000,000,000,
8130     000,000,000,000,000,000,'~',000,
8131     000,'A','B','C','D','E','F','G',
8132     'H','I','J','K','L','M','N','O',
8133     'P','Q','R','S','T','U','V','W',
8134     'X','Y','Z',000,000,000,000,000,
8135 };
8136 /* -------------------------       */
8137 /* The actual structure of a clist block manipulated by
8138  * getc and putc (mch.s)
8139  */
8140 struct cblock {
8141     struct cblock *c_next;
8142     char info[6];
8143 };
8144 /* -------------------------       */
8145 /* The character lists-- space for 6*NCLIST characters */
8146     struct cblock cfree[NCLIST];
8147
8148 /* List head for unused character blocks. */
8149     struct cblock *cfreelist;
```

```
8150 /* structure of device registers for KL, DL, and DC
8151  * interfaces-- more particularly, those for which the
8152  * SSTART bit is off and can be treated by general routines
8153  * (that is, not DH).
8154  */
8155 struct {
8156     int ttrcsr;
8157     int ttrbuf;
8158     int tttcsr;
8159     int tttbuf;
8160 };
8161 /* -------------------------       */
8162 /* The routine implementing the stty system call.
8163  * Just call lower level routine and pass back values.
8164  */
8165 stty()
8166 {
8167     int v[3];
8168     register *up, *vp;
8169
8170     vp = v;
8171     sgtty(vp);
8172     if (u.u_error)
8173             return;
8174     up = u.u_arg[0];
8175     suword(up, *vp++);
8176     suword(++up, *vp++);
8177     suword(++up, *vp++);
8178 }
8179 /* -------------------------       */
8180 /* The routine implementing the stty system call.
8181  * Read in values and call lower level.
8182  */
8183 stty()
8184 {
8185     register int *up;
8186
8187     up = u.u_arg[0];
8188     u.u_arg[0] = fuword(up);
8189     u.u_arg[1] = fuword(++up);
8190     u.u_arg[2] = fuword(++up);
8191     sgtty(0);
8192 }
8193 /* -------------------------       */
8194 /* Stuff common to stty and stty.
8195  * Check legality and switch out to individual
8196  * device routine.
8197  * v is 0 for stty; the parameters are taken from u.u_arg[].
8198  * c is non-zero for stty and is the place in which the
8199  * device routines place their information.
```

```
8200  */
8201  sstty(v)
8202  int *v;
8203  {
8204      register struct file *fp;
8205      register struct inode *ip;
8206      if ((fp = getf(u.u_ar0[R0])) == NULL)
8207          return;
8208      ip = fp->f_inode;
8209      if ((ip->i_mode&IFMT) != IFCHR) {
8210          u.u_error = ENOTTY;
8211          return;
8212      }
8213      (*cdevsw[ip->i_addr[0].d_major].d_sstty)(ip->i_addr[0],v);
8214  }
8215  /* ------------------------      */
8216  /* Wait for output to drain, then flush input waiting. */
8217  wflushtty(atp)
8218  struct tty *atp;
8219  {
8220      register struct tty *tp;
8221      tp = atp;
8222      sp15();
8223      while (tp->t_outq.c_cc) {
8224              tp->t_state =| ASLEEP;
8225              sleep(&tp->t_outq, TTOPRI);
8226      }
8227      flushtty(tp);
8228      sp10();
8229  }
8230  /* ------------------------      */
8231  /* Initialize clist by freeing all character blocks, & count
8232   * number of character devices. (Once-only routine)
8233   */
8234  cinit()
8235  {
8236      register int ccp;
8237      register struct cblock *cp;
8238      register struct cdevsw *cdp;
8239      ccp = cfree;
8240      for (cp=(ccp+07)&~07; cp <= &cfree[NCLIST-1]; cp++) {
8241              cp->c_next = cfreelist;
8242              cfreelist = cp;
8243      }
8244      ccp = 0;
8245      for(cdp = cdevsw; cdp->d_open; cdp++)
8246              ccp++;
8247      nchrdev = ccp;
8248  }
8249  /* ------------------------      */
```

```
8250  /* flush all TTY queues
8251   */
8252  flushtty(atp)
8253  struct tty *atp;
8254  {
8255      register struct tty *tp;
8256      register int sps;
8257      tp = atp;
8258      while (getc(&tp->t_canq) >= 0);
8259      while (getc(&tp->t_outq) >= 0);
8260      wakeup(&tp->t_rawq);
8261      wakeup(&tp->t_outq);
8262      sps = PS->intes;
8263      sp15();
8264      while (getc(&tp->t_rawq) >= 0);
8265      tp->t_delct = 0;
8266      PS->intes = sps;
8267  }
8268  /* ------------------------      */
8269  /* transfer raw input list to canonical list,
8270   * doing erase-kill processing and handling escapes.
8271   * It waits until a full line has been typed in cooked mode,
8272   * or until any character has been typed in raw mode.
8273   */
8274  canon(atp)
8275  struct tty *atp;
8276  {
8277      register char *bp;
8278      char *bp1;
8279      register struct tty *tp;
8280      register int c;
8281
8282      tp = atp;
8283      sp15();
8284      while (tp->t_delct==0) {
8285              if ((tp->t_state&CARR_ON)==0)
8286                      return(0);
8287              sleep(&tp->t_rawq, TTIPRI);
8288      }
8289      sp10();
8290  loop:
8291      bp = &canonb[2];
8292      while ((c=getc(&tp->t_rawq)) >= 0) {
8293              if (c==0377) {
8294                      tp->t_delct--;
8295                      break;
8296              }
8297              if ((tp->t_flags&RAW)==0) {
8298                      if (bp[-1]!='\\') {
8299                              if (c==tp->t_erase) {
```

```
8300                                    if (bp > &canonb[2])
8301                                            bp--;
8302                                    continue;
8303                            }
8304                            if (c==tp->t_kill)
8305                                    goto loop;
8306                            if (c==CEOT)
8307                                    continue;
8308                    } else
8309            if (maptab[c] && (maptab[c]==c || (tp->t_flass&LCASE))) {
8310                            if (bp[-2] != '\\')
8311                                    c = maptab[c];
8312                            bp--;
8313                    }
8314            }
8315            *bp++ = c;
8316            if (bp>=canonb+CANBSIZ)
8317                    break;
8318    }
8319    bp1 = bp;
8320    bp = &canonb[2];
8321    c = &tp->t_canq;
8322    while (bp<bp1)
8323            putc(*bp++, c);
8324    return(1);
8325 }
8326 /* --------------------------       */
8327 /* Place a character on raw TTY input queue, putting in
8328  * delimiters and waking up top half as needed.
8329  * Also echo if required.
8330  * The arguments are the character and the appropriate
8331  * tty structure.
8332  */
8333 ttyinput(ac, atp)
8334 struct tty *atp;
8335 {
8336    register int t_flass, c;
8337    register struct tty *tp;
8338
8339    tp = atp;
8340    c = ac;
8341    t_flass = tp->t_flass;
8342    if ((c =& 0177) == '\r' && t_flass&CRMOD)
8343            c = '\n';
8344    if ((t_flass&RAW)==0 && (c==CQUIT || c==CINTR)) {
8345            signal(tp, c==CINTR? SIGINT:SIGQIT);
8346            flushtty(tp);
8347            return;
8348    }
8349    if (tp->t_rawq.c_cc>=TTYHOG) {
8350            flushtty(tp);
8351            return;
8352    }
8353    if (t_flass&LCASE && c>='A' && c<='Z')
8354            c =+ 'a'-'A';
8355    putc(c, &tp->t_rawq);
8356    if (t_flass&RAW || c=='\n' || c==004) {
8357            wakeup(&tp->t_rawq);
8358            if (putc(0377, &tp->t_rawq)==0)
8359                    tp->t_delct++;
8360    }
8361    if (t_flass&ECHO) {
8362            ttyoutput(c, tp);
8363            ttstart(tp);
8364    }
8365 }
8366 /* --------------------------       */
8367 /* put character on TTY output queue, adding delays,
8368  * expanding tabs, and handling the CR/NL bit.
8369  * It is called both from the top half for output, and from
8370  * interrupt level for echoing.
8371  * The arguments are the character and the tty structure.
8372  */
8373 ttyoutput(ac, tp)
8374 struct tty *tp;
8375 {
8376    register int c;
8377    register struct tty *rtp;
8378    register char *colp;
8379    int ctype;
8380
8381    rtp = tp;
8382    c = ac&0177;
8383    /* Ignore EOT in normal mode to avoid hanging up
8384     * certain terminals.
8385     */
8386    if (c==004 && (rtp->t_flass&RAW)==0)
8387            return;
8388    /* Turn tabs to spaces as required
8389     */
8390    if (c=='\t' && rtp->t_flass&XTABS) {
8391            do
8392                    ttyoutput(' ', rtp);
8393            while (rtp->t_col&07);
8394            return;
8395    }
8396    /* for upper-case-only terminals,
8397     * generate escapes.
8398     */
8399    if (rtp->t_flass&LCASE) {
```

```
8400                colp = "({)}!!^~'`";
8401                while(*colp++) {
8402                        if(c == *colp++) {
8403                                ttyoutput('\\', rtp);
8404                                c = colp[-2];
8405                                break;
8406                        }
8407                if ('a'<=c && c<='z')
8408                        c =+ 'A' - 'a';
8409        }
8410        /* turn <nl> to <cr><lf> if desired.
8411         */
8412        if (c=='\n' && rtp->t_flags&CRMOD)
8413                ttyoutput('\r', rtp);
8414        if (putc(c, &rtp->t_outq))
8415                return;
8416        /* Calculate delays.
8417         * The numbers here represent clock ticks
8418         * and are not necessarily optimal for all terminals.
8419         * The delays are indicated by characters above 0200,
8420         * thus (unfortunately) restricting the transmission
8421         * path to 7 bits.
8422         */
8423        colp = &rtp->t_col;
8424        ctype = partab[c];
8425        c = 0;
8426        switch (ctype&077) {
8427        /* ordinary */
8428        case 0:
8429                (*colp)++;
8430        /* non-printing */
8431        case 1:
8432                break;
8433        /* backspace */
8434        case 2:
8435                if (*colp)
8436                        (*colp)--;
8437                break;
8438        /* newline */
8439        case 3:
8440                ctype = (rtp->t_flags >> 8) & 03;
8441                if(ctype == 1) { /* tty 37 */
8442                        if (*colp)
8443                                c = max((*colp>>4) + 3, 6);
8444                } else
8445                if(ctype == 2) { /* vt05 */
8446                        c = 6;
8447                }
8448                *colp = 0;
8449                break;
```

```
8450        /* tab */
8451        case 4:
8452                ctype = (rtp->t_flags >> 10) & 03;
8453                if(ctype == 1) { /* tty 37 */
8454                        c = 1 - (*colp ! ~07);
8455                        if(c < 5)
8456                                c = 0;
8457                }
8458                *colp =! 07;
8459                (*colp)++;
8460                break;
8461        /* vertical motion */
8462        case 5:
8463                if(rtp->t_flags & VTDELAY) /* tty 37 */
8464                        c = 0177;
8465                break;
8466        /* carriage return */
8467        case 6:
8468                ctype = (rtp->t_flags >> 12) & 03;
8469                if(ctype == 1) { /* tn 300 */
8470                        c = 5;
8471                } else
8472                if(ctype == 2) { /* ti 700 */
8473                        c = 10;
8474                }
8475                *colp = 0;
8476        }
8477        if(c)
8478                putc(c!0200, &rtp->t_outq);
8479 }
8480 /* ------------------------------ */
8481 /* Restart typewriter output following a delay
8482  * timeout.
8483  * The name of the routine is passed to the timeout
8484  * subroutine and it is called during a clock interrupt.
8485  */
8486 ttrstrt(atp)
8487 {
8488        register struct tty *tp;
8489
8490        tp = atp;
8491        tp->t_state =& ~TIMEOUT;
8492        ttstart(tp);
8493 }
8494 /* ------------------------------ */
8495 /* Start output on the typewriter. It is used from the top
8496  * half after some characters have been put on the output
8497  * queue, from the interrupt routine to transmit the next
8498  * character, and after a timeout has finished.
8499  * If the SSTART bit is off for the tty the work is done
```

```
8500   * here, using the protocol of the single-line interfaces
8501   * (kl, dl, dc);   otherwise the address word of the tty
8502   * structure is taken to be the name of the device-dependent
8503   * start-up routine.
8504   */
8505  ttstart(atp)
8506  struct tty *atp;
8507  {
8508      register int *addr, c;
8509      register struct tty *tp;
8510      struct { int (*func)(); };
8511
8512      tp = atp;
8513      addr = tp->t_addr;
8514      if (tp->t_state&SSTART) {
8515              (*addr.func)(tp);
8516              return;
8517      }
8518      if ((addr->tttcsr&DONE)==0 || tp->t_state&TIMEOUT)
8519              return;
8520      if ((c=getc(&tp->t_outq)) >= 0) {
8521              if (c<=0177)
8522                      addr->tttbuf = c | (partab[c]&0200);
8523              else {
8524                      timeout(ttrstrt, tp, c&0177);
8525                      tp->t_state =| TIMEOUT;
8526              }
8527      }
8528  }
8529  /* --------------------------      */
8530  /* Called from device's read routine after it has
8531   * calculated the tty-structure given as argument.
8532   * The pc is backed up for the duration of this call.
8533   * In case of a caught interrupt, an RTI will re-execute.
8534   */
8535  ttread(atp)
8536  struct tty *atp;
8537  {
8538      register struct tty *tp;
8539
8540      tp = atp;
8541      if ((tp->t_state&CARR_ON)==0)
8542              return;
8543      if (tp->t_canq.c_cc || canon(tp))
8544        while (tp->t_canq.c_cc && passc(getc(&tp->t_canq))>=0);
8545  }
8546  /* --------------------------      */
8547  /* Called from the device's write routine after it has
8548   * calculated the tty-structure given as argument.
8549   */
8550  ttwrite(atp)
8551  struct tty *atp;
8552  {
8553      register struct tty *tp;
8554      register int c;
8555      tp = atp;
8556      if ((tp->t_state&CARR_ON)==0)
8557              return;
8558      while ((c=cpass())>=0) {
8559              sp15();
8560              while (tp->t_outq.c_cc > TTHIWAT) {
8561                      ttstart(tp);
8562                      tp->t_state =| ASLEEP;
8563                      sleep(&tp->t_outq, TTOPRI);
8564              }
8565              sp10();
8566              ttyoutput(c, tp);
8567      }
8568      ttstart(tp);
8569  }
8570  /* --------------------------      */
8571  /* Common code for gtty and stty functions on typewriters.
8572   * If v is non-zero then stty is being done and information
8573   * is passed back therein;
8574   * if it is zero gtty is being done and the input inform-
8575   * ation is in the u_arg array.
8576   */
8577  ttystty(atp, av)
8578  int *atp, *av;
8579  {
8580      register *tp, *v;
8581      tp = atp;
8582      if(v = av) {
8583              *v++ = tp->t_speeds;
8584              v->lobyte = tp->t_erase;
8585              v->hibyte = tp->t_kill;
8586              v[1] = tp->t_flags;
8587              return(1);
8588      }
8589      wflushtty(tp);
8590      v = u.u_arg;
8591      tp->t_speeds = *v++;
8592      tp->t_erase = v->lobyte;
8593      tp->t_kill = v->hibyte;
8594      tp->t_flags = v[1];
8595      return(0);
8596  }
8597  /* --------------------------      */
8598
8599
```

```
8600 #
8601 /* PC-11 Paper tape reader/punch driver */
8602
8603 #include "../param.h"
8604 #include "../conf.h"
8605 #include "../user.h"
8606
8607 #define     PCADDR  0177550
8608
8609 #define     CLOSED  0
8610 #define     WAITING 1
8611 #define     READING 2
8612 #define     EOF     3
8613
8614 #define     RDRENB  01
8615 #define     IENABLE 0100
8616 #define     DONE    0200
8617 #define     BUSY    04000
8618 #define     ERROR   0100000
8619
8620 #define     PCIPRI  30
8621 #define     PCOPRI  40
8622 #define     PCOLWAT 50
8623 #define     PCOHWAT 100
8624 #define     PCIHWAT 250
8625
8626 struct {
8627     int pcrcsr;
8628     int pcrbuf;
8629     int pcpcsr;
8630     int pcpbuf;
8631 };
8632 /* --------------------------- */
8633
8634 struct clist {
8635     int     cc;
8636     int     cf;
8637     int     cl;
8638 };
8639 /* --------------------------- */
8640
8641 struct pc11 {
8642     int     pcstate;
8643     struct  clist pcin;
8644     struct  clist pcout;
8645 } pc11;
8646 /* --------------------------- */
8647
8648 pcopen(dev, flag)
8649 {
```

```
8650     extern lbolt;
8651
8652     if (flag==0) {
8653             if (pc11.pcstate!=CLOSED) {
8654                     u.u_error = ENXIO;
8655                     return;
8656             }
8657             pc11.pcstate = WAITING;
8658             while(pc11.pcstate==WAITING) {
8659                     PCADDR->pcrcsr = IENABLE!RDRENB;
8660                     sleep(&lbolt, PCIPRI);
8661             }
8662     } else {
8663             PCADDR->pcpcsr =! IENABLE;
8664             pcleader();
8665     }
8666 }
8667 /* --------------------------- */
8668
8669 pcclose(dev, flag)
8670 {
8671     if (flag==0) {
8672             sp14();
8673             while (getc(&pc11.pcin) >= 0);
8674             PCADDR->pcrcsr = 0;
8675             pc11.pcstate = CLOSED;
8676             sp10();
8677     } else
8678             pcleader();
8679 }
8680 /* --------------------------- */
8681
8682 pcread()
8683 {
8684     register int c;
8685
8686     sp14();
8687     do {
8688             while ((c = getc(&pc11.pcin)) < 0) {
8689                     if (pc11.pcstate==EOF)
8690                             goto out;
8691                     if ((PCADDR->pcrcsr&(ERROR!BUSY!DONE))==0)
8692                             PCADDR->pcrcsr =! IENABLE!RDRENB;
8693                     sleep(&pc11.pcin, PCIPRI);
8694             }
8695     } while (passc(c)>=0);
8696 out:
8697     sp10();
8698 }
8699 /* --------------------------- */
```

```
8700
8701 pcwrite()
8702 {
8703     register int c;
8704
8705     while ((c=cpass())>=0)
8706             pcoutput(c);
8707 }
8708 /* ------------------------        */
8709
8710 pcstart()
8711 {
8712     register int c;
8713
8714     if (PCADDR->pcpcsr&DONE && (c = getc(&pc11.pcout)) >= 0)
8715             PCADDR->pcpbuf = c;
8716 }
8717 /* ------------------------        */
8718
8719 pcrint()
8720 {
8721     if (pc11.pcstate==WAITING) {
8722             if (PCADDR->pcrcsr&ERROR)
8723                     return;
8724             pc11.pcstate = READING;
8725     }
8726     if (pc11.pcstate==READING) {
8727             if (PCADDR->pcrcsr&ERROR)
8728                     pc11.pcstate = EOF;
8729             else {
8730                     putc(PCADDR->pcrbuf, &pc11.pcin);
8731                     if (pc11.pcin.cc < PCIHWAT)
8732                             PCADDR->pcrcsr =| IENABLE!RDRENB;
8733             }
8734             wakeup(&pc11.pcin);
8735     }
8736 }
8737 /* ------------------------        */
8738
8739 pcpint()
8740 {
8741
8742     pcstart();
8743     if (pc11.pcout.cc <= PCOLWAT)
8744             wakeup(&pc11.pcout);
8745 }
8746 /* ------------------------        */
8747
8748 pcoutput(c)
8749 {
```

```
8750     if (PCADDR->pcpcsr&ERROR) {
8751             u.u_error = EIO;
8752             return;
8753     }
8754     if (pc11.pcout.cc >= PCOHWAT)
8755             sleep(&pc11.pcout, PCOPRI);
8756     putc(c, &pc11.pcout);
8757     spl4();
8758     pcstart();
8759     spl0();
8760 }
8761 /* ------------------------        */
8762
8763 pcleader()
8764 {
8765     register int i;
8766
8767     i = 100;
8768     do
8769             pcoutput(0);
8770     while (--i);
8771 }
8772 /* ------------------------        */
8773
8774
8775
8776
8777
8778
8779
8780
8781
8782
8783
8784
8785
8786
8787
8788
8789
8790
8791
8792
8793
8794
8795
8796
8797
8798
8799
```

```
8800 #
8801 /*
8802  */
8803
8804 /*
8805  * LP-11 Line printer driver
8806  */
8807
8808 #include "../param.h"
8809 #include "../conf.h"
8810 #include "../user.h"
8811
8812 #define    LPADDR   0177514
8813
8814 #define    IENABLE 0100
8815 #define    DONE    0200
8816
8817 #define    LPPRI    10
8818 #define    LPLWAT   50
8819 #define    LPHWAT   100
8820 #define    EJLINE   60
8821 #define    MAXCOL   80
8822
8823 struct {
8824     int lpsr;
8825     int lpbuf;
8826 };
8827 /* ------------------------         */
8828
8829 struct   {
8830     int     cc;
8831     int     cf;
8832     int     cl;
8833     int     flag;
8834     int     mcc;
8835     int     ccc;
8836     int     mlc;
8837 } lp11;
8838 /* ------------------------         */
8839
8840 #define CAP       01   /* Set to 0 for 96-char printer,
8841                          else to 01 */
8842 #define EJECT     02
8843 #define OPEN      04
8844 #define IND       010 /* Set to 0 for no indent,
8845                          else to 010 */
8846
8847 #define FORM      014
8848
8849
```

```
8850 lpopen(dev, flag)
8851 {
8852
8853     if(lp11.flag & OPEN || LPADDR->lpsr < 0) {
8854             u.u_error = EIO;
8855             return;
8856     }
8857     lp11.flag =| (IND|EJECT|OPEN);
8858     LPADDR->lpsr =| IENABLE;
8859     lpcanon(FORM);
8860 }
8861 /* ------------------------         */
8862
8863 lpclose(dev, flag)
8864 {
8865     lpcanon(FORM);
8866     lp11.flag = 0;
8867 }
8868 /* ------------------------         */
8869
8870 lpwrite()
8871 {
8872     register int c;
8873
8874     while ((c=cpass())>=0)
8875             lpcanon(c);
8876 }
8877 /* ------------------------         */
8878
8879 lpcanon(c)
8880 {
8881     register c1, c2;
8882
8883     c1 = c;
8884     if(lp11.flag&CAP) {
8885             if(c1>='a' && c1<='z')
8886                     c1 =+ 'A'-'a'; else
8887             switch(c1) {
8888
8889             case '{':
8890                     c2 = '(';
8891                     goto esc;
8892
8893             case '}':
8894                     c2 = ')';
8895                     goto esc;
8896
8897             case '`':
8898                     c2 = '\'';
8899                     goto esc;
```

```
8900
8901            case '!':
8902                    c2 = '!';
8903                    goto esc;
8904
8905            case '~':
8906                    c2 = '~';
8907
8908            esc:
8909                    lpcanon(c2);
8910                    lp11.ccc--;
8911                    c1 = '-';
8912            }
8913    }
8914
8915    switch(c1) {
8916
8917    case '\t':
8918            lp11.ccc = (lp11.ccc+8) & ~7;
8919            return;
8920
8921    case FORM:
8922    case '\n':
8923            if((lp11.flag&EJECT) == 0 ||
8924               lp11.mcc!=0 || lp11.mlc!=0) {
8925                    lp11.mcc = 0;
8926                    lp11.mlc++;
8927                    if(lp11.mlc >= EJLINE && lp11.flag&EJECT)
8928                            c1 = FORM;
8929                    lpoutput(c1);
8930                    if(c1 == FORM)
8931                            lp11.mlc = 0;
8932            }
8933
8934    case '\r':
8935            lp11.ccc = 0;
8936            if(lp11.flag&IND)
8937                    lp11.ccc = 8;
8938            return;
8939
8940    case 010:
8941            if(lp11.ccc > 0)
8942                    lp11.ccc--;
8943            return;
8944
8945    case ' ':
8946            lp11.ccc++;
8947            return;
8948
8949    default:
```

```
8950            if(lp11.ccc < lp11.mcc) {
8951                    lpoutput('\r');
8952                    lp11.mcc = 0;
8953            }
8954            if(lp11.ccc < MAXCOL) {
8955                    while(lp11.ccc > lp11.mcc) {
8956                            lpoutput(' ');
8957                            lp11.mcc++;
8958                    }
8959                    lpoutput(c1);
8960                    lp11.mcc++;
8961            }
8962            lp11.ccc++;
8963    }
8964 }
8965 /* ------------------------         */
8966
8967 lpstart()
8968 {
8969    register int c;
8970
8971    while (LPADDR->lpsr&DONE && (c = getc(&lp11)) >= 0)
8972            LPADDR->lpbuf = c;
8973 }
8974 /* ------------------------         */
8975
8976 lpint()
8977 {
8978    register int c;
8979
8980    lpstart();
8981    if (lp11.cc == LPLWAT || lp11.cc == 0)
8982            wakeup(&lp11);
8983 }
8984 /* ------------------------         */
8985
8986 lpoutput(c)
8987 {
8988    if (lp11.cc >= LPHWAT)
8989            sleep(&lp11, LPPRI);
8990    putc(c, &lp11);
8991    spl4();
8992    lpstart();
8993    spl0();
8994 }
8995 /* ------------------------         */
8996
8997
8998
8999
```

```
9000 #
9001 /*
9002  */
9003
9004 /*
9005  * Memory special file
9006  * minor device 0 is physical memory
9007  * minor device 1 is kernel memory
9008  * minor device 2 is EOF/RATHOLE
9009  */
9010
9011 #include "../param.h"
9012 #include "../user.h"
9013 #include "../conf.h"
9014 #include "../seg.h"
9015
9016 mmread(dev)
9017 {
9018     register c, bn, on;
9019     int a, d;
9020
9021     if(dev.d_minor == 2)
9022             return;
9023     do {
9024             bn = lshift(u.u_offset, -6);
9025             on = u.u_offset[1] & 077;
9026             a = UISA->r[0];
9027             d = UISD->r[0];
9028             spl7();
9029             UISA->r[0] = bn;
9030             UISD->r[0] = 077406;
9031             if(dev.d_minor == 1)
9032                     UISA->r[0] = (ka6-6)->r[(bn>>7)&07]
9033                                     + (bn & 0177);
9034             c = fuibyte(on);
9035             UISA->r[0] = a;
9036             UISD->r[0] = d;
9037             spl0();
9038     } while(u.u_error==0 && passc(c)>=0);
9039 }
9040 /* ------------------------          */
9041
9042 mmwrite(dev)
9043 {
9044     register c, bn, on;
9045     int a, d;
9046
9047     if(dev.d_minor == 2) {
9048             c = u.u_count;
9049             u.u_count = 0;
```

```
9050             u.u_base =+ c;
9051             dpadd(u.u_offset, c);
9052             return;
9053     }
9054     for(;;) {
9055             bn = lshift(u.u_offset, -6);
9056             on = u.u_offset[1] & 077;
9057             if ((c=cpass())<0 || u.u_error!=0)
9058                     break;
9059             a = UISA->r[0];
9060             d = UISD->r[0];
9061             spl7();
9062             UISA->r[0] = bn;
9063             UISD->r[0] = 077406;
9064             if(dev.d_minor == 1)
9065                     UISA->r[0] = (ka6-6)->r[(bn>>7)&07]
9066                                     + (bn & 0177);
9067             suibyte(on, c);
9068             UISA->r[0] = a;
9069             UISD->r[0] = d;
9070             spl0();
9071     }
9072 }
9073 /* ------------------------          */
9074
9075
9076
9077
9078
9079
9080
9081
9082
9083
9084
9085
9086
9087
9088
9089
9090
9091
9092
9093
9094
9095
9096
9097
9098
9099
```

A COMMENTARY ON THE UNIX™ OPERATING SYSTEM

J. Lions
Department of Computer Science
The University of New South Wales
June, 1977

This booklet is intended as a companion to, and commentary on, the booklet UNIX* Operating System Source Code, Level Six. The UNIX Software System was written by K. Thompson and D. Ritchie of Bell Telephone Laboratories, Murray Hill, NJ.

* UNIX is a Trademark of Bell Laboratories.

CONTENTS

* UNIX is a Trademark of Bell Laboratories.

it runs on a system which was already available to us;

it is compact and accessible;

it provides an extensive set of very usable facilities;

it is intrinsically interesting, and in fact breaks new ground in a number of areas.

Not least amongst the charms and virtues of the UNIX Time-sharing System is the compactness of its source code. The source code for the permanently resident "nucleus" of the system when only a small number of peripheral devices is represented, is comfortably less than 9000 lines of code.

It has often been suggested that 10,000 lines of code represents the practical limit in size for a program which is to be understood and maintained by a single individual.

Most operating systems either exceed this limit by one or even two orders of magnitude, or else offer the user a very limited set of facilities, i.e. either the details of the system are inaccessible to all but the most determined, dedicated and long-suffering student, or else the system is rather specialised and of little intrinisic interest.

There seem to be three main approaches to teaching Operating Systems.

First there is the "general principles" approach, wherein fundamental principles are expounded, and illustrated by references to various existing systems, (most of which happen to be outside the students' immediate experience). This is the approach advocated by the COSINE Committee, but in our view, many students are not mature or experienced enough to profit from it.

The second approach is the "building block" approach, wherein the students are enabled to synthesise a small scale or "toy" operating system for themselves. While undoubtedly this can be a valuable exercise, if properly organised, it cannot but fail to encompass the complexity and sophistication of real operating systems, and is usually biased towards one aspect of operating system design, such as process synchronisation.

The third approach is the "case study" approach. This is the one originally recommended for the Systems Programming course in "Curriculum '68", the report of the ACM Curriculum Committee on Computer Science, published in the March, 1968 issue of the "Communications of the ACM".

Ten years ago, this approach, which advocates devoting "most of the course to the study of a single system" was unrealistic because the cost of providing adequate student access to a suitable system was simply too high.

Ten years later, the economic picture has changed significantly, and the costs are no longer a decisive disadvantage if a minicomputer system can be the subject of study. The considerable advantages of the approach which undertakes a detailed analysis of an existing system are now attainable.

In our opinion, it is highly beneficial for students to have the opportunity to study a working operating system in all its aspects.

Moreover it is undoubtedly good for students majoring in Computer Science, to be confronted at least once in their careers, with the task of reading and understanding a program of major dimensions.

PREFACE

This book is an attempt to explain in detail the nucleus of one of the most interesting computer operating systems to appear in recent years.

It is the UNIX' Time-sharing System, which runs on the larger models of Digital Equipment Corporation's PDP11 computer system, and was developed by Ken Thompson and Dennis Ritchie at Bell Laboratories. It was first announced to the world in the July, 1974 issue of the "Communications of the ACM".

Very soon in our experience with UNIX, it suggested itself as an interesting candidate for formal study by students, for the following reasons:

In 1976 we adopted UNIX as the subject for case study in our courses in Operating Systems at the University of New South Wales. These notes were prepared originally for the assistance of students in those courses (6.602B and 6.657G).

The courses run for one semester each. Before entering either course, students are presumed to have studied the PDP11 architecture and assembly language, and to have had an opportunity to use the UNIX operating system during exercises for earlier courses.

In general, students seem to find the new courses more onerous, but much more satisfying than the previous courses based on the "general principles" approach of the COSINE Committee.

Some mention needs to be made regarding the documentation provided by the authors of the UNIX system. As reproduced for use on our campus, this comprises two volumes of A4 size paper, with a total thickness of 3 cm, and a weight of 1250 grams.

A first observation is that the whole documentation is not unreasonably transportable in a student's brief case. However it must not be assumed that this amount of documentation, which is written in a fresh, terse, whimsical style, is necessarily inadequate.

In fact the second observation (which is only made after considerable experience) is that for reference purposes, the documentation is remarkably comprehensive. However there is plenty of scope for additional tutorial material, one part of which, it is hoped, is satisfied by these notes.

The actual UNIX operating system source code is recorded in a separate companion volume entitled "UNIX Operating System Source Code", which was first printed in July, 1976. This is a specially edited selection of code from the Level Six version of UNIX, as received by us in December, 1975.

During 1976, an initial version of the present notes was distributed in roneoed form, and only in the latter part of the year were the facilities of the "nroff" text formatting program exploited. The opportunity has recently been taken to revise and "nroff" the earlier material, to make some revisions and corrections, and to integrate them into their present form.

A decision had to be made quite early regarding the order of presentation of the source code. The intention was to provide a reasonably logical sequence for the student who wanted to learn the whole system. With the benefit of hindsight, a great many improvements in detail are still possible, and it is intended that these changes will be made in some future edition.

It is our hope that this book will be of interest and value to many students of the UNIX Time-sharing System. Although not prepared primarily for use as a reference work, some will wish to use it as such. The indices provided at the end should go some of the way towards satisfying the requirement for reference material at this level.

Since these notes refer to proprietary material administered by the Western Electric Company, they can only be made available to licensees of the UNIX Time-sharing System, and hence are unable to be published through more usual channels.

Corrections, criticism and suggestions for improvement of these notes will be very welcome.

Acknowledgements

The preparation of these notes has been encouraged and supported by many of my colleagues and students including David Carrington, Doug Crompton, Ian Hayes, David Horsfall, Peter Ivanov, Ian Johnstone, Chris Maltby, Dave Milway, John O'Brien and Greg Rose.

Pat Mackie and Mary Powter did much of the initial typing, and Adele Green has assisted greatly in the transfer of the notes to "nroff" format.

David Millis and the Publications Section of the University of New South Wales have assisted greatly with the mechanics of publication, and Ian Johnstone and the Australian Graduate School of Management provided facilities for the preparation of the final draft.

Throughout this project, my wife Marianne has given me unfailing moral support and much practical support with proof-reading.

Finally Ken Thompson and Dennis Ritchie started it all.

To all the above, I wish to express my sincere thanks.

The co-operation of the "nroff" program must also be mentioned. Without it, these notes could never have been produced in this form. However it has yielded some of its more enigmatic secrets so reluctantly, that the author's gratitude is indeed mixed. Certainly "nroff" itself must provide a fertile field for future practitioners of the program documenter's art.

John Lions
Kensington, NSW
May, 1977

CHAPTER ONE

Introduction

UNIX* is the name of a time-sharing system for PDP11 computers, written by Ken Thompson and Dennis Ritchie at Bell Laboratories. It was described by them in the July, 1974 issue of the "Communications of the ACM".

UNIX has proved to be effective, efficient and reliable in operation and was in use at more than 150 installations by the end of 1976.

The amount of effort to write UNIX, while not inconsiderable in itself (~10 man years up to the release of the Level Six system) is insignificant when compared to other systems. (For instance, by 1968, OS/360 was reputed to have consumed more then five man millennia and TSS/360, another IBM operating system, more than one man millennium.)

Much of the effectiveness of UNIX derives from the simple and direct implementation, by two people (presumably sharing the same office!) using an appropriate high level language called "C", and restrained by the very definite size limitations of the PDP11.

Not only is UNIX effective, but it is accessible in a way that most other systems are not: the amount of material which must be mastered in order to gain a reasonably deep understanding of the system is not impossibly large. By way of comparison, OS/360 and its successors are far too complex to be completely understood by any one individual. Most major operating systems require many months of study before an individual will be ready to make major modifications to the system.

Of course there are systems which are easier to understand than UNIX but, it may be asserted, these are invariably much simpler and more modest in what they attempt to achieve. As far as the list of features offered to users is concerned, UNIX is in the "big league". In fact it offers many features which are notable by their absence from some of the well-known major systems.

The UNIX Operating System

The purpose of this document, and its companion, the "UNIX Operating System Source Code", is to present in detail that part of the UNIX time-sharing system which we choose to call the "UNIX Operating System", namely the code which is permanently resident in the main memory during the operation of UNIX. This code has the following major functions:

        initialisation;
        process management;
        system calls;
        interrupt handling;
        input/output operations;
        file management.

Utilities

The remaining part of UNIX (which is much larger!) is composed of a set of suitably tailored programs which run as "user programs", and which, for want of a better term, may be termed "utilities".

Under this heading come a number of programs with a very strong symbiotic relationship with the operating system such as

    the "shell" (the command language interpreter)

    "/etc/init" (the terminal configuration controller)

and a number of file system management programs such as:

check	du	rmdir
chmod	mkdir	sync
clri	mkfs	umount
df	mount	update

It should be pointed out that many of the functions carried out by the above-named programs are regarded as operating system functions in other computer systems, and that this certainly does contribute significantly to the bulk of these other systems as compared with the UNIX Operating System (in the way we have defined it).

Descriptions of the function and use of the above programs may be found in the "UNIX Programmer's Manual" (UPM), either in Section I (for the commonly used programs) or in Section VIII (for the programs used only by the System Manager).

Other Documentation

These notes make frequent reference to the "UNIX Programmer's Manual" (UPM), occasional reference to the "UNIX Documents" booklet, and constant

---

* UNIX is a Trademark of Bell Laboratories.

reference to the "UNIX Operating System Source Code".

All these are relevant to a complete understanding of the system. In addition, a full study of the assembly language routines requires reference to the "PDP11 Processor Handbook", published by Digital Equipment Corporation.

UNIX Programmer's Manual

The UPM is divided into eight major sections, preceded by a table of contents and a KWIC (Key Word In Context) index. The latter is mostly very useful but is occasionally annoying, as some indexed material does not exist, and some existing material is not indexed.

Within each section of the manual, the material is arranged alphabetically by subject name. The section number is conventionally appended to the subject name, since some subjects appear in more than one section, e.g. "CHDIR(I)" and "CHDIR(II)".

Section I contains commands which either are recognised by the "shell" command interpreter, or are the names of standard user utility programs;

Section II contains "system calls" which are operating system routines which may be invoked from a user program to obtain operating system service. A study of the operating system will render most of these quite familiar;

Section III contains "subroutines" which are library routines which may be called from a user program. To the ordinary programmer, the distinctions between Sections II and III often appear somewhat arbitrary. Most of Section III is irrelevant to the operating system;

Section IV describes "special files", which is another name for peripheral devices. Some of these are relevant, and some merely interesting. It depends where you are;

Section V describes "File Formats and Conventions". A lot of highly relevant information is tucked away in this section;

Sections VI and VII describe "User Maintained" programs and subroutines. No UNIXophile will ignore these sections, but they are not particularly relevant to the operating system;

Section VIII describes "system maintenance" (software, not hardware!). There is lots of useful information here, especially if you are interested in how a UNIX installation is managed.

UNIX Documents

This is a somewhat miscellaneous collection of essays of varying degrees of relevance:

Setting up UNIX really belongs in Section VIII of the UPM (it's relevant);

The UNIX Time-sharing System is an updated version of the original "Communications of the ACM" paper. It should be re-read at least once per month;

UNIX for Beginners is useful if your UNIX experience is still limited;

The tutorials on "C" and the editor, and the reference manuals for "C" and the assembler are highly useful unless you are completely expert;

The UNIX I/O System provides a good overview of many features of the operating system;

UNIX Summary provides a check list which will be useful in answering the question "what does an operating system do?"

UNIX Operating System Source Code

This is an edited version of the operating system as supplied by Bell Laboratories.

The code selection presumes a "model" system consisting of:

PDP11/40 processor;

RK05 disk drives;

LP11 line printer;

PC11 paper tape reader/punch;

KL11 terminal interface.

The principal editorial changes to the source code are as follows:

the order of presentation of files has been changed;

the order of material within several files has been changed;

to a very limited extent, code has been transferred between files (with hindsight a lot more of this would have been desirable);

about 5% of the lines have been shortened in various ways to less than 66 characters (by elimination of blanks, rearrangement of comments, splitting into two lines, etc.);

a number of comments consisting of a line of underscore characters have been introduced, particularly at the end of procedures;

the size of each file has been adjusted to an exact multiple of 50 lines by padding with blank lines;

a four digit line number has been inserted at the beginning of each line to identify it for cross-referencing.

The source code has been printed in a double column format with fifty lines per column, giving one hundred lines per sheet (or page). Thus there is a convenient relationship between line numbers and sheet numbers.

A number of summaries have been included at the beginning of the Source Code volume:

A Table of Contents showing files in order of appearance, together with the procedures they contain;

An alphabetical list of procedures with line numbers;

A list of Defined Symbols with their values;

A Cross Reference Listing giving the line numbers where each symbol is used. (Reserved words in "C" and a number of commonly used symbols such as "p" and "u" have been omitted.)

Source Code Sections

The source code has been divided into five sections, each devoted primarily to a single major aspect of the system.

The intention, which has been largely achieved, has been to make each section sufficiently self-contained so that it may be studied as a unit and before its successors have been mastered:

Section One deals with system initialisation, and process management. It also contains all the assembly language routines;

Section Two deals with interrupts, traps, system calls and signals (software interrupts);

Section Three deals primarily with disk operations for program swapping and basic, block oriented input/output. It also deals with the manipulation of the pool of large buffers;

Section Four deals with files and file systems: their creation, maintenance, manipulation and destruction;

Section Five deals with "character special files", which is the UNIX term for slow speed peripheral devices which operate out of a common, character oriented, buffer pool.

The contents of each section is outlined in more detail in Chapter Four.

Source Code Files

Each of the five sections just described consists of several source code files. The name of each file includes a suffix which identifies its type:

".s" denotes a file of assembly language statements;

".c" denotes a file of executable "C" language statements;

".h" denotes a file of "C" language statements which is not for separate compilation, but for inclusion in other ".c" files when they are compiled i.e. the ".h" files contain global declarations.

Use of these notes

These notes, which are intended to supplement the comments already present in the source code, are not essential for understanding the UNIX operating system. It is perfectly possible to proceed without them, and you should attempt to do so as long as you can.

The notes are a crutch, to aid you when the going becomes difficult. If you attempt to read each file or procedure on your own first, your initial progress is likely to be slower, but your ultimate progress much faster. Reading other people's programs is an art which should be learnt and practised – because it is useful!

A Note on Programming Standards

You will find that most of the code in UNIX is of a very high standard. Many sections which initially seem complex and obscure, appear in the light of further investigation and reflection, to be perfectly obvious and "the only way to fly".

For this reason, the occasional comments in the notes on programming style, almost invariably refer to apparent lapses from the usual standard of near perfection.

What caused these? Sometimes it appears that the original code has been patched expediently. More than once apparent lapses have proved not to be such: the "bad" code has been found in fact to incorporate some subtle feature which was not at all apparent initially. And some allowance is certainly needed for occasional human weakness.

But on the whole you will find that the authors of UNIX, Ken Thompson and Dennis Ritchie, have created a program of great strength, integrity and effectiveness, which you should admire and seek to emulate.

-oOo-

The Processor

The processor, which is designed around a sixteen bit word length for instructions, data and program addresses, incorporates a number of high speed registers.

Processor Status Word

This sixteen bit register has subfields which are interpreted as follows:

bits	description
14,15	current mode (00 = kernel;)
12,13	previous mode (11 = user;)
5,6,7	processor priority (range 0..7)
4	trap bit
3	N, set if the previous result was negative
2	Z, set if the previous result was zero
1	V, set if the previous operation gave an overflow
0	C, set if the previous operation gave a carry

The processor can operate in two different modes: kernel and user. Kernel mode is the more privileged of the two and is reserved by the operating system for its own use. The choice of mode determines:

The set of memory management segmentation registers which is used to translate program virtual addresses to physical addresses;

The actual register used as r6, the "stack pointer";

Whether certain instructions such as "halt" will be obeyed.

General Registers

The processor incorporates a number of sixteen bit registers of which eight are accessible at any time as "general registers". These are known as

r0, r1, r2, r3, r4, r5, r6 and r7.

The first six of the general registers are available for use as accumulators, address pointers or index registers. The convention in UNIX for the use of these registers is as follows:

r0, r1 are used as temporary accumulators during expression evaluation, to return results from a procedure, and in some cases to communicate actual parameters during a procedure call;

r2, r3, r4 are used for local variables during procedure execution. Their values are almost always stored upon procedure entry, and restored upon procedure exit;

r5 is used as the head pointer to a "dynamic chain" of procedure activation records stored in the current stack. It is referred to as the "environment pointer".

The last two of the "general registers" do have a special significance and are to all intents, "special purpose":

r6 (also known as "sp") is used as the stack pointer. The PDP11/40 processor incorporates two separate registers which may be used as "sp", depending on whether the processor is in kernel or user mode. No other one of the general registers is duplicated in this way;

r7 (also known as "pc") is used as the program counter, i.e. the instruction address register.

CHAPTER TWO

Fundamentals

UNIX runs on the larger models of the PDP11 series of computers manufactured by Digital Equipment Corporation. This chapter provides a brief summary of certain selected features of these computers with particular reference to the PDP11/40.

If the reader has not previously made the acquaintance of the PDP11 series then he is directed forthwith to the "PDP11 Processor Handbook", published by DEC.

A PDP11 computer consists of a processor (also called a CPU) connected to one or more memory storage units and peripheral controllers via a bi-directional parallel communication line called the "Unibus".

Instruction Set

The PDP11 instruction set includes double, single and zero operand instructions. Instruction length is usually one word, with some instructions being extended to two or three words with additional addressing information.

With single operand instructions, the operand is usually called the "destination"; with double operand instructions, the two operands are called the "source" and "destination". The various modes of addressing are described later.

The following instructions have been used in the file "m40.s" i.e. the file of assembly language support routines for use with the 11/40 processor. Note that N, Z, V and C are the condition codes i.e. bits in the processor status word ("ps"), and that these are set as side effects of many instructions besides just "bit", "cmp" and "tst" (whose stated function is to set the condition codes).

adc Add the contents of the C bit to the destination;

add Add the source to the destination;

ash Shift the contents of the defined register left the number of times specified by the shift count. (A negative value implies a right shift.);

ashc Similar to "ash" except that two registers are involved;

asl Shift all bits one place to the left. Bit 0 becomes 0 and bit 15 is loaded into C;

asr Shift all bits one place to the right. Bit 15 is replicated and bit 0 is loaded into C;

beq Branch if equal, i.e. if Z = 1;

bge Branch if greater than or equal to, i.e. if N = V;

bhi Branch if higher, i.e. if C = 0 and Z = 0;

bhis Branch if higher or the same, i.e. if C = 0;

bic Clear each bit to zero in the destination that corresponds to a non-zero bit in the source;

bis Perform an "inclusive or" of source and destination and store the result in the destination;

bit Perform a logical "and" of the source and destination to set the condition codes;

ble Branch if greater than or equal to, i.e. if Z = 1 or N = V;

blo Branch if lower (than zero), i.e. if C = 1;

bne Branch if not equal (to zero), i.e. if Z = 0;

br Branch to a location within the range (.-128,.+127) where "." is the current location;

clc Clear C;

clr Clear destination to zero;

cmp Compare the source and destination to set the condition codes. N is set if the source value is less than the destination value;

dec Subtract one from the contents of the destination;

div The 32 bit two's complement integer stored in rn and r(n+1) (where n is even) is divided by the source operand. The quotient is left in rn, and the remainder in r(n+1);

inc Add one to the contents of the destination;

jmp Jump to the destination;

jsr Jump to subroutine. Register values are shuffled as follows:

pc, rn, -(sp) = dest., pc, rn

mfpi Push onto the current stack the value of the designated word in the "previous" address space;

mov Copy the source value to the destination;

mtpi Pop the current stack and store the value in the designated word in the "previous" address space;

mul Multiply the contents of rn and the source. If n is even, the product is left in rn and r(n+1);

reset Set the INIT line on the Unibus for 10 milliseconds. This will have the effect of reinitialising all the device controllers;

ror Rotate all bits of the destination one place to the right. Bit 0 is loaded into C, and the previous value of C is loaded into bit 15;

rts Return from subroutine. Reload pc from rn, and reload rn from the stack;

rtt Return from interrupt or trap. Reload both pc and ps from the stack;

sbc Subtract the carry bit from the destination;

sob Subtract one from the designated register. If the result is not zero, branch back "offset" words;

sub Subtract the source from the destination;

swab Exchange the high and low order bytes in the destination;

tst Set the condition codes, N and Z, according to the contents of the destination;

wait Idle the processor and release the Unibus until a hardware interrupt occurs.

The "byte" version of the following instructions are used in the file "m40.s", as well as the "word" versions described above:

```
bis        inc
clr        mov
cmp        tst
```

Addressing Modes

Much of the novelty and complexity of the PDP11 instruction set lies in the variety of addressing modes which may be used for defining the source and destination operands.

The addressing modes which are used in "m40.s" are described below.

Register Mode. The operand resides in one of the general registers, e.g.

```
clr        r0
mov        r1,r0
add        r4,r2
```

In the following modes, the designated register contains an address value which is used to locate the operand.

Register Deferred Mode. The register contains the address of the operand, e.g.

```
inc        (r1)
asr        (sp)
add        (r2),r1
```

Autoincrement Mode. The register contains the address of the operand. As a side effect, the register is incremented after the operation, e.g.

```
clr        (r1)+
mfpi       (r0)+
mov        (r1)+,r0
mov        r2,(r0)+
cmp        (sp)+,(sp)+
```

Autodecrement Mode. The register is decremented and then used to locate the operand, e.g.

```
inc        -(r0)
mov        -(r1),r2
mov        (r0)+,-(sp)
clr        -(sp)
```

Index Mode. The register contains a value which is added to a sixteen bit word following the instruction to form the operand address, e.g.

```
clr        2(r0)
movb       6(sp),(sp)
movb       _reloc(r0),r0
mov        -10(r2),(r1)
```

Depending on your viewpoint, in this mode the register is either an index register or a base register. The latter case actually predominates in "m40.s". The third example above is actually one of the few uses of a register as an index register. (Note that "_reloc" is an acceptable variable name.)

There are two addressing modes whose use is limited to the following two examples:

```
jsr        pc,*(r0)+
jmp        *0f(r0)
```

The first example involves the use of the "autoincrement deferred" mode. (This occurs in the routine "call1" on lines 0785, 0799.) The address of a routine intended for execution is to be found in the word addressed by r0, i.e. two levels of indirection are involved. The fact that r0 is incremented as a side effect is not relevant in this usage.

The second example (which occurs on lines 1055, 1066) is an instance of the "index deferred" mode. The destination

of the "jump" is the content of the word whose address is labelled by "0f" plus the value of r0 (a small positive integer). This is a standard way to implement a multi-way switch.

The following two modes use the program counter as the designated register to achieve certain special effects.

Immediate Mode. This is the pc autoincrement mode. The operand is thus extracted from the program string, i.e. it becomes an immediate operand, e.g.

```
add        $2,r0
add        $2,(r1)
bic        $!7,r0
mov        $KISA0,r0
mov        $77406,(r1)+
```

Relative Mode. This is the pc index mode. The address relative to the current program counter value is extracted from the program string and added to the pc value to form the absolute address of the operand, e.g.

```
bic,       $340,PS
bit        $1,SSR0
inc        SSR0
mov        (sp),KISA6
```

It may be noted that each of the modes "index", "index deferred", "immediate" and "relative" extends the instruction size by one word.

The existence of the "autoincrement" and "autodecrement" modes, together with the special attributes of r6, make it conveniently possible to store many operands in a stack, or LIFO list, which grows downwards in memory. There are a number of advantages which flow from this: code string lengths are shorter and it is easier to write position independent code.

Unix Assembler

The UNIX assembler is a two pass assembler without macro facilities. A full description may be found in the "UNIX Assembler Reference Manual" which is contained in the "UNIX Documents"

The following brief notes should be of some assistance:

(a) a string of digits may define a constant number. This is assumed to be an octal number unless the string is terminated by a period ("."), when it is interpreted as a decimal number.

(b) The character "/" is used to signify that the rest of the line is a comment;

(c) If two or more statements occur on the same line, they must be separated by semicolons;

(d) The character "." is used to denote the current location;

(e) UNIX assembler uses the characters "$" and "*" where the DEC assemblers use "#" and "@" respectively.

(f) An identifier consists of a set of alphanumeric characters (including the underscore). Only the first eight characters are significant and the first may not be numeric;

(g) Names which occur in "C" programs for variables which are to be known globally, are modified by the addition of a prefix consisting of a single underscore. Thus for example the variable "_regloc" which occurs on line 1025 in the assembly language file, "m40.s", refers to the same variable as "regloc" at line 2677 of the file, "trap.c";

(h) There are two kinds of statement labels: name labels and numeric labels. The latter consist of a single digit followed by a colon, and need not be unique. A reference to "nf" where "n" is a digit, refers to the first occurrence of the label "n:" found by searching forward.

A reference to "nb" is similar except that the search is conducted in the backwards direction;

(i) An assignment statement of the form

        identifier = expression

associates a value and type with the identifier. In the example

        . = 60^.

the operator '^' delivers the value of the first operand and the type of the second operand (in this case, "location");

(j) The string quote symbols are "<" and ">";

(k) Statements of the form

        .globl x, y, z

serve to make the names "x", "y" and "z" external;

(l) The names "_edata" and "_end" are loader pseudo variables which the define the size of the data segment, and the data segment plus the bss segment respectively.

Memory Management

Programs running on the PDP11 may address directly up to 64K bytes (32K words) of storage. This is consistent with an address size of sixteen bits. Since it is economical and not unreasonable to do so the larger PDP11 models may be equipped with larger amounts of memory (up to 256K bytes for the PDP11/40) plus a mechanism for converting sixteen bit virtual (program) addresses into physical addresses of eighteen bits or more. The mechanism, which is known as the memory management unit, is simpler on the PDP11/40 than on the 11/45 or the 11/70.

On the PDP11/40 the memory management unit consists of two sets of registers for mapping virtual addresses to physical addresses. These are known as "active page registers" or "segmentation registers". One set is used when the processor is in user mode and the other set, in kernel mode. Changing the contents of these registers changes the details of these mappings. The ability to make these changes is a privilege that the operating system keeps firmly to itself.

Segmentation Registers.

Each set of segmentation registers is composed of eight pairs, each consisting of a "page address register" (PAR) and a "page description register" (PDR).

Each pair of registers controls the mapping of one page i.e. one eighth part of the virtual address space which has a size of 8K bytes (4K words).

Each page may be regarded as an aggregate of 128 blocks, each of 64 bytes (32 words). This latter size is the "grain size" for the memory mapping function, and as a practical consequence, it is also the "grain size" for memory allocation.

Any virtual address belongs to one page or other. The corresponding physical address is generated by adding the relative address within the page to the contents of the corresponding PAR to form an extended address (18 bits on the PDP11/40 and 11/45; 22 bits on the 11/70).

Thus each page address register acts as a relocation register for one page.

Each page can be divided on a 32 word boundary into two parts, an upper part and lower part. Each such part has a size which is a multiple of 32 words. In particular one part may be null, in which case the other part coincides with the whole page.

One of the two parts is deemed to contain valid virtual addresses. Addresses in the remaining part are declared invalid. Any attempt to reference an invalid address will be trapped by the hardware. The advantage of this scheme is that space in the physical memory need only be allocated for the valid part of a page.

Page Description Register

The page description register defines:

(a) the size of the lower part of the page. (The number stored is actually the number of 32 word blocks less one);

(b) a bit which is set when the upper part is the valid part. (Also known as the "expansion direction" bit);

(c) access mode bits defining "no access" or "read only access" or "read/write access".

Note that if the valid part is null, this fact must be shown by setting the access bits to "no access".

Memory Allocation

The hardware does not dictate the way areas in physical memory which correspond to the valid parts of pages

should be allocated (except to the extent that they must begin and end on a 32 word boundary). These areas may be allocated in any order and may overlap to any extent.

In practice the allocation of areas of physical memory is much more disciplined as we shall see in Chapter Seven. Areas for pages which are related are most often allocated contiguously and in the order of their page numbers, so that all the segment areas associated with a single program are contained within one or at most two large areas of physical memory.

Memory Management Status Registers

In addition to the segmentation registers, on the PDP11/40 there are two memory management status registers:

SR0 contains abort error flags and other essential information for the operating system. In particular memory management is enabled when bit 0 of SR0 is on;

SR2 is loaded with the 16 bit virtual address at the beginning of each instruction fetch.

"i" and "d" Spaces

In the PDP11/45 and 11/70 systems, there are additional sets of segmentation registers. Addresses created using the pc register (r7) are said to belong to "i" space, and are translated by a different set of segmentation registers from those used for the remaining addresses which are said to belong to "d" space.

The advantage of this arrangement is that both "i" and "d" spaces may occupy up to 32K words, thus allowing the maximum space which can be allocated to a program to be increased to twice the

space available on the PDP11/40.

Initial Conditions

When the system is first started after all the devices on the Unibus have been reinitialised, the memory management unit is disabled and the processor is in kernel mode.

Under these circumstances, virtual (byte) addresses in the range 0 to 56K are mapped into identically valued physical addresses. However the highest page of the virtual address space is mapped into the highest page of the physical address space, i.e. on the PDP11/40 or 11/45, addresses in the range

0160000 to 0177777

are mapped into the range

0760000 to 0777777

Special Device Registers

The high page of physical memory is reserved for various special registers associated with the processor and the peripheral devices. By sacrificing one page of memory space in this way, the PDP11 designers have been able to make the various device registers accessible without the need to provide special instruction types.

The method of assignment of addresses to registers in this page is a black art: the values are hallowed by tradition and are not to be questioned.

-oOo-

CHAPTER THREE

Reading "C" Programs

Learning to read programs written in the "C" language is one of the hurdles that must be overcome before you will be able to study the source code of UNIX effectively.

As with natural languages, reading is an easier skill to acquire than writing. Even so you will need to be careful lest some of the more subtle points pass you by.

There are two of the "UNIX Documents" which relate directly to the "C" language:

"C Reference Manual", by Dennis Ritchie

"Programming in C - A Tutorial",
                    by Brian Kernighan

You should read them now, as far as you can, and return to reread them from time to time with increasing comprehension.

Learning to write "C" programs is not required. However if you have the opportunity, you should attempt to write at least a few small programs. This does represent the accepted way to learn a programming language, and your understanding of the proper use of such items as:

        semicolons;
        "=" and "==";
        "{" and "}";
        "++" and "--";
        declarations;
        register variables;
        "if" and "for" statements;
        etc.

will be quickly reinforced.

You will find that "C" is a very convenient language for accessing and manipulating data structures and character strings, which is what a large part of operating systems is about. As befits a terminal oriented language, which requires concise, compact expression, "C" uses a large character set and makes many symbols such as "*" and "&" work hard. In this respect it invites comparison with APL.

There many features of "C" which are reminiscent of PL/1, but it goes well beyond the latter in the range of facilities provided for structured programming.

Some Selected Examples

The examples which follow are taken directly from the source code.

Example 1

The simplest possible procedure, which does nothing, occurs twice(!) in the source code as "nullsys" (2864) and "nulldev" (6577), sic.

```
6577 nulldev ()
        {
        }
```

While there are no parameters, the parentheses, "(" and ")", are still required. The brackets "{" and "}" delimit the procedure body, which is empty.

Example 2

The next example is a little less trivial:

```
6566 nodev ()
        {
        u.u_error = ENODEV;
        }
```

The additional statement is an assignment statement. It is terminated by a semicolon which is part of the statement, not a statement separator as in Algol-like languages.

"ENODEV" is a defined symbol, i.e. a symbol which is replaced by an associated character string by the compiler preprocessor before actual compilation. "ENODEV" is defined on line 0484 as 19. The UNIX convention is that defined symbols are written in upper case, and all other symbols in lower case.

"=" is the assignment operator, and "u.u_error" is an element of the structure "u". (See line 0419.) Note the use of "." as the operator which selects an element of a structure. The element name is "u_error" which may be taken as a paradigm for the way names of structure elements are constructed in the UNIX source code: a distinguishing letter is followed by an underscore followed by a name.

Example 3

```
6585 bcopy (from, to, count)
     int *from, *to;
     {
       register *a, *b, c;
       a = from;
       b = to;
       c = count;
       do
         *b++ = *a++;
       while (--c);
     }
```

The function of this procedure is very simple: it copies a specified number of words from one set of consecutive locations to another set.

There are three parameters. The second line

        int *from, *to;

specifies that the first two variables are pointers to integers. Since no specification is supplied for the third parameter, it is assumed to be an integer by default.

The three local variables, a, b, and c, have been assigned to registers, because registers are more accessible and the object code to reference them is shorter. "a" and "b" are pointers to integers and "c" is an integer. The register declaration could have been written more pedantically as

        register int *a, *b, c;

to emphasise the connection with integers.

The three lines beginning with "do" should be studied carefully. If "b" is a "pointer to integer" type, then

        *b

denotes the integer pointed to. Thus to copy the value pointed to by "a" to the location designated by "b", we could write

        *b = *a;

If we wrote instead

        b = a;

this would make the value of "b" the same as the value of "a", i.e. "b" and "a" would point to the same place. Here at least, that is not what is required.

Having copied the first word from source to destination, we need to increase the values of "b" and "a" so that the point to the next words of their respective sets. This can be done by writing

        b = b+1; a = a+1;

but "C" provides a shorter notation (which is more useful when the variable names are longer) viz.

        b++; a++;

or alternatively

        ++b; ++a;

Now there is no difference between the statements "b++;" and "++b;" here.

However "b++" and "++b" may be used as terms in an expression, in which case they are different. In both cases the effect of incrementing "b" is retained, but the value which enters the expression is the initial value for "b++" and

the final value for "++b".

The "--" operator obeys the same rules as the "++" operator, except that it decrements by one. Thus "--c" enters an expression as the value after decrementation.

The "++" and "--" operators are very useful, and are used throughout UNIX. Occasionally you will have to go back to first principles to work out exactly what their use implies. Note also there is a difference between

        *b++ and (*b)++

These operators are applicable to pointers to structures as well as to simple data types. When a pointer which has been declared with reference to a particular type of structure is incremented, the actual value of the pointer is incremented by the size of the structure.

We can now see the meaning of the line

        *b++ = *a++;

The word is copied and the pointers are incremented, all in one hit.

The line

        while (--c);

delimits the end of the set of statements which began after the "do". The expression in parentheses "--c", is evaluated and tested (the value tested is the value after decrementation). If the value is non-zero, the loop is repeated, else it is terminated.

Obviously if the initial value for "count" were negative, the loop would not terminate properly. If this were a serious possibility then the routine would have to be modified.

Example 4

```
6619 getf (f)
     {
         register *fp, rf;
         rf = f;
         if (rf < 0 || rf >= NOFILE)
           goto bad;
         fp = u.u_ofile[rf];
         if (fp != NULL)
           return (fp);
     bad:
         u.u_error = EBADF;
         return (NULL);
     }
```

The parameter "f" is a presumed integer, and is copied directly into the register variable "rf". (This pattern will become so familiar that we will now cease to remark upon it.)

The three simple relational expressions

```
    rf < 0     rf >=NOFILE    fp != NULL
```

are each accorded the value one if true, and the value zero if false. The first tests if the value of "rf" is less than zero, the second, if "rf" is greater than the value defined by "NOFILE" and the third, if the value of "fp" is not equal to "NULL" (which is defined to be zero).

The conditions tested by the "if" statements are the arithmetic expressions contained within parentheses.

If the expression is greater than zero, the test is successful and the following statement is executed. Thus if for instance, "fp" had the value 001375, then

```
             fp != NULL
```

is true, and as a term in an arithmetic expression, is accorded the value one. This value is greater than zero, and hence the statement

```
             return (fp);
```

would be executed, to terminate further execution of "getf", and to return the value of "fp" to the calling procedure as the result of "getf".

The expression

```
     rf < 0 || rf >= NOFILE
```

is the logical disjunction ("or") of the two simple relational expressions.

An example of a "goto" statement and associated label will be noted.

"fp" is assigned a value, which is an address, from the "rf"-th element of the array of integers "u_ofile", which is embedded in the structure "u".

The procedure "getf" returns a value to its calling procedure. This is either the value of "fp" (i.e. an address) or "NULL".

Example 5

```
2113 wakeup (chan)
     {
         register struct proc *p;
         register c, i;
         c = chan;
         p = &proc[0];
         i = NPROC;
         do {
           if (p->p_wchan == c) {
             setrun (p);
           }
           p++;
         } while (--i);
     }
```

There are a number of similarities between this example and the previous one. We have a new concept however, an array of structures. To be just a little confusing, in this example it turns out that both the array and the structure are called "proc" (yes, "C" allows this). They are declared on

Sheet 03 in the following form:

```
0358 struct proc
     {
         char p_stat;
         ..........
         int p_wchan;
         ..........
     } proc [NPROC];
```

"p" is a register variable of type pointer to a structure of type "proc".

```
         p = &proc[0];
```

assigns to "p" the address of the first element of the array "proc". The operator "&" in this context means "the address of ".

Note that if an array has n elements, the elements have subscripts 0, 1, .., (n-1). Also it is permissible to write the above statement more simply as

```
         p = proc;
```

There are two statements in between the "do" and the "while".

The first of these could be rewritten more simply as

```
     if (p->p_wchan == c) setrun (p);
```

i.e. the brackets are superfluous in this case, and since "C" is a free form language, the arrangement of text between lines is not significant.

The statement

```
         setrun (p);
```

invokes the procedure "setrun" passing the value of "p" as a parameter. (All parameters are passed by value.)

The relation

```
         p->p_wchan == c
```

tests the equality of the value of "c" and the value of the element "p_wchan" of the structure pointed to by "p". Note that it would have been wrong to have written

        p.p_wchan == c

because "p" is not the name of a structure.

The second statement, which cannot be combined with the first, increments "p" by the size of the "proc" structure, whatever that is. (The compiler can figure it out.)

In order to do this calculation correctly, the compiler needs to know the kind of structure pointed at. When this is not a consideration, you will notice that often in similar situations, "p" will be declared simply as

        register *p;

because it was easier for the programmer, and the compiler does not insist.

The latter part of this procedure could have been written equivalently but less efficiently as

```
        ............
        i = 0;
        do
          if (proc[i].p_wchan == c)
             setrun (&proc[i]);
        while (++i < NPROC);
```

Example 6

```
5336 geterror (abp)
     struct buf *abp;
     {
       register struct buf *bp;
       bp = abp;
       if (bp->b_flags&B_ERROR)
         if((u.u_error=bp->b_error)==0)
            u.u_error = EIO;
     }
```

This procedure simply checks if there has been an error, and if the error indicator "u.u_error" has not been set, sets it to a general error indication ("EIO").

"B_ERROR" has the value 04 (see line 4575) so that, with only one bit set, it can be used as mask to isolate bit number 2. The operator "&" as used in

        bp->b_flags&B_ERROR

is the bitwise logical conjunction ("and") applied to arithmetic values.

The above expression is greater than one if bit 2 of the element "b_flags" of the "buf" structure pointed to by "bp", is set.

Thus if there has been an error, the expression

        (u.u_error = bp->b_error)

is evaluated and compared with zero. Now this expression includes an assignment operator "=". The value of the expression is the value of "u.u_error" after the value of "bp->b_flags" has been assigned to it.

This use of an assignment as part of an expression is useful and quite common.

Example 7

```
3428 stime ()
     {
       if (suser()) {
         time[0] = u.u_ar0[R0];
         time[1] = u.u_ar0[R1];
         wakeup (tout);
       }
     }
```

In this example, you should note that the procedure "suser" returns a value which is used for the "if" test. The

three statements whose execution depends on this value are enclosed in the brackets "{" and "}".

Note that a call on a procedure with no parameters must still be written with a set of empty parentheses, sic.

        suser ()

Example 8

"C" provides a conditional expression. Thus if "a" and "b" are integer variables,

        (a > b ? a : b)

is an expression whose value is that of the larger of "a" and "b".

However this does not work if "a" and "b" are to be regarded as unsigned integers. Hence there is a use for the procedure

```
6326 max (a, b)
     char *a, *b;
     {
       if (a > b)
         return(a);
       return (b);
     }
```

The trick here is that "a" and "b", having been declared as pointers to characters are treated for comparison purposes as unsigned integers.

The body of the procedure could have been written as

```
     {
       if (a > b)
         return (a);
       else
         return (b);
     }
```

but the nature of "return" is such that the "else" is not needed here!

Example 9

Here are two "quickies" which introduce some different and exotic looking expressions. First:

```
7679 schar()
     {
     return (*u.u_dirp++ & 0377);
     }
```

where the declaration

```
          char *u_dirp;
```

is part of the declaration of the structure "u".

"u.u_dirp" is a character pointer. Therefore the value of "*u.u_dirp++" is a character. (Incrementation of the pointer occurs as a side effect.)

When a character is loaded into a sixteen bit register, sign extension may occur. By "and"ing the word with 0377 any extraneous high order bits are eliminated. Thus the result returned is simply a character.

Note that any integer which begins with a zero (e.g. 0377) is interpreted as an octal integer.

The second example is:

```
1771 nseg(n)
     {
     return ((n+127)>>7);
     }
```

The value returned is "n divided by 128 and rounded up to the next highest integer".

Note the use of the right shift operator ">>" in preference to the division operator "/".

Example 10

Many of the points which have been introduced above are collected in the following procedure:

```
2134 setrun (p)
     {
     register struct proc *rp;
     rp = p;
     rp->p_wchan = 0;
     rp->p_stat = SRUN;
     if (rp->p_pri < curpri)
         runrun++;
     if (runout != 0 &&
         (rp->p_flag&SLOAD) == 0) {
         runout = 0;
         wakeup (&runout);
     }
     }
```

Check your understanding of "C" by figuring out what this one does.

There are two additional features you may need to know about:

"&&" is the logical conjunction ("and") for relational expressions. (Cf. "||" introduced earlier.)

The last statement contains the expression

```
          &runout
```

which is syntactically an address variable but semantically just a unique bit pattern.

This is an example of a device which is used throughout UNIX. The programmer needed a unique bit pattern for a particular purpose. The exact value did not matter as long as it was unique. An adequate solution to the problem was to use the address of a suitable global variable.

Example 11

```
4856 bawrite (bp)
     struct buf *bp;
     {
     register struct buf *rbp;
     rbp = bp;
     rbp->b_flags =| B_ASYNC;
     bwrite (rbp);
     }
```

The second last statement is interesting because it could have been written as

```
rbp->b_flags = rbp->b_flags | B_ASYNC;
```

In this statement the bit mask "B_ASYNC" is "or"ed into "rbp->b_flags". The symbol "|" is the logical disjunction for arithmetic values.

This is an example of a very useful construction in UNIX, which can save the programmer much labour. If "ø" is any binary operator, then

$$x = x \; ø \; a;$$

where "a" is an expression, can be rewritten more succinctly as

$$x =ø \; a;$$

A programmer using this construction has to be careful about the placement of blank characters. Since

$$x =+ 1;$$

is different from

$$x = +1;$$

what is to be the meaning of

$$x =+1; \quad ?$$

Example 12

```
6824 ufalloc ()
     {
        register i;
        for (i=0; i<NOFILE; i++)
          if (u.u_ofile[i]==NULL) {
             u.u_ar0[R0] = i;
             return (i);
          }
        u.u_error = EMFILE;
        return (-1);
     }
```

This example introduces the "for" statement, which has a very general syntax making it both powerful and compact.

The structure of the "for" statement is adequately described on page 10 of the "C Tutorial", and that description is not repeated here.

The Algol equivalent of the above "for" statement would be

```
     for i:=1 step 1 until NOFILE-1 do
```

The power of the "for" statement in "C" derives from the great freedom the programmer has in choosing what to include between the parentheses. Certainly there is nothing which restricts the calculations to integers, as the next example will demonstrate.

Example 13

```
3949 signal (tp, sig)
     {
        register struct proc *p;
        for (p=proc;p<&proc[NPROC];p++)
          if (p->p_ttyp == tp)
             psignal (p,sig);
     }
```

In this example of the "for" statement, the pointer variable "p" is stepped through each element of the array "proc" in turn.

Actually the original code had

```
     for (p=&proc[0];p<&proc[NPROC];p++)
```

but it wouldn't fit on the line! As noted earlier, the use of "proc" as an alternative to the expression "&proc[0]" is acceptable in this context.

This kind of "for" statement is almost a cliche in UNIX so you had better learn to recognise it. Read it as

```
     for p = each process in turn
```

Note that "&proc[NPROC]" is the address of the (NPROC+1)-th element of the array (which does not of course exist) i.e. it is the first location beyond the end of the array.

At the risk of overkill we would point out again that whereas in the previous example

```
                    i++
```

meant "add one to the integer i", here

```
                    p++
```

means "skip p to point to the next structure".

Example 14

```
8870 lpwrite ()
     {
        register int c;
        while ((c=cpass()) >= 0)
          lpcanon(c);
     }
```

This is an example of the "while" statement, which should be compared with the "do ... while ..." construction encountered earlier. (Cf. the "while" and "repeat" statements of Pascal.)

The meaning of the procedure is

     Keep calling "cpass" while the result is positive, and pass the result as a parameter to a call on "lpcanon".

Note the redundant "int" in the declaration for "c". It isn't always omitted!

Example 15

The next example is abbreviated from the original:

```
5861 seek ()
     {
        int n[2];
        register *fp, t;
        fp = getf (u.u_ar0[R0]);
        ...........
        t = u.u_arg[1];
        ...........
        switch (t) {

        case 1:
        case 4:
          n[0] =+ fp->f_offset[0];
          dpadd (n, fp->f_offset[1]);
          break;

        default:
          n[0] =+ fp->f_inode->i_size0
             &0377;
          dpadd(n,fp->f_inode->i_size1);

        case 0:
        case 3:
          ;
        }
        ...........
     }
```

Note the array declaration for the two word array "n", and the use of "getf" (which appeared in Example 4).

The "switch" statement makes a multi-way branch depending on the value of the expression in parentheses. The individual parts have "case labels":

If "t" is one or four, then one set of actions is in order.

If "t" is zero or three, nothing is to be done at all.

If "t" is anything else, then a set of actions labelled "default" is to be executed.

Note the use of "break" as an escape to the next statement after the end of the "switch" statement. Without the "break", the normal execution sequence would be followed within the "switch" statement.

Thus a "break" would normally be required at the end of the "default" actions. It has been omitted safely here because the only remaining cases actually have null actions associated with them.

The two non-trivial pairs of actions represent the addition of one 32 bit integer to another. The later versions of the "C" compiler will support "long" variables and make this sort of code much easier to write (and read).

Note also that in the expression

        fp->f_inode->i_size0

there are two levels of indirection.

Example 16

```
6672 closei (ip, rw)
     int *ip;
     {
     register *rip;
     register dev, maj;
     rip = ip;
     dev = rip->i_addr[0];
     maj = rip->i_addr[0].d_major;
     switch (rip->i_mode&IFMT) {

     case IFCHR:
        (*cdevsw[maj].d_close)(dev,rw);
        break;
```

```
     case IFBLK:
        (*bdevsw[maj].d_close)(dev,rw);
     }
     iput (rip);
     }
```

This example has a number of interesting features.

The declaration for "d_major" is

```
     struct {
        char d_minor;
        char d_major;
     }
```

so that the value assigned to "maj" is the high order byte of the value assigned to "dev".

In this example, the "switch" statement has only two non-null cases, and no "default". The actions for the recognised cases, e.g.

        (*bdevsw[maj].d_close)(dev,rw);

look formidable at first glance.

First it should be noted that this is a procedure call, with parameters "dev" and "rw".

Second "bdevsw" (and "cdevsw") are arrays of structures, whose "d_close" element is a pointer to a function, i.e.

        bdevsw[maj]

is the name of a structure, and

        bdevsw[maj].d_close

is an element of that structure which happens to be a pointer to a function, so that

        *bedsw[maj].d_close

is the name of a function. The first pair of parentheses is "syntactical sugar" to put the compiler in the right frame of mind!

Example 17

We offer the following as a final example:

```
4043 psig ()
     {
     register n, p;
     .........
     switch (n) {

     case SIGQIT:
     case SIGINS:
     case SIGTRC:
     case SIGIOT:
     case SIGEMT:
     case SIGFPT:
     case SIGBUS:
     case SIGSEG:
     case SIGSYS:
        u.u_arg[0] = n;
        if (core())
           n =+ 0200;
     }
     u.u_arg[0]=(u.u_ar0[R0]<<8) | n;
     exit ();
     }
```

Here the "switch" selects certain values for "n" for which the one set of actions should be carried out.

An alternative would have been to write a "monster" "if" statement such as

```
     if (n==SIGQIT || n==SIGINS || ...
           ... || n==SIGSYS)
```

but that would not have been either transparent or efficient.

Note the addition of an octal constant to "n" and the method of composing a 16 bit value from two eight bit values.

                    -oOo-

CHAPTER FOUR

An Overview

The purpose of this chapter is to survey the source code as a whole i.e. to present the "wood" before the "trees".

Examination of the source code will reveal that it consists of some 44 distinct files, of which:

> two are in assembly language, and have names ending in ".s";
>
> 28 are in the "C" language and have names ending in ".c";
>
> 14 are in the "C" language, but are not intended for independent compilation, and have names ending in ".h".

The files and their contents were arranged by the programmers presumably to suit their convenience and not for ours. In many ways the divisions between files is irrelevant to the present discussion and might well be abolished entirely.

As mentioned already in Chapter One, the files have been organised into five sections. As far as was possible, the sections were chosen to be of roughly equal size, to cluster files which are strongly associated and to separate files which are only weakly associated.

Variable Allocation

The PDP11 architecture allows efficient access to variables whose absolute address is known, or whose address relative to the stack pointer can be determined exactly at compile time.

There is no hardware support for multiple lexical levels for variable declarations such as are available in block structured languages such as Algol or Pascal. Thus "C" as implemented on the PDP11 supports only two lexical levels: global and local.

Global variables are allocated statically; local variables are allocated dynamically within the current stack area or in the general registers (r2, r3 and r4 are used in this way).

Global Variables

In UNIX with very few exceptions, the declarations for global variables have been all gathered into the set of ".h" files. The exceptions are:

(a) the static variable "p" (2180) declared in "swtch" which is stored globally, but is accessible only from within the procedure "swtch". (Actually "p" is a very popular name for local variables in UNIX.);

(b) a number of variables such as "swbuf" (4721) which are referenced only by procedures within a single file, and are declared at the beginning of that file.

Global variables may be declared separately within each file in which they are referenced. It is then the job of the loader, which links the compiled versions of the program files together to match up the different declarations for the same variable.

The 'C' Preprocessor

If global declarations must be repeated in full in each file (as is required by Fortran, for instance) then the bulk of the program is increased, and modifying a declaration is at best a nuisance, and at worst, highly error-prone.

These difficulties are avoided in UNIX by use of the preprocessor facility of the "C" compiler. This allows declarations for most global variables to be recorded once only in one of the few ".h" files.

Whenever the declaration for a particular global variable is required the appropriate ".h" file can then be "included" in the file being compiled.

UNIX also uses the ".h" files as vehicles for lists of standard definitions for many symbolic names which represent constants and adjustable parameters, and for declaration of some structure types.

For example, if the file "bottle.c" contains a procedure "glug" which references a global variable called "gin" which is declared in the file "box.h", then a statement:

#include "box.h"

must be inserted at the beginning of the file "bottle.c". When the file "bottle.c" is compiled, all declarations in "box.h" are compiled, and since they are found before the beginning of any procedure in "bottle.c" they are flagged as external in the relocatable module which is produced.

When all the object modules are linked together, a reference to "gin" will be found in every file for which the source included "box.h". All these references will be consistent and the loader will allocate a single space for "gin" and adjust all the references accordingly.

Section One

Section One contains many of the ".h" files and the assembly language files.

It also contains a number of files concerned with system initialisation and process management.

The First Group of '.h' Files

param.h [Sheet 01] contains no variable declarations, but many definitions for operating system constants and parameters, and the declarations for three simple structures. The convention will be noted of using "upper case only" for defined constants.

systm.h [Sheet 02; Chapter 19] consists entirely of declarations (with definitions of the structures "callout" and "mount" as side-effects). Note that none of the variables is initialised explicitly, and hence all are initialised to zero.

The dimensions for the first three arrays are parameters defined in "param.h". Hence any file which "includes" "systm.h" must have

previously "included" "param.h".

seg.h [Sheet 03] contains a few definitions and one declaration, which are used for referencing the segmentation registers. This file could be absorbed into "param.h" and "systm.h" without any real loss;

proc.h [Sheet 03; Chapter 7] contains the important declaration for "proc", which is both a structure type and an array of such structures. Each element of the "proc" structure has a name which begins with "p_", and no other variable is so named. Similar conventions are used for naming the elements of the other structures.

The sets of values for the first two elements, "p_stat" and "p_flag", have individual names which are defined.

user.h [Sheet 04; Chapter 7] contains the declaration for the very important "user" structure, plus a set of defined values for "u_error".

Only one instance of the "user": structure is ever accessible at one time. This is referenced under the name "u" and is in the low address part of a 1024 byte area known as the "per process data area".

In general the complete ".h" files are not analysed in detail later in this text. It is expected that the reader will refer to them from time to time (with increasing familiarity and understanding).

Assembly Language Files

There are two files in assembly language which comprise about 10% of the source code. A reasonable acquaintance with these files is necessary.

low.s [Sheet 05; Chapter 9] contains information, including the trap vector, for initialising the low address part of main memory. This file is generated by a utility program called "mkconf" to suit the set of peripheral devices present at a particular installation;

m40.s [Sheets 06..14; Chapters 6, 8, 9, 10, 22] contains a set of routines appropriate to the PDP11/40, to carry out a variety of specialised functions which cannot be implemented directly in "C".

Sections of this file are introduced into the discussion as and where appropriate. (The largest of the assembler procedures, "backup", has been left to the reader to survey as an exercise.)

There is an alternative to "m40.s", which is not presented here, namely "m45.s", which is used on PDP11/45's and 70's.

Other Files in Section One

main.c [Sheets 15..17; Chapters 6, 7] contains "main" which performs various initialisation tasks to get UNIX running. It also contains "sureg" and "estabur" which set the user segmentation registers.

slp.c [Sheets 18..22; Chapters 6, 7, 8, 14] contains the major procedures required for process management including "newproc", "sched", "sleep" and "swtch".

prf.c [Sheets 23, 24; Chapter 5] contains "panic" and a number of other procedures which provide a simple mechanism for displaying initialisation messages and error messages to the operator.

malloc.c [Sheet 25; Chapter 5] contains "malloc" and "mfree" which are used to manage memory resources.

Section Two

Section Two is concerned with traps, hardware interrupts and software interrupts.

Traps and hardware interrupts introduce sudden switches into the CPU's normal instruction execution sequence. This provides a mechanism for handling special conditions which occur outside the CPU's immediate control.

Use is made of this facility as part of another mechanism called the "system call", whereby a user program may execute a "trap" instruction to cause a trap deliberately and so obtain the operating system's attention and assistance.

The software interrupt (or "signal") is a mechanism for communication between processes, particularly when there is "bad news".

reg.h [Sheet 26; Chapter 10] defines a set of constants which are used in referencing the previous user mode register values when they are stored in the kernel stack.

trap.c [Sheets 26..28; Chapter 12] contains the "C" procedure "trap" which recognises and handles traps of various kinds.

sysent.c [Sheet 29; Chapter 12] contains the declaration and initialisation of the array "sysent" which is used by "trap" to associate the appropriate kernel mode routine with each system call type.

sys1.c [Sheets 30..33; Chapters 12, 13] contains various routines associated with system calls, including "exec", "exit", "wait" and "fork".

sys4.c [Sheets 34..36; Chapters 12, 13, 19] contains routines for "unlink", "kill" and various other minor system calls.

clock.c [Sheets 37, 38; Chapter 11] contains "clock" which is the handler for clock interrupts, and which does much of the incidental housekeeping and basic accounting.

sig.c [Sheets 39..42; Chapter 13] contains the procedures which handle "signals" or "software interrupts". These provide facilities for inter-process communication and tracing.

Section Three

Section Three is concerned with basic input/output operations between the main memory and disk storage.

These operations are fundamental to the activities of program swapping and the creation and referencing of disk files.

This section also introduces procedures for the use and manipulation of the large (512 byte) buffers.

text.h [Sheet 43; Chapter 14] defines the "text" structure and array. One "text" structure is used to define the status of a shared text segment.

text.c [Sheets 43, 44; Chapter 14] contains the procedures which manage the shared text segments.

buf.h [Sheet 45; Chapter 15] defines the "buf" structure and array, the structure "devtab", and names for the values of "b_error". All these are needed for the management of the large (512 byte) buffers.

conf.h [Sheet 46; Chapter 15] defines the arrays of structures "bdevsw" and "cdevsw", which specify the device oriented procedures needed to carry out logical file operations.

conf.c [Sheet 46; Chapter 15] is generated, like "low.s", by the "mkconf" utility to suit the set of peripheral devices present at a particular installation. It contains the initialisation for the arrays "bdevsw" and "cdevsw", which control the basic i/o operations.

bio.c [Sheets 47..53; Chapters 15, 16, 17] is the largest file after "m40.s". It contains the procedures for manipulation of the large buffers, and for basic block oriented i/o.

rk.c [Sheets 53, 54; Chapter 16] is the device driver for the RK11/RK05 disk controller.

Section Four

Section Four is concerned with files and file systems.

A file system is a set of files and associated tables and directories organised onto a single storage device such as a disk pack.

This section covers the means of
    creating and accessing files;
    locating files via directories;
    organising and maintaining
            file systems.

it also includes the code for an exotic breed of file called a "pipe".

file.h [Sheet 55; Chapter 18] defines the "file" structure and array.

filsys.h [Sheet 55; Chapter 20] defines the "filsys" structure which is copied to and from the "super block" on "mounted" file systems.

ino.h [Sheet 56] describes the structure of "inodes" as recorded on the "mounted" devices. Since this file is not "included" in any other, it really exists for information only.

inode.h [Sheet 56; Chapter 18] defines the "inode" structure and array. "inodes" are of fundamental importance in managing the accesses of processes to files.

sys2.c [Sheets 57..59; Chapters 18, 19] contains a set of routines associated with system calls including "read", "write", "creat", "open" and "close".

sys3.c [Sheets 60, 61; Chapters 19, 20] contains a set of routines associated with various minor system calls.

rdwri.c [Sheets 62, 63; Chapter 18] contains intermediate level routines involved with reading and writing files.

subr.c [Sheets 64, 65; Chapter 18] contains more intermediate level routines for i/o, especially "bmap" which translates logical file pointers into physical disk addresses.

fio.c [Sheets 66..68; Chapters 18, 19] contains intermediate level routines for file opening, closing and control of access.

alloc.c [Sheets 69..72; Chapter 20] contains procedures which manage the allocation of entries in the "inode" array and of blocks of disk storage.

iget.c [Sheets 72..74; Chapters 18, 19, 20] contains procedures concerned with referencing and updating "inodes".

nami.c [Sheets 75, 76; Chapter 19] contains the procedure "namei" which searches the file directories.

pipe.c [Sheets 77, 78; Chapter 21] is the "device driver" for "pipes", which are a special form of short disk file used to transmit information from one process to another.

Section Five

Section Five is the final section. It is concerned with input/output for the slower, character oriented peripheral devices.

Such devices share a common buffer pool, which is manipulated by a set of standard procedures.

The set of character oriented peripheral devices are exemplified by the following:

```
KL/DL11    interactive terminal
PC11       paper tape reader/punch
LP11       line printer.
```

tty.h [Sheet 79; Chapters 23, 24] defines the "clist" structure (used as a list head for character buffer queues), the "tty" structure (stores

relevant data for controlling an individual terminal), declares the "partab" table (used to control transmission of individual characters to terminals) and defines names for many associated parameters.

kl.c [Sheet 80; Chapters 24, 25] is the device driver for terminals connected via KL11 or DL11 interfaces.

tty.c [Sheets 81..85; Chapters 23, 24, 25] contains common procedures which are independent of the attaching interfaces, for controlling transmission to or from terminals, and which take into account various terminal idiosyncrasies.

pc.c [Sheets 86, 87; Chapter 22] is the device handler for the PC11 paper tape reader/punch controller.

lp.c [Sheets 88, 89; Chapter 22] is the device handler for the LP11 line printer controller.

mem.c [Sheet 90] contains procedures which provide access to main memory as though it were an ordinary, file. This code has been left to the reader to survey as an exercise.

-oOo-

Section One contains many of the global declaration files and the assembly language files.

It also contains a number of files concerned with system initialisation and process management.

CHAPTER FIVE

Two Files

This chapter is intended to provide a gentle introduction to the source code by looking at two files in Section One which can be isolated reasonably well from the rest.

The discussion of these files supplements the discussion of Chapter Three and includes a number of additional comments regarding the syntax and semantics of the "C" language.

The File 'malloc.c'

This file is found on Sheet 25 of the Source code, and consists of just two procedures:

malloc (2528) mfree (2556)

These are concerned with the allocation and subsequent release of two kinds of memory resources, namely:

main memory in units of 32 words (64 bytes);

disk swap area in units of 256 words (512 bytes).

For each of these two kinds of resource, a list of available areas is maintained within a resource "map" (either "coremap" or "swapmap"). A pointer to the appropriate resource "map" is always passed to "malloc" and "mfree" so that the routines themselves do not have to know the kind of resource with which they are dealing.

Each of "coremap" and "swapmap" is an array of structures of the type "map" as declared at line 2515. This structure consists of two character pointers i.e. two unsigned integers.

The declarations of "coremap" and "swapmap" are on lines 0203, 0204. Here the "map" structure is completely ignored - a regrettable programming short-cut which is possible because it is not detected by the loader. Thus the actual numbers of list elements in "coremap" and "swapmap" are "CMAPSIZ/2" and "SMAPSIZ/2" respectively.

Rules for List Maintenance

(A) Each available area is defined by its size and relative address (reckoned in the units appropriate to the resource);

(B) The elements of each list are arranged at all times in order of increasing relative address. Care is taken that no two list elements represent contiguous areas - the alternative course, to merge the two areas into a single larger area is always taken;

(C) The whole list can be scanned by looking at successive elements of the array, starting with the first, until an element with a zero size is encountered. This last element is a "sentinel" which is not part of the list proper.

The above rules provide a complete specification for "mfree", and a specification for "malloc" which is complete except in one respect:

We need to specify how the resource allocation is actually made when there exists more than one way of performing it.

The method adopted in "malloc" is one known as "First Fit" for reasons which should become obvious.

As an illustration of how the resource "map" is maintained, suppose the following three resource areas were available:

an area of size 15 beginning at location 47 and ending at location 61;

an area of size 13 spanning addresses 27 to 39 inclusive;

an area of size 7 beginning at location 65.

Then the "map" would contain:

Entry	Size	Address
0	13	27
1	15	47
2	7	65
3	0	??
4	??	??

If a request for a space of size 7 were received, the area would be allocated starting at location 27, and the "map" would become:

Entry	Size	Address
0	6	34
1	15	47
2	7	65
3	0	??
4	??	??

If the area spanning addresses 40 to 46 inclusive is returned to the available list, the "map" would become

Entry	Size	Address
0	28	34
1	7	65
2	0	?
3	??	??

Note how the number of elements has actually decreased by one because of amalgamation though the total available resources have of course increased.

Let us now turn to a consideration of the actual source code.

malloc (2528)

The body of this procedure consists of a "for" loop to search the "map" array until either:

(a) the end of the list of available resources is encountered; or

(b) an area large enough to honour the current request is found;

2534: The "for" statement initialises "bp" to point to the first element of the resource map. At each succeeding iteration "bp" is incremented to point to the next "map" structure.

Note that the continuation condition "bp->m_size" is an expression, which becomes zero with the sentinel is referenced. This expression could have been written equivalently but more transparently as "bp->m_size>0".

Note also that no explicit test for the end of the array is made. (It can be shown that this latter is not necessary provided CMAPSIZ, SMAPSIZ >= 2*NPROC !)

2535: If the list element defines an area at least as large as that requested, then ...

2536: Remember the address of the first unit of the area;

2537: Increment the address stored in the array element;

2538: Decrement the size stored in the element and compare the result with zero (i.e. was it an exact fit?);

2539: In the case of an exact fit, move all the remaining list elements (up to and including the sentinel) down one place.

Note that "(bp-1)" points to the structure before the one referenced by "bp";

2542: The "while" continuation condition does not test the equality of "(bp-1)->m_size" and "bp->m_size"!

The value tested is the value assigned to "(bp-1)->m_size" copied from "bp->m_size".

(You are forgiven for not recognising this at once.);

2543: Return the address of the area. This represents the end of the procedure and hence very definitely the end of the "for" loop.

Note that a value of zero returned means "no luck". This is based on the assumption that no valid area can ever begin at location zero.

mfree (2556)

This procedure returns the area of size "size" at address "aa" to the "resource map" designated by "mp". The body of the procedure consists of a one line "for" statement, followed by a multi-line "if" statement.

2564: The semicolon at the end of this line is extremely significant, terminating as it does the empty statement. (It would aid legibility if this character were moved to a line on its own, as is done on line 2394.)

Depending on your point of view, this statement demonstrates either the power or the obscurity of the "C" language. Try writing equivalent code to this statement in another language such as Pascal or PL/1.

Step "bp" through the list until an element is encountered either with an address greater than the address of the area being returned.

i.e. not "bp->m_addr <= a"

or which indicates the end of the list

i.e. not "bp->m_size != 0";

2565: We have now located the element in front of which we should insert the new list element. The question is: Will the list grow larger by one element or will amalgamation keep the number of elements the same or even reduce it by one?

If "bp > mp" we are not trying to insert at the beginning of the list. If

(bp-1)->m_addr+(bp-1)->m_size==a

then the area being return abuts the previous element in the list;

2566: Increase the size of the previous list element by the size of the area being returned;

2567: Does the area being returned also abut the next element of the list? If so...

2568: Add the size of the next element of the list to the size of the previous element;

2569: Move all the remaining list elements (up to the one containing the final zero size) down one place.

Note that if the test on line 2567 fortuitously gives a true result when "bp->m_size" is zero no harm is done;

2576: This statement is reached if the test on line 2565 failed i.e. the area being returned cannot be amalgamated with the previous element on the list.

Can it be amalgamated with the next element? Note the check that the next element is not null;

2579: Provided the area being returned is genuinely non-null (perhaps this test should have been made sooner?) add a new element to the list and push all the remaining elements up one place.

In conclusion...

The code for these two procedures has been written very tightly. There is little, if any, "fat" which could be removed to improve run time efficiency. However it would be possible write these procedures in a more transparent fashion.

If you feel strongly on this point, then as an exercise, you should rewrite "mfree" to make its function more easily discernible.

Note also that the correct functioning of "malloc" and "mfree" depends on correct initialisation of "coremap" and "swapmap". The code to do this occurs in the procedure "main" at lines 1568, 1583.

The File 'prf.c'

This file is found on Sheets 23 and 24, and contains the following procedures:

printf	(2340)	panic	(2416)
printn	(2369)	prdev	(2433)
putchar	(2386)	deverror	(2447)

The calling relationship between these procedures is illustrated below:

```
panic  deverror
  |       |
  |     prdev
  |       |
   \     /
   printf
     |
   printn
     |
   putchar
```

printf (2340)

The procedure "printf" provides a direct, unsophisticated low-level, unbuffered way for the operating system to send messages to the system console terminal. It is used during initialisation and to report hardware errors or the imminent collapse of the system.

(These versions of "printf" and "putchar" run in kernel mode and are similar to, but not the same as, the versions invoked by a "C" program which runs in user mode. The latter versions of "printf" and "putchar" live in the library "/lib/libc.a". You may still find it useful to read the sections "PRINTF(III)" and "PUTCHAR(III)" of the UPM at this point.)

2340: The programmer must have been carried away when he declared all the parameters for this procedure. In fact the procedure body only contains references to "xl" and "fmt".

This serves to reveal one of the facts of "C" programming. The rules for matching parameters in procedure calls and procedure declarations are not enforced, not even with respect to the numbers of parameters.

Parameters are placed on the stack in reverse order. Thus when "printf" is called "fmt" will be nearer to the "top of stack" than "xl", etc.

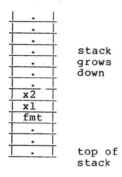

"xl" has a higher address then "fmt" but a lower address then "x2", because stacks grow downwards on the PDP11.

2341: "fmt" may be interpreted as a constant character pointer. This declaration is (almost) equivalent to
            "char *fmt;"
The difference is that here the value of "fmt" cannot be changed;

2346: "adx" is set to point to "xl". The expression "&xl" is the address of "xl". Note that since "xl" is a stack location, this expression cannot be evaluated at compile time.

(Many of the expressions you will find elsewhere involving the addresses of variables or arrays are effective because they <u>can</u> be evaluated at compile or load time.);

2348: Extract into the register "c" successive characters from the format string;

2349: If "c" is not a '%' then ...

2350: If "c" is a null character ('\0'), this indicates the end of the format string in the normal way, and "printf" terminates;

2351: Otherwise call "putchar" to send the character to the system console terminal;

2353: A '%' character has been seen. Get the next character (it had better not be the '\0'!);

2354: If this character is a 'd' or 'l' or 'o', call "printn" passing as parameters the value referenced by "adx" and either the value "8" or "10" depending on whether "c" is 'o' or not. (The 'd' and 'l' codes are clearly equivalent.)

"printn" expresses the binary numbers as a set of digit characters according to the radix supplied as the second parameter;

2356: If the editing character is 's', then all but the last character of a null terminated string is to be sent to the terminal. "adx" should point to a character pointer in this case;

2361: Increment "adx" to point to the next word in the stack i.e. to the next parameter passed to "printf";

2362: Go back to line 2347 and continue scanning the format string. Enthuisiasts for structured programming will prefer to replace lines 2347 and this by
    "while (1) {"   and   "}"
respectively.

printn (2369)

This procedure calls itself recursively in order to generate the required digits in the required order. It might be possible to code this procedure more efficiently but not more completely. (Anyway, in view of the implementation of "putchar", efficiency is hardly a consideration here.)

Suppose n = A*b + B where A = ldiv(n,b) and where B = lrem(n,b) satisfies 0<=B<b. Then in order to display the value for n, we need to display the value for A followed by the value for B.

The latter is easy for b = 8 or 10: it consists of a single character. The former is easy if A = 0. It is also easy if "printn" is called recursively. Since A < n, the chain of recursive calls must terminate.

2375: Arithmetic values corresponding to digits are conveniently converted to their corresponding character representations by the addition of the character '0'.

The procedures "ldiv" and "lrem" treat their first parameter as an unsigned integer (i.e. no sign extension, when a 16 bit value is extended to a 32 bit value before the actual division operation). They may be found beginning on lines 1392 and 1400 respectively.

putchar (2386)

This procedure transmits to the system console the character which was passed as a parameter.

It illustrates in a small way the basic features of i/o operations on the PDP11 computer.

2391: "SW" is defined on line 0166 as the value "0177570". This is the kernel address of a read only processor register which stores the setting of the console switch register.

The meaning of the statement is clear: get the contents at location 0177570 and see if they are zero. The problem is to express this in "C". The code

        if (SW == 0)

would not have conveyed this meaning. Clearly "SW" is a pointer value which should be dereferenced. The compiler might have been changed to accept

        if (SW -> == 0)

but as it stands, this is syntactically incorrect. By inventing a dummy structure, with an element "integ" (see line 0175), the programmer has found a satisfactory solution to his problem.

Several other examples of this programming device will be found in this procedure and elsewhere.

In hardware terms, the system console terminal interface consists of four 16 bit control registers which are given consecutive addresses on the Unibus beginning at kernel address 0177560 (see the declaration for "KL" on line 0165.) For a description of the formats and usage of these registers, see Chapter Twenty-Four or the "PDP11 Peripherals Handbook".

In software terms, this interface is the unnamed structure which is defined beginning on line 2313, with four elements which name the four control registers. It does not matter that the structure is unnamed because it is not necessary to allocate any instances of it (the one we are interested in is essentially predefined, at the address given by "KL").

2393: While bit 7 of the transmitter status register ("XST") is off, keep doing nothing, because the interface is not ready to accept another character.

This is a classic case of "busy waiting" where the processor is allowed to cycle uselessly through a set of instructions until some externally defined event occurs. Such waste of processing power cannot normally be tolerated but this procedure is only used in unusual situations.

2395: The need for this statement is tied up with the statement on line 2405;

2397: Save the current contents of the transmitter status register;

2398: Clear the transmitter status register preparatory to sending the next character;

2399: With bit 7 of the control status register reset, move the next character to be transmitted to the transmitter buffer register. This initiates the next output operation;

2400: A "new line" character needs to be accompanied by a "carriage return" character and this is accomplished by a recursive call on "putchar".

A couple of extra "delete" characters are thrown in also, to allow for any delays in completing the carriage return operation at the terminal;

2405: This call on "putchar" with an argument of zero effectively results in a re-execution of lines 2391 to 2394.

(It is very hard to see why the programmer chose to use a recursive call here in preference to simply repeating lines 2393 and 2394, since both code efficiency

and compactness not to mention clarity seem to have suffered.);

2406: Restore the contents of the transmitter status register. In particular if bit 6 was formerly set to enable interrupts then this resets it.

panic (2419)

This procedure is called from a number of locations in the operating system. (e.g. line 1605). When circumstances exist under which continued operation of the system seems undesirable.

UNIX does not profess to be a "fault tolerant" or "fail soft" system, and in many cases the call on "panic" can be interpreted as a fairly unsophisticated response to a straightforward problem.

However more complicated responses require additional code, lots of it, and this is contrary to the general UNIX philosophy of "keep it simple".

2419: The reason for this statement is given in the comment beginning at line 2323;

2420: "update" causes all the large block buffers to be written out. See Chapter Twenty;

2421: "printf" is called with a format string and one parameter, which was passed to "panic";

2422: This "for" statement defines an infinite loop in which the only action is a call on the assembly language procedure "idle" (1284).

"idle" drops the processor priority to zero, and performs a "wait". This is a "do nothing" instruction of indefinite duration. It terminates when a hardware interrupt occurs.

An infinite set of calls on "idle" is better than the execution of a "halt" instruction, since any i/o activities which were under way can be allowed to complete and the system clock can keep ticking.

The only way for the operator to recover from a "panic" is to reinitialise the system, (after taking a core dump, if desired)..

prdev (2433)

deverror (2447)

These procedures provide warning messages when errors are occurring in i/o operations. At this stage, their only interest is as examples of the use of "printf".

Included Files

It will be noted that whereas the file "malloc.c" contains no request to include other files, requests to include four separate files are included at the beginning of "prf.c".

(The observant reader will note that these files are presumed to reside one level higher in the file hierarchy than "prf.c" itself.)

The statement on line 2304 is to be understood as if it were replaced by the entire contents of the file "param.h". This then supplies definitions for the identifiers "SW", "KL" and "integ" which occur in "putchar".

We noted earlier that declarations for "KL", "SW" and "integ" occurred on lines 0165, 0166 and 0175 respectively, but this would have been meaningless, if the file "param.h" had not been "included" in "prf.c".

The files "buf.h" and "conf.h" have been included to provide declarations for "d_major". "d_minor", "b_dev" and "b_blkno", which are used in "prdev" and "deverror".

The reason for the inclusion of the fourth file, "seg.h", is a little harder to find. In fact it is not necessary as the code stands, and the author owes his readers an apology. In editing the source code, it seemed like a good idea to move the declaration for "integ" from "seg.h" to "param.h". Q.E.D.

Note that the variable "panicstr" (2328) is also global but since it is not referenced outside "prf.c", its declaration has not been placed in any ".h" file.

-oOo-

CHAPTER SIX

Getting Started

This chapter considers the sequence of events which occur when UNIX is "rebooted" i.e. it is loaded and initiated in an idle machine.

A study of the initialisation process is of interest in itself, but more importantly, it allows a number of important features of the system to be presented in an orderly manner.

The operating system may have to be restarted in the aftermath of a system crash. It will also have to be restarted frequently for quite ordinary, operational reasons, e.g. after an overnight shutdown. If we assume the

latter case, then we can assume that all the disk files are intact and that no special circumstance needs to be recognised or dealt with.

In particular, we can assume there is a file in the root directory called "/unix", which is the object code for the operating system.

This file began life as a set of source files such as we are investigating. These were compiled and linked together in the normal way to form a single object program file, and stored in the root directory.

Operator Actions

Reinitialisation requires operator action at the processor console. The operator must:

    stop the processor by setting the "enable/halt" switch to "halt";

    set the switch register with the address of the hardware bootstrap loader program;

    depress and release the "load address" switch;

    move the "enable/halt" switch to "enable";

    depress and release the "start" switch.

This activates the bootstrap program which is permanently recorded in a ROM in the processor.

The bootstrap loader program loads a larger loader program (from block #0 of the system disk), which looks for and loads a file called "/unix" into the low part of memory.

It then transfers control to the instruction loaded at address zero.

Address zero is occupied by a branch instruction (line 0508), which branches to location 000040, which contains a jump instruction (line 0522), which jumps to the instruction labelled "start" in the file "m40.s" (line 0612).

start (0612)

0613: The "enabled" bit of the memory management status register, SR0, is tested. If this set, the processor will dwell forever in a two instruction loop. This register will normally be cleared when the operator activates the "clear" button on the console before starting the system.

A number of reasons have been suggested for the necessity for this loop. The most likely is that in the case of a double bus timeout error, the processor will branch to location zero, and in this situation it should not be allowed to go further.

0615: "reset" clears and initialises all the peripheral device control and status registers;

The system will now be running in kernel mode with memory management disabled.

0619: KISA0 and KISD0 are the high core addresses of the first pair of kernel mode segmentation registers. The first six kernel descriptor registers are initialised to 077406, which is the description of a full size, 4K word, read/write segment.

The first six kernel address registers are initialised to 0, 0200, 0400, 0600, 01000 and 01200 respectively.

As a result the first six kernel segments are initialised (without any reference to the actual size of UNIX) to point to the first six 4K word segments of physical memory. Thus the "kernel to physical" address translation is trivial for kernel addresses in the range 0 to 0137777;

0632: "_end" is a loader pseudo variable which defines the extent of the program code and data area. This value is rounded up to the next multiple of 64 bytes and is stored in the address register for the seventh segment (segment #6).

Note that the address of this register is stored in "ka6", so that the content of this register is accessible as "*ka6";

0634: The corresponding descriptor register is loaded with a value which (since "USIZE" is equal to 16) is the description of a read/write segment which is 16 x 32 = 512 words long.

The value 007406 is obtained by shifting the octal value 017 eight places to the left and then "or"ing in the value 6;

0641: The eighth segment is mapped into the highest 4K word segment of the physical address space.

It should be noted that with memory management disabled, the same translation is already in force i.e. addresses in the highest 4K word segment of the 32K program address space are automatically mapped into the highest 4K word segment of the physical address space.

We may note that from this point on, all the kernel mode segmentation registers will remain unchanged with the single exception of the seventh kernel segmentation address register.

This register is explicitly manipulated by UNIX to point to a variety of locations in physical memory. Each such location is the beginning of an area 512 words long, known as a "per process data area".

The seventh kernel address register is now set to point to the segment which will become the per process data area for process #0.

0646: The stack pointer is set to point to the highest word of the per process data area;

0647: By incrementing the value of SR0 from zero to one, the "memory management enabled" bit is conveniently set.

From this point, all program addresses are translated to physical addresses by the memory management hardware.

0649: "bss" refers to the second part of the program data area, which is not initialised by the loader (see "A.OUT(V)" in the UPM). The lower and upper limits of this area are defined by the loader pseudo variables, "_edata" and "_end" respectively;

0668: The processor status word (PS) is changed to indicate that the "previous mode" was "user mode".

This prepares the way for the investigation and initialisation of the areas of physical memory which are not part of the kernel address space. (This involves use of the special instructions "mtpi" and "mfpi" (Move To/From Previous Instruction space) together with some manipulation of the user mode segmentation registers.);

0669: A call is then made to the procedure "main" (1550).

It will be seen later that "main" calls "sched" which never terminates. The need for or use of the last three instructions of "start" (lines 0670,

0671 and 0672) is therefore somewhat enigmatic. The reason will come later. In the meantime you might like to ponder "why?". What do these lines do anyway?

main (1550)

Upon entry to this procedure:

(a)   the processor is running at priority zero, in kernel mode and with the previous mode shown as user mode;

(b)   the kernel mode segmentation registers have been set and the memory management unit has been enabled;

(c)   all the data areas used by the operating system have been initialised;

(d)   the stack pointer (SP or r6) points to a word which contains a return address in "start".

1559: The first action of "main" would appear to be redundant, since "updlock" should have already been set to zero as part of the initialisation performed by "start";

1560: "i" is initialised to the ordinal of the first 32 word block beyond the "per process data area" for process #0;

1562: The first pair of user mode segmentation registers are used to provide a "moving window" into higher areas of the physical memory.

At each position of the window an attempt is made (using "fuibyte") to read the first accessible word in the window. If this is not successful, it is assumed that the end of the physical memory has been reached.

Otherwise the next 32 word block is initialised to zero (using "clearseg" (0676)) and added to the list of available memory, and the window is advanced by 32 words.

"fuibyte" and "clearseg" are both to be found in "m40.s". "fuibyte" will normally return a positive value in the range 0 to 255. However, in the exceptional case where the memory location referenced does not respond, the value -1 is returned. (The way this is brought about is a little obscure, and will be explained later in Chapter Ten.)

1582: "maxmem" defines the maximum amount of main memory which may be used by a user program. This is the minimum of:

the physically available memory ("maxmem");

an installation definable parameter ("MAXMEM") (0135);

the ultimate limit imposed by the PDP11 architecture;

1583: "swapmap" defines available space on the swapping disk which may be used when user programs are swapped out of main memory. It is initialised to a single area of size "nswap", starting at relative address "swplo". Note that "nswap" and "swplo" are initialised in "conf.c" (lines 4697, 4698);

1589: The significance of this and the next four lines will be discussed shortly;

1599: The design of UNIX assumes the existence of a system clock which interrupts the processor at line frequency (i.e 50 Hz or 60 Hz).

There are two possible clock types available: a line frequency clock (KW11-L) which has a control register on the Unibus at address 777546, or a programmable, real-time clock (KW11-P) located at address 777540 (lines 1509, 1510).

UNIX does not presume which clock will be present. It attempts to read the status word for the line frequency clock first. If successful, that clock is initialised and the other (if present) remains unused. If the first attempt is unsuccessful, then the other clock is tried. If both attempts are unsuccessful, there is a call on "panic" which effectively halts the system with an error message to the operator.

Since the absence of a clock will be indicated by a bus timeout error, it is convenient to make the reference via "fuiword", preceded by the setting of a user mode segmentation register pair (1599, 1600).

1607: Either type of clock is initialised by the statement

*lks = 0115;

As a consequence of this action, the clock will interrupt the processor within the next 20 milliseconds. This interrupt may occur at any time, but it will be convenient for this discussion to assume that no interrupt will occur before initialisation is complete;

1613: "cinit" (8234) initialises the pool of character buffers. See Chapter 23;

1614: "binit" (5055) initialises the pool of large buffers. See Chapter 17;

1615: "iinit" (6922) initialises table entries for the root device. See Chapter Twenty.

Processes

"process" is a term which has occurred more than once already. A definition which will suit our purposes reasonably well at present is simply "a program in execution".

Details of the representation of processes in UNIX will be discussed in the next chapter. For now we just note that each process involves a "proc" structure from the array called "proc" and a "per process data area" which includes one copy of the structure "u".

Initialisation of proc[0]

The explicit initialisation of the structure "proc[0]" is performed starting at line 1589. Only four elements are changed from the overall initial value of zero:

(a) "p_stat" is set to "SRUN" which implies that process #0 is "ready to run";

(b) "p_flag" is set to show both "SLOAD" and "SSYS". The former implies that the process is to be found in core (it has not been swapped out onto the disk), and the second, that it should never be swapped out;

(c) "p_size" is set to "USIZE";

(d) "p_addr" is set to the contents of the kernel segmentation address register #6.

It will be seen that process #0 has acquired an area of "USIZE" blocks (exactly the size of a "per process data area") which begins immediately after the official end ("_end") of the operating system data area.

The ordinal number of the first block of this area has been stored for future reference in "p_addr". This area, which was cleared to zero in "start"

(0661), contains a single copy of the "user" structure called "u".

On line 1593, the address of "proc[0]" is stored in "u.u_procp", i.e. the "proc" structure and the "u" structure are mutually linked.

The story continues ...

1627: "newproc" (1826) will be discussed in detail in the next chapter.

In brief this initialises a second "proc" structure viz. "proc[1]", and allocates a second "per process data area" in core. This is a copy of the "per process data area" for process #0, exact in all but one respect: the value of "u.u_procp" in the second area is "&proc[1]".

We should note here that at line 1889, there is a call on "savu" (0725) which saves the current values of the environment and the stack pointers in "u.u_rsav" before the copy is made.

Also from line 1918 we can see that the value returned by "newproc" will be zero, so that the statements on lines 1628 to 1635 will not be executed;

1637: A call is made to "sched" (1940) which, it may be observed, contains an infinite loop, so that it never returns!

sched (1940)

At this stage we are only interested in what happens when "sched" is entered for the first time.

1958: "spl6" is an assembler routine (1292) which sets the processor priority level to six. (Cf. also "spl0", "spl4", "spl5" and "spl7" in "m40.s").

When the processor is at level six, only devices with priority seven can interrupt it. The clock whose priority level is six is thus inhibited from interrupting the processor between this point and the subsequent call on "spl0" at line 1976.

1960: A search is made through "proc" for a process whose status is "SRUN" and which is not "loaded".

(Processes #0 and #1 have status "SRUN" and are loaded. All remaining processes, have a status of zero, which is equivalent to "undefined" or "NULL").

1966: The search fails ("n" is still -1). The flag "runout" is made non-zero, indicating that there are no processes which are both ready to run and "swapped out" onto disk;

1968: "sleep" is called (to wait for such an event) with a priority "PSWP" (== -100) for when it wakes up, which is in the category of "very urgent".

sleep (2066)

2070: "PS" is the address of the processor status word. The processor status is stored in the register "s" (0164, 0175);

2071: "rp" is set to the address of the entry in the array "proc" of the current process (still "proc[0]" at this stage!);

2072: "pri" is negative, so the "else" branch is taken, setting the status of the current process (#0) to "SSLEEP". The reason for "going to sleep" and the "awakening priority" are noted.

2093: "swtch" is then called.

swtch (2178)

2184: "p" is a static variable (2180), which means that its value is initialised to zero (1566) and is preserved between calls. For the very first call on "swtch", "p" is set to point to "proc[0]";

2189: "savu" is called to save the stack pointer and the environment pointer for the current process in "u.u_rsav";

2193: "retu" is called:

(a) to reset the kernel address register for segment #6 to the value passed as an argument (this causes a change in the current process!);

(b) to reset the stack and environment pointers to values appropriate to the revised current process, whose execution is about to be resumed.

The combination of successive calls on "savu" and "retu" at this point constitutes a so-called "coroutine jump" (Cf. "exchange jump" on the Cyber or "Load PSW" on the /360 or "Move Stack" on the B6700).

This time however the coroutine jump is from process #0 to process #0 (not very interesting!).

2201: The set of processes is searched to find the process whose state is "SRUN" and which is loaded and for which "p_pri" is a maximum.

The search is successful and process #1 is found. (N.B. The state of process #0 was just changed from "SRUN" to "SSLEEP" in "sleep" so it no longer satisfies the search criterion);

2218: Since "p" is not "NULL", the idle loop is not entered;

2228: "retu" (0740) causes a coroutine jump to process #1 which becomes the current process.

What is process #1 ? It is a copy of process #0, made at a previous stage of the latter's existence.

This call on "retu" was not preceded by a call on "savu" because the necessary information has in fact been saved already. (Where?)

2229: "sureg" is a routine (1738) which copies into the user mode segmentation registers, the values appropriate for the current process. These have been stored earlier in the arrays "u.u_uisa" and "u.u_uisd".

The very first call on "sureg" copies zeros and serves no real purpose.

2240: The "SSWAP" flag is not set, so that this enigmatic (2239) section can be ignored for now;

2247: Finally "swtch" returns with a value of "1". But where does the "return" return to? <u>Not</u> <u>to</u> <u>"sleep"</u> !

The "return" follows values set by the stack pointer and the environment pointer. These (just before the return) have values equal to those in force when the most recent "savu(u.u_rsav)" was performed.

Now process #1, which is only just starting has never performed a "savu", but values were stored in "u.u_rsav" before the copy of process #0 was made by "newproc", which had been called from "main".

Thus in this case, <u>the return from</u> <u>"swtch"</u> <u>is made to "main", with a value</u> <u>of one</u>. (Look over this again, to be sure you understand!)

main revisited

The story so far: process #0, having created a copy of itself in the form of process #1, has gone to sleep. As a result process #1 has become the current process and has returned to "main" with a value of one. Now read on ...

1627: The statements in "main" which are conditional on "newproc" are now executed;

1628: "expand" (2268) finds a new, larger area (from USIZE*32 to (USIZE+1)*32 words) for process #1, and copies the original data area into it.

In this case, the original user data area consists only of a "per process data area", with zero length data and stack areas. The original area is released;

1629: "estabur" is used to set the "prototype" segmentation registers which are stored in "u.u_uisa" and "u.u_uisd" for later use by "sureg". "estabur" calls "sureg" as its last action.

The parameters for "estabur" are the sizes of the text, data and stack areas plus an indicator to decide whether the text and data areas should be in separate address spaces. (Never true on the PDP11/40.) The sizes are all in units of 32 words;

1630: "copyout" (1252) is an assembler routine which copies an array in kernel space of specified size into a region in user space. Here the array "icode" is copied into an area starting at location zero in user space;

1635: The "return" is not special. From "main" it goes to "start" (0670) where the three last instructions have the effect of causing <u>execution in user mode of the instruction at user mode address zero</u>. i.e. the execution of a

copy of the first instruction in "icode". The instructions subsequently executed are copies also of instructions in "icode".

AT THIS POINT, THE INITIALISATION OF THE SYSTEM IS COMPLETE.

Process #1 is running and to all intents and purposes, is a normal process. Its initial form is (almost) that which would come from compilation, loading and execution of the simple, but non-trivial "C" program:

```
char *init "/etc/init";
main ( ) {
    execl (init, init, 0);
    while (1);
}
```

The equivalent assembler program is

```
        sys exec
        init
        initp
        br
initp:  init
        0
init:   </etc/init\0>
```

If the system call on "exec" fails (e.g. the file "/etc/init" cannot be found) the process falls into a tight loop, and there the processor will stay, except when the occasional clock interrupt occurs.

A description of the functions performed by "/etc/init" can be found in the section "INIT (VIII)" of the UPM.

-oOo-

CHAPTER SEVEN

Processes

The previous chapter traced the developments which occur after the operating system has been "rebooted", and in so doing introduced a number of significant features of the process concept. One of the aims of this chapter is to go back and re-explore some of the same ground more thoroughly.

There are a number of serious difficulties in providing a generally acceptable definition of "process". These are akin to the difficulties faced by the philosopher who would answer "what is life?" We will be in good company if we brush the more subtle points lightly aside.

The definition for "process" already given, "a program in execution", does reasonably well in suggesting what is intended. However it does not fit the case of either process #0 throughout its life or process #1 during its first moments. All other processes in the system however are clearly associated with the execution of some program file or other.

Processes can be introduced into discussions of operating systems at two levels.

At the upper level, "process" is an important organising concept for describing the activity of a computer system as a whole. It is often expedient to view the latter as the combined activity of a number of processes, each associated with a particular program such as the "shell", or the "editor". A discussion of UNIX at this level is given in the second half of Ritchie's and Thompson's paper, "The UNIX Time-sharing System".

At this level the processes themselves are considered to be the active entities in the system, while the identities of the true active elements, the processor and the peripheral devices, are submerged: the processes are born, live and die; they exist in varying numbers; they may acquire and release resources; they may interact, cooperate, conflict, share resources; etc.

At the lower level, "processes" are inactive entities which are acted on by active entities such as the processor. By allowing the processor to switch frequently from the execution of one process image to another, the impression can be created that each of the process images is developing continuously and this leads to the upper level interpretation.

Our present concern is with the low level interpretation: with the structure of the process image, with the details of execution and with the means for switching the processor between processes.

The following observations may be made about processes in the UNIX context:

(a) the existence of a process is implied by the existence of a non-null structure in the "proc" array, i.e. a "proc" structure for which the element "p_stat" is non-null;

(b) for each process there is a "per process data area" containing a copy of the "user" structure;

(c) the processor spends its entire life executing one process or another (except when it is resting between instructions);

(d) it is possible for one process to create or destroy another process;

(e) a process may acquire and possess resources of various kinds.

The Process Image

Ritchie and Thompson in their paper define a "process" as the execution of an "image", where the "image" is the current state of a pseudo-computer, i.e. an abstract data structure, which may be represented in either main memory or on disk.

The process image involves two or three physically distinct areas of memory:

(1) the "proc" structure, which is contained within the core resident "proc" array and is accessible at all times;

(2) the data segment, which consists of the "per process data

area", combined with a segment containing the user program data, (possibly) program text, and stack;

(3) the text segment, which is not always present, consists of a segment containing only pure program text i.e. re-entrant code and constant data.

Many programs do not have a separate text segment. Where one is defined, a single copy will be shared among all processes which are executions of the same particular program.

The proc Structure (0358)

This structure, which is permanently resident in main memory, contains fifteen elements, of which eight are characters, six are integers, and one a pointer to an integer. Each element represents information that must be accessible at any time, especially when the main part of the process image has been swapped out to disk:

"p_stat" may take one of seven values which define seven mutually exclusive states. See lines 0381 to 0387;

"p_flag" is an amalgam of six one bit flags which may be set independently. See lines 0391 to 0396;

"p_addr" is the address of the data segment:

If the data segment is in main memory this is a block number;

otherwise, if the data segment has been swapped out, this is a disk record number;

"p_size" is the size of the data segment, measured in blocks;

"p_pri" is the current process priority. This may be recalculated

from time to time as a function of "p_nice", "p_cpu" and "p_time";

"p_pid", "p_ppid" are numbers which uniquely identify a process and its parent;

"p_sig", "p_uid", "p_ttyp" are involved with external communication i.e. with messages or "signals" from outside the process's normal domain;

"p_wchan" identifies, for a "sleeping" process ("p_stat" equals either "SSLEEP" or "SWAIT"), the reason for sleeping;

"p_textp" is either null or a pointer to an entry in the "text" array (4306), which contains vital statistics regarding the text segment.

The user Structure (0413)

One copy of the "user" structure is an essential ingredient of each "per process data area". At any one time there is exactly one copy of the "user" structure which is accessible. This goes under the name "u" and is always to be found at kernel address 0140000 i.e. at the beginning of the seventh page of the kernel address space.

The "user" structure has more elements than can be conveniently or usefully introduced here. The comment accompanying each declaration on Sheet 04 succinctly suggests the function of each element.

For the moment you should notice:

(a) "u_rsav", "u_qsav", "u_ssav" which are two word arrays used to store values for r5, r6;

(b) "u_procp" which gives the address of the corresponding "proc" structure in the "proc" array;

(c) "u_uisa[16]", "u_uisd[16]" which store prototypes for the page address and description registers;

(d) "u_tsize", "u_dsize", "u_ssize" which are the size of the text segment and two parameters defining the size of the data segment, measured in 32 word blocks.

The remaining elements are concerned with:

- saving floating point registers (not for the PDP11/40);

- user identification;

- parameters for input/output operations;

- file access control;

- system call parameters;

- accounting information.

The Per Process Data Area

The "per process data area" corresponds to the valid part (lower part) of the seventh page of the kernel address space. It is 1024 bytes long. The lower 289 bytes are occupied by an instance of the "user" structure, leaving 367 words to be used as a kernel mode stack area. (Obviously there will be as many kernel mode stacks as there are processes.)

While the processor is in kernel mode, the values of r5 and r6, the environment and stack pointers, should remain within the range
     0140441 to 01437777.
Transition beyond the upper limit would be trapped as a segmentation violation, but the lower limit is protected only by the integrity of the software. (It may be noted that the hardware stack limit option is not used by UNIX.)

The Segments

The data segment is allocated as one single area of physical memory but consists of three distinct parts:

(a) a "per process data area";

(b) a data area for the user program. This may be further divided into areas for program text, initialised data and uninitialised data;

(c) a stack for the user program.

The size of (a) is always "USIZE" blocks. The sizes of (b) and (c) are given in blocks by "u.u_dsize" and "u.u_ssize". (It may be noted in passing that the latter two may change during the life of a process.)

A separate text segment containing only pure text is allocated as one single area of physical memory. The internal structure of the segment is not important here.

Execution of an Image

The image currently being executed (and hence the identity of the current process) is determined by the setting of the seventh kernel segmentation address register. If process #i is the current process, then the register has the value "proc[i].p_addr".

It is often desirable to distinguish between a process being executed in kernel mode and the same one being executed in user mode. We will use the terms "kernel process #i" and "user process #i" to denote "process #i executing in kernel mode" and "process #i executing in user mode" respectively.

If we chose to associate processes with particular execution stacks rather than with an entry in the "proc" array, then we would consider kernel process #i and user process #i to be separate processes, rather than different aspects of a single process #i.

Kernel Mode Execution

The seventh kernel segmentation address register must be set appropriately. None of the other kernel segmentation registers is ever disturbed and so their values are assumed. As was seen earlier, the first six kernel pages are mapped to the first six pages of physical memory, while the eighth is mapped into the highest page of physical memory. The size of the seventh segment is always the same.

In kernel mode the setting of the user mode segmentation registers is in general irrelevant. However they are normally set correctly for the user process.

The environment and stack pointers point into the kernel stack area in the seventh page, above the "user" structure.

User Mode Execution

Each activation of a user process is preceded and succeeded by an activation of the corresponding kernel process. Accordingly both the user mode and kernel mode registers will be properly set whenever a process image is being executed in user mode.

The environment and stack pointers point into the user stack area. This begins as the upper part of the eighth user page, but may be extended downwards, e.g. to occupy the whole of eighth page and part or all of the seventh page, etc.

Whereas the setting of the kernel segmentation registers is fairly trivial, setting the user segmentation registers is much less so.

An Example

Consider a program on the PDP11/40 which uses 1.7 pages of text, 3.3 pages of data, and 0.7 pages of stack area. (Our use of fractions in this example is admittedly a little crude.) The set of virtual addresses would be divided as shown in the following diagram:

888	///	sl	stack
888	///	sl	area
888			
777			
777			
777			
666			
666			
666	\\\	d4	
555	\\\	d3	
555	\\\	d3	
555	\\\	d3	
444	\\\	d2	data
444	\\\	d2	
444	\\\	d2	area
333	\\\	dl	
333	\\\	dl	
333	\\\	dl	
222			
222	///	t2	
222	///	t2	text
111	///	tl	
111	///	tl	area
111	///	tl	

Virtual Address Space

Two whole pages in the virtual address space must be allocated to the text segment, even though the physical area required is only 1.7 pages.

222	///	t2	
222	///	t2	text
111	///	tl	
111	///	tl	area
111	///	tl	

Text Segment

The data and stack areas require the dedication of four and one pages of virtual address space, and 3.3 and 0.7 pages of physical memory respectively.

The whole data segment requires four and one eighth pages of physical memory. The extra eighth is for the "per process data area" which corresponds (from time to time) to the seventh kernel address page.

```
| 888 /// s1 | stack
| 888 /// s1 | area
| 666 \\\ d4 |
| 555 \\\ d3 |
| 555 \\\ d3 |
| 555 \\\ d3 |
| 444 \\\ d2 | data
| 444 \\\ d2 |
| 444 \\\ d2 | area
| 333 \\\ d1 |
| 333 \\\ d1 |
| 333 \\\ d1 |
|      ppda  |
```

Data Segment

Note the order of the components of the data segment, and that there is no embedded unused space.

The user mode segmentation need to be set to reflect the values in the following table, where "t", "d" denote the block numbers of beginning of the text and data segments respectively:

Page	Address	Size	Comment
====	=======	====	=======
1	t+0	1.0	read only
2	t+128	0.7	read only
3	d+16	1.0	
4	d+144	1.0	
5	d+272	1.0	
6	d+400	0.3	
7	?	0.0	not used
8	d+400	0.7	grows downwards

Note the setting of the eighth address register. The address prototypes stored in the array "u.u_uisa" are obtained by setting "t" and "d" to zero.

Setting the Segmentation Registers

Prototypes for the user segmentation registers are set up by "estabur" which is called when a program is first launched into execution, and again whenever a significant change in memory allocation requires it. The prototypes are stored in the arrays "u.u_uisa", "u.u_uisd".

Whenever process #i is about to be re-activated, the procedure "sureg" is called to copy the the prototypes into the appropriate registers. The description registers are copied directly, but the address registers must be adjusted to reflect the actual location in physical memory of the area used.

estabur (1650)

1654: Various checks on consistency are performed, to ensure that the requested sizes for the text, data and stack are reasonable.

   Note that a non-zero value for "sep" implies separate mappings for the text area ("i" space) and the data area ("d" space). This is never possible on the PDP11/40;

1664: "a" defines the address of a segment relative to an arbitrary base of zero. "ap" and "dp" point to the set of prototype segmentation address and descriptor registers respectively.

The first eight of each of these sets are intended to refer to "i" space, and the second eight, to "d" space.

1667: "nt" measures the number of 32 word blocks needed for the text segment. If "nt" is non-zero, one or more pages must be allocated for this purpose.

Where more than one page is allocated, all but the last will consist of 128 blocks (4096 words), and will be read only, and will have relative addresses starting at zero and increasing successively by 128.

1672: If some fraction of a page of text is still to be assigned, allocate the appropriate part of the next page;

1677: if "i" and "d" spaces are being used separately, mark the segmentation registers for the remaining "i" pages as null;

1682: "a" is reset because all remaining addresses refer to the data area (not the text area) and are relative to the beginning of this area. The first "USIZE" blocks of this area are reserved for the "per process data area";

1703: The stack area is allocated from the top of the address space towards the lower addresses ("downwards");

1711: If a partial page must be allocated for the stack area, it is the high address part of the page which is valid. (For text and data areas, which grow "upwards", it is the lower part of a partial page which is valid.) This requires an extra bit in the descriptor, hence "ED" ("expansion downwards");

1714: If separate "i" and "d" spaces are not used, only the first eight of the sixteen prototype register pairs will have been initialised by this point. In this case, the second eight are copied from the first eight.

sureg (1739)

This routine is called by "estabur" (1724), "swtch" (2229) and "expand" (2295), to copy the prototype

1743: Get the base address for the data area from the appropriate element of the "proc" array;

1744: The prototype address registers (of which there are only eight for the PDP11/40) are modified by the addition of "a" and stored in the hardware segmentation address registers;

1752: Test if a separate text area has been allocated, and if so, reset "a" to the relative address of the text area to the data area. (Note this value may be negative! Fortunately at this point, addresses are in terms of 32 word blocks.);

1754: The pattern of code now followed is similar to the beginning of the routine, except ...

1762: a rather obscure piece of code adjusts the setting of the address register for segments which are not "writable" i.e. which presumably are text segments.

The code in "estabur" and "sureg" shows evidence of having been developed in several stages and is not as elegant as could be desired.

newproc (1826)

It is now time to take a good look at the procedure which creates new processes as (almost exact) replicas of their creators.

1841: "mpid" is an integer which is stepped through the values 0 to 32767. As each new process is created, a new value for "mpid" is created to provide a unique distinguishing number for the process. Since the cycle of values may eventually repeat, a check is made that the number is not still in use; if so a new value is tried;

1846: A search is made through the "proc" array for a null "proc" structure (indicated by "p_stat" having a null value);

1860: At this point, the address of the new entry in the "proc" array is stored as both "p" and "rpp", and the address of "proc" entry for the current process is stored both as "up" and "rip";

1861: The attributes of the new process are stored in the new "proc" entry. Many of these are copied from the current process;

1876: The new process inherits the open files of its parent. Increment the reference count for each of these;

1879: If there is a separate text segment increment the associated reference counts. Notice that "rip", "rpp" are used for temporary reference here;

1883: Increment the reference count for the parent's current directory;

1889: Save the current values of the environment and stack pointers in "u.u_rsav". "savu" is an assembler routine defined at line 0725;

1890: Restore the values of "rip" and "rpp". Temporarily change the value of "u.u_procp" from the value appropriate to the current process to the value appropriate to the new process;

1896: Try to find an area in main memory in which to create the new data segment;

1902: If there is no suitable area in main memory, the new copy will have to be made on disk. The next section of code should be analysed carefully because of the inconsistency introduced at line 1891 i.e.
      u.u_procp->p_addr != *ka6

1903: Mark the current process as "SIDL" to head off temporarily any further attempt to swap it out (i.e. initiated by "sched" (1940));

1904: Make the new "proc" entry consistent, i.e. set
      rpp->p_addr = *ka6;

1905: Save the current values of the environment and stack pointers in "u.u_ssav";

1906: Call "xswap" (4368) to copy the data segment into the disk swap area. Because the second parameter is zero, the main memory area will not be released;

1907: Mark the new process as "swapped out";

1908: Return the current process to its normal state;

1913: There was room in main memory, so store the address of the new "proc" entry and copy the data segment a block at a time;

1917: Restore the current process's "per process data area" to its previous state;

1918: Return with a value of zero.

Obviously "newproc" on its own is not sufficient to produce an interesting and varied set of processes. The procedure "exec" (3020) which is discussed in Chapter Twelve provides the necessary additional facility: the means for a process to change its character, to be reincarnated.

-oOo-

This may be done for example if a process has reached a point beyond which it cannot proceed immediately. The process calls "sleep" (2066) which calls "swtch".

Alternatively a kernel process which is ready to revert to user mode will test the variable "runrun" and if this is non-zero, implying that a process with a higher precedence is ready to run, the kernel process will call "swtch".

"swtch" searches the "proc" table, for entries for which "p_stat" equals "SRUN" and the "SLOAD" bit is set in "p_flag". From these it selects the process for which the value of "p_pri" is a minimum, and transfers control to it.

Values for "p_pri" are recalculated for each process from time to time by use of the procedure "setpri" (2156). Obviously the algorithm used by "setpri" has a significant influence.

A process which has called "sleep" and suspended itself may be returned to the "ready to run" state by another process. This often occurs during the handling of interrupts when the process handling the interrupt calls "setrun" (2134) either directly or indirectly via a call on "wakeup" (2113).

Interrupts

It should be noted that a hardware interrupt (see Chapter Nine) does not directly cause a call on "swtch" or its equivalent. A hardware interrupt will cause a user process to revert to a kernel process, which as just noted, may call "swtch" as an alternative to reverting to user mode after the interrupt handling is complete.

If a kernel process is interrupted, then after the interrupt has been handled, the kernel process resumes where

it had left off regardless. This point is important for understanding how UNIX avoids many of the pitfalls associated with "critical sections" of code, which are discussed at the end of this chapter.

Program Swapping

In general there will be insufficient main memory for all the process images at once, and the data segments for some of these will have to be "swapped out" i.e. written to disk in a special area designated as the swap area.

While on disk the process images are relatively inaccessible and certainly unexecutable. The set of process images in main memory must therefore be changed regularly by swapping images in and out. Most decisions regarding swapping are made by the procedure "sched" (1940) which is considered in detail in Chapter Fourteen.

"sched" is executed by process #0, which after completing its initial tasks, spends its time in a double role: openly as the "scheduler" i.e. a normal kernel process; and surreptitiously as the intermediate process of "swtch" (discussed in Chapter Seven). Since the procedure "sched" never terminates, kernel process #0 never completes its task, and so the question of a user process #0 does not arise.

Jobs

There is no concept of "job" in UNIX, at least in the sense in which this term is understood in more conventional, batch processing oriented systems.

Any process may "fork" a new copy of itself at any time, essentially without delay, and hence create the equivalent of a new job. Hence job scheduling, job classes, etc. are non-events here.

CHAPTER EIGHT

Process Management

Process management is concerned with the sharing of the processor and the main memory amongst the various processes, which can be seen as competitors for these resources.

Decisions to reallocate resources are made from time to time, either on the initiative of the process which holds the resource, of for some other reason.

Process Switching

An active process may suspend itself i.e relinquish the processor, by calling "swtch" (2178) which calls "retu" (0740).

The next three procedures are written in assembler and run with the processor priority level set to seven. These procedures do not observe the normal procedure entry conventions so that r5 and r6, the environment and stack pointers, are not disturbed during procedure entry and exit.

As has already been noted, "savu" and "retu" can combine to produce the effect of a coroutine jump. The third procedure, "aretu", when followed by a "return" statement produces the effect of a non-local "goto".

savu (0725)

This procedure is called by "newproc" (1889, 1905), "swtch" (2189, 2281), "expand" (2284), "trapl" (2846) and "xswap" (4476,4477).

The values of r5 and r6 are stored in the array whose address is passed as a parameter.

retu (0740)

This procedure is called by "swtch" (2193, 2228) and "expand" (2294).

It resets the seventh kernel segmentation address register, and then resets r6 and r5 from the newly accessible copy of "u.u_rsav" (which it may be noted, is at the beginning of "u").

aretu (0734)

This procedure is called by "sleep" (2106) and "swtch" (2242).

It reloads r6 and r5 from the address passed as a parameter.

swtch (2178)

"swtch" is called by "trap" (0770, 0791), "sleep" (2084, 2093), "expand" (2287), "exit" (3256), "stop" (4027) and "xalloc" (4480).

This procedure is unique in that its execution is in three phases which in general involve three separate kernel processes. The first and third of these processes will be called the "retiring" and the "arising" processes respectively. Process #0 is always the intermediate process; it may be the "retiring" or the "arising" process as well.

Note that the only variables used by "swtch" are either registers, or global or static (stored globally).

2184: The static structure pointer, "p", defines a starting point for searching through the "proc" array to locate the next process to activate. Its use reduces the bias shown to processes entered early in the "proc" array. If "p" is null, set its value to the beginning of the "proc" array. This should only occur upon the very first call on "swtch";

2189: A call on "savu" (0725) saves the current values of the environment and stack pointers (r5 and r6);

2193: "retu" (0740) resets r5 and r6, and, most importantly, resets the kernel address register #6 to address the "scheduler's" data segment;

2195: Phase Two begins:

The code from this line to line 2224 is only ever executed by kernel process #0. There are two nested loops, from which there is no exit until a runnable process can be found.

At slack periods, the processor

spends most of its time executing line 2220. It is only disturbed thence by an interrupt (e.g. from the clock);

2196: The flag "runrun" is reset. (It is used to indicate that a higher priority process than the current process is ready to run. "swtch" is about to look for the highest priority process.);

2224: The priority of the "arising" process is noted in "curpri" (a global variable) for future reference and comparison;

2228: Another call on "retu" resets r5, r6 and the seventh kernel address register to values appropriate for the "arising" process;

2229: Phase Three begins:

"sureg" (1739) resets the user mode hardware segmentation registers using the stored prototypes for the arising process;

2230: The comment which begins here is not encouraging. We will return to this point again towards the end of this chapter;

2247: If you check, you will find that none of the procedures which call "swtch" directly examines the value returned here.

Only the procedures which call "newproc" which are interested in this value, because of the way the child process is first activated!

setpri (2156)

2161: Process priorities are calculated according to the formula:

$$priority = \min \{127, (time\ used + PUSER + p\_nice)\}$$

where

(1) time used = accumulated central processor time (usually since the process was last swapped in), measured in clock ticks divided by 16 i.e. thirds of a second. (More on this later when we discuss the clock interrupt.);

(2) PUSER == 100;

(3) "p_nice" is a parameter used to bias the process priority. It is normally positive and hence reduces the process's effective precedence.

Note the somewhat confusing convention in UNIX that the lower the priority, the higher the precedence. Thus a priority of -10 beats a priority of 100 every time.

2165: Set the rescheduling flag if the process, whose priority has just been recalculated, has less precedence than the current process.

The sense of the test on line 2165 is surprising, especially when it is compared with line 2141. We leave it to the reader to satisfy himself that this is not an error. (Hint: look at the parameters for the calls on "setpri".)

sleep (2066)

This procedure is called (from nearly 30 different places in the code) when a kernel process chooses to suspend itself. There are two parameters:

- the reason for sleeping;

- a priority with which the process will run after being awakened.

If this priority is negative the process cannot be aroused from its sleep by the arrival of a "signal". "signals" are discussed in Chapter Thirteen.

2070: The current processor status is saved to preserve the incoming processor priority and previous mode information;

2072: If the priority is non-negative, a test is made for "waiting signals";

2075: A small critical section begins here, wherein the process status is changed and the parameters are stored in generally accessible locations (viz. within the array "proc").

This code is critical because the same information fields may be interrogated and changed by "wakeup" (2113) which is frequently called by interrupt handlers;

2080: When "runin" is non-zero, the scheduler (process #0) is waiting to swap another process into main memory;

2084: The call on "swtch" represents a delay of unknown extent during which a relevant external event may have occurred. Hence the second test on "issig" (2085) is not irrelevant;

2087: For negative priority "sleeps", where the process typically waits for freeing of system table space, the occurrence of a "signal" is not allowed to deflect the course of the activity.

wakeup (2113)

This procedure complements "sleep". It simply searches the set of all processes, looking for any processes which are "sleeping" for a specified reason (given as the parameter "chan"), and reactivating these individually by a call on "setrun".

setrun (2134)

2140: The process status is set to "SRUN". The process will now be considered by "swtch" and "sched" as a candidate for execution again;

2141: If the aroused process is more important (lower priority!) than the current process, the rescheduling flag, "runrun" is set for later reference;

2143: If "sched" is sleeping, waiting for a process to "swap in", and if the newly aroused process is on disk, wake up "sched".

Since it turns out that "sched" is the only procedure which calls "sleep" with "chan" equal to "&runout", line 2145 could be replaced by the recursive call

        setrun (&proc[0]);

or better still, by just

        rp = &proc[0];
        goto sr;

where "sr" is a label to be inserted at the beginning of line 2139.

expand (2268)

The comment at the beginning of this procedure (2251) says most of what needs to be said about the procedure, except for the question of "swapping out" when not enough core is available.

Note that "expand" takes no particular notice of the contents of the user data area or stack area.

2277: If the expansion is actually a contraction, then trim off the excess from the high address end;

2281: "savu" stores the values of r5 and r6 in "u.u_rsav";

2284: The environment pointer and stack pointer are recorded again in "u.u_ssav". But note that since no new procedures have been entered, and since there has been no cumulative stack growth, the values recorded are the same as at line 2281;

2285: "xswap" (4368) copies the core image for the process designated by its first parameter to disk.

Since the second parameter is non-zero the main memory area occupied by the data segment is returned to the list of available space.

However the computation continues using the same area in main memory until the next call on "retu" (2193) in "swtch".

Note also that the call on "savu" at line 2189 in "swtch" stores new values in "u.u_rsav" after the disk image has been made (and therefore serves no useful purpose since the core image has already been officially "abandoned");

2286: The "SSWAP" flag is set in the process's "proc" array element. (This is not swapped out, so the effect is not lost!);

2287: "swtch" is called, and the process, still running in its old area suspends itself. Since the call on "xswap" will have resulted in the "SLOAD" flag being switched off, there is no way that "swtch" will choose the process for immediate reactivation.

Only after the disk image has been copied back into core again can the process be activated again. The "return" executed by "swtch" is a return to the procedure which called "expand".

swtch revisited

What happens to the process when it is reactivated i.e. it becomes the "arising" process in "swtch"?

2228: The stack and environment pointers are restored from "u.u_rsav" (Note that a pointer to "u" is also a pointer to "u.u_rsav" (0415) but ...

2240: If the core image was "swapped out" e.g. by expand" ...

2242: No reliance is placed on the values of the stack and environment pointers, and they are reset from "u.u_ssav".

The question is "if the values stored in "u.u_ssav" at line 2284 are the same as values stored in "u.u_rsav" at line 2281, how did they get to be different?"

Presumably this is what "you are not expected to understand" (line 2238) ... clearly "xswap" should be investigated ... the trail finally ends at Chapter Fifteen ... in the meantime you may wish to investigate for yourself so that you may join the "2238" club that much sooner.

Critical Sections

If two or more processes operate on the same set of data, then the combined output of the set of processes may depend on the relative synchronisation of the various processes.

This is usually considered to be highly undesirable and to be avoided at all costs. The solution is usually to define "critical sections" (it is the programmer's responsibility to recognise these) in the code which is executed by each process. The programmer must then ensure that at any time no more than one process is executing a section of code which is critical with respect to a particular set of data.

In UNIX user processes do not share data and so do not conflict in this way. Kernel processes however have shared access to various system data and can conflict.

In UNIX an interrupt does not cause a change in process as a direct side effect. Only where kernel processes may suspend themselves in the middle of a critical section by an explicit call on "sleep", does an explicit lock variable (which may be observed by a group of processes) need to be introduced. Even then the actions of testing and setting the locks do not usually have to be made inseparable.

Some critical sections of code are executed by interrupt handlers. To protect other sections of code whose outcome may be affected by the handling of certain interrupts, the processor priority is raised temporarily high enough before the critical section is entered to delay such interrupts until it is safe, when the processor priority is reduced again. There are of course a number of conventions which interrupt handling code should observe, as will be discussed later in Chapter Nine.

In passing it may be noted that the strategy adopted by UNIX works only for a single processor system and would be totally inappropriate in a multi-processor system.

-oOo-

Section Two is concerned with traps, hardware interrupts and software interrupts.

Traps and hardware interrupts introduce sudden switches into the CPU's normal instruction execution sequence. This provides a mechanism for handling special conditions which occur outside the CPU's immediate control.

Use is made of this facility as part of another mechanism called the "system call", whereby a user program may execute a "trap" instruction to cause a trap deliberately and so obtain the operating system's attention and assistance.

The software interrupt (or "signal") is a mechanism for communication between processes, particularly when there is "bad news".

CHAPTER NINE

Hardware Interrupts and Traps

In the PDP11 computer, as in many other computers, there is an "interrupt" mechanism, which allows the controllers of peripheral devices (which are devices external to the CPU) to interrupt the CPU at appropriate times, with requests for operating system service.

The same mechanism has been usefully and conveniently applied to "traps" which are events internal to the CPU, which relate to hardware and software errors, and to requests for service from user programs.

Hardware Interrupts

The effect of an interrupt is to divert the CPU from whatever it was doing and to redirect it to execute another program.

During a hardware interrupt:

The CPU saves the current processor status word (PS) and the current program count (PC) in its internal registers;

the PC and PS are then reloaded from two consecutive words located in the low area of main memory. The address of the first of these two words is known as the "vector location" of the interrupt;

finally the original PC and PS values are stored into the newly current stack. (Whether this is the kernel or user stack depends on the new value of the PS.)

Different peripheral devices may have different vector locations. The actual vector location for a particular device is determined by hard wiring, and can only be changed with difficulty. Moreover there are well entrenched conventions for choosing vector locations for the various devices.

Thus after the interrupt has occurred, because the PC has been reloaded, the source of instructions executed by the CPU has been changed. The new source should be a procedure associated with the peripheral device controller which caused the interrupt.

Also since the PS has also been changed, the processor mode may have changed. In UNIX, the initial mode may be either "user" or "kernel", but after the interrupt, the mode is always "kernel". Recall also that a change in mode implies:

(a) a change in memory mappings. (Note that to avoid any confusion, vector locations are always interpreted as kernel mode addresses.);

(b) a change in stack pointers. (Recall that the stack pointer,

SP of r6, is the only special
register which is replicated for
each mode. This implies that
after a mode change, the stack
pointer value will have changed
even though it has not been
reloaded!)

The Interrupt Vector

For our sample system, the representative peripheral devices chosen are
listed in Table 9.1, along with their
conventional hardware defined vector
locations and priorities.

vector location	peripheral device	interrupt priority	process priority
========	==========	=========	========
060	teletype input	4	4
064	teletype output	4	4
070	paper tape input	4	4
074	paper tape output	4	4
100	line clock	6	6
104	programmable clock	6	6
200	line printer	4	4
220	RK disk drive	5	5

Table 9.1 Interrupt
Vector Locations and Priorities

Interrupt Handlers

Within this selection of UNIX source
code, there are seven procedures known
as "interrupt handlers", i.e. which are
executed as the result of, and only as
the result of, interrupts:

clock	(3725)	pcrint	(8719)
rkintr	(5451)	pcpint	(8739)
klxint	(8070)	lpint	(8976)
klrint	(8078)		

"clock" will be examined in detail in
Chapter 11. The others are discussed
with the code for their associated devices.

Priorities

An interrupt does not necessarily occur
immediately the peripheral device controller requests it, but only when the
CPU is ready to accept it. It is usually desirable that a request for a low
priority service should not be allowed
to interrupt an activity with a higher
priority.

Bits 7 to 5 of the PS determine the
processor priority at one of eight levels (labelled zero to seven). Each
interrupt also has an associated priority level determined by hardware wiring. An interrupt will be inhibited as
long as the processor priority is
greater than or equal to the interrupt
priority.

After the interrupt the processor
priority will be determined from the PS
stored in the vector location and this
does not have to be the same as the
interrupt priority. Whereas the interrupt priority is determined by
hardware, it is possible for the
operating system to change the contents
of the vector location at any time.

As a matter of curiosity, it may be
noted that the PDP11 hardware restricts
the possible interrupt priorities to 4,
5, 6 and 7 i.e. levels 1, 2 and 3 are
not supported by the Unibus.

Interrupt Priorities

In UNIX, interrupt handling routines
are initiated at the same priority as
the interrupt priority.

This means that during the handling of
the interrupt, a second interrupt from
a device of the same priority class
will be delayed until the processor
priority is reduced, either by the execution of one of the "spl" procedures,
which are intended for just this purpose (see lines 1293 to 1315), or by

reloading the processor status word
e.g. upon returning from the interrupt.

During interrupt handling, the processor priority may be raised temporarily
to protect the integrity of certain
operations. For instance, character
oriented devices such as the paper tape
reader/punch or the line printer interrupt at level four. Their interrupt
handlers call "getc" (0930) or "putc"
(0967), which raise the processor
priority temporarily to level five,
while the character buffer queues are
manipulated.

The interrupt handler for the console
teletype makes use of a "timeout"
facility. This involves a queue which
is also manipulated by the clock interrupt handler, which runs at level six.
To prevent possible interference, the
"timeout" procedure (3835) runs at
level seven (the highest possible
level).

Usually it does not make sense to run
an interrupt handler at a processor
priority lower than the interrupt
priority, for this would then risk a
second interrupt of the same type, even
from the same device, before completion
of the processing of the first interrupt. This likely to be at best inconvenient and at worst disastrous. However the clock interrupt handler, which
once per second has a lot of extra work
to do, does exactly this.

Rules for Interrupt Handlers

As discussed above, interrupt handlers
need to be careful about the manipulation of the processor priority to avoid
allowing other interrupts to happen
"too soon". Likewise care needs to be
taken that the other interrupts are not
delayed excessively, lest the performance of the whole system be degraded.

It is important to note that when an interrupt occurs, the process which is currently active will very likely not be the process which is interested in the occurrence. Consider the following scenario:

User process #m is active and initiates an i/o operation. It executes a trap instruction and transfers to kernel mode. Kernel process #m initiates the required operation and then calls "sleep" to suspend itself to await completion of the operation ...

Some time later, when some other process, user process #n say, is active, the operation is completed and an interrupt occurs. Process #n reverts to kernel mode, and kernel process #n deals with the interrupt, even though it may have no interest in or prior knowledge of the operation.

Usually kernel process #n will include waking process #m as part of its activity. This will not always be the case though, e.g. where an error has occurred and the operation is retried.

Clearly, the interrupt handler for a peripheral device should not make references to the current "u" structure for this is not likely to be the appropriate "u" structure. (The appropriate "u" structure could quite possibly be inaccessible, if it has been temporarily swapped out to the disk.)

Likewise the interrupt handler should not call "sleep" because the process thus suspended will most likely be some innocent process.

Traps

"Traps" are like "interrupts" in that they are events which are handled by the same hardware mechanism, and hence by similar software mechanisms.

"Traps" are unlike "interrupts" in that they occur as the result of events internal to the CPU, rather than externally. (In other systems the terminology "internal interrupt" and "external interrupt" is used to draw this distinction more forcefully.) Traps may occur unexpectedly as the result of hardware or power failures, or predictably and reproducibly, e.g. as the result of executing an illegal instruction or a "trap" instruction.

"Traps" are always recognised by the CPU immediately. They cannot be delayed in the way low priority interrupts may be. If you like, "traps" have an "interrupt priority" of eight.

"Trap" instructions may be deliberately inserted in user mode programs to catch the attention of the operating system with a request to perform a specified service. This mechanism is used as part of the facility known as "system calls".

Like interrupts, traps result in the reloading of the PC and PS from a vector location, and the saving of the old values of the PC and PS in the current stack. Table 9.2 lists the vector locations for the various "trap" types.

vector location	trap type	process priority
========	=========	========
004	bus timeout	7
010	illegal instruction	7
014	bpt-trace	7
020	iot	7
024	power failure	7
030	emulator trap instruction	7
034	trap instruction	7
114	11/70 parity	7
240	programmed interrupt	7
244	floating point error	7
250	segmentation violation	7

Table 9.2 Trap Vector Locations and Priorities

The contents of Tables 9.1 and 9.2 should be compared with the file "low.s" on Sheet 05. As noted earlier, this file is generated at each installation (along with the file "conf.c" (sheet 46)), as the product of the utility program "mkconf", so as to reflect the actual set of peripherals installed.

Assembly Language 'trap'

From "low.s" it appears that traps and interrupts are handled separately by the software. However closer examination reveals that "call" and "trap" are different entry points to a single code sequence in the file "m40.s" (see lines 0755, 0776). This sequence is examined in detail in the next chapter.

During the execution of this sequence, a call is made on a "C" language procedure to carry out further specific processing. In the case of an interrupt, the "C" procedure is the interrupt handler specific to the particular device controller.

In the case of a trap, the "C" procedure is another procedure called "trap" (yes, the word "trap" is definitely overworked!), which in the case of a system error will most likely call "panic" and in the case of a "system call", will invoke (indirectly via "trapl"(2841)) the appropriate system call procedure.

Return

Upon completion of the handling of an interrupt or trap, the code follows a common path ending in an "rtt" instruction (0805). This reloads both the PC and PS from the current stack, i.e. the kernel stack, in order to restore the processor environment that existed before the interrupt or trap.

-oOo-

(a) "main" (1564) calls "fuibyte" repeatedly until a negative value is returned. This will occur after a "bus timeout error" has been encountered with a subsequent trap to vector location 4 (line 0512);

(b) The clock has been set running and will generate an interrupt every clock tick i.e. 16.7 or 20 milliseconds;

(c) Process #1 is about to execute a "trap" instruction as part of the system call on "exec".

fuibyte (0814)

fuiword (0844)

"main" uses both "fuibyte" and "fuiword". Since the former is more complicated in a non-essential way, we leave it to the reader, and concentrate on the latter.

"fuiword" is called (1602) when the system is running in kernel mode with one argument which is an address in user address space. The function of the routine is to fetch the value of the corresponding word and to return it as a result (left in r0). However if an error occurs, the value −1 is to be returned.

Note that with "fuiword", there is an ambiguity which does not occur with "fuibyte", namely a returned value of −1 may not necessarily be an error indication but the actual value in the user space. Convince yourself that for the way it is used in "main", this does not matter.

Also the code does not distinguish between a "bus timeout error" and a "segmentation error".

The routine proceeds as follows:

0846: The argument is moved to r1;

0848: "gword" is called;

0852: The current PS is stored on the stack;

0853: The priority level is raised to 7 (to disable interrupts);

0854: The contents of the location "nofault" (1466) are saved in the stack;

0855: "nofault" is loaded with the address of the routine "err";

0856: An "mfpi" instruction is used to fetch the word from user space.

If nothing goes wrong this value will be left on the kernel stack.

0857: The value is transferred from the stack to r0;

0876: The previous values of "nofault" and PS are restored;

0878: Return via line 0849.

Now suppose something does go wrong with the "mfpi" instruction, and a bus time-out does occur.

0856: The "mfpi" instruction will be aborted. PC will point to the next instruction (0857) and a trap via vector location 4 will occur;

0512: The new PC will have the value of "trap". The new PS will indicate:

present mode = kernel mode
previous mode = kernel mode
priority   = 7;

0756: The next instruction executed is the first instruction of "trap". This saves the processor status word two words beyond the current "top of stack". (This is not relevant here.);

CHAPTER TEN

The Assembler "Trap" Routine

The principal purpose of this chapter is to examine the assembly language code in "m40.s" which is involved in the handling of interrupts and traps.

This code is found between lines 0750 and 0805, and has two entry points, "trap" (0755) and "call" (0766). There are several different and relevant paths through this code and we shall trace some examples of these.

Sources of Traps and Interrupts

The discussion in Section One introduced three places where the occurrence

0757: "nofault" contains the address of "err" and is non-zero;

0765: Moving 1 to SR0 reinitialises the memory management unit;

0766: The contents of "nofault" are moved on top of the stack, overwriting the previous contents, which was the return address in "gword";

0767: The "rtt" returns, not to "gword" but to the first word of "err";

0880: "err" restores "nofault" and PS, skips the return to "fuiword", places -1 in r0, and returns directly to the calling routine.

Interrupts

Suppose the clock has interrupted the processor.

Both clock vector locations, 100 and 104, have the same information. PC is set to the address of the location labelled "kwlp" (0568) and PS is set to show:

```
present mode  = kernel mode
previous mode = kernel or user mode
priority      = 6
```

Note. The PS will contain the true previous mode, regardless of the value picked up from the vector location.

0570: The vector location contains a new PC value which is the address of the statement labelled "kwlp". This instruction is a subroutine call on "call" via r0.

After the execution of this instruction, r0 is left with the address of the code word after the instruction which contains "_clock", i.e. r0 contains the address of the address of the "clock" routine in the file "clock.c" (3725).

call (0776)

0777: Copy PS onto the stack;

0779: Copy r1 onto the stack;

0780: Copy the stack pointer for the previous address space onto the stack. (This is only significant if the previous mode was user mode).

This represents a special case of the "mfpi" instruction. See the "PDP11 Processor Handbook", page 6-20;

0781: Copy the copy of PS onto the stack and mask out all but the lower five bits. The resulting value designates the cause of the interrupt (or trap). The original value of the PS had to be captured quickly;

0783: Test if the previous mode is kernel or user.

If the previous mode is kernel mode the branch is taken (0784). PS is changed to show the previous mode as user mode (0798);

0799: The specialised interrupt handling routine pointed to by r0 is entered. (In this case it is the routine "clock", which is discussed in detail in the next chapter.)

0800: When the "clock" routine (or some other interrupt handler) returns, the top two words of the stack are deleted. These are the masked copy of the PS and the copy of the stack pointer;

0802: r1 is restored from the stack;

0803: Delete the copy of PS from the stack;

0804: Restore the value of r0 from the stack;

0805: Finally the "rtt" instruction returns to the "kernel" mode

routine that was interrupted;

If the previous mode was user mode it is not certain that the interrupted routine will be resumed immediately;

0788: After the specialised interrupt routine (in this case "clock") returns, a check ("runrun > 0") is made to see if any process of higher priority than the current process is ready to run. If the decision is to allow the current process to continue, then it is important that it be not interrupted as it restores its registers prior to the "return from interrupt" instruction. Hence before the test, the processor priority is raised to seven (line 0787), thus ensuring that no more interrupts occur until user mode is resumed. (Another interrupt may occur immediately thereafter, however.)

If "runrun > 0", then another, higher priority, process is waiting. The processor priority is reset to 0, allowing any pending interrupt to be taken. A call is then made to "swtch" (2178), to allow the higher priority process to proceed. When the process returns from "swtch", the program loops back to repeat the test.

The above discussion obviously extends to all interrupts. The only part which relates specifically to the clock interrupt is the call on the specialised routine "clock".

User Program Traps

The "system call" mechanism which enables user mode programs to call on the operating system for assistance, involves the execution by the user mode program of one of 256 versions of the "trap" instruction. (The "version" is the value of the low order byte of the instruction word.)

tion in a user mode program causes a trap to occur to vector location 34 which causes the PC to be loaded with the value of the label "trap" (lines 0512, 0755). A new PS is set which indicates

    present mode = kernel mode
    previous mode = user mode
    priority   = 7

0756: The next instruction executed is the first instruction of "trap". This saves the processor status word in the stack two words beyond the current "top of stack".

It is important to save the PS as soon as possible, before it can be changed, since it contains information defining the type of trap that occurred. The somewhat unconventional destination of the "move" is to provide compatibility with the handling of interrupts, so that the same code can be used further on;

0757: "nofault" will be zero so the branch is not taken;

0759: The memory management status registers are stored just in case they will be needed, and the memory management unit is reinitialised;

0762: A subroutine entry is made to "call1" using r0. (This neatly stores the old value of r0 in the stack, but not a return address. The new value is the address of the address of the routine to be entered next (in this case the "trap" routine in the file "trap.c" (2693));

0772: The stack pointer is adjusted to point to the location which already contains the copy of PS;

0773: The CPU priority is set to zero;

0774: A branch is taken to the second instruction of "call".

From here the same path as for an interrupt is followed.

The Kernel Stack

The state of the kernel stack at the time that the "trap" procedure ("C" version) or one of the specialised interrupt handling routines is entered, is shown in Figure 10.1.

					previous top of stack
(rps	2)	7	ps	old PS	
(r7	1)	6	pc	old PC (r7)	
(r0	0)	5->	r0	old r0	
		4	nps	new PS after trap	
(rl	-2)	3	rl	old rl	
(r6	-3)	2	sp	old SP for previous mode	
		1	dev	masked new PS	
		0->	tpc	return address in "call"	
(r5	-6)	-1	(r5)	old r5	
(r4	-7)	-2	(r4)	old r4	
(r3	-8)	-3	(r3)	old r3	
(r2	-9)	-4	(r2)	old r2	

(1)   (2)   (3)   (4)   (5)
                   stack

Figure 10.1

Columns (2) and (3) give the positions of stack words relative to the positions in the stack of the words labelled "r0" and "tpc" respectively.

Columns (1) and (2) define (or explain) the contents of the file "reg.h" (Sheet 26).

"dev", "sp", "rl", "nps" "r0", "pc" and "ps" in that order are the names of the parameters used in the declaration of the procedures "trap" (2693) and "clock" (3725).

Note that just before entry to "trap" ("C" version) or the other interrupt handling routines, the values for the registers r2, r3, r4 and r5 have not yet been saved in the stack. This is performed by a call on "csv" (1420) which is automatically included by the "C" compiler at the beginning of every compiled procedure. The form of the call on "csv" is equivalent to the assembler instruction

        jsr r5,csv

This saves the current value of r5 on the stack and replaces it by the address of the next instruction in the "C" procedure.

1421: This value of r5 is copied into r0;

1422: the current value of the stack pointer is copied into r5.

Note that at this point, r5 points to a stack location containing the previous value of r5 i.e. it points to the beginning of a chain of pointers, one per procedure, which "thread" the stack. When a "C" procedure exits, it actually returns to "cret" (1430) where the value of r5 is used to restore the stack and r2, r3 and r4 to their earlier condition (i.e. as they were immediately prior to entering the procedure). For this reason r5 is often called the environment pointer.

                  -oOo-

The procedure "clock" (3725) handles interrupts from either the line frequency time clock (type KW11-L, interrupt vector address 100) or the programmable real-time clock (type KW11-P, interrupt vector address 104).

UNIX requires that at least one of these should be available. (If both are present, only the line time clock is used.)

Whichever clock is used, interrupts are generated at line frequency (i.e. with a 50 Hz power supply, every 20 milliseconds). The clock interrupt priority level is six, higher than for any other peripheral device on our typical system, so that there will usually be very little delay in the initiation of "clock" once the interrupt has been requested by the clock controller.

clock (3725)

The function of "clock" is one of general housekeeping:

the display register is updated (PDP11/45 and 11/70 only);

various accounting values such as the time of day, accumulated processing times and execution profiles are maintained;

processes sleeping for a fixed time interval are awakened as per schedule;

core swapping activity is initiated once per second.

"clock" breaks most of the rules for peripheral device handlers: it does reference the current "u" structure, and it also runs at a low priority for some of the time. It abbreviates its activity if a previous execution has not yet completed.

3740: "display" is a no-op on the PDP11/40;

3743: The array "callout" (0265) is an array of "NCALL" (0143) structures of type "callo" (0260). The "callo" structure contains three elements: an incremental time, an argument and the address of a function. When the function element is not null, the function is to be executed with the supplied argument after a specified time.

(For the systems under study, the only function ever executed in this way is "ttrstrt" (8486), which is part of the teletype handler. (See Chapter 25.));

3748: If the first element of the list is null, the whole list is null;

3750: The "callout" list is arranged in the desired order of execution. The time recorded is the number of clock ticks between events. Unless the first time (the time before the next event) is already zero, (meaning that the execution is already due) this time should be decremented by one.

If this time has already been counted to zero, decrement the next time unless it is already zero also, etc. i.e. decrement the first non-zero time in the list. All the leading entries with zero times represent operations which are already due. (The operations are actually carried out a little later.);

3759: Examine the previous processor status word, and if the priority was non-zero, bypass the next section, which executes those operations which are due;

3766: Reduce the processor priority to five (other level six interrupts may now occur);

3767: Search the "callout" array looking for operations which are due and execute them;

3773: Move the entries for operations which are still not yet due, to the beginning of the array;

3787: The code from here until line 3797 is executed, whatever the previous processor priority, at either priority level five or six;

3788: If the previous mode was "user mode", then increment the user time counter, and if an execution profile is being accumulated, call "incupc" (0895) to make an entry in a histogram for the user mode program counter (PC).

"incupc" is written in Assembler, presumably for efficiency and convenience. A description of what it does may be found in the section "PROFIL(II)" of the UPM. See also the procedure "profil" (3667);

3792: If the previous mode was not user mode, increment the system (kernel) time counter for the process.

basic time accounting for the system. Every clock tick results in the incrementing of either "u.u_utime" or "u.u_stime" for some process. Both "u.u_utime" and "u.u_stime" are initialised to zero in "fork" (3322). Their values are interrogated in "wait" (3270). The values will go negative after 32K ticks (about 10 hours)!

3795: "p_cpu" is used in determining process priorities. It is a character value which is always interpreted as a positive integer (0 to 255). When it is moved to a special register, sign extension occurs so that 255, for instance, becomes like -1. Adding one then leaves a zero result. In this case the value is reduced to -1 again, and stored as 255 unsigned. Note that in the other places where "p_cpu" is referenced (2161, 3814), the top eight bits are masked off after the value has been transferred to a special register;

3797: Increment "lbolt" and if it exceeds "HZ", i.e. a second or more has elapsed ...

3798: Then provided the processor was not previously running at a non-zero priority, do a whole lot of housekeeping;

3800: Decrement "lbolt" by "HZ";

3801: Increment the time of day accumulator;

3803: The events which follow may take some time, but they may reasonably be interrupted to service other peripherals. So the processor priority is dropped below all the device priority levels i.e. below four.

However there is now a possibility of another clock interrupt before this activation of the "clock" procedure is completed. By setting the processor priority to one rather than to zero, a second activation of "clock" will not attempt to execute the code from line 3804 on also. Note however that to the hardware, priority one is functionally the same as priority zero;

3804: If the current time (measured in seconds) is equal to the value stored in "tout", wake all processes which have elected to suspend themselves for a period of time via the "sleep" system call i.e. via the procedure "sslep" (5979).

"tout" stores the time at which the next process is to be awakened. If there is more than one such process, then the remainder, which will have been disturbed, must reset "tout" between them. This mechanism, while quite effective, will not be efficient if the number of such processes ever becomes large.

In this situation, a mechanism similar to the "callout" array (see 3767) would need to be provided. (In fact, how difficult would it be to merge the two mechanisms? What would be the disadvantages ??);

3806: When the last two bits of "time[1]" are zero i.e. every four seconds, reset the scheduling flag "runrun" and wake up everything waiting for a "lightning bolt". ("lbolt" represents a general event which is caused every four seconds, to initiate miscellaneous housekeeping. It is used by "pcopen" (8648).);

3810: For all currently defined processes:

increment "p_time" up to a maximum of 127 (it is only a character variable);

decrement "p_cpu" by "SCHMAG" (3707) but do not allow it to go negative. Note that as discussed earlier (line 3795) "p_cpu" is

treated as a positive integer in the range 0 to 255;

if the processor priority is currently set at a depressed level, recalculate it.

Note that "p_cpu" enters into the calculation of process priorities, "p_pri", by "setpri" (2156). "p_pri" is used by "swtch" (2209) in choosing which process, from among those which are in core ("SLOAD") and ready to run ("SRUN"), should next receive the CPU's attention.

"p_time" is used to measure how long (in seconds) a process has been either in core or swapped out to disk. "p_time" is set to zero by "newproc" (1869), by "sched" (2047) and by "xswap" (4386). It is used by "sched" (1962, 2009) to determine which processes to swap in or out.

3820: If the scheduler is waiting to rearrange things, wake it up. Thus the normal rate for scheduling decisions is once per second;

3824: If the previous mode before the interrupt was "user mode", store the address of "r0" in a standard place, and if a "signal" has been received for the process, call "psig" (4043) for the appropriate action.

timeout (3845)

This procedure makes new entries in the "callout" array. In this system it is only called from the routine "ttstart" (8505), passing the procedure "ttrstrt" (8486). Note that "ttrstrt" calls "ttstart", which may call "timeout", for a thoroughly incestuous relationship!

Note also that most of "timeout" runs at priority level seven, to avoid clock interrupts.

CHAPTER TWELVE

Traps and System Calls

This chapter is concerned with the way
the system handles traps in general and
system calls in particular.

There are quite a number of conditions
which can cause the processor to
"trap". Many of these are quite
clearly error conditions, such as
hardware or power failures, and UNIX
does not attempt any sophisticated
recovery procedures for these.

The initial focus for our attention is
the principal procedure in the file
"trap.c".

trap (2693)

The way that this procedure is invoked
was explored in Chapter Ten. The
assembler "trap" routine carries out
certain fundamental housekeeping tasks
to set up the kernel stack, so that
when this procedure is called, everything appears to be kosher.

The "trap" procedure can operate as
though it had been called by another
"C" procedure in the normal way with
seven parameters

dev, sp, r1, nps, r0, pc, ps.

(There is a special consideration which
should be mentioned here in passing.
Normally all parameters passed to "C"
procedures are passed by value. If the
procedure subsequently changes the
values of the parameters, this will not
affect the calling procedure directly.

However if "trap" or the interrupt
handlers change the values of their
parameters, the new values will be
picked up and reflected back when the
"previous mode" registers are
restored.)

The value of "dev" was obtained by cap-
turing the value of the processor
status word immediately after the trap
and masking out all but the lower five
bits. Immediately before this, the processor status word had been set using
the prototype contained in the
appropriate vector location.

Thus if the second word of the vector
location was "br7+n;" (e.g. line 0516)
then the value of "dev" will be n.

2698: "savfp" saves the floating point
registers (for the PDP11/40, this
is a no-op!);

2700: If the previous mode is "user
mode", the value of "dev" is
modified by the addition of the
octal value 020 (2662);

2701: The stack address where r0 is
stored is noted in "u.u_ar0" for
future reference. (Subsequently
the various register values can
be referenced as "u.u_ar0[Rn]".);

2702: There is now a multi-way "switch"
depending on the value of "dev".

At this point we can observe that UNIX
divides traps into three classes,
depending on the prior processor mode
and the source of the trap:

(A)   kernel mode;

(B)   user mode, not due to a "trap"
      instruction;

(C)   user mode, due to a "trap"
      instruction.

Kernel Mode Traps

The trap is unexpected and with one
exception, the reaction is to "panic".
The code executed is the "default" of
the "switch" statement:

2716: Print:

the current value of the seventh
kernel segment address register
(i.e. the address of the current
per process data area);

the address of "ps" (which is in
the kernel stack); and

the trap type number;

2719: "panic", with no return.

Floating point operations are only used
by programs, and not by the operating
system. Since such operations on the
PDP11/45 and 11/70 are handled asynchronously, it is possible that when a
floating point exception occurs, the
processor may have already switched to
kernel mode to handle an interrupt.

Thus a kernel mode floating point
exception trap can be expected occasionally and is the concern of the
current user program.

flag to show that a floating point exception has occurred;

2794: Return.

This raises an interesting question: "Why are the kernel mode and user mode floating point exceptions handled slightly differently?"

User Mode Traps

Consider first of all a trap which is not generated as the result of the execution of a "trap" instruction. This is regarded as a probable error for which the operating system makes no provision apart from the possibility of a "core dump". However the user program itself may have anticipated it and provided for it.

The way this provision is made and implemented is the subject of the next chapter. At this stage, the principal requirement is to "signal" that the trap has occurred.

2721: A bus error has occurred while the system is in user mode. Set "i" to the value "SIGBUS" (0123);

2723: The "break" causes a branch out of the "switch" statement to line 2818;

2733: Apart from the one special case noted, the treatment of illegal instructions is the same at this level as for bus errors;

2739:
2743:
2747:
2796: Cf. the comment for line 2721.

Note that cases "4+USER" (power fail) and "7+USER" (programmed interrupt) are handled by the "default" case (line 2715).

2810: This represents a case where operating system assistance is required to extend the user mode stack area.

The assembler routine "backup" (1012) is used to reconstruct the situation that existed before execution of the instruction that caused the trap.

"grow" (4136) is used to do the actual extension.

The procedure "backup" is non-trivial and its comprehension involves a careful consideration of various aspects of the PDP11 architecture. It has been left for the interested reader to pursue privately.

As noted for the PDP11/40, "backup" may not always succeed because the processor does not save enough information to resolve all possibilities.

2818: Call "psignal" (3963) to set the appropriate "signal". (Note that this statement is only reached from those cases of the "switch" which included a "break" statement.);

2821: "issig" checks if a "signal" has been sent to the user program, either just now or at some earlier time and has not yet been attended to;

2822: "psig" performs the appropriate actions. (Both "issig" and "psig" are discussed in detail in the next chapter.);

2823: Recalculate the priority for the current process.

System Calls

User mode programs use "trap" instructions as part of the "system call" mechanism to call upon the operating system for assistance.

Since there are many possible "versions" of the "trap" instruction, the type of assistance requested can be and is encoded as part of the "trap" instruction.

Parameters which are part of a system call may be passed from the user program in different ways:

(a) via the special register r0;

(b) as a set of words embedded in the program string following the "trap" instruction;

(c) as a set of words in the program's data area. (This is the "indirect" call.)

Indirect calls have a higher overhead than direct system calls. Indirect calls are needed when the parameters are data dependent and cannot be determined at compile time.

Indirect calls may sometimes be avoided if there is only one data dependent parameter, which is passed via r0. In choosing which parameters should be passed via r0, the system designers have presumably been guided by their own experience, since the pattern doesn't satisfy the law of least astonishment.

The "C" compiler does not give special recognition to system calls, but treats them in the same way as other procedures. When the loader comes to resolve undetermined references, it satisfies these with library routines which contain the actual "trap" instructions.

2752: The error indicators are reset;

2754: The user mode instruction which caused the trap is retrieved and all but the least significant six bits are masked off. The result is used to select an entry from the array of structures, "sysent". The address of the selected entry is stored in "callp";

2755: The "zeroeth" system call is the "indirect" system call, in which the parameter passed is actually the address in the user program data space of a system call parameter sequence.

Note the separate uses of "fuword" and "fuiword". The distinction between these is unimportant on the PDP11/40, but is most important on machines with separate "i" and "d" address spaces;

2760: "i=077" simulates a call on the very last system call (2975), which results in a call on "nosys" (2855), which results in an error condition which will usually be fatal for the user mode program;

2762:
2765: The number of arguments specified in "sysent" is the actual number provided by the user programmer, or that number less one if one argument is transferred via r0. The arguments are copied from the user data or instruction area into the five element array "u.u_arg". (From "sysent" (Sheet 29) it would seem that four elements would have been sufficient for "u_arg[ ]" - is this an allowance for future inflation?);

2770: The value of the first argument is copied into "u.u_dirp", which seems to function mainly as a convenient temporary storage location;

2771: "trap1" is called with the address of the desired system routine. Note the comment beginning on line 2828;

2776: When an error occurs, the "c-bit" in the old processor status word is set (see line 2658) and the error number is returned via r0.

System Call Handlers

The full set of system calls may be reviewed in the file "sysent.c" on Sheet 29, but more relevantly, these are discussed in full detail in Section II of the UPM.

The procedures which handle the system calls are found mostly in the files "sys1.c", sys2.c", sys3.c" and "sys4.c".

Two important "trivial" procedures are "nullsys" (2855) and "nosys" (2864) which are found in the file "trap.c".

The File 'sys1.c'

This file contains the procedures for five system calls, of which three will be considered now, and two ("rexit" and "wait") will be deferred to the next chapter.

The first procedure in this file, and also the first system call we have encountered, is "exec".

exec (3020)

This system call, #11, changes a process executing one program into a process executing a different program. See Section "EXEC(II)" of the UPM. This is the longest and one of the most important system calls.

3034: "namei" (6618) (which is discussed in detail in Chapter 19) converts the first argument (which is a pointer to a character string defining the name of the new program) into an "inode" reference. ("inodes" are essential parts of the file referencing mechanism.);

3037: Wait if the number of "exec"s currently under way is too large. (See the comment on line 3011.);

3040: "getblk(NODEV)" results in the allocation of a 512 byte buffer from the pool of buffers. This buffer is used temporarily to store in core, that information which is currently in the user data area, and which is needed to start the new program. Note that the second argument in "u.u_arg" is a pointer to this information;

3041: "access" returns a non-zero result if the file is not executable. The second condition examines whether the file is a directory or a special character file. (It would seem that by making this test earlier, e.g. just after line 3036, the efficiency of the code could be improved.);

3052: Copy the set of arguments from the user space into the temporary buffer;

3064: If the argument string is too large to fit in the buffer, take an error exit;

3071: If the number of characters in the argument string is odd, add an extra, null character;

3090: The first four words (8 bytes) of the named file are read into "u.u_arg". The interpretation of these words is indicated in the comment beginning on line 3076 and, more fully, in the section "A.OUT(V)" of the UPM.

Note the setting of "u.u_base", "u.u_count", "u.u_offset" and "u.u_segflg" preparatory to the read operation;

3095: If the text segment is not to be protected, add the text area size to the data area size, and set the former to zero;

3105: Check whether the program has a "pure" text area, but the program file has already been opened by some other program as a data file. If so, take the error exit;

decision to execute the new program is irrevocable i.e. there is no longer the opportunity to return to the original program with an error flag set;

3129: "expand" here actually implies a major contraction, to the "per process data" area only;

3130: "xalloc" takes care of allocating (if necessary) and linking to the text area;

3158: The information stored in the buffer area is copied into the stack in the user data area of the new program;

3186: The locations in the kernel stack which contain copies of the "previous" values of the registers in user mode are set to zero, except for r6, the stack pointer, which was set at line 3155;

3194: Decrement the reference count for the "inode" structure;

3195: Release the temporary buffer;

3196: Wake up any other process waiting at line 3037.

fork (3322)

A call on "exec" is frequently preceded by a call on "fork". Most of the work for "fork" is done by "newproc" (1826), but before the latter is called, "fork" makes an independent search for a slot in the "proc" array, and remembers the place as "p2" (3327).

"newproc" also searches "proc" but independently. Presumably it always locates the same empty slot as "fork", since it does not report the value back. (Why is there no confusion on this point?)

3335: for the new process, "fork" returns the value of the parent's process identification, and initialises various accounting parameters;

3344: For the parent process, "fork" returns the value of the child's process identification, and skips the user mode program counter by one word.

Note that the values finally returned to a "C" program are slightly different from the above. Refer to the section "FORK(II)" of the UPM.

sbreak (3354)

This procedure implements system call #17 which is described in the Section "BREAK (II)" of the UPM. The comment at the head of the procedure has confused more than one reader: clearly the identifier "break" is used in "C" programs (leave an enclosing program loop) in an entirely different way from that intended here (change the size of the program data area).

"sbreak" has clear similarities with the procedure "grow" (4136) but unlike the latter, it is only invoked explicitly and may in fact cause a contraction of the data area as well as an expansion (depending on the new desired size).

3364: Calculate the new size for the data area (in 32 word blocks);

3371: Check that the new size is consistent with the memory segmentation constraints;

3376: The area is shrinking. Copy the stack area down into the former data area. Call "expand" to trim off the excess;

3386: Call "expand" to increase the total area. Copy the stack area up into the new part, and clear

the areas which were formerly occupied by the stack.

The following procedures which are also contained in "sys1.c" are described in Chapter 13:

rexit   (3205)   wait   (3270)
exit   (3219)

The Files 'sys2.c' and 'sys3.c'

"sys2.c" and "sys3.c" are mainly concerned with the file system and input/output, and they have been relegated to Section Four of the operating system source code.

The File 'sys4.c'

All the procedures in this file implement system calls. The following procedures are described in Chapter 13:

ssig   (3614)   kill   (3630)

The following procedures are straightforward and have been left for the amusement and edification of the reader:

getswit (3413)   sync   (3486)
gtime   (3420)   getgid (3472)
stime   (3428)   getpid (3480)
setuid (3439)   nice   (3493)
getuid (3452)   times   (3656)
setgid (3460)   profil (3667)

The following procedures which are concerned with file systems, are described later:

unlink (3510)   chown   (3575)
chdir   (3538)   smdate (3595)
chmod   (3560)

-oOo-

CHAPTER THIRTEEN

Software Interrupts

The principal concern of this chapter
is the content of the file "sig.c",
which appears on Sheets 39 to 42. This
file introduces a facility for communication between processes. In particular
it provides for the course of one "user
mode" process to be interrupted,
diverted or terminated by the action of
another process or as the result of an
error or operator action.

In this discussion the term "software
interrupt" has been deliberately used
in place of the term "signal". This
latter has been eschewed because it has
obtained connotations in the UNIX
milieu which are rather different from
the usage of ordinary English.

UNIX recognises 20 ("NSIG", line 0113)
different types of software interrupts,
of which (as the reader may discover
for himself by perusal of the the Section "SIGNAL (II)" of the UPM) thirteen
have standard names and associations.
Interrupt type #0 is interpreted as "no
interrupt".

Within the "per process data area" of
each process is an array, "u.u_signal",
of "NSIG" words. Each word corresponds
to a different software interrupt type
and defines the action which should be
taken if the process encounters that
kind of software interrupt:

u_signal[n]	when interrupt #n occurs
===========	=========================
zero	the process will terminate itself;
odd non-zero	the software interrupt is ignored;
even non-zero	the value is taken as the address in user space of a procedure which should be executed forthwith.

Interrupt type #9 ("SIGKIL") is especially distinguished because UNIX
ensures that "u.u_signal[9]" remains
zero until the very end of a process's
existence, so that if a process is ever
interrupted for that reason, it will
always terminate itself.

Anticipation

Each process can set the contents of
the array "u.u_signal[]" (with the
exception of "u.u_signal[9]" as just
noted) in anticipation of future interrupts so that the appropriate action is
taken. The user programmer does this
via the "signal" system call (see "SIG-
NAL (II)" of the UPM).

Thus if for example the programmer
wishes to ignore software interrupts of
type #2 (which result if the user hits
the "delete" key on his terminal), he
should set "u.u_signal[2]" to one by
executing the system call

"signal (2,1);"

from his "C" program.

Causation

An interrupt is "caused" for a process
quite simply by setting the value of
"p_sig" (0363) in the process's "proc"
entry, to the type number appropriate
to the interrupt (i.e. a value in the
range 1 to "NSIG"-1).

"p_sig" is always directly accessible,
even when the affected process and its
"per process data area" have been
swapped out to disk. Obviously this
mechanism only allows one interrupt per
process to be outstanding at any one
time. The outstanding interrupt will
always be the most recent one, unless
one of the interrupts was of type #9,
which always prevails.

Effect

The effect of a software interrupt
never takes place immediately. It may
occur after only some slight delay if
the affected process is currently running, or possibly after a considerable
delay if the affected process is
suspended and has been swapped out.

The action dictated by the interrupt is
always inflicted on the affected process by _itself_, and hence can only
occur when the affected process is
active.

Where the effect is to execute a user
defined procedure, the kernel mode process adjusts the user mode stack to

been entered and immediately interrupted (hardware style) before executing the first instruction. The system
then returns from kernel mode to user
mode in the usual manner. The result
of all this is that the next user mode
instruction which is executed is the
first instruction of the designated
procedure.

Tracing

The software interrupt facility has
been extended to provide a powerful but
somewhat inefficient mechanism whereby
a parent process may monitor the progress of one or more child processes.

Procedures

Since the interrelationships of the
procedures associated with software
interrupts are somewhat confusing at
first sight, it is worthwhile introduc-
ing the procedures briefly before
plunging in with both feet ....

A. Anticipation

"ssig" (3614) implements system call
#48 ("signal") to set the value in one
element of the array "u.u_signal".

B. Causation

"kill" (3630) implements system call
#37 ("kill") to cause a specified
interrupt to a process defined by its
process identifying number.

"signal" (3949) causes a specified
interrupt to be caused for all
processes controlled and/or initiated
from a specified terminal.

"psignal" (3963) is called by "kill"
(3649) and "signal" (3955) (also "trap"
(2793, 2818) and "pipe" (7828)) to do
the actual setting of "p_sig".

C. Effect

"issig" (3991) is called by "sleep"
(2073, 2085), "trap" (2821) and "clock"
(3826) to enquire whether there is an
outstanding non-ignorable software
interrupt for the active process "just
waiting to happen".

"psig" (4043) is called whenever
"issig" returns a non-zero result
(except in "sleep" where things are a
little more complex) to implement the
action triggered by the interrupt.

"core" (4094) is called by "psig" if a
core dump is indicated for a terminating process.

"grow" (4136) is called by "psig" to
enlarge the user mode stack area if
necessary.

"exit" (3219) terminates the currently
active process.

D. Tracing

"ptrace" (4164) implements the "ptrace"
system call #26.

"stop" (4016) is called by "issig"
(3999) for a process which is being
traced to allow the supervising parent
to have a "look-see".

"procxmt" (4204) is a procedure called
from "stop" (4028) whereby the child
carries out certain operations related
to tracing, at the behest of the
parent.

ssig (3614)

This procedure implements the "signal"
system call.

3619: If the interrupt reason is out of
range or is equal to "SIGKIL"
(9), take an error exit;

3623: Capture the initial value in
"u.u_signal[a]" for return as the
result of the system call;

3624: Set the element of "u.u_signal"
to the desired value ...

3625: If an interrupt for the current
reason is pending, cancel it. (It
is not clear why this step should
be necessary or even desirable.
Any suggestions??)

kill (3630)

This procedure implements the "kill"
system call to cause a specified type
of software interrupt to another designated process.

3637: If "a" is non-zero, it is the
process identifying number of a
process to be interrupted. If
"a" is zero, then all processes
originating from the same terminal as the current process are to
be interrupted;

3639: Consider each entry in the "proc"
table in turn and reject it if:
it is the current process (3640);
it is not the designated process
(3642);
no particular process was designated ("a" == 0) but it does not
have the same controlling terminal, or it is one of the two initial processes (3644);
the user is not the "super user"
and the user identities do not
match (3646);

3649: For any process that survives the
above tests, call "psignal" to
change "p_sig".

signal (3949)

For every process, if it is controlled by the specified terminal (denoted by "tp"), hit it with "psignal".

psignal (3963)

3966: Reject the call if "sig" is too large (but why not if negative?? "kill" does not check this parameter before passing it to "psignal". Admittedly the "kill" command could only result in a positive value for "sig" ...);

3971: If the current value of "p_sig" is NOT set to "SIGKIL", then overwrite it (i.e. once a process has been "killed outright" there is no way to revive it.);

3973: Seems to be an error here ... for "p_stat" read "p_pri" ... improve the priority of the process if it is not too good;

3975: If the process is waiting for a non-kernel event i.e. it called "sleep" (2066) with a positive priority, then set it running again.

issig (3991)

3997: If "p_sig" is non-zero, then ...

3998: If the "tracing" flag is on, call "stop" (this topic will be resumed later);

4000: Return a zero value if "p_sig" is zero. (This apparently redundant test is necessary because "stop" may reset "p_sig" as a side effect.);

4003: If the value in the corresponding element of "u.u_signal" is even (may be zero) return a non-zero value;

4006: Otherwise return a zero value.

The comment regarding the frequency of calls on "issig" which occurs on lines 3983 to 3985 needs some clarification. At least one call on "issig" is a part of every execution of "trap" but only of one interrupt routine ("clock", which calls "issig" only once per second). In cases where "pri" is positive, "sleep" (2073, 2085) calls "issig" before and after calling "swtch".

psig (4043)

This procedure is only called if "u.u_signal[n]" was found by "issig" to have an even value. If this value is found (4051) to be non-zero, it is taken as the address of a user mode function which has to be executed.

4054: Reset "u.u_signal[n]" except in the case where the interrupt is for an illegal instruction or a trace trap;

4055: Calculate the user space addresses of the lower of two words which are to be inserted into the user mode stack ...

4056: Call "grow" to check the current user mode stack size, and to extend it (downwards!) if necessary;

4057: Put the values of the processor status register and the program counter which were captured at the time of the "trap" or hardware interrupt (in the case of a "clock" interrupt) into the user stack, and update the "remembered" values of r6, r7 and the processor status word. Upon returning to user mode, execution will resume at the beginning of the designated procedure. When this procedure returns, the procedure which was originally interrupted will be resumed;

4066: If "u.u_signal[n]" is zero, then for the interrupt types listed, generate a core image via the procedure "core";

4079: Store a value in "u.u_arg[0]" composed of the low order byte of the remembered value of r0, and of "n", which records the interrupt type and whether a core image was successfully created;

4080: Call "exit" for the process to terminate itself.

core (4094)

This procedure copies the swappable program image into a file called "core" in the user's current directory. A detailed explanation of this procedure must wait until the material of Sections Three and Four, which deal with input/output and file systems, have been covered.

grow (4136)

The parameter, "sp", of this procedure defines the address of a word which should be included in the user mode stack.

4141: If the stack already extends far enough, simply return with a zero value.

Note that this test relies on the idiosyncrasies of 2's complement arithmetic, and if both

$$|sp| > 2^{15}$$

and

$$|u.u\_size * 64| > 2^{15}$$

the decision to extend the stack may be taken wrongly at this juncture;

4143: Calculate the stack size increment needed to include the new stack point plus a 20*32 word margin;

positive (i.e. we are not dealing
with a failure of the test on
line 4141.);

4146: Check that the new stack size
does not conflict with the memory
segmentation constraints ("estabur" sets "u.u_error" if they do)
and reset the segmentation register prototypes;

4148: Get a new, enlarged data area,
copy the stack segments (32 words
at a time) into the high end of
the new data area, and clear the
segments which now become the
stack expansion;

4156: Update the stack size,
"u.u_ssize" and return a "successful" result.

exit (3219)

This procedure is called when a process
is to terminate itself.

3224: Reset the "tracing" flag;

3225: Set all of the values in the
array "u.u_signal" (including
"u.u_signal[SIGKIL]") to one so
that no future execution of
"issig" will ever be followed by
execution of "psig";

3227: Call "closef" (6643) to close all
the files which the process has
open. (For the most part, "closing" simply involves decrementing
a reference count.);

3232: Reduce the reference count for
the current directory;

3233: Sever the process's connection
with any text segment;

3234: A place is needed to store "per
process" information until the
parent process can look at it. A
block (256 words) in the swap
area of the disk is a convenient
place;

3237: Find a suitable buffer (256
words) and ...

3238: Copy the lower half of the "u"
structure into the buffer area;

3239: Write the buffer into the swap
area;

3241: Enter the core space occupied by
the process into the free list.
(This space is of course still in
use, but the use will terminate
before any other process gets to
dip into the free list again.
This could not be done any
sooner, because, as will be seen
later, both "getblk" and "bwrite"
can call "sleep", during which
all sorts of things might happen.
In view of all this, it might be
reasonable if the statement
        "expand (USIZE);"
were inserted after line 3226.);

3243: Set the process state to "zombie"
(i.e. "a corpse said to be
revived by witchcraft" (O.E.D.));

3245: The remaining code searches the
"proc" array to find the parent
process and to wake it up, to
make any children "wards of the
state", and, if they have
"stopped" for tracing, to release
them. Finally the code includes
(for this process) a last call on
"swtch".

Before going on to consider tracing,
there are two routines which are
closely associated with "exit", which
can be conveniently disposed of now.

rexit (3205)

This procedure implements the "exit"
system call, #1. It simply salvages the
low order byte of the user supplied
parameter and saves it in "u.u_arg[0]"

which is in the lower half of the "u"
structure i.e. the part that is written
to the "swap area" as a "zombie".

wait (3270)

For every call on "exit", there should
be a matching call on "wait" by an anx-
ious parent or ancestor. The principal
function of the latter procedure, which
implements the "wait" system call, is
for the parent or ancestor to find and
dispose of a "zombie" child.

"wait" also has a secondary function,
to look for children which have
"stopped" for tracing (which is the
next major topic).

3277: Search the whole "proc" array
looking for child processes. (If
none exist, take an error exit
(line 3317));

3280: If the child is a "zombie":

save the child's process identifying number, to report back to
the parent;

read the 256 word record back
from the disk swap area, and
release the swap space;

reinitialise the "proc" array
entry;

accumulate the various time
accounting entries;

save the "u_arg[0]" value also to
report back to the parent;

3298: Finally, release the buffer area;

3300: Is the child in a "stopped"
state? (If so, wait for the discussion on tracing);

3313: If one or more children were
found but none were "zombies" or
"stopped", "sleep" and then look
again.

Tracing

The tracing facilities are provided through a modification and extension of the software interrupt facilities. Briefly, if a parent process is tracing the progress of child process, every time the child process encounters a software interrupt, the parent process is given the opportunity to intervene as part of the total response to the interrupt.

The parent's intervention may involve interrogation of values within the child process's data areas, including the "per process data area". Subject to certain constraints, the parent process may also change values within these data areas.

The source of the software interrupts may be the parent process, the user himself (e.g. by entering "kill" commands or "delete"s through his terminal) or the child process itself (e.g. if it is prone to executing illegal instructions or other maladies).

The communication between child and parent processes is a kind of ritual dance:

(1) the child experiences a software interrupt and "stops";

(2) the waiting parent discovers the "stopped" child (line 3301), and revives. Subsequently ...

(3) the parent may execute the "ptrace" system call which has the effect of leaving a request message in the system defined structure "ipc" (3939) for the child process;

(4) the parent then goes to "sleep" while the child "wakes up";

(5) the child reads the message in "ipc" and acts upon it (e.g. copying one of its own values into "ipc.ip_data");

(6) the child then goes to "sleep" while the parent "wakes up";

(7) the parent inspects the result, as recorded in "ipc", of the operation;

(8) steps (3) to (7) may be repeated several times in succession.

Finally the parent may allow the child to continue its normal execution, possibly without ever knowing that a software interrupt had occurred.

A discussion of the tracing facility is contained in the Section "PTRACE (II)" of the UPM. To the list of functional limitations noted in the "Bugs" paragraph, we can add the following comments on efficiency:

There should be a mechanism for transferring large blocks (e.g. up to 256 words at a time) of information from the child to the parent (though not necessarily in the reverse direction);

There should be a proper coroutine procedure (analogous to "swtch") to allow rapid transfer of control between child and parent.

stop (4016)

This procedure is called by "issig" (3999) if the tracing flag ("STRC", 0395) is set.

4022: If your parent is process #1 (i.e. "/etc/init"), then call "exit" (line 4032);

4023: Otherwise look through "proc" for your parent ... wake him up ... declare yourself "stopped" and ... call "swtch" (Note do **NOT** call "sleep". Why?);

4028: If the tracing flag has been reset, or the result of the procedure "procxmt" is true, return to "issig";

4029: Otherwise start again.

wait (3270) (continued)

3301: If the child process has "stopped" and ...

3302: If the "SWTED" flag is not set (i.e. the parent hasn't noticed this child lately) ...

3303: As an "aide-memoire" set the "SWTED" flag. Set "u.u_ar0[R0]", "u.u_ar0[R1]" so that the child process status word is returned to the parent;

3309: The "SWTED" flag was set. This means that the parent, by performing at least two "waits" in succession without any intervening call on "ptrace", is not very interested in the child. So reset both the "STRC" and the "SWTED" flags and release the child. (Note the use of "setrun" (not "wakeup") to complement the call on "swtch" (4027)).

ptrace (4164)

This procedure implements the "ptrace" system call, #26.

4168: "u.u_arg[2]" corresponds to the first parameter in the "C" program calling sequence. If this is zero, a child process is asking to be traced by its parent, so set the "STRC" flag and return.

Note that this code handles the only explicit action the child process is asked to take with respect to tracing. There is no real reason why even this action should be taken by the child process and not by the parent process.

most probably desirable that a child process should only be traceable if it gives its permission. On the other hand, if the child asks to be traced and is then ignored by the parent, the child process may be blocked indefinitely. Perhaps the best solution would be for the "STRC" flag to be set only after explicit action by _both_ the parent _and_ the child.

4172: Search the "proc" table looking for a process which:
is stopped;
matches the given process identifying number;
is a child of the current process;

4181: Wait for the "ipc" structure to become available if it is currently in use;

4183: Copy the parameters into "ipc" ...

4187: reset the "SWTED" flag, and ...

4188: return the child to a "ready to run" state;

4189: Sleep until "ipc.ip_req" is non-positive (4212);

4191: Extract a value that is to be returned to the parent process, check for errors, unlock "ipc" and "wake up" any processes waiting for "ipc".

Note that the "sleeps" on lines 4182, 4190 are for essentially different reasons, and could be differentiated to good effect by replacing "&ipc" by "&ipc.ip_req" on lines 4190 and 4213.

procxmt (4204)

This procedure is executed by the child process under the influence of data left by the parent in the "ipc" structure.

4209: If "ipc.ip_lock" is set wrongly for the current process, then certainly the rest of "ipc" should be ignored.

After "stop" (4027) calls "swtch", the child process is restarted by one of three calls on "setrun" which leave the "STRC" and "SWTED" flags in the state indicated:

		STRC	SWTED	ipc.ip_lock
exit	(3254)	set	set	arbitrary
wait	(3310)	reset	reset	arbitrary
ptrace	(4188)	set	reset	properly set

In the third case "ptrace" will always set "ipc.ip_lock" properly, before the child is restarted, so that there is then no chance of the test on 4209 failing.

In the second case, where the parent has ignored the child, "procxmt" will never in fact be called.

By executing the statement "return (0);" on line 4210, "procxmt" forces "stop" to loop back to line 4020. In the case where the parent has already died, the test on line 4022 will then fail, and a call on "exit" (4032) will result.

4211: Store the value of "ipc.ip_req" before resetting the latter, "wake up" the parent, and select the next action as indicated.

The various actions are adequately explained in Section "PTRACE (II)" of the UPM, with the one qualification that cases 1, 2 and 4, 5 are documented the wrong way around (i.e. "I" and "D" spaces respectively, not "D" and "I"!).

-oOo-

Section Three is concerned with basic input/output operations between the main memory and disk storage.

These operations are fundamental to the activities of program swapping and the creation and referencing of disk files.

This section also introduces procedures for the use and manipulation of the large (512 byte) buffers.

CHAPTER FOURTEEN

Program Swapping

UNIX, like all time-sharing systems, and some multiprogramming systems uses "program swapping" (also called "roll-in/roll-out") to share the limited resource of the main physical memory among several processes.

Processes which are suspended may be selectively "swapped out" by writing their data segments (including the "per process data") into a "swap area" on disk

The main memory area which was occupied can then be reassigned to other processes, which quite probably will be "swapped in" from the "swap area".

Most of the decisions regarding "swapping out", and all the decisions regarding "swapping in", are made by the procedure "sched". "Swapping in" is handled by a direct call (2034) on the procedure "swap" (5196), whereas "swapping out" is handled by a call (2024) on "xswap" (4368).

For those archaeologists who like to ponder the "bones" of earlier versions of operating systems, it seems that originally "sched" called "swap" directly to "swap out" processes, rather than via "xswap". The extra procedure (one of several to be found in the file "text.c") has been necessitated by the implementation of the sharable "text segments".

It is instructive to estimate how much extra code has been necessitated by the text segment feature: in "text.c" are four procedures "xswap", "xalloc", "xfree" and "xccdec", which manipulate an array of structures called "text", which is declared in the file "text.h". Additional code has also been added to "sys1.c" and "slp.c".

Text Segments

Text segments are segments which contain only "pure" code and data i.e. code and data which remain unaltered throughout the program execution, so that they may be shared amongst several processes executing the same program.

The resulting economies in space can be quite substantial when many users of the system are executing the same program simultaneously e.g. the editor or the "shell".

Information about text segments must be stored in a central location, and hence the existence of the "text" array. Each program which shares a text segment keeps a pointer to the corresponding text array element in "u.u_textp".

beginning of the code file. The first program to begin execution causes a copy of the text segment to be made in the "swap" area.

When subsequently no programs are left which reference the text segment, the resources absorbed by the text segment are released. The main memory resource is released whenever there are no programs which reference the text segment currently in main memory; the "swap" area is released in general whenever there are no programs left running which reference the text segment.

The numbers in each of these states are denoted by "x_ccount" and "x_count" respectively. Decrementing these numbers is handled by the routines "xccdec" and "xfree" which also take care of releasing resources when the counts reach zero. ("xccdec" is called whenever a program is swapped out or terminates. "xfree" is called by "exit" whenever a program terminates.)

sched (1940)

Process #0 executes "sched". When it is not waiting for the completion of an input/output operation that it has initiated, it spends most of its time waiting in one of the following situations:

A. (runout)
None of the processes which are swapped out is ready to run, so that there is nothing to do. The situation may be changed by a call to "wakeup", or to "xswap" called by either "newproc" or "expand".

B. (runin)
There is at least one process swapped out and ready to run, but it hasn't been out more than 3 seconds and/or none of the processes presently in main memory is inactive or has been there more than 2 seconds. The situation may

be changed by the effluxion of time as measured by "clock" or by a call to "sleep".

When either of these situations terminate:

1958: With the processor running at priority six, so that the clock can't interrupt and change values of "p_time", a search is made for the process which is ready to run and has been swapped out for the longest time;

1966: If there is no such process then situation A holds;

1976: Search for a main memory area of adequate size to hold the data segment. If an associated text segment must be present also but is not currently in main memory, the area is increased by the size of the text segment;

1982: If an area of adequate size is available the program branches to "found2" (2031). (Note that the program does not handle the case where there is sufficient space for both text and data segments but in distinct areas of main memory. Would it be worth while to extend the code to cover this possibility?);

1990: Search for a process which is in main memory, but which is not the scheduler or locked (i.e. already being swapped out), and whose state is "SWAIT" or "SSTOP" (but not "SSLEEP") (i.e. the process is waiting for an event of low precedence, or has stopped during tracing (see Chapter Thirteen)). If such a process is found, go to line 2021, to swap the image out.

Note that there seems to be a bias here against processes whose "proc" entries are early in the "proc" array;

2003: If the image to be swapped in has been out less than 3 seconds, then situation B holds;

2005: Search for the process which is loaded, but is not the scheduler or locked, whose state is "SRUN" or "SSLEEP" (i.e. ready to run, or waiting for an event of high precedence) and which has been in main memory for the longest time;

2013: If the process image to be swapped out has been in main memory for less than 2 seconds, then situation B holds.

The constant "2" here (also the "3" on line 2003) is somewhat arbitrary. For some reason the programmer has departed from his usual practice of naming such constants to emphasise their origins;

2022: The process image is flagged as not loaded and is swapped out using "xswap" (4368).

Note that the "SSWAP" flag is not set here because the process swapped out is not the current process. (Cf. lines 1907, 2286);

2032: Read the text segment into main memory if necessary. Note that the arguments for the "swap" procedure are:

an address within the swap area of the disk;

a main memory address (ordinal number of a 32 word block);

a size (number of 32 word blocks to be transferred);

a direction indicator ("B_READ==1" denotes "disk to main memory");

2042: Swap in the data segment and ...

2044: Release the disk swap area to the available list, record the main memory address, set the "SLOAD" flag and reset the accumulated time indicator.

xswap (4368)

4373: If "oldsize" data was not supplied, use the current size of the data segment stored in "u";

4375: Find a space in the disk swap area for the process's data segment. (Note that the disk swap area is allocated in terms of 512 character blocks);

4378: "xccdec" (4490) is called (unconditionally!) to decrease the count, associated with the text segment, of the number of "in main memory" processes which reference that text segment. If the count becomes zero, the main memory area occupied by the text segment is simply returned to the available space. (There is no need to copy it out, since, as we shall see, there will be a copy already in the disk swap area);

4379: The "SLOCK" flag is set while the process is being swapped out. This is to prevent "sched" from attempting to "swap out" a process which is already in the process of being "swapped out". (This can only happen if "swapping out" was started initially by some routine other than "sched" e.g. by "expand");

4382: The main memory image is released except when "xswap" is called by "newproc";

4388: If "runout" is set, "sched" is waiting for something to "swap in", so wake it up.

xalloc (4433)

"xalloc" is called by "exec" (3130), when a new program is being initiated, to handle the allocation of, or linking to, the text segment. The argument, "ip", is a pointer to the "mode" of the code file. At the time of this call, "u.u_arg[1]" contains the text segment size in bytes.

4439: If there is no text segment, return immediately;

4441: Look through the "text" array for both an unused entry and an entry for the text segment. If the latter can be found, do the bookkeeping and go to "out" (4474);

4452: Arrange to copy the text segment into the disk swap area. Initialise the unused text entry, and get space in the disk swap area;

4459: Change the space occupied by the process to one large enough to contain the "per process data" area and the text segment;

4460: The call on "estabur" is necessary to set the user mode segmentation registers before reading the code file;

4461: A UNIX process can only initiate one input/output operation at a time. Hence it is possible to store i/o parameters at standard locations in the "u" structure, viz. "u.u_count", "u.u_offset []" and "u.u_base";

4462: The octal value 020 (decimal 16) is an offset into the code file;

4463: Information is to be read into the area beginning at location zero in the user address space;

4464: Read the text segment part of the code file into the current data segment;

4467: "Swap out" the data segment (minus the "per process data") into the disk swap area reserved for the text segment;

4473: "Shrink" the data segment - it is about to be swapped out;

4475: "sched" always "swaps in" the text segment before the data segment i.e. there is no mechanism for bringing the text segment into main memory once the data segment is present. If the text

segment is not in main memory, get back into step by "swapping out" the data segment to disk.

It will be noted that the code to handle text segments is very conservative whenever the situation starts to get complicated. For example, the "panic" (4451) when no more text entries are available would seem to be a rather extreme reaction. However the strategy of being generous with "text" array space is quite likely to be less expensive than the code needed to do "better". What do you think?

xfree (4398)

"xfree" is called by "exit" (3233), when a process is being terminated, and by "exec" (3128), when a process is being transmogrified.

4402: Set the text pointer in the "proc" entry to "NULL";

4403: Decrement the main memory count and if it is now zero ...

4406: and if the text segment has <u>not</u> been flagged to be saved, ...

4408: Abandon the image of the text segment in the disk swap area;

4411: Call "iput" (7344) to decrement the "inode" reference count and if necessary delete it.

"ISVTX" (5695) is a mask which defines the "sticky bit" mentioned in section "CHMOD(I)" of the UPM. If this bit is set, the disk copy of the text segment is allowed to remain in the disk swap area even when no programs are running which reference it, in the expectation that it will be required again shortly. This is an efficient device for commonly used programs such as the "shell" or the editor.

−oOo−

CHAPTER FIFTEEN

Introduction to Basic I/O

There are three files whose contents need to be thoroughly absorbed before the subject of UNIX input/output is broached in detail.

The File 'buf.h'

This file declares two structures called "buf" (4520) and "devtab" (4551). Instances of the structure "buf" are declared as "bfreelist" (4567) and as the array "buf" (!) (4535) with "NBUF" elements.

The structure "buf" is possibly misnamed because it is in fact a buffer header (or buffer control block). The buffer areas proper are allocated separately and declared (4720) as

"char buffers [NBUF] [514];"

Pointers from the "buf" array to the "buffers" array are set up by the procedure "binit".

Other instances of the structure "buf" are declared as "swbuf" (4721) and "rrkbuf" (5387). No 514 character buffer areas are associated with "bfreelist" or "swbuf" or "rrkbuf".

The "buf" structure may be divided into three parts:

(a) flags: These convey status information and are contained within a single word. Masks for setting these flags are defined as "B_WRITE", ."B_READ" etc. in lines 4572 to 4586.

(b) list pointer: Forward and backward pointers for two doubly linked lists, which we shall refer to as the "b"-list and the "av"-list.

(c) i/o parameters: A set of values associated with the actual data transfer.

devtab (4551)

The "devtab" structure has five words, the last four of which are forward and backward pointers.

One instance of "devtab" is declared within the device handler for each block type of peripheral device. For our model system the only block device is the RK05 disk, and "rktab" is declared as a "devtab" structure at line 5386.

The "devtab" structure contains some status information for the the device and serves as a list head for:

(a) the list of buffers associated with the device, and simultaneously on the "av"-list;

(b) the list of outstanding i/o requests for the device.

The File 'conf.h'

The file "conf.h" declares:

yet another way to dissect an integer into two parts ("d_minor" and "d_major"). Note that "d_major" corresponds to "hibyte" (0180);

two arrays of structures;

two integer variables, "nblkdev" and "nchrdev".

The two arrays of structures, "bdevsw" and "cdevsw", are declared but not dimensioned or initialised in "conf.h". The initialisation of these arrays is performed in the file "conf.c".

The file 'conf.c'

This file, along with "low.s", is generated individually at each installation (to reflect the set of peripherals actually installed) by the program "mkconf". (In our case, "conf.c" reflects the representative devices for our model system.)

This file initialises the following:

bdevsw (4656)	swapdev (4696)
cdevsw (4669)	swplo (4697)
rootdev (4695)	nswap (4698)

System generation

System generation at a UNIX installation consists mainly of:

   running "mkconf" with appropriate input;

   recompiling the output files (created as "c.c" and "l.s");

   reloading the system with the revised object files.

This process only takes a few minutes (not the several hours of some other operating systems). Note that "bdevsw" and "cdevsw" are defined differently in "conf.c" from elsewhere, namely as a one dimensional array of pointers to functions which return integer values. This quietly ignores the fact that, for example, "rktab" is not a function, and relies on the linking program not to enquire too closely into the nature of the work which it is performing.

swap (5196)

Before plunging into all the detail of the file "bio.c", it will be instructive as well as convenient to examine one routine which was introduced earlier, namely "swap".

The buffer head "swbuf" was declared to control swapping input/output, which must share access to the disk with other activity. No element of "buffers" is associated with "swbuf". Instead the core area occupied (or to be occupied) by the program serves as the data buffer.

5200: The address of the flags in "swbuf" is transferred to the register variable "fp" for convenience and economy;

5202: The "B_BUSY" flag is tested, and if it is on, a swap operation is already under way, so that the "B_WANTED" flag is set and the

process must wait via a call on "sleep".

   Note that the code loop on lines 5202 to 5205 runs at priority level six, i.e. one higher than the disk interrupt priority.

   Can you see why this is necessary? Under what conditions will the "B_BUSY" flag be set?

5206: The flags are set to reflect:

   "swbuf" is in use ("B_BUSY");

   physical i/o implying a large transfer direct to/from the user data segment ("B_PHYS");

   whether the operation is read or write. ("rdflg" is a parameter to "swap");

5207: The "b_dev" field is initialised. (Presumably this could have been performed once during initialisation rather than every time "swbuf" is used, i.e. in "binit".);

5208: "b_wcount" is initialised. Note the negative value and the effective multiplication by 32;

5210: The hardware device controller requires a full physical address (18 bits on the PDP/11-40). The block number of a 32 word block must be converted into two parts: the low order ten bits are shifted left six places and stored as "b_addr", and the remaining six high order bits as "b_xmem". (On the PDP 11/40 and 11/45 only two of these bits are significant.);

5212: A mouthful at first glance! Shift "swapdev" eight places to the right to obtain the major device number. Use the result to index "bdevsw". From the structure thus selected, extract the strategy routine and execute it with the address of "swbuf" passed as a parameter;

5213: Explain why this call on "spl6" is necessary;

5214: Wait until the i/o operation is complete. Note that the first parameter to "sleep" is in effect the address of "swbuf";

5216: Wakeup those processes (if any) which are waiting for "swbuf";

5218: Reset the process or priority to zero, thus allowing any pending interrupts to "happen";

5219: Reset both the "B_BUSY" and "B_WANTED" flags.

Race Conditions

The code for "swap" has a number of interesting features. In particular it displays in microcosm the problems of race conditions when several processes are running together.

Consider the following scenario:

No swapping is taking place when process A initiates a swapping operation. Denoting "swbuf.b_flags" by simply "flags", we have initially

   flags == null

Process A is not delayed at line 5204, initiates its i/o operation and goes to sleep at line 5215. We now have

   flags == B_BUSY | B_PHYS | rdflg

which was set at line 5206.

Suppose now while the i/o operation is proceeding, process B also initiates a swapping operation. It too begins to execute "swap", but finds the "B_BUSY" flag set, so it sets the "B_WANTED" flag (5203) and goes to sleep also (5204). We now have

B_WANTED

At last the i/o operation completes. Process C takes the interrupt and executes "rkintr", which calls (5471) "iodone" which calls (5301) "wakeup" to awaken process A <u>and</u> process B. "iodone" also sets the "B_DONE" flag and resets the "B_WANTED" flag so that

    flags == B_BUSY | B_PHYS | rdflg |
        B_DONE

What happens next depends on the order in which process A and process B are reactivated. (Since they both have the same priority, "PSWP", it is a toss-up which goes first.)

<u>Case (a)</u>: Process A goes first. "B_DONE" is set so no more sleeping is needed. "B_WANTED" is reset so there is no one to "wakeup". Process A tidies up (5219), and leaves "swap" with

    flags == B_PHYS | rdflg | B_DONE

Process B now runs and is able to initiate its i/o operation without further delay.

<u>Case (b)</u>: Process B goes first. It finds "B_BUSY" on, so it turns the "B_WANTED" flag back on, and goes to sleep again, leaving

    flags == B_BUSY | B_PHYS | rdflg |
        B_DONE | B_WANTED

Process A starts again as in Case (a), but this time finds "B_WANTED" on so it must call "wakeup" (5217) in addition to its other chores. Process B finally wakes again and the whole chain completes.

Case (b) is obviously much less efficient than case (a). It would seem that a simple change to line 5215 to read

    sleep (ip, PSWP-1);"

would cost virtually nothing and ensure that Case (b) never occurred!

The necessity for the raising of processor priority at various points should be studied: for example if line 5201 was omitted and if process B had just completed line 5203 when the "i/o complete" interrupt occurred for Process A's operation, then "iodone" would turn off "B_WANTED" and perform "wakeup" before process B went to sleep ... forever! A bad scene.

Reentrancy

Note also the assumption made above, that both process A and process B could execute "swap" simultaneously. All UNIX procedures are in general "re-entrant" (which means multiple simultaneous executions are possible). How would UNIX have to change if re-entrancy were not allowed?

For the Uninitiated

we can now return to complete an investigation started in Chapter Eight concerning "aretu" and "u.u_ssav":

After setting "u.u_ssav" (2284), "expand" calls (2285) "xswap", which calls (4380) "swap", which calls (5215) "sleep", which calls (2084) "swtch", which <u>resets</u> "u.u_rsav" (2189).

Thus in fact "u.u_rsav" finally gets reset to a value appropriate to four procedure calls deeper than that for "u.u_ssav".

The article "The UNIX I/O System" by Dennis Ritchie is highly pertinent.

-oOo-

CHAPTER SIXTEEN

The RK Disk Driver

The RK disk storage system employs a removable disk cartridge containing a single disk, which is mounted inside a drive with moving read/write heads.

The device designated RK11-D consists of a disk controller together with a single drive. Additional drives, designated RK05, up to a total of seven, may be added to a single RK11-D.

A requirement for more than eight drives would require an additional controller with a different set of UNIBUS addresses. Also the code in the file "rk.c" would have to be modified to handle the case of two or more controllers. This case is most unlikely because requirements for large amounts of on-line disk storage will be more economically provided otherwise e.g. by the RP04 disk system.

```
Cartridge capacity: 1,228,800 words
                    (4800 512 byte records)
Surfaces/cartridge: 2
Tracks/surface:     200(plus 3 spare)
Sectors/Track:      12
Words/Sector:       256
Recording density:  2040 bpi maximum
Rotation speed:     1500 rpm
Half revolution:    20 msecs
Track positioning:
        10 msecs (one track)
        50 msecs (average)
        85 msecs (worst case)
Interrupt Vector Address:   220
Priority Level:     5

Unibus Register Addresses
  Drive Status        RKDS 777400
  Error               RKER 777402
  Control Status      RKCS 777404
  Word Count          RKWC 777406
  Current bus address RKBA 777410
  Disk address        RKDA 777412
  Data Buffer         RKDB 777416
```

Table 16.1 RK Vital Statistics

The average total access time is 70 milliseconds. With multi-drive subsystems, seeking by one drive may be overlapped with reading or writing by another drive. However this feature is not used by UNIX because of bugs which existed at one time in the hardware controller.

In initiating a data transfer, RKDA, RKBA and RKWC are set, and then RKCS is set. Upon completion, status information is available in RKCS, RKER and RKDS. When an error occurs, UNIX simply calls "deverror" (2447) to display RKER and RKDS on the system console, without any attempt at analysis. An operation is repeated up to ten times before an error is reported by the device driver.

The register formats which are described fully in the "PDP11 Peripherals Handbook" are reflected in the program code at several points. The following summaries suffice to describe the features used by UNIX:

Control Status Register (RKCS)

bit   description

15   Set when any bit of RKER (the Error Register) is set;

7   Set when the control is no longer engaged in actively executing a function and is ready to accept a command;

6   When set, the control will issue an interrupt to vector address 220 upon operation completion or error;

5-4   Memory Extension. The two most significant bits of the 18 bit physical bus address. (The other 16 bits are recorded in RKBA.);

3-1   Function to be performed:

```
        CONTROL RESET  000
        WRITE          001
        READ           010
        etc.,
```

0   Initiate the function designated by bits 1 to 3 when set. (write only);

Word Count Register (RKWC)

Contains the twos complement of the number of words to be transferred.

bit	description
15-13	Drive number (0 to 7)
12-5	Cylinder number (0 to 199)
4	Surface number (0,1)
3-0	Sector address (0 to 11)

The file 'rk.c'

This file contains the code which is specific to the RK disk system, i.e. which is the RK "device driver".

rkstrategy (5389)

The strategy routine is called, e.g. from "swap" (5212), to handle both read and write requests.

5397: The test and call on "mapalloc" here is a "no-op" except on the PDP11/70 system;

5399: The code from here to line 5402 appears to be unnecessarily devious! See the discussion of "rkaddr" below. If the block number is too large, set the "B_ERROR" flag and report "completion";

5407: Link the buffer into a FIFO list for the controller. The list is singly linked, uses the "av_forw" pointer of the "buf" structures, and has head and tail pointers in "rktab". Interrupts from disk devices may not be allowed after the first step;

5414: If the RK controller is not currently active, wake it up via a call on "rkstart" (5440), which checks that there is something to do (5444), flags the controller as busy (5446) and calls "devstart" (5447), passing as parameters:

a pointer to the first enqueued buffer header;

the address of the RKDA disk address register. (The value passed is in effect 0177412. See lines 5363, 5382.);

a "disk address" computed by "rkaddr";

zero (not really important in our discussion, and may be ignored).

rkaddr (5420)

The code in this procedure incorporates a special feature for files which extend over more than one disk drive. This feature is described in the UPM Section "RK(IV)". Its usefulness seems to be restricted.

The value returned by "rkaddr" is formatted for direct transmission to the control register, RKDA.

devstart (5096)

This procedure when called for the RK disk loads appropriate values into the registers RKDA, RKBA, RKWC and RKCS in succession. Only the last value needs to be computed at this stage.

The calculation, though messy in appearance, is straight forward. Note that "hbcom" is zero and "rbp->b_xmem" contains the two high order bits of the physical core address. The loading of RKCS initialises the disk controller i.e. the operation is now entirely under the control of the hardware.

"devstart" returns to "rkstart" (5448), which returns to "rkstrategy" (5416). which resets the processor priority and returns to "swap" (5213), which ...

rkintr (5451)

This procedure is invoked to handle the interrupts which occur when RK disk operations are completed.

5455: Check for a false alarm!

5459: Inspect the error bit; if set ...

5460: Call "deverror" (2447) to display a message on the system console terminal;

5461: Clear the internal registers of the disk controller and ...

5462: Wait till this is completed (usually a few microseconds);

5463: If the operation has been retried less than ten times, call "rkstart" to try again. Otherwise give up and report an error;

5469: Set the "retry" (!) count back to zero, remove the current operation from the "actf" list, and complete the operation by calling "iodone";

5472: "rkstart" is called unconditionally here. If the call is not necessary (because the "actf" list is empty) "rkstart" will return immediately (5444).

iodone (5018)

This routine is primarily concerned with the return of resources when a block i/o operation has completed. It:

frees up the Unibus map (for 11/70's, if appropriate);

sets the "B_DONE" flag;

releases the buffer if the i/o was asynchronous, or else resets the "B_WANTED" flag and wakes up any process waiting for the i/o operation to complete.

-oOo-

CHAPTER SEVENTEEN

Buffer Manipulation

In this chapter we look at the file "bio.c" in detail. It contains most of the basic routines used to manipulate buffer headers and buffers (4535, 4720).

Individual buffer headers are tagged by a device number "b_dev", (4527) and a block number "b_blkno", (4531). (Note the way in which the latter is declared as an unsigned integer.)

Buffer headers may be linked simultaneously into two lists:

the b -lists are lists, one per device controller, which link together buffers associated with that device type;

the av -list is a list of buffers which may be detached from their current use and converted to an alternate use.

Both the "av"-list and the various "b"-lists are doubly linked to facilitate insertion and deletion at any point.

Flags

If a buffer is withdrawn temporarily from the "av"-list, then its "B_BUSY" flag is raised.

If the contents of a buffer correctly reflect the information that is or should be stored on disk, then the "B_DONE" flag is raised.

If the "B_DELWRI" flag is raised, the contents of the buffer are more up to date than the contents of the corresponding disk block, and hence the buffer must be written out before it can be reassigned.

A Cache-like Memory

It will be seen that the large buffers in UNIX are manipulated in a way which is analogous to the operation of a hardware cache attached to the main memory of a computer e.g. the PDP11/70.

Buffers are not assigned to any particular program or file, except for very short intervals at a time. In this way a relatively small number of buffers can be shared effectively amongst a large number of programs and files.

Information is left in the buffers until the buffer is needed i.e. immediate "write through" is avoided if only part of the buffer has recently been changed. Programs which read or write records which are small compared with the buffer size are then not penalised unduly.

Finally when programs are terminated and files are closed, the problems of ensuring that the program's buffers are flushed properly (problems which have plagued other operating systems) have largely disappeared.

There is one area of practical concern: if the decision "when to write" is left to the operating system alone, then some buffers may not be written out for a very long time. Accordingly there is a utility program which runs twice per minute and forces all such buffers to be written out unconditionally. This limits the likely amount of damage that a sudden system crash may cause.

clrbuf (5038)

This routine zeros out the first 256 words (512 bytes) of the buffer. Note that the parameter passed to "clrbuf" is the address of the buffer header. "clrbuf" is called by "alloc" (6982).

incore (4899)

This routine searches for a buffer that is already assigned to a particular (device, block number) pair. It searches the circular "b"-list whose head is the "devtab" structure for the device type. If a buffer is found, the address of the buffer header is returned. "incore" is called by "breada" (4780, 4788).

getblk (4921)

This routine performs the same search as "incore" but goes further in that if the initial search is unsuccessful, a buffer is allocated from the "av"-list (available list).

By a call on "notavail" (4999), the buffer is removed from the "av"-list and flagged as "B_BUSY".

parameters than "incore". It is called by

exec	(3040)	writei	(6304)
exit	(3237)	iinit	(6928)
bread	(4758)	alloc	(6981)
breada	(4781,4789)	free	(7016)
smount	(6123)	update	(7216)

4940: At this point the required buffer has been located by searching the "b"-list. Either it is "B_BUSY" in which case a "sleep" must be taken (4943), or else it is appropriated (4948);

4953: If the required buffer has not been located, and if the "av"-list is empty, set the "B_WANTED" flag for the "av"-list and go to "sleep" (4955);

4960: If the "av"-list is not empty, select the first member, and if it represents a "delayed write" arrange to have it written out asynchronously (4962);

4966: "B_RELOC" is a relic! (See 4583);

4967: The code from here until 4973 unconditionally removes the buffer from the "b"-list for its current device type and reinserts it into the "b"-list for the new device type. Since this will fre-quently be a "no-op" i.e. the new and old device type will be the same, it would seem desirable to insert a test
   if (bp->b_dev == dev)
before executing lines 4967 to 4974.

Note the special handling for calls where "dev == NODEV" (-1). (Such calls incidently are made without a second parameter - tut! tut! See e.g. 3040).

"bfreelist" serves as the "devtab" structure for the "b"-list for "NODEV".

This procedure takes the buffer passed as a parameter and links it back into the "av"-list.

Any process which is either waiting for the particular buffer or any available buffer is woken up.

Note however that since both "sleeps" (4943, 4955) are at the same priority, if two processes are waiting - one for the particular buffer and one for any buffer - it will be a toss-up which will get it.

By giving the first priority over the second (e.g. by biasing by one) the race should be resolved more satisfac-torily. The disadvantage of such a change might be that it could lead to a deadlock situation in certain rather peculiar circumstances.

If an error has occurred e.g. upon reading information into the buffer, the information in the buffer may be incorrect. The assignment on line 4883 ensures that the information in the buffer will not be mistakenly retrieved subsequently. The "B_ERROR" flag is set e.g. by "rkstrategy" (5403) and "rkintr" (5467).

To see how this could occur, consider what happens to a buffer when a disk i/o operation is completed:

5471 "rkintr" calls "iodone";
5026 "iodone" sets the "B_DONE" flag;
5028 "iodone" calls "brelse";
4887 "brelse" resets the "B_WANTED", "B_BUSY" and "B_ASYNC" flags but not the "B_DONE" flag;

   . . . .

4948 "getblk" finds the buffer and calls "notavail";
5010 "notavail" sets the "B_BUSY" flag;
4759 "bread" (which called "getblk") finds the "B_DONE" flag set and exits.

Note that buffer headers are removed from the "av"-list by "notavail" and are returned by "brelse". Buffer headers are moved from one "b"-list to another by "getblk".

binit (5055)

This procedure is called by "main" (1614) to initialise the buffer pool. Empty, doubly linked circular lists are set up:

   for the "av"-list ("bfreelist" is head);

   the "b"-list for null devices ("dev == NODEV") ("bfreelist" is again head);

   a "b"-list for each major device type.

For each buffer:

   the buffer header is linked into the "b"-list for the device "NODEV" (-1);

   the address of the buffer is set in the header (5067);

   the buffer flags are set as "B_BUSY" (this doesn't seem to be really necessary) (5072);

   the buffer header is linked into the "av"-list by a call on "brelse" (5073);

The number of block devices is recorded as "nblkdev". This is used for checking values for "dev" in "getblk" (4927), "getmdev" (6192) and "openi" (6720). Inspection of "bdevsw" (4656) shows that "nblkdev" will be set to eight whereas the value one is what is really required.

This result could be obtained by "edit-ing" as follows:
   /5084/m/5081/   "nblkdev=i;
   /5083/m/5077/   "i++

bread (4754)

This is the standard procedure for reading from block devices. It is called by:

wait	(3282)	iinit	(6927)
breada	(4799)	alloc	(6973)
statl	(6051)	ialloc	(7097)
smount	(6116)	iget	(7319)
readi	(6258)	iupdat	(7386)
writei	(6305)	itrunc	(7426,7431)
bmap	(6472,6488)	namei	(7625)

"getblk" finds a buffer. If the "B_DONE" flag is set no i/o is needed.

breada (4773)

This procedure has an additional parameter, as compared with "bread". It is called only by "readi" (6256).

4780: Check if the desired block has already been assigned to a buffer. (It may not yet be available, but at least is it there?);

4781: If not initiate the necessary read operation but don't wait for it to finish;

4788: Look around for the "read ahead" block. If it is not there, allocate a buffer (4789) but release it (4791) if the buffer is already ready;

4793: The "read ahead" block is not ready, so initiate an asynchronous read operation;

4798: If a buffer was assigned to the current block call "bread" to wrap it up, else...

4800: Wait for the completion of the operation which was started at line 4785.

bwrite (4809)

This is the standard procedure for writing to block devices. It is called by "exit" (3239), "bawrite" (4863), "getblk" (4963), "bflush" (5241), "free" (7021), "update" (7221) and "iupdat" (7400). N.B. "writei" calls "bawrite" (6310)!

4820: If the "B_ASYNC" flag is not set, the procedure does not return until the i/o operation is completed;

4823: If the "B_ASYNC" flag is set, but "B_DELWRI" was not set (note "flag" is set at line 4816) call "geterror" (5336) to check on the error flag. (If "B_DELWRI" was set, and there is an error, sending the error indication to the right process is "too hard."). The call (4824) on "geterror" will only report errors related to the initiation of the write operation.

bawrite (4856)

This procedure is called by "writei" (6310) and "bdwrite" (4845). "writei" calls either "bawrite" or "bdwrite" depending on whether the block to be written has been wholly or partially filled.

bdwrite (4836)

This procedure is called by "writei" (6311) and "bmap" (6443, 6449, 6485, 6500 and 6501 !).

4844: Don't delay the write if the device is a magnetic tape drive ... keep everything in order;

4847: Set the "B_DONE", "B_DELWRI" flags and call "brelse" to link the buffer into the "av"-list.

bflush (5229)

This procedure is called by "update" (7201), which is called by "panic" (2420), "sync" (3489) and "sumount" (6150).

"bflush" searches the "av"-list for "delayed write" blocks and forces them to be written out asynchronously.

Note that as "notavail" adjusts the links of the "av"-list, the search (which runs at processor priority six) is reinitiated after each "delayed write" block is encountered.

Note also that since it happens that "bflush" is only called by "update" with "dev" equal to "NODEV", line 5238, in particular, could be simplified.

physio (5259)

This routine is called to handle "raw" input/output i.e. operations which ignore the normal 512 character block size.

"physio" is called by "rkread" (5476) and "rkwrite" (5483) which appear as entries in the array "cdevsw" (4684) i.e. as entries for a character device.

"Raw i/o" is not an essential feature of UNIX. For disk devices it is used mainly for copying whole disks and checking the integrity of the file system as a whole (see e.g. ICHECK (VIII) in the UPM), where it is convenient to read whole tracks, rather than single blocks, at a time.

Note the declaration of "strat" (5261). Since the actual parameter used e.g. "rkstrategy" (5389) does not return any value, is this form of declaration really necessary?

-oOo-

Section Four is concerned with files and file systems.

A file system is a set of files and associated tables and directories organised onto a single storage device such as a disk pack.

This section covers the means of

creating and accessing files;
locating files via directories;
organising and maintaining
file systems.

It also includes the code for an exotic breed of file called a "pipe".

A large part of every operating system seems to be concerned with data management and file management, and UNIX turns out to be no exception.

Section Four

Section Four of the source code contains thirteen files.

The first four contain common declarations needed by various of the other routines:

"file.h" describes the structure of the "file" array;

"filsys.h" describes the structure of the "super block" for "mounted" file systems;

"ino.h" describes the structure of "inodes" recorded on "mounted" devices;

"inode.h" describes the structure of the "inode" array;

The next two files, "sys2.c" and "sys3.c" contain code for system calls. ("sys1.c" and "sys4.c" were presented in Section Two).

The next five files, "rdwri.c", "subr.c", "fio.c", "alloc.c" and "iget.c", together present the principal routines for file management, and provide a link between the i/o oriented system calls and the basic i/o routines.

The file "nami.c" is concerned with searching directories to convert file pathnames into "inode" references.

Finally, "pipe.c" is the "device driver" for pipes.

File Characteristics

A UNIX file is conceptually a named character string, stored on one of a variety of peripheral devices (or in the main memory), and accessible via mechanisms appropriate to the usual peripheral devices.

It will be noted that there is no record structure associated with UNIX files. However "newline" characters may be inserted into the file to define substrings analogous to records.

UNIX carries the ideas of device independence to their logical extreme by allowing the file name in effect to determine uniquely all relevant attributes of the file.

System Calls

The following system calls are provided expressly for file manipulation:

#	Name	Line	#	Name	Line
=	====	====	=	====	====
3	read	5711	14	mknod	5952
4	write	5720	15	chmod	3560
5	open	5765	16	chown	3575
6	close	5846	19	seek	5861
8	creat	5781	21	mount	6086
9	link	5909	22	umount	6144
10	unlink	3510	41	dup	6069
12	chdir	3538	42	pipe	7723

Control Tables

The arrays "file" and "inode" are essential components of the file access mechanism.

file (5507)

The array "file" is defined as an array of structures (also named "file").

An element of the "file" array is considered to be unallocated if "f_count" is zero.

Each "open" or "creat" system call results in the allocation of an element of the "file" array. The address of this element is stored in an element of the calling process's array "u.u_ofile". It is the index of the newly allocated element of the latter array which is passed back to the user process. Descendants of a process created by "newproc" inherit the contents of the parent's "u.u_ofile" array.

Each element of "file" includes a counter, "f_count", to determine the number of current processes which reference it.

"f_count" is incremented by "newproc" (1878), "dup" (6079) and "falloc" (6857); it is decremented by "closef" (6657) and (if the file can't be opened) by "open1" (5836).

The "f_flag" (5509) of the "file" element notes whether the file is open for reading and/or writing or whether it is a "pipe" or not. (Further discussion of "pipes" will be deferred till Chapter Twenty-One.)

The "file" structure also contains a pointer, "f_inode" (5511) to an entry in the "inode" table, and a 32 bit integer, "f_offset" (5512), which is a logical pointer to a character within the file.

inode (5659)

"inode" is defined as an array of structures (also named "inode").

An element of the "inode" array is considered to be unallocated if the reference count, "i_count", is zero.

At each point in time, "inode" contains a single entry for each file which may be referenced for normal i/o operations, or which is being executed or which has been executed and has the "sticky" bit set, or which is the working directory for some process.

Several "file" table entries may point to a single "inode" entry. The inode entry describes the general disposition of the file.

Resources Required

Each file requires the dedication of certain system resources. When a file exists, but is not being referenced in any way, it requires:

(a) a directory entry (16 characters in a directory file);

(b) a disk "inode" entry (32 characters in a table stored on the disk);

(c) zero, one or more blocks of disk storage (512 characters each).

In addition if the file is being referenced for some purpose, it requires

(d) a core "inode" entry (32 characters in the "inode" array);

Finally if a user program has "opened" the file for reading or writing, a number of resources are required:

(e) a "file" array entry (8 characters);

(f) an entry in the user program's "u.u_ofile" array (one word per file, pointing to a "file" array entry);

Mechanisms have to be set up for allocating and deallocating each of these resources in an orderly manner. The following table gives the names of the principal procedures involved:

resource	obtain	free
========	======	====
directory entry	namei	namei
disk "inode" entry	ialloc	ifree
disk storage block	alloc	free
core "inode" entry	iget	iput
"file" table entry	falloc	closef
"u_ofile" entry	ufalloc	close

When a program wishes to reference a file which already exists, it must "open" the file to create a "bridge" to the file. (Note that in UNIX, processes usually inherit the open files of their parents or predecessors, so that often all needed files are already implicitly open.) If the file does not already exist, it must be "created".

This second case will be investigated first:

creat (5781)

5786: "namei" (7518) converts a pathname into an "inode" pointer. "uchar" is the name of a procedure which recovers the pathname, character by character, from the user program data area;

5787: A null "inode" pointer indicates either an error or that no file of that name already exists;

5788: For error conditions, see "CREAT (II)" in the UPM;

5790: "maknode" (7455) creates a core "inode" via a call on "ialloc" and then initialises it and enters it into the appropriate directory. Note the explicit resetting of the "sticky" bit ("ISVTX").

openl (5804)

This procedure is called by "open" (5774) and "creat" (5793, 5795), passing values of the third parameter, "trf", of 0, 2 and 1 respectively. The value 2 represents the case where no file of the desired name already exists.

5812: The second parameter, "mode", can take the values 01 ("FREAD"), 02 ("FWRITE") of 03 ("FREAD|FWRITE") when "trf" is 0, but only 02 otherwise;

5813: Where a file of the desired name already exists, check the access permissions for the desired mode(s) of activity via calls on "access" (6746), which may set "u.u_error" as a side-effect;

5824: If the file is being "created", eliminate its previous contents via a call on "itrunc" (7414). The code here could be improved by changing the test to "(trf == 1)". Verify that this would be so.

5826: "prele" (7882) is used to "unlock" "inodes". Where, you may ask, did the "inode" get "locked", and why?

5827: Note that "falloc" (6847) calls "ufalloc" (6824) as the first thing it does;

5831: "ufalloc" leaves the user file identifying number in "u.u_ar0[R0]". Why does this statement occur where it does, instead of after line 5834?

5832: "openi" (6702) is called to call handlers for special files, in case any device specific actions are required (for disk files there is no action);

5839: In the case of an error while making the "file" array entry, the "inode" entry is released by a call on "iput".

It will be seen that responsibility is quite widely distributed. The "file" table entry is initialised by "falloc" and "openl"; the "inode" table entry, by "iget", "ialloc" and "maknode".

Note that "ialloc" clears out the "i_addr" array of a newly allocated "inode" and "itrunc" does the same for a pre-existing "inode", so that after the "creat" system call, there are no disk blocks associated with the file, now classed as "small".

open (5763)

We now turn to consider the case where a program wishes to reference a file which already exists.

"namei" is called (5770) with a second parameter of zero to locate the named file. ("u.u_arg[0]" contains the address in the user space of a character string which defines a file path name.)

"u.u_arg[1]" has to be incremented by one, because there is a mismatch between the user programming conventions and the internal data representations.)

openl revisited

"trf" is now zero, so access permissions are checked (5813) but the existing file (if any) is not deallocated (5824).

What is a little disconcerting here is that, apart from the call on "falloc" (5827), there is no direct call on any of the "resource allocation" routines. Of course, for an existing file, neither directory entry nor disk "inode" entry nor disk blocks need be allocated. The core "inode" entry is allocated (if necessary) as a side-effect of the call on "namei", but ... where is it initialised?

close (5846)

The "close" system call is used to sever explicitly the connection between a user program and a file and thus can be regarded as the inverse of "open".

The user program's file identification is passed via r0. The value is validated by "getf" (6619), the "u.u_ofile" entry is erased, and a call is made on "closef".

closef (6643)

"closef" is called by "close" (5854) and by "exit" (3230). (The latter is more common since most files do not get closed explicitly but only implicitly when the user program terminates.)

6649: If the file is a pipe, reset the mode of the pipe and "wakeup" any process which is waiting for the pipe, either for information or for space;

6655: If this is the last process to reference the file, call "closei" (6672) to handle any special end of file processing for special files and then call "iput";

6657: Decrement the "file" entry reference count. If this now zero, the entry is no longer allocated.

iput (7344)

"closei", as its last action calls "iput". This routine is in fact called from many places, whenever a connection to a core "inode" is to be severed and the reference count decremented.

7350: If the reference count is one at this point, the "inode" is to be released. While this is happening, it should be locked.

7352: If the number of "links" to the file is zero (or less) the file is to be deallocated (see below);

7357: "iupdat" (7374) updates the accessed and update times as

recorded on the disk "inode";

7358: "prele" unlocks the "inode". Why should it be called here as well as at line 7363?

Deletion of Files

New files are automatically entered into the file directory as permanent files as soon as they are "opened". Subsequent "closing" of a file does not automatically cause its deletion. As was seen at line 7352, deletion will occur when the field "i_nlink" of the core "inode" entry is zero. This field is set to one initially by "maknode" (7464) when the file is first created. It may be incremented by the system call "link" (5941) and decremented by the system call "unlink" (3529).

Programs which create temporary "work files" should remove these files before terminating, by executing an "unlink" system call. Note that the "unlink" call does not of itself remove the file. This can only happen when the reference count ("i_count") is about to be decremented to zero (7350, 7362).

To minimise the problems associated with "temporary" files which survive program or system crashes, programmers should observe the conventions that:

(a) temporary files should be "unlinked" immediately after they are opened;

(b) temporary files should always be placed in the "tmp" directory. Unique file names can be generated by incorporating the process's identifying number into the file name (See "getpid" (3480)).

Reading and Writing

It is of interest to work through an abbreviated summary of the code which is invoked when a user process performs a "read" system call before examining the code in detail.

```
    .... read (f, b, n); /*user program*/

            {trap occurs}

2693 trap

            {system call #3}

5711 read ( );
5713     rdwr (FREAD);
```

Execution of the system call by the user process results in the activation of "trap" running in kernel mode. "trap" recognises system call #3, and calls (via "trap1") the routine "read", which calls "rdwr".

```
5731 rdwr

5736    fp = getf (u.u_ar0[R0]);
5743    u.u_base = u.u_arg[0];
5744    u.u_count = u.u_arg[1];
5745    u.u_segflg = 0;
5751    u.u_offset[1] = fp->f_offset[1];
5752    u.u_offset[0] = fp->f_offset[0];
5754    readi(fp->f_inode);
5756    dpadd(fp->f_offset,
            u.u_arg[1]-u.u_count);
```

"rdwr" includes much code which is common to both "read" and "write" operations. It converts, via "getf" (6619), the file identification supplied by the user process into the address of an entry in the "file" array.

Note that the first parameter of the system call is passed in a different way from the remaining two parameters.

"u.u_segflg" is set to zero to indicate that the operation destination is in the user address space. After "readi"

"inode" pointer, the final accounting is performed by adding the number of characters requested for transfer less the residual number not transferred (left in "u.u_count") to the file offset.

6221 readi

```
6239  lbn = lshift (u.u_offset, -9);
6240  on = u.u_offset[1] & 0777;
6241  n = min (512 - on, u.u_count);
6248  bn = bmap(ip, lbn);
6250  dn = ip->i_dev;
6258  bp = bread (dn, bn);
6260  iomove (bp, on, n, B_READ);
6261  brelse (bp);
```

"readi" converts the file offset into two parts: a logical block number, "lbn", and an index into the block, "on". The number of characters to be transferred is the minimum of "u.u_count" and the number of characters left in the block (in which case additional block(s) must be read (not shown)) (and the number of characters remaining in the file (this case is not shown)).

"dn" is the device number which is stored within the "inode". "bn" is the actual block number on the device (disk), which is computed by "bmap" (6415) using "lbn".

The call on "bread" finds the required block, copying it into core from disk if necessary. "iomove" (6364) transfers the appropriate characters to their destination, and performs accounting chores.

rdwr (5731)

"read" and "write" perform similar operations and share much code. The two system calls, "read" (5711) and

"write" (5720), call "rdwr" immediately to:

5736: Convert the user program file identification to a pointer in the file table;

5739: Check that the operation (read or write) is in accordance with the mode with which the file was opened;

5743: Set up various standard locations in "u" with the appropriate parameters;

5746: "pipes" get special treatment right from the start!

5755: Call "readi" or "writei" as appropriate;

5756: Update the file offset by, and set the value returned to the user program to, the number of characters actually transferred.

readi (6221)

6230: If no characters are to be transferred, do nothing;

6232: Set the "inode" flag to indicate that the "inode" has been accessed;

6233: If the file is a character special file, call the appropriate device "read" procedure, passing the device identification as parameter;

6238: Begin a loop to transfer data in amounts up to 512 characters at a time until (6262) either an irrecoverable error condition has been encountered or the requested number of characters has been transferred;

6239: "lshift" (1410) concatenates the two words of the array "u.u_offset", shifts right by nine places, and truncates to 16 bits. This defines the "logical

block number" of the file which is to be referenced;

6240: "on" is a character offset within the block;

6241: "n" is determined initially as the minimum of the number of characters beyond "on" in the block, and the number requested for transfer. (Note that "min" (6339) treats its arguments as unsigned integers.)

6242: If the file is not a special block file then ...

6243: Compare the file offset with the current file size;

6246: Reset "n" as the minimum of the characters requested and the remaining characters in the file;

6248: Call "bmap" to convert the logical block number for the file to a physical block number for its host device. There will be more on "bmap" shortly. For now, note that "bmap" sets "rablock" as a side effect;

6250: Set "dn" as the device identification from the "inode";

6251: If the file is a special block file then ...

6252: Set "dn" from the "i_addr" field of the "inode" entry. (Presumably this will nearly always be the same as the "i_dev" field, so why the distinction?)

6253: Set the "read ahead block" to the next physical block;

6255: If the blocks of the file are apparently being read sequentially then ...

6256: Call "breada" to read the desired block and to initiate reading of the "read ahead block";

6258: else just read the desired block;

6260: Call "iomove" to transfer information from the buffer to the user area;

6261: Return the buffer to the "av"-list.

writei

6303: If less than a full block is being written the previous contents of the buffer must be read so that the appropriate part can be preserved, otherwise just get any available buffer;

6311: There is no "write ahead" facility, but there is a "delayed write" for buffers whose final characters have not been changed;

6312: If the file offset now points beyond the recorded end of file character, the file has obviously grown bigger!

6318: Why is it necessary/desirable to set the "IUPD" flag again? (See line 6285.)

iomove (6364)

The comment at the beginning of this procedure says most of what needs to be said. "copyin", "copyout", "cpass" and "passc" may be found at lines 1244, 1252, 6542 and 6517 respectively.

bmap (6415)

A general description of the function of "bmap" may be found on Page 2 of "FILE SYSTEM (V)" of the UPM.

6423: Files of more than 2**15 blocks (2**24 characters) are not supported;

6427: Start with the "small" file algorithm (file is not greater than eight blocks i.e. 4096 characters);

6431: If the block number is 8 or more, the "small" file must converted into a large file. Note this is a side effect of "bmap", and should occur only when "bmap" has been called by "writei" (and never by "readi" - see line 6245). Thus all files start life as "small" files and are never explicitly changed to "large" files. Note also that the change is irreversible!

6435: "alloc" (6956) allocates a block on device "d" from the device's free list. It then assigns a buffer to this block and returns a pointer to the buffer header;

6438: The eight buffer addresses in the "i_addr" array for the "inode" are copied into the buffer area and then erased;

6442: "i_addr[0]" is set to point to the buffer which is set up for a "delayed" write;

6448: The file is still small. Get the next block if necessary;

6456: Note the setting of "rablock";

Leftovers

You should investigate the following procedures for yourself:

seek	(5861)	statl	(6045)
sslep	(5979)	dup	(6069)
fstat	(6014)	owner	(6791)
stat	(6028)	suser	(6811)

-oOo-

each file must have at least one name.
A file may have more than one distinct
name, but the same name may not be
shared by two distinct files, i.e.
each name must define a unique file.

A name may be multipart. When written,
the parts or components of the name are
separated by slashes ("/"). The order
of components within a name is significant i.e. "a/b/c" is different from
"a/c/b".

If file names are divided into two
parts: an initial part or "stem" and a
final part or "ending", then two files
whose names have identical stems are
usually related in some way. They may
reside on the same disk, they may
belong to the same user, etc.

The Directory Data Structure

Users make initial reference to files
by quoting the file name, e.g. in the
"open" system call. An important
operating system function is to decode
the name into the corresponding "inode"
entry. To do this, UNIX creates and
maintains a directory data structure.
This structure is equivalent to a
directed graph with named edges.

In its purest form, the graph is a tree
i.e. it has a single root node, with
exactly one path between the root and
any node. More commonly in UNIX (but
not so commonly in other operating systems) the graph is a lattice which may
be obtained from a tree by coalescing
one or more groups of leaves.

In this case, while there is still only
one path between the root and any interior node, there may be more than one
path between the root and a leaf.
Leaves are nodes without successors and
correspond to data files. Interior
nodes are nodes with successors and
correspond to directory files.

CHAPTER NINETEEN
File Directories and Directory Files

As we have seen, much important information about individual files is contained in the "inode" tables. If the
file is currently accessible, or being
accessed, the relevant information is
held in the core "inode" table. If a
file is on disk (more generally, on
some "file system volume") and is not
currently accessible, then the relevant
"inode" table is the one recorded on
the disk (file system volume).

File Names

Notably absent from the "inode" table
is any information regarding the "name"
of the file. This is stored in the
directory files.

The name for a file is obtained from
the names of the edges of the path
between the root and the node
corresponding to the file. (For this
reason, the name is often referred to
as a "pathname".) If there are several
paths, then the file has several names.

Directory Files

A directory file is in many respects
indistinguishable from a non-directory
file. However it contains information
which is used in locating other files
and hence its contents are carefully
protected, and are manipulated by the
operating system alone.

In every file, the information is
stored as one or more 512 character
blocks. Each block of a directory file
is divided into 32 * 16 character
structures. Each structure consists of
a 16 bit "inode" table pointer and a 14
character name. The "inode" pointer is
to the "inode" table on the same disk
or file system volume as the files
which the directory references. (More
on this later.) An "inode" value of
zero defines a null entry in the directory.

The procedures which reference directories are:

```
namei  (7518)  search directory
link   (5909)  create alternate name
wdir   (7477)  write directory entry
unlink (3510)  delete name
```

namei (7518)

7531: "u.u_cdir" defines the "inode" of
       a process's current directory. A
       process inherits its parent's
       current directory at birth
       ("newproc", 1883). The current
       directory may be changed using
       the "chdir" (3538) system call;

7532: Note that "func" is a parameter to "namei" and is always either "uchar" (7689) or "schar" (7679);

7534: "iget" (7276) is called to:

wait until such time as the "inode" corresponding to "dp" is no longer locked;

check that the associated file system is still mounted;

increment the reference count;

lock the "inode";

7535: Multiple slashes are acceptable! (i.e. "////a///b/" is the same as "/a/b");

7537: Any attempt to replace or delete the current working directory or the root directory is bounced immediately!

7542: The label "cloop" marks the beginning of a program loop that extends to line 7667. Each cycle analyses a component of the pathname (i.e. a string terminated by a null character or one or more slashes). Note that a name may be constructed from many different characters (7571);

7550: The end of the pathname has been reached (successfully). Return the current value of "dp";

7563: "search" permission for directories is coded in the same way as "execute" permission for other files;

7570: Copy the name into a more accessible location before attempting to match it with a directory entry. Note that a name of greater than "DIRSIZ" characters is truncated;

7589: "u.u_count" is set to the number of entries in the directory;

7592: The label "eloop" marks the beginning of a program loop which extends to line 7647. Each cycle of the loop handles a single directory entry;

7600: If the directory has been searched (linearly!) without matching the supplied pathname component, then there must be an error unless:
(a) this is the last component of the pathname, i.e. "c=='\0'";
(b) the file is to be created, i.e. "flag == 1"; and
(c) the user program has "write" permission for the directory;

7606: Record the "inode" address for the directory for the new file in "u.u_pdir";

7607: If a suitable slot for a new directory entry has previously been encountered (7642), store the value in "u.u_offset[1]"; else set the "IUPD" flag for the "dp" designated "inode" (but why?);

7622: When appropriate, read a new block from the directory file (note the use of "bread") (why not "breada"?), after carefully releasing any previously held buffer;

7636: Copy the eight words of the directory entry into the array "u.u_dent". The reason for copying before comparing is obscure! Can this actually be more efficient? (The reason for copying the whole directory at all is rather perplexing to the author of these notes.);

7645: This comparison makes efficient use of a single character pointer register variable, "cp". The loop would be even more efficient if word by word comparison were used;

7647: The "eloop" cycle is terminated by one of:

"return (NULL);" (7610)

"goto out;" (7605, 7613)

a successful match so that the branch to "eloop" (7647) is not taken;

7657: If the name is to be deleted ("flag==2"), if the pathname has been completed, and if the user program has "write" access to the directory, then return a pointer to the directory "inode";

7662: Save the device identity temporarily (why not in the register "c"?) and call "iput" (7344) to unlock "dp", to decrement the reference count on "dp" and to perform any consequent processing;

7664: Revalidate "dp" to point to the "inode" for the next level file;

7665: "dp==NULL" shouldn't happen, since the directory says the file exists! However "inode" table overflows and i/o errors can occur, and sometimes the file system may be left in an inconsistent state after a system crash.

Some Comments

"namei" is a key procedure which would seem to have been written very early, to have been thoroughly debugged and then to have been left essentially unchanged. The interface between "namei" and the rest of the system is rather complex, and for that reason alone, it would not win the prize for "Procedure of the Year".

"namei" is called thirteen times by twelve different procedures:

3034	exec	uchar	0
3543	chdir	uchar	0
5770	open	uchar	0
5914	link	uchar	0
6033	stat	uchar	0
6097	smount	uchar	0
6186	getmdev	uchar	0
6976	owner	uchar	0
5786	creat	uchar	1
5928	link	uchar	1
5958	mknod	uchar	1
3515	unlink	uchar	2
4101	core	schar	1

It will be seen that:

(a) there are two calls from "link";

(b) the calls can be divided into four categories, of which the first is by far the largest;

(c) the last two categories have only one representative each;

(d) in particular, there is only one call involving the routine "schar", which is always for a file called "core". (If this case were handled as a special case e.g. where the second parameter had the value "3", then the "uchar"s and "schar" could be eliminated.)

"namei" may terminate in a variety of ways:

(a) if there has been an error, then a "NULL" value is returned and the variable "u.u_error" is set.

(Most errors result in a branch to the label "out" (7669) so that reference counts for the "inode"s are properly maintained (7670). This is not necessary if the failure occurs in "iget" (7664).);

(b) if "flag==2" (i.e. the call is from "unlink"), the value returned (in normal circumstances) is an "inode" pointer for the parent directory of the named file (7660);

(c) if "flag==1" (i.e. the call is from "creat" or "link" or "mknod", and a file is to be created if it does not already exist) and if the named file does not exist, then a "NULL" value is returned (7610). In this case a pointer to the "inode" for the directory which will point to the new file, is left in "u.u_pdir" (7606). (Note also that in this case, "u.u_offset" is left pointing either at an empty directory entry or at the end of the directory file.);

(d) if in the remaining cases, the file exists, an "inode" pointer for the file is returned (7551). The "inode" is locked and the reference count has been incremented. A call to "iput" is needed subsequently to undo both these side effects.

link (5909)

This procedure implements a system call which enters a new name for an existing file into the directory structure. Arguments to the procedure are the existing and the new names of the file;

5914: Look up the existing file name;

5917: If the file already has 127 different names, quit in disgust;

5921: If the existing file turns out to be a directory, then only the super-user may rename it;

5926: Unlock the existing file "inode" This is locked when the first call on "namei" does an "iget" (7534,7664).

Under what conditions would the failure to unlock the "inode" here be disastrous? The chances that the existing file would be a directory encountered in the search for the new name would seem slight, if not impossible. Most probably the relevant circumstance is where the system is attempting to recreate an alternative file name or alias, which already exists;

5927: Search the directory for the second name, with the intention of creating a new entry;

5930: There is an existing file with the second name;

5935: "u.u_pdir is set as a side effect of the call on "namei" (5928). Check that the directory resides on the same device as the file;

5940: Write a new directory entry (see below);

5941: Increase the "link" count for the file.

wdir (7477)

This procedure enters a new name into a directory. It is called by "link" (5940) and "maknode" (7467) with a pointer to a (core) "inode" as parameter.

The sixteen characters of the directory entry are copied into the structure "u.u_dent", and written from there into the directory file. (Note that the previous content of "u.u_dent" will have been the name of the last entry in the directory file.)

The procedure assumes that the directory file has already been searched, that the "inode" for the directory file has already been allocated and that the values of "u.u_offset" have been set appropriately.

maknode (7455)

This procedure is called from "core" (4105), "creat" (5790) and "mknod" (5966), after a previous call on "namei" with a second parameter of one, has revealed that no file of the specified name existed.

unlink (3510)

This procedure implements a system call which deletes a file name from the directory structure. (When all references to a file are deleted, the file itself will be deleted.)

3515: Search for a file with the specified name, and if it exists, return a pointer to the "inode" of the immediate parent directory;

3518: Unlock the parent directory;

3519: Get an "inode" pointer to the file itself;

3522: Unlinking directories is forbidden, except for super-users;

3528: Rewrite the directory entry with the "inode" value set to zero;

3529: Decrement the "link" count.

Note that there is no attempt to reduce the size of a directory below its "high water" mark.

mknod (5952)

This procedure, which implements a system call of the same name, is only executable by the super-user. As explained in the Section "MKNOD(II)" of the UPM, this system call is used to create "inodes" for special files.

"mknod" also solves the problem of "where do directories come from"? The

second parameter passed to "mknod" is used, without modification or restriction to set "i_mode". (Compare "creat" (5790) and "chmod" (3569)). This is the only way an "inode" can get flagged as a directory, for instance.

In such cases, the third parameter passed to "mknod" must be zero. This value is copied into "i_addr[0]" (as is appropriate for special files), and, if non-zero, will be accepted uncritically by "bmap" (6447). It might be prudent to insert a test

if (ip->i_mode & (IFCHR & IFBLK) != 0)

before line 5969, rather than rely indefinitely on the infallibility of the super-user.

access (6746)

This procedure is called by "exec" (3041), "chdir" (3552), "core" (4109), "open1" (5815, 5817), "namei" (7563, 7664, 7658) to check access permission to a file. The second parameter, "mode", is equal to one of "IEXEC", "IWRITE" and "IREAD", with octal values of 0100, 0200 and 0400 respectively.

6753: "write" permission is denied if the file is on a file system volume which has been mounted as "read only" or if the file is functioning as the text segment for an executing program;

6763: the super-user may not execute a file unless it is "executable" in at least one of the three "permission" groups. In any other situation he is always allowed access;

6769: If the user is not the owner of the file, shift "m" three places to the right so that group permissions will be operative ... If the groups don't match, shift "m" again;

6774: Compare "m" and the access permissions.

Note that there is an anomaly here in that if a file has a "mode" of 0077, the owner cannot reference it at all, but everyone else can. This situation could be changed satisfactorily by inserting a statement

m =| (m | (m >> 3)) >> 3;

after line 6752, and replacing lines 6764, 6765 by

if (m & IEXEC && (m & ip->i_mode) == 0)

-oOo-

a storage device is only accessible if it is inserted in an access device. In this situation, reference to the storage device is made via a reference to the access device;

a storage device is acceptable as a file system volume if:

(a) information is recorded as addressable blocks of 512 characters each, which can be independently read or written.

(Note IBM compatible magnetic tape does not satisfy this condition.);

(b) the information recorded on the device satisfies certain consistency criteria:

block #1 is formatted as a "super block" (see below);

blocks #2 to #(n+1) (where n is recorded in the "super block") contain an "inode" table which references all files recorded on the storage device, and does not reference any other files;

directory files recorded on the storage device reference all, and only, files on the same storage device, i.e. a file system volume constitutes a self-contained set of files, directories and "inode" table;

a file system volume is mounted if the presence of the storage device in an access device has been formally recognised by the operating system.

The 'Super Block' (5561)

The "super block" is always recorded as block #1 on the storage device. (Block #0 is always ignored and is available for miscellaneous uses not necessarily concerned with UNIX.)

CHAPTER TWENTY

File Systems

In most computer systems more than one peripheral storage device is used for the storage of files. It is now necessary to discuss a number of matters pertaining to the management by UNIX of the whole set of files and file storage devices. First, some definitions:

file system: an integrated collection of files with a hierarchical system of directories recorded on a single block oriented storage device;

storage device: a device which can store information (especially disk pack or DECtape, etc.);

access device: a mechanism for transferring information to or from a storage device;

The "super block" contains information used in allocating resources, viz. the storage blocks and the entries in the "inode" table recorded on the file system. While the file system volume is mounted a copy of the "super block" is maintained in core and updated there. To prevent the storage device copy becoming too far out of date, its contents are written out at regular intervals.

The 'mount' table (0272)

The "mount" table contained an entry for each mounted file system volume. Each entry defines the device on which the file system volume is mounted, a pointer to the buffer which stores the "super block" for the device, and an "inode" pointer. The table is referenced as follows:

iinit (6922) which is called by "main" (1615), makes an entry for the root device;

smount (6086) is a system call which makes entries for additional devices;

iget (7276) searches the "mount" table if it encounters an "inode" with the 'IMOUNT' flag set;

getfs (7167) searches the "mount" table to find and return a pointer to the "super block" for a particular device;

update (7201) is called periodically and searches the "mount" table to locate information which should be written from core tables into the tables maintained on the file system volumes;

sumount (6144) is a system call which deletes entries from the table.

iinit (6922)

This routine is called by "main" (1615) to initialise the "mount" table entry for the root device.

6926: Call the "open" routine for the root device. Note that "rootdev" is defined in "conf.c" (4695);

6931: Copy the contents of the root device "super block" into a buffer area not associated with any particular device;

6933: The zeroeth entry in the "mount" table is assigned to the root device. Only two of the three elements are explicitly initialised. The third, the "inode" pointer, will never be referenced;

6936: The "locks" stored in the "super block" are explicitly reset. (These locks may have been set when the "super block" was last written onto the file system volume);

6938: The root device is mounted in a "writable" state;

6939: The system sets its idea of the current time and date from the time recorded in the "super block". (If the system has been stopped for an appreciable period, the computer operator will need to reset the contents of "time".)

Mounting

From an operational view point, "mounting" a file system volume involves placing it in a suitable access device, readying the device, and then entering a command such as

        "/etc/mount /dev/rk2 /rk2"

to the "shell", which forks a program to perform a "mount" system call, passing pointers to the two file names as parameters.

smount (6086)

6093: "getmdev" decodes the first argument to locate a block oriented access device;

6096: "u.u_dirp" is reset preparatory to calling "namei" to decode the second file name. (Note that "u.u_dirp" is set by "trap" to "u.u_arg[0]" (2770);

6100: Check that the file named by the second parameter is in a satisfactory condition, i.e. no one else is currently accessing the file, and that the file is not a special file (block or character);

6103: Search the "mount" table looking for an empty entry ("mp->m_bufp==NULL") or an entry already made for the device. (The "mount" data structure is defined at line 0272);

6111: "smp" should point to a suitable entry in the "mount" table;

6113: Perform the appropriate "open" routine, with the device name and a read/write flag as arguments. (As was seen earlier, for the RK05 disk the "open" routine is a "no-op");

6116: Read block #1 from the device. This block is the "super block";

6124: Copy the "super block" into a buffer associated with "NODEV", from the buffer associated with "d". The second buffer will not be released again until the device is unmounted;

6130: "ip" points to the "inode" for the second named file. This "inode" is now flagged as "IMOUNT". The effect of this is to force "iget" (7292) to ignore the normal contents of the file,

while the file system volume is mounted. (In practice, the second file is an empty file created especially for this purpose.)

Notes

1. The "read/write" status of a mounted device depends only on the parameters provided to "smount". No attempt is made to sense the hardware "read/write" status. Thus if a disk is readied with "write protect" on, but is not mounted "read only", then the system will complain vigorously.

2. The "mount" procedure does not carry out any kind of label checking on the "mounted" file system volume. This is reasonable in a situation where file system volumes are rarely rearranged. However in situations where volumes are mounted and remounted frequently, some means of verifying that the correct volume has been mounted would seem desirable. (Further, if a file system volume contains sensitive information, it may be desirable to include some form of password protection as well. There is room in the "super block" (5575) for the storage of a name and an encrypted password.)

iget (7276)

This procedure is called by "main" (1616,1618), "unlink" (3519), "ialloc" (7078) and "namei" (7534, 7664) with two parameters which together uniquely identify a file: a device, and the "inode" number of a file on the device. "iget" returns a reference to an entry in the core "inode" table.

When "iget" is called, the core "inode" table is searched first to see if an entry already exists for the file in the core "inode" table. If not, then "iget" creates one.

7286: If an entry for the designated file already exists ...

7287: Then if it is locked go to sleep;

7290: Try again. (Note the whole table needs to be searched again from the beginning, because the entry may have vanished!);

7292: If the "IMOUNT" flag is on ... this is an important possibility for which we will delay the discussion;

7302: If the "IMOUNT" flag is not set, increase the "inode" reference count, set the "ILOCK" flag and return a pointer to the "inode";

7306: Make a note of the first empty slot in the "inode" table;

7309: If the "inode" table is full, send a message to the operator, and take an error exit;

7314: At this point, a new entry is to be made in the "inode" table;

7319: Read the block which contains the file system volume "inode". Note the use of "bread" instead of "readi", the assumption that "inode" information begins in block #2 and the convention that valid "inode" numbers begin at one (not zero);

7326: A read error at this point isn't very well reported to the rest of the system;

7328: Copy the relevant "inode" information. This code makes implicit use of the contents of the file "ino.h" (Sheet 56), which isn't referenced explicitly anywhere.

Let us now return to unfinished business:

7292: The "IMOUNT" flag is found to be set. This flag was set by "smount", when a file system volume was mounted;

7293: Search the "mount" table to find the entry which points to the current "inode". (Although searching this table is not a horrendous overhead, it does seem possible that a "back pointer" could be conveniently stored in in the "inode" e.g. in the "i_lastr" field. This would save both time and code space.);

7396: Reset "dev" and "ino" to the mounted device number and the "inode" number of the root directory on the mounted file system volume. Start again.

Clearly, since "iget" is called by "namei" (7534, 7664), this technique allows the whole directory structure on the mounted file system volume to be integrated into the pre-existing directory structure. If we momentarily ignore the possible deviations of directory structures away from tree structures, we have the situation where a leaf of the existing tree is being replaced by an entire subtree.

getfs (7167)

There is little that needs to be said about this procedure in addition to the author's comment. This procedure is called by

```
"access"  (6754)    "ialloc"  (7072)
"alloc"   (6961)    "ifree"   (7138)
"free"    (7004)    "iupdat"  (7383)
```

Note the cunning use of "n1", "n2" which are declared as character pointers i.e. as unsigned integers. This allows only one sided tests on the two variables at line 7177.

update (7201)

The function of this procedure, in its broadest terms, is to ensure that information on the file system volumes is kept up to date. The comment for this procedure (beginning on line 7190) describes the three main sub-functions, (in the reverse order!).

"update" is the whole business of the "sync" system call (3486). This may be invoked via the "sync" shell command. Alternatively there is a standard system program which runs continuously and whose only function is to call "sync" every 30 seconds. (See "UPDATE(VIII)" in the UPM.)

"update" is called by "sumount" (6150) before a file system volume is unmounted, and by "panic" (2420) as the last action of the system before activity ceases.

7207: If another execution of "update" is under way, then just return;

7210: Search the "mount" table;

7211: For each mounted volume, ...

7213: Unless the file system has not been recently modified or the "super block" is locked or the volume has been mounted "read only" ...

7217: Update the "super block", copy it into a buffer and write the buffer out onto the volume;

7223: Search the "inode" table, and for each non-null entry, lock the entry and call "iupdat" to update the "inode" entry on the volume if appropriate;

7229: Allow additional executions of "update" to commence;

7230: "bflush" (5229) forces out any "delayed write" blocks.

sumount (6144)

This system call deletes an entry for a mounted device from the "mount" table. The purpose of this call is to ensure that traffic to and from the device is terminated properly, before the storage device is physically removed from the access device.

6154: Search the "mount" table for the appropriate entry;

6161: Search the "inode" table for any outstanding entries for files on the device. If any such exist, take an error exit, and do not change the "mount" table entry;

6168: Clear the "IMOUNT" flag.

Resource Allocation

Our attention now turns to the management of the resources of an individual FSV (file system volume).

Storage blocks are allocated from the free list by "alloc" at the request of "bmap". Storage blocks are returned to the free list by "free" at the behest of "itrunc" (which is called by "core", "openl" and "iput").

Entries in the FSV "inode" tables are made by "ialloc", which is called by "maknode" and "pipe". Entries in this table are cancelled by "ifree", which is called by "iput".

The "super block" for the FSV is central to the resource management procedures. The "super block" (5561) contains:

   size information (total resources available);

   list of up to 100 available storage blocks;

list of up to 100 available "inode" entries;

   locks to control manipulation of the above lists;

   flags;

   current date of last update.

If the list in core of available "inode" entries for the file system volume ever becomes exhausted, then the entire table on the FSV is read and searched to rebuild the list. Conversely if the available "inode" table overflows, additional entries are simply forgotten to be rediscovered later.

A different strategy is used for the list of available storage blocks. These blocks are arranged in groups of up to one hundred blocks. The first block in each group (except the very first) is used to store the addresses of the blocks belonging to the previous group. Addresses of blocks in the last incomplete group are stored in the "super block".

The first entry in the first list of block numbers is zero, which acts as a sentinel. Since the whole list is subject to a LIFO discipline, discovery of a block number of zero in the list signifies that the list is in fact empty.

alloc (6956)

This is called by "bmap" (6435, 6448, 6468, 6480, 6497) whenever a new storage block is needed to store part of a file.

6961: Convert knowledge of the device name into a pointer to the "super block";

6962: If "s_flock" is set, the list of available blocks is currently being updated by another process;

6967: Obtain the block number of the next available storage block;

6968: If the last block number on the list is zero, the entire list is now empty;

6970: "badblock" (7040) is used to check that the block number obtained from the list seems reasonable;

6971: If the list of available blocks in the "super block" is now empty, then the block just located will contain the addresses of the next group of 100 free blocks;

6972: Set "s_flock" to delay any other process from getting a "no space" indication before the list of available blocks in the "super block" can be replenished;

6975: Determine the number of valid entries in the list to be copied;

6978: Reset "s_flock", and "wakeup" anyone waiting;

6982: Clear the buffer so that any information recorded in the file by default will be all zeros;

6983: Set the "modified" flag to ensure that the "super block" will be written out by "update" (7213).

itrunc (7414)

This procedure is called by "core" (4112), "openl" (5825) and "iput" (7353). In the first two cases, the contents of the "file" are about to be replaced. In the third case, the file is about to be abandoned.

7421: If the file is a character or block special file then there is nothing to do;

7423: Search backwards the list of block numbers stored in the "inode";

indirect fetch is needed. (A double indirect fetch is needed for
blocks numbered seven and
higher.);

7427: Reference all 257 elements of the
buffer in reverse order. (Note
this seems to be the only place
where characters #512, #513 of
the buffer area are referenced.
Since they will presumably contain zero, they will contribute
nothing to the calculation. Hence
if "510" were substituted for
"512" here, and again on line
7432, a general improvement all
round would result (?));

7438: "free" returns an individual
block to the available list;

7439: This is the end of the "for"
statement commencing on line
7427. (Likewise the statement
which begins at 7432 ends at
7435.);

7443: Clear the entry in "i_addr[ ]";

7445: Reset size information, and flag
the "inode" as "updated".

free (7000)

This procedure is called by "itrunc"
(7435, 7438, 7442) to reinsert a simple
storage block into the available list
for a device.

7005: It is not clear why the "s_fmod"
flag is set here as well as at
the end of the procedure (line
7026). Any suggestions?

7006: Observe the locking protocol;

7010: If no free blocks previously
existed for the device, restore
the situation by setting up a one
element list containing an entry
for block #0. This value will
subsequently be interpreted as an
"end of list" sentinel;

"super block" is already full, it
is time to write it out onto the
FSV. Set "s_flock";

7016: Get a buffer, associated with the
block now being entered in the
free list;

7019: Copy the contents of the super
block list, preceded by a count
of the number of valid blocks,
into the buffer; write the
buffer; unset the lock and
"wakeup" anybody waiting;

7025: Add the returned block to the
available list.

iput (7344)

This procedure is one of the most popular in UNIX (called from nearly thirty
different places) and its use will have
already been frequently observed.

In essence it simply decrements the
reference count for the "inode" passed
as a parameter, and then calls "prele"
(7882) to reset the "inode" lock and to
perform any necessary "wakeup"s.

"iput" has an important side effect. If
the reference count is going to be
reduced to zero, then a release of
resources is indicated. This may be
simply the core "inode", or both that
and the file itself, if the number of
links is also zero.

ifree (7134)

This procedure is called by "iput"
(7355) to return a FSV "inode" to the
available list maintained in the "super
block". If this list is already full
(as noted above) or if the list is
locked (using "s_ilock") the information is simply discarded.

iupdat (7374)

This procedure is called by "statl"
(6050), "update" (7226) and "iput"
(7357) to revise a particular "inode"
entry on a FSV. It does nothing if the
corresponding core "inode" is not
flagged ("IUPD" or "IACC");

The "IUPD" flag may be set by one of

unlink (3530)	bmap (6452,6467)
chmod (3570)	itrunc (7448)
chown (3583)	maknode (7462)
link (5942)	namei (7609)
writei (6285,6318)	pipe (7751)

The "IACC" flag may be set by one of

readi (6232)	maknode (7462)
writei (6285)	pipe (7751)

The flags are reset by "iput" (7359).

7383: Forget it, if the FSV has been
mounted as "read only";

7386: Read the appropriate block containing the FSV "inode" entry.
As observed earlier with respect to "iget", note the the use of
"bread" instead of "readi", the
assumption that the "inode" table
begins at block #2 and the convention that valid "inode"
numbers begin at one;

7389: Copy the relevant information
from the core "inode";

7391: If appropriate, update the time
of last access;

7396: If appropriate, update the time
of last modification;

7400: Write the updated block back to
the FSV.

-oOo-

CHAPTER TWENTY-ONE

Pipes

A "pipe" is a FIFO character list, which is managed by UNIX as yet another variety of file.

One group of processes may "write" into a "pipe" and another group may "read" from the same "pipe". Hence "pipe"s may be, and are used, primarily for inter-process communication.

By exploiting the concept of a "filter", which is a program which reads an input file and transforms it into an output file, and by using "pipes" to link two or more programs of this type together, UNIX offers its users a surprisingly comprehensive and sophisticated set of facilities.

pipe (7723)

A "pipe" is created as the result of a system call on the "pipe" procedure.

7728: Allocate an "inode" for the root device;

7731: Allocate a "file" table entry;

7736: Remember the "file" table entry as "r" and allocate a second "file" table entry;

7744: Return user file identifications in R0 and R1;

7746: Complete the entries in the "file" array and the "inode" entry.

readp (7758)

"pipes" are different from other files in that two separate offsets into the file are kept - one for "read" operations and one for "write" operations. The "write" offset is actually the same as the file size.

7763: the parameter passed to "readp" is a pointer to a "file" array entry, from which an "inode" pointer can be extracted;

7768: "plock" (7862) ensures that only one operation takes place at a time: either "read" or "write";

7776: If a process wishing to write to a "pipe" has been blocked because the pipe was "full" (or rather because the valid part of the file had reached the file limit), it will have signified its predicament by setting the "IWRITE" flag in "ip->i_mode";

7786: Release the lock before going to sleep;

7787: "i_count" is the number of file table entries pointing at the "inode". If this is less than two, then the group of "writers" must be extinct;

7789: A process waiting for input will raise the "IREAD" flag. Since a pipe cannot be full and empty simultaneously, no more than one of the flags "IWRITE" or "IREAD" should be set at one time;

7799: "prele" unlocks the file and "wakes up" any process waiting for the pipe.

writep (7805)

The structure of this procedure echoes that of "readp" in many respects.

7828: Note that a "writer", which finds that there are no more "readers" left, receives a "signal" just in case he is not monitoring the result of his "write" operation.

(A "reader" in the analogous situation receives a zero character count as the result of the read, and this is the standard end-of-file indication.)

7835: The "pipe" size is not allowed to grow beyond "PIPSIZ" characters. As long as "PIPSIZ" (7715) is no greater than 4096, the file will not be converted to a "large" file. This is highly desirable from the viewpoint of access efficiency.

(Note that "PIPSIZ" limits the "write" offset pointer value. If the "read" offset pointer is not far behind, the true content of the "pipe" may be quite small).

plock (7862)

Lock the "inode" after waiting if necessary. This procedure is called by "readp" (7768) and "writep" (7815).

prele (7882)

Unlock the "inode" and "wake" any waiting processes. This procedure is called by several others (especially "iput"), in addition to "readp" and "writep".

-oOo-

Section Five is the final section: last but not least. It is concerned with input/output for the slower, character oriented peripheral devices.

Such devices share a common buffer pool, which is manipulated by a set of standard procedures.

The set of character oriented peripheral devices are exemplified by the following:

```
KL/DL11  interactive terminal
PC11     paper tape reader/punch
LP11     line printer.
```

CHAPTER TWENTY-TWO

Character Oriented Special Files

Character oriented peripheral devices are relatively slow (< 1000 characters per second) and involve character by character transmission of variable length, usually short, records.

A device handler (as its name suggests) is the software part of the interface between a device and the general system. In general, the device handler is the only part of the software which recognises the idiosyncrasies of a particular device.

As far as possible or reasonable, a single device driver is written to serve many separate devices of similar types, and, where appropriate, several such devices simultaneously. The group of "interactive terminals" (with keyboard input and a serial printer or visual display output) can just be coerced with difficulty into a single device driver, as the reader may judge during his perusal of the file "tty.c".

The standard UNIX device handlers for character devices make use of the procedures "putc" and "getc" which store and retrieve characters into and from a standard buffer pool. This will be described in more detail in Chapter Twenty-Three.

The "PDP11 Peripherals Handbook" should be consulted for more complete information on the device controller hardware and the devices themselves.

LP11 Line Printer Driver

This driver is to be found in the file "lp.c" (Sheets 88, 89). Much of the complexity of this driver is contained in the procedure "lpcanon" (8879). This procedure is involved in the proper handling of special characters and this is a separate issue from the one we wish to study first.

Initially one may ignore "lpcanon" by assuming that all calls upon it (lines 8859, 8865, 8875) are simply replaced by similar calls upon "lpoutput" (8986). "lpcanon" acts as a "final filter" for characters going to the line printer: handling code conversions, special format characters, etc.

lpopen (8850)

When a line printer file is opened, the normal calling sequence is followed:

"open" (5774) calls "open1", which (5832) calls "openi", which (6716) calls, in the case of a character special file, "cdevsw[..].d_open". In the case of the line printer, this latter translates (4675) to "lpopen".

8853: Take the error exit if either another line printer file is already open, or if the line printer is not ready (e.g. the power is off, or there is no paper, or the printer drum gate is open, or the temperature is too high, or the operator has switched the printer off-line.)

8857: Set the "lp11.flag" to indicate that the file is open, the printer has a "form feed" capability and lines are to be indented by eight characters.

Notes

(A). "lp11" is a seven word structure defined beginning at line 8829. The first three words of the structure in fact constitute a structure of type "clist" (7908). Only the first element is explicitly manipulated in "lp.c". The next two are used implicitly by "putc" and "getc".

(B). "flag" is the fourth element of the structure. The remaining three elements are

"mcc"	maximum character count
"ccc"	current character count
"mlc"	maximum line count

(C). The line printer controller has two registers on the UNIBUS.

Line Printer Status Register ("lpsr")

bit 15 Set when an error condition exists (see above);

bit 7 "DONE" Set when the printer

controller is ready to receive the next character;

bit 6 "IENABLE" Set to allow "DONE" or "Error" to cause an interrupt;

Line Printer Data Buffer Register ("lpbuf")

Bits 6 through 0 hold the seven bit ASCII code for the character to be printed. This register is "write only".

8858: Set the "enable interrupts" bit in the line printer status register.

8859: Send a "form feed" (or "new page") character to the printer, to ensure that characters which follow will start on a new page. (As already noted above, at this stage we are ignoring "lpcanon" and assuming line 8859 to be simply "lpoutput (FORM)". "lpcanon" does things like suppressing all but the first "form feed" in a string of "form feed"s and "new line"s, to avoid wasting paper.);

lpoutput (8986)

This procedure is called with a character to be printed, as a parameter.

8988: "lp11.cc" is a count of the number of characters waiting to be sent to the line printer. If this is already large enough ("LPHWAT", 8819), "sleep" for a while (so as not to flood the character buffer pool);

8990: Call "putc" (0967) to store the character in a safe place. (The function of "putc" and its companion "getc" is a major topic to be discussed in Chapter Twenty-Three.) It should be noted that no check is made that "putc" was successful in storing the character. (There may have been no space in the character buffers.) In practice there seems to be no

real problem here, but one can wonder.

8991: Raise the processor priority sufficiently to inhibit the interrupts from the line printer, call "lpstart" and then drop the priority again.

lpstart (8967)

While the line printer is ready, and while there are still characters stored away in the "safe place", keep sending characters to the printer controller.

The presumption is that while the controller is building up a set of characters for a complete line, the "DONE" bit will reset faster than the CPU can feed characters to the controller.

However once a print cycle has been initiated, the "DONE" bit will not be reset again for a period of the order of 100 milliseconds (depending on the speed of the printer).

Note that during this series of data transfers, interrupts will be inhibited and so "lpint" will not be getting into the act whenever the "DONE" bit is set, except possibly once at the very end when the processor priority is reduced again.

lpint (8976)

This procedure is called to handle interrupts from the line printer. As mentioned above, most potential interrupts are ignored by the processor. Those interrupts which are accepted by the CPU will be associated with either

(a) completion of a print cycle; or

(b) the printer going ready after a period during which the "Error" bit was set; or

character transfers;

8980: Start transferring characters into the printer buffer again;

8981: Wakeup the process waiting to feed characters to the printer if the number of characters waiting to be sent is either zero or exactly "LPLWAT" (8818).

This latter condition is somewhat puzzling in that it will only occasionally be satisfied. The intention surely is "if the number of characters in the list is getting low, start refilling". However if "lpstart" carries out a series of transfers without interruption (at least by "lpint") the number of characters could go from a value greater than "LPLWAT" to one less than this without this test ever being made. Accordingly the waiting process will not be awakened until the list is completely empty. The result could be frequently to delay the initiation of the next print cycle, and hence to allow the printer to run below its rated capacity.

One solution to this problem is to change entirely the buffering strategy for line printers. A less drastic change would involve inventing a new flag, "lpll.wflag" say, replacing lines 8981, 8982 by something like

```
    if (lpll.cc <= LPLWAT && lpll.wflag)
    {
        wakeup (&lpll);
        lpll.wflag = 0
    }
```
and replacing line 8989 by

```
    {
        lpll.wflag++;
        sleep (&lpll, LPPRI);
    }
```

lpwrite (8870)

This is the procedure which is invoked as a result of the "write" system call:

which (5755) calls "writei", which (6287) calls "cdevsw[..].d_write", which translates (4675) to "lpwrite".

"lpwrite" takes the non-null characters of a null terminated string recorded in the user area, and passes them to "lpoutput" (via "lpcanon") one at a time.

lpclose (8863)

The list of procedure calls which leads to the invocation of this procedure is similar to that for "lpopen". A "form feed" character is output to clear the current page, and the "open" flag is reset.

Discussion

"lpwrite" is called one or more times to send a string of characters to the printer. In turn it calls "lpcanon" which calls "lpoutput". If at any point too many characters are stored away, the process will "sleep" in "lpoutput". Sooner or later "lpoutput" will continue, will store the character in a buffer area, and will then call "lpstart" to send, if possible, a string of characters to the printer controller.

"lpstart" is called both when more characters are available to be sent, and when an interrupt from the printer is taken.

The majority of calls on "lpstart" will in fact achieve nothing. Occasionally (usually when the printer has just completed a print cycle) "lpstart" will be able to send a whole string of characters to the printer controller.

lpcanon (8879)

This procedure interprets characters being sent to the line printer and make various modifications, insertions and deletions. It thus functions as a filter.

8884: The section of code from here to line 8913 is concerned with character translation when the full 96 character set is not available, and a 64 character set is in use.

Since the capabilities of a printer do not usually change with time, the defined variable "CAP" (8840) must be set once and for all (at a particular installation).

The run-time test on
        (lpll.flag & CAP)
could be replaced by a compile-time test on
        (CAP)
and if the compiler has its "druthers", if CAP turns out to be zero, the whole section of code to line 8913 could be compiled down to nothing.

The present code could be said to plan ahead for a situation where an installation may have two or more printers of different types. Even so there is a basic inconsistency here in the use of "CAP", "IND" and "EJECT" on the one hand, and "EJLINE" and "MAXCOL" on the other. In fact since forms of different sizes are not uncommonly used on a single printer, the last two should not be constants at all, but should be dynamically settable.

8885: Lower case alphabetics are translated by the addition of a constant, which is conveniently defined as "'A' - 'a'";

8887: Certain of the remaining characters are special characters which are printed as a similar character with an overprinted minus sign, e.g. "{" (8889) is printed as "{";

8909: The "similar" character is output via a recursive call on "lpcanon", which will increment "lpll.ccc" by one as a side effect;

8910: Decrement the current character count (for the same effect as a "back space" character) and ...

8911: prepare to output a minus sign;

8915: The "switch" statement beginning here extends to line 8963. Certain characters involved in vertical and horizontal spacing are given special interpretations with delayed actions;

8917: For a horizontal tab character, round the current character count up to the next multiple of eight. Do not output any blank characters immediately;

8921: For a "form feed" or "new line" character, if:

  (a) the printer does not have a "page restore" capability; or

  (b) the current line is not empty; or

  (c) some lines have been completed since the last "form feed" character. then ...

8925: reset "lpll.mcc" to zero;

8926: Increment the completed line count;

8927: Convert a "new line" character to a "form feed" if sufficient lines have been completed on the current page, and the printer has a "form feed" capability;

8929: Output the character, and if it was a "form feed", reset the number of completed lines to zero;

Examination of this code will show that:

  (a) Any string of "form feed"s or "new line"s which begins with a "form feed", will, if sent to a printer with "form feed" capability, be reduced to a single "form feed";

  (b) A "form feed" character sent to a printer without the "form feed" capability, will cause a new line to be started but will be passed on otherwise without comment.

8934: For "carriage return"s, and, note, "form feed"s and "new line"s, reset the current character count to zero or eight, depending on "IND", and return;

8949: For all other characters ...

8950: If a string of "backspace"s (real or contrived) and/or "carriage return"s has been received, output a single "carriage return" and reset the maximum character count to zero;

8954: Provided the current character count does not exceed the maximum line length, output blank characters to bring the maximum character count to the current character count. (Perhaps these two variables would be more accurately called the "actual character count" and the "logical character count".);

8959: Output the actual character.

For idle readers: A suggestion

It will be observed that backspaces for overprinting or underscoring characters introduce separate print cycles, and where these features are in heavy use, the effective output rate of the printer may be drastically reduced. If this is considered a serious problem, "lpcanon" could be rewritten to ensure that no more than two print cycles are used per line in such cases.

========================

PC-11 Paper Tape Reader/Punch Driver

This driver is to be found in the file "pc.c" on Sheets 86, 87. It is simpler than the line printer driver in that there is no routine analogous to "lpcanon". However it is more complicated in that there is both an input and an output device which can be simultaneously and independently active.

A description of the operation of this device is included in the document "The UNIX I/O System" by D. Ritchie. Certain special features may be noted:

(1). Only one process may open the file for reading at a time, but there is no limit on the number of writers;

(2). This routine pays a little more attention to error conditions than the line printer driver, but the treatment is still not exhaustive;

(3). "passc" (8695) knows how many characters are required and returns a negative value when "enough" is reached;

(4). "pcclose" is careful to flush out any remaining characters in the input queue if and only if it believes the device was opened for input.

-oOo-

CHAPTER TWENTY-THREE

Character Handling

Buffering for character special devices is provided via a set of four word blocks, each of which provides storage for six characters. The prototype storage block is "cblock" (8140) which incorporates a word pointer (to a similar structure) along with the six characters.

Structures of type "clist" (7908) which contain a character counter plus a head and tail pointer are used as "headers" for lists of blocks of type "cblock".

"cblock"s which are not in current use are linked via their head pointers into a list whose head is the pointer "cfreelist" (8149). The head pointer for the last element of the list has the value "NULL".

A list of "cblock"s provides storage for a list of characters. The procedure "putc" may be used to add a character to the tail of such a list, and "getc", to remove a character from the head of such a list.

Figures 23.1 through 23.4 illustrate the development of a list as characters are deleted and added.

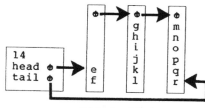

Figure 23.1

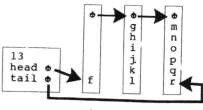

Figure 23.2

Initially the list is assumed to contain the fourteen characters "efghijklmnopqr". Note that the head and tail pointers point to <u>characters</u>. If the first character, "e", is removed by "getc", the situation portrayed in Figure 23.1 changes to that of Figure 23.2. The character count has been decremented and the head pointer has been advanced by one character position.

If a further character, "f", is removed from the head of the list, the situation becomes as in Figure 23.3. The character count has been decremented; the first "cblock" no longer contains any useful information and has been returned to "cfreelist"; and the head pointer now points to the first character in the second "cblock".

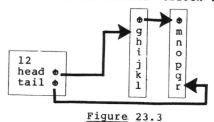

Figure 23.3

The question now poses itself: "how is the difference between the first and second situations detected so that the action taken is always appropriate?":

The answer (if you have not already guessed) involves looking at the value of the pointer address modulo 8. Since division by eight is easily performed on a binary computer, the reason for the choice of six characters per "cblock" should now also be apparent.

The addition of a character to the list is illustrated in the change between Figure 23.3 and Figure 23.4.

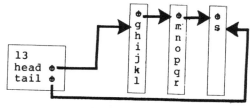

Figure 23.4

Since the last "cblock" in Figure 23.3 was full, a new one has been obtained from "cfreelist" and linked into the list of "cblock"s. The character count and tail pointer have been adjusted appropriately.

cinit (8234)

This procedure, which is called once by "main" (1613), links the set of character buffers into the free list, "cfreelist", and counts the number of character device types.

8239: "ccp" is the address of the first word in the array "cfree" (8146);

8240: Round "ccp" up to the next highest multiple of eight, and mark out "cblock" sized pieces, taking care not to exceed the boundary of "cfree".
Note. In general there will be "NCLIST - 1" (rather than "NCLIST") blocks so defined;

8241: Set the first word of the "cblock" to point to the current head of the free list.
Note that "c_next" is defined on line 8141, and that the initial value of "cfreelist" is "NULL".

8242: Update "cfreelist" to point to the new head of the list;

8244: Count the number of character device types. Upon reference to "cdevsw" on Sheet 46, it will be seen that "nchrdev" will be set to 16, whereas a more appropriate value would be 10.

getc (0930)

This procedure is called by

    flushtty (8258, 8259, 8264)
    canon   (8292) pcread (8688)
    ttstart   (8520) pcstart (8714)
    ttread   (8544) lpstart (8971)
    pcclose   (8673)

with a single argument which is the address of a "clist" structure.

0931: Copy the parameter to r1 and save the initial processor status word and value of r2 on the stack;

0934: Set the processor priority to five (higher than the interrupt priority of a character device);

0936: r1 points to the first word of a "clist" structure (i.e. a character count). Move the second word of this structure (i.e. a pointer to the head character) to r2;

0937: If the list is empty (head pointer is "NULL") go to line 0961;

0938: Move the head character to r0 and increment r2 as a side effect;

0939: Mask r0 to get rid of any extended negative sign;

0940: Store the updated head pointer back in the "clist" structure. (This may have to be altered later.);

0941: Decrement the character count and if this is still positive, go to line 0947;

0942: The list is now empty, so reset the head and tail character pointers to "NULL". Go to line 0952;

0947: Look at the three least significant bits of r2. If these are non-zero, branch to line 0957 (and return to the calling routine forthwith);

0949: At this point, r2 is pointing at the next character position beyond the "cblock". Move the value stored in the first word of the "cblock" (i.e. at r2 - 8), which is the address of the next "cblock" in the list, to the head pointer in the "clist". (Note that r1 was incremented as a side effect at line 0941);

0950: The last value stored needs to incremented by two (Consult

---

Figures 23.2 and 23.3);

0952: At this point, a "cblock" determined by r2 is to be returned to "cfreelist". Either r2 points into the "cblock" or just beyond it. Decrement r2 so that r2 will point into the "cblock";

0953: Reset the three least significant bits of r2, leaving a pointer to the "cblock";

0954: Link the "cblock" into "cfreelist";

0957: Restore the values of r2 and PS from the stack and return;

0961: At this point the list is known to be empty because a "NULL" head pointer was encountered. Make sure that the tail pointer is "NULL" also;

0962: Move -1 to r0 as the result to be returned when the list is empty.

putc (0967)

This procedure is called by

    canon   (8323)
    ttyinput (8355,8358)
    ttyoutput (8414, 8478)
    pcrint   (8730)
    pcoutput (8756)
    lpoutput (8990)

with two arguments: a character and the address of a "clist" structure.

"getc" and "putc" have related functions and the codes for the two procedures are similar in many respects. For this reason the code for "putc" will not be examined in detail, but is left for the reader.

It should be noted that "putc" can fail if a new "cblock" is needed and "cfreelist" is empty. In this case a non-zero value (line 1002) is returned

<u>Note</u>. The procedures "getc" and "putc" discussed here are <u>NOT</u> directly related to the procedures discussed in the Sections "GETC(III)" and "PUTC(III)" of the UPM.

Character Sets

UNIX makes use of the full ASCII character set, which is displayed in Section "ASCII(V)" of the UPM. Since knowledge of this character set is often assumed without comment, not always justifiably, some comment here would seem to be in order.

"ASCII" is an acronym for "American Standard Code for Information Interchange".

Control Characters

The first 32 of the 128 ASCII characters are non-graphic and are intended for the control of some aspect of transmission or display. The control characters explicitly used or recognised by UNIX are

Numeric Value	Mnemonic	Description	UNIX Name
004	eot	end of transmission or (control-D)	004
010	bs	back space	010
011	ht	(horizontal) tab	'\t'
012	nl	new line or line feed	FORM
014	np	new page or form feed	'\n'
015	cr	carriage return	'\r'
034	fs	file separator or quit	CQUIT
040	sp	forward space or blank	' '
0177	del	delete	CINTR

It will be noted that the last two of these belong to the last 96 characters, or the graphic portion, of the code.

Graphic Characters

There are 96 graphic characters. Two of these, the space and the delete, are not "visible", and may be classified with the control characters.

The graphic characters may be divided into three groups of 32 characters, which may be roughly characterised as

I.   numeric and special characters
II.   upper case alphabetic characters
III.   lower case alphabetic characters.

Of course, since there are only 26 alphabetic characters, the latter two groups include some special characters as well. In particular, the last group includes the following six non-alphabetic characters:

140		reverse apostrophe
173	{	left brace
174	l	vertical bar
175	}	right brace
176	~	tilde
177		delete

Graphic Character Sets

Devices such as line printers or terminals which support <u>all</u> the ASCII graphic symbols are often said to support the 96 ASCII character set (though there are only 94 graphics actually involved).

Devices which support all the ASCII graphic symbols except those in the last group of 32, are said to support the 64 ASCII character set. Such devices lack the lower case alphabetics and the symbols listed above, namely "~", "{", "l", "}" and "~". Note that "delete", since it is not a visible character, can still be supported.

Devices in this latter group may be referred to as "upper case only".

Sometimes some of the graphic symbols may be non-standard, e.g."⌐" instead of "_", and this can be inconvenient, though not usually fatal.

UNIX Conventions

UNIX prefers, as the reader is no doubt well aware, to view the world through "lower case" spectacles. Alphabetic characters received from an "upper case only" terminal are translated <u>immediately</u> upon receipt from upper case to lower case. A lower case alphabetic may subsequently be translated back to upper case if it is preceded by a single backslash. For output to such a terminal, both upper and lower case alphabetic characters are mapped to upper case.

Equivalences for the five "upper case" special characters are as follows:

character	line printer	terminal
{	⊥	\'
l	≠	\(
}	≠	\!
~	±	\)
	≐	\^

The conventions for line printers and terminals are different because:

(a)   for line printers, horizontal alignment is usually important, and it is possible (without too much difficulty) to print composite, overstruck characters (using the minus sign in this case); and

(b)   for terminals, horizontal alignment is not considered to be so important; backspacing to provide overstruck characters does not work on most VDUs; and, since the same graphic conventions are used for both input and output, the symbols should be as convenient to type as possible.

maptab (8117)

This array is used in the translation of character input from a terminal preceded by a single backslash, "\".

There are three characters, 004 (eot), '#' and '@', which always have special meanings and need to be asserted by a backslash whenever they are to be interpreted literally. These three characters occur in "maptab" in their "natural" locations (i.e. their locations in the ASCII table). Thus for example '#' has code 043 and

$$maptab[043] == 043.$$

The other non-null characters in "maptab" are involved in the translation of input characters from "upper case only" devices and do not occur in their "natural" locations but in the location of their equivalent character, e.g. "{" occurs in the natural location for "(", since "\(" will be interpreted as "{", etc.

Note the situation regarding alphabetic characters. This is only explicable when it is remembered that the alphabetic characters are all translated to lower case before any backslash is recognised.

partab (7947)

This array consists of 256 characters, like "maptab". Unfortunately the initialisation of "partab" was omitted from the UNIX Operating System Source Code booklet. It is certainly needed, and so is given now:

```
char partab [] {

0001,0201,0201,0001,0201,0001,0001,0201,
0202,0004,0003,0205,0005,0206,0201,0201,
0201,0001,0001,0201,0001,0201,0201,0001,
0001,0201,0201,0001,0201,0001,0001,0201,
0200,0000,0000,0200,0000,0200,0200,0000,
0000,0200,0200,0000,0200,0000,0000,0200,
0000,0200,0200,0000,0200,0000,0000,0200,
0200,0000,0000,0200,0000,0200,0200,0000,
0200,0000,0000,0200,0000,0200,0200,0000,
0000,0200,0200,0000,0200,0000,0000,0200,
0000,0200,0200,0000,0200,0000,0000,0200,
0200,0000,0000,0200,0000,0200,0200,0000,
0000,0200,0200,0000,0200,0000,0000,0200,
0200,0000,0000,0200,0000,0200,0200,0000,
0200,0000,0000,0200,0000,0200,0200,0000,
0000,0200,0200,0000,0200,0000,0000,0201

};
```

Each element of "partab" is an eight bit character, which, with the use of appropriate bitmasks (0200 and 0177), can be interpreted as a two part structure:

bit 7   parity bit;
bits 3-6   not used. Always zero;
bits 0-2   code number.

The parity bit is appended to the seven bit ASCII code when a character is transmitted by the computer, to form an eight bit code with even parity.

The code number is used by "ttyoutput" (8426) to classify the character into one of seven categories for determining the delay which should ensue before the transmission of the next character. (This is particularly important for mechanical printers which require time for the carriage to return from the end of a line, etc.)

-oOo-

(d) output technique: serial printer or visual display;

(e) miscellaneous: combined carriage return/line feed character; half duplex terminal (input characters do not need echoing); recognition of tab characters;

(f) characteristic delays for certain control functions, e.g. carriage returns may not be completed within a single character transmission time, etc.

Interfaces

As well as the wide variety of terminals which are available and in use, there is also a variety of hardware devices which may be used to interface a terminal to a PDP 11 computer. For example:

DL11/KL11 single line, asynchronous interface; 13 standard transmission rates between 40 and 9600 baud;

DJ11 16 line, asynchronous, buffered serial line multiplexer; 11 speeds between 75 and 9600 baud, selectable in four line groups;

DH11 16 line, asynchronous, buffered, serial line multiplexer; 14 speeds, individually selectable; DMA transmission

Each of the above interfaces will work in full or half duplex mode; handle 5, 6, 7 or 8 level codes; generate odd, even or no parity; and generate a stop code of 1, 1.5 or 2 bits.

In addition to the above asynchronous interfaces, there are a number of synchronous interfaces, e.g. DQ11.

CHAPTER TWENTY-FOUR

Interactive Terminals

Our remaining task, to be completed in this and the following chapter, is to consider the code which controls interactive terminals (or "terminals", for short).

A wide variety of terminals is available and several different types may be simultaneously attached to a single computer. Distinguishing characteristics for different classes of terminal include (besides such non-essential features as shape, size and colour):

(a) transmission speed, e.g. 110 baud for an ASR33 teletype, 300 baud for a DECwriter, 2400 baud or 9600 baud for a Visual Display Unit ("VDU");

(b) graphic character set, notably the full ASCII graphic set and the 64 graphic subset;

(c) transmission parity: odd, even, none or inoperative;

Each interface has its own control characteristics and it requires a separate operating system device driver. The common code which can be shared between these is gathered into a single file "tty.c", to be found on Sheets 81 to 85. A set of common definitions is gathered in the file "tty.h" on Sheet 79.

By way of example, Sheet 80 contains the file "kl.c", which constitutes the device driver for a set of DL11/KL11 interfaces. This device driver always needs to be present, since one KL11 interface is invariably included in a system for the the operator's console terminal.

The 'tty' Structure (7926)

An instance of "tty" is associated with every terminal port to the system (no matter what type of hardware interface is used). A "port" in this context is a place to attach a terminal line. Hence a DL11 supplies only one port, whereas a DJ11 supplies up to sixteen ports.

The "tty" structure consists of sixteen words and includes:

A. t_dev   fixed for a particular
   t_addr   terminal port;

B. t_speeds   fixed for a particular
   t_erase   terminal. These values may
   t_kill   be set by "stty" and
   t_flags   interrogated by "gtty";

C. t_rawq   list heads for three char-
   t_canq   acter queues: the so-
   t_outq   called "raw" input,
              "cooked" input and the
              output queues;

D. t_state   status information which
   t_delct   changes frequently during
   t_col   normal processing;
   t_char

Table 24.1

Note

The reader should study the information on Sheet 79 carefully. Certain items listed below are not referenced in any essential way in the selection of code examined here.

t_char	(7940)	NLDELAY	(7974)
t_speeds	(7941)	TBDELAY	(7975)
HUPCL	(7966)	CRDELAY	(7976)
ODDP	(7972)	WOPEN	(7985)
EVENP	(7973)	ASLEEP	(7993)

Initialisation

Initialisation of the "tty" structures is the responsibility of the various "open" routines in the device drivers, for example, "klopen" (8023).

The items in Group B of Table 24.1 may be changed by a "stty" system call. The current values may be interrogated by a "gtty" system call.

A description of these is contained in the sections, "STTY(II)" and "GTTY(II)" of the UPM. These calls are invoked by the "stty" shell command which is described in the section "STTY(I)".

Since the "stty" and "gtty" system calls require a file descriptor as a parameter, they can only be applied to an "open" character special file.

The two system calls share a good deal of common code. We will trace the progress of an execution of "stty" below and leave the tracing of a similar execution of "gtty" to the reader.

stty (8183)

This procedure implements the "stty" system call. It copies three words of user parameter information into

"u.u_arg[..]" using the parameter supplied as a pointer, and then calls "sgtty".

sgtty (8201)

8206: Get a validated pointer to a "file" array entry;

8209: Check that the file is a "character special";

8213: Call the appropriate "d_sgtty" routine for the device type. (See Sheet 46.)

Note that the "d_sgtty" routine is "nodev" for the line printer and paper tape reader/punch.

klsgtty (8090)

This is an example of a "d_sgtty" routine. It calls "ttystty" passing a pointer to the appropriate "tty" structure as a parameter.

ttystty (8577)

A call originating from "stty" will have a second parameter of zero.

8589: Empty all the queues associated with the terminal forthwith. They quite likely contain nonsense;

8591: Reset the speed information (useful in the case of a DH11 interface, but of little interest for the present selection of code);

8592: Reset the "erase" character and the "kill" character. ("kill" here denotes "throw away the current input line".) Note that if these characters are changed away from their normal values of "#" and "@" respectively, no corresponding changes are made to "maptab". Nor should they!);

8593: Reset the "flags" defining some relevant terminal characteristics (see Sheet 79):

flag bit if set ...

XTABS 1 the terminal will not interpret horizontal tab characters correctly;

LCASE 2 the terminal supports only the 64 character ASCII subset;

ECHO 3 the terminal is operating in full duplex mode, and input characters must be echoed back;

CRMOD 4 upon input, a "carriage return" is replaced by a "line feed"; upon output, a "line feed" is replaced by a "carriage return" and a "line feed";

RAW 5 input characters are to be sent to the program exactly as received, without "erase" or "kill" processing, or adjustment for backslash characters.

In addition, the following bits are interrogated by "ttyoutput" (8373) in choosing the delay which should ensue after the character indicated is sent, before sending the next character:

8,9	line feed;
10,11	horizontal tab;
12,13	carriage return;
14	vertical tab or form feed.

The DL11/KL11 Terminal Device Handler

The file "kl.c" constitutes the device handler for terminals connected to the system via DL11/KL11 interfaces. This group always has at least one member - the operator's console terminal. Hence this device handler will always be present.

vides an asynchronous, serial interface to connect a single terminal to a PDP 11 system. For more complete details regarding this interface, the reader should consult the "PDP11 Peripherals Handbook".

Device Registers

Each DL11/KL11 unit has a group of four registers occupying four consecutive words on the UNIBUS. UNIX maps a structure of type "klregs" (8016) onto each register group.

Receiver Status Register (klrcsr)

bit 7   Receiver Done. (A character has been transferred into the Receiver Data Buffer Register.);

bit 6   Receiver Interrupt Enable. (When set, an interrupt is caused every time bit 7 is set.);

bit 1   Data terminal ready;

bit 0   Reader Enable. Write only. (When set, bit 7 is cleared.).

Receiver Data Buffer Register (klrbuf)

bit 15   Error indication, when set.

bits 7-0   Received character, Read only.

Transmitter Status Register (kltcsr)

bit 7   Transmitter ready. This is cleared when data is loaded into the Transmitter Data Buffer, and is set when the latter is ready to receive another character;

bit 6   Transmitter Interrupt Enable. (When set, causes an interrupt to be generated whenever bit 7 is set.)

Transmitter Data Buffer Register (kltbuf)

bits 7-0   Transmitted data. Write only.

UNIBUS Addresses

The Receiver Status Register always has its lowest address starting on a four word boundary. (The addresses which follow are all 18 bit octal addresses.)

	Receiver Status	Transmitter Data
Operator's console	777560 ->	777566
Group Two	776500 ->	776506
	776510 ->	776516
	------	------
	776670 ->	776676
Group Three	775610 ->	775616
	775620 ->	775626
	------	------
	776170 ->	776176

Apart from the operator's console interface which has its own standard UNIBUS location, the interfaces are gathered into two groups (for reasons which are irrelevant here). Within each group, by convention, registers are allocated in consecutive locations starting at the lowest address.

Software Considerations

"NKL11" (8011) must be set to define, for a particular installation, the number of interfaces in the first two groups, and "NDL11" (8012), the number in the third group. Any hardware alterations which changed the actual number of interfaces would have to be reflected in the software by changing and recompiling "kl.c", and relinking the operating system.

It will be seen that "klopen" calculates the correct kernel mode address (16 bits) for the Receiver Status Register for each interface, and this is stored (8044) into the the "t_addr" element of the appropriate "tty" structure.

Interrupt Vector Addresses

The vector addresses for the first interface are 060 and 064 (for receiver and transmitter interrupts, respectively). Additional DL11/KL11 interfaces have vector addresses which are always at least 0300, and which are assigned according to rules which take into consideration other interfaces which may be present.

The second word of an interrupt doublet is the "new processor status" word. The five low order bits of this word may be chosen arbitrarily, and are in fact used to define the minor device number (cf. a similar use to distinguish the various kinds of "traps" - see Sheet 05). A masked version of the new processor status word is provided to the interrupt handling routines as the parameter "dev" (see e.g. line 8070).

Source Code

We can now turn to a detailed study of the code in the files "kl.c" (Sheet 80) and "tty.c" (Sheets 81 to 85). We shall look first at "opening" and "closing" terminals as character special files and the handling of interrupts. Then in the next chapter we shall look at the receipt of data from the terminal, and finally transmission of data to the terminal.

"klread" (8062), "klwrite" (8066) and "klsgtty" (8090) have already been discussed above.

klopen (8023)

This procedure is called to "open" a terminal as a character special file. This call is usually made by the program "/etc/init" for each terminal which is to be active in the system. Since child processes inherit the open files of their parents, it is not usually necessary for other processes to "open" the device again. It will be noted that the there is no attempt to stop two unrelated processes having the terminal as an open file simultaneously.

8026: Check the minor device number;

8030: Locate the appropriate "tty" structure;

8031: If the process opening the file has no associated controlling terminal designate the current terminal for this role. (Note that the reference stored is the address of a "tty" structure.);

8033: Store the terminal device number in the "tty" structure;

8039: Calculate the address of the appropriate set of device registers for the terminal and store in "t_addr";

8045: If the terminal is not already "open", do some initialisation of the "tty" structure ..

8046: "t_state" is set to show the file is "open", so that the next three lines will not be executed if the file is opened a second time, possibly undoing the effect of a "stty" system call;
"t_state" is also set to show "CARR_ON" ("carrier on"). This is a software flag which shows that the terminal is logically enabled, regardless of the true hardware status of the terminal. If "CARR_ON" is reset for a terminal, the system should ignore all input from the terminal.

(This does not seem to be entirely true, and this point will be taken up again later.);

8047: The standard terminal is assumed to be unable to interpret horizontal tabs, to support only the 64 character ASCII subset, to run in full duplex mode and to require both "carriage return" and "line feed" characters to provide normal "new Line" processing. (Could this be a Model 33 teletype?);

8048: The "erase" and "kill" characters are set according to the UNIX convention;

8051: The Receiver Control Status register is initialised with the pattern "0103" so that the terminal is made ready, reading is enabled and receiver interrupts are enabled;

8052: The Transmitter Control Status register is initialised so that an interrupt will be generated whenever the interface is ready to receive another character.

Note that the "open" routine does not distinguish between the cases where the file is opened for reading only, or writing only, or for both reading and writing.

klclose (8055)

8057: Find the address of the appropriate "tty" structure in the array of such structures, "kl11" (8015). (This operation may be observed in all the procedures in the second column of Sheet 80, and its relevance should be noted.);

8058: "wflushtty" (8217) allows the output queue for the terminal to "drain" and then flushes the input queue;

8059: "t_state" is reset so that "ISOPEN" and "CARR_ON" are no longer true.

klxint (8070)

This procedure is executed in response to a transmitter interrupt. It should be compared with "pcpint" (8739) and "lpint" (8976). Note that the parameter "dev" is a masked version (low order five bits preserved) of the "new processor status" word in the interrupt vector. Provided the vector was properly initialised, the minor device number will be properly identified.

The second part of the test on line 8074 will be discussed at the end of the next chapter.

klrint (8078)

This procedure is executed in response to a receiver interrupt. It is not so readily compared with "pcrint" (8719) although similarities certainly exist.

8083: Read the input character from the Receiver Data Buffer register;

8084: Enable the receiver for the next character;

8085: The comment says "hardware botch". Better believe it;

8086: Pass the character to "ttyinput" to insert it into the appropriate "raw" input queue.

-oOo-

"wflushtty" is called (8058) by
"klclose". This does not happen very
often - in fact only when all files
referencing the terminal are closed
i.e. usually only when the user logs
off.

The purpose of this procedure is to
"normalise" the queries associated with
a particular terminal. Its effect is
to terminate transmission to the terminal forthwith and to throw away any
accumulated input characters.

8258: Throw away everything in the
"cooked" input queue;

8259: ditto for the output queue;

8260: Wakeup any process waiting to
extract a character from the
"raw" input queue;

8261: ditto for the output queue;

8263: Raise the processor priority to
prevent an interrupt from the
terminal while ...

8264: the "raw" input queue is flushed,
and ...

8265: the "delimiter count" is properly
set to zero.

"flushtty" is called by "wflushtty"
(see below) and "ttyinput" (8346,8350)
when either:

(a)   the terminal is not operating in
"raw" mode and a "quit" or
"delete" character is received
from the terminal; or

(b)   the "raw" input queue has grown
unreasonably large (presumably
because no process is reading
input from the terminal);

wflushtty (8217)

This procedure waits until the queue of
characters for a terminal is empty
(because they"ve all been sent!) and
then calls "flushtty" to clean up the
input queues.

It is also called by "ttystty" (8589)
just before the terminal environment
parameters are adjusted.

Character Input

For a program requesting input from a
terminal, there is a chain of procedure
calls which extends to "ttread" ...

ttread (8535)

8541: Check that the terminal is
logically active;

8543: If there are characters in the
"cooked" input queue or a call on
"canon" (8274) is successful ...

8544: transfer characters from the
"cooked" input queue until either
it is empty or enough characters
have been transferred to suit the
user's requirements.

canon (8274)

This procedure is called by "ttread"
(8543) to transfer characters from the
"raw input queue to the "cooked" input
queue (after processing "erase" and
"kill" characters and, in the case of
upper case only terminals, processing
"escaped" characters, i.e. characters
preceded by the character '\'). "canon"
returns a non-zero value if the
"cooked" input queue is no longer
empty.

8284: If the number of delimiters in
the "raw" input queue is zero
then ...

CHAPTER TWENTY-FIVE

The File "tty.c"

In this, the last chapter, the intrica-
cies of interactive terminal handlers
are finally unveiled, including:

(a)   the handling of the "erase" and
"kill" characters;

(b)   the conversion of characters
during input and output for
upper case only terminals;

(c)   the insertion of delays after
various special characters such
as "carriage return".

The routines "gtty" (8165), "stty"
(8183), "sgtty" (8201) and "ttystty"
(8577) were dealt within the previous
chapter.

8285: if the terminal is logically inactive, then just return;

8286: otherwise go to "sleep".

Note that delimiters in this context are characters of all ones (octal value is 377) and are inserted by "ttyinput" (8358).

8291: Set "bp" to point to the third character of the work array, "canonb";

8292: Begin a loop (extending to line 8318) which removes one character from the "raw" queue per cycle;

8293: If the character is a delimiter, reduce the delimiter count by one and exit the loop i.e. go to line 8319;

8297: If the terminal is not operating in "raw" mode ...

8298: If the previous character (note the "bp[-1]" notation!) was not a backslash, '\', execute the code from line 8299 to 8307, otherwise execute the code beginning at line 8309.

Previous character was not a backslash

8299: If the character is an "erase" and ...

8300: if there is at least one character to erase, backup the pointer "bp";

8302: Start on the next cycle of the loop beginning at line 8292;

8304: If the character is a "kill", throw away all the characters accumulated for the current line, by going back to line 8290;

8306: If the character is an "eot" (004) (usually generated at the terminal as "control-D"), ignore it (and do not put it into "canonb") and start on the next

cycle;
(If this character occurs at the beginning of a line, then subsequently "ttread" (8544) will find no characters in the "cooked" input queue i.e. it will read a zero length record, which then leads to the program receiving the normal "end of file" indication.)

Previous character was a backslash

8309: If "maptab[c]" is non-zero, and either "maptab[c] == c" or the terminal is upper case only, then ...

8310: if the last character but one was not a backslash ('\'), then replace "c" by "maptab[c]" and back up "bp" (so that the backslash will be erased).

Character ready

8315: Move "c" into the next character in "canonb", and if this array is now full, leave the loop.

line completed

8319: At this point, an input line has been assembled in the array "canonb";

8322: Shift the contents of "canonb" into the "cooked" input queue, and return a "successful" result.

Notes

(A) The reason why "bp" starts (8291) at the third character of "canonb" can be found on line 8310.

(B) A number of subtleties in the handling of backslashes (which the reader will no doubt have encountered in his

practical use of UNIX) are still not immediately apparent. Since "maptab[c]" is zero for "c == '\'" (octal value of 134), all backslashes get copied into "canonb". A single backslash will be subsequently over-written if the following character is to be asserted (as in the case of '#' or '@' or eot (004), or if the case of an alphabetic character is to be changed for an upper case only terminal

ttyinput (8333)

"canon" removes characters from the "raw" input queue. They are put there in the first place by "ttyinput" which is called by "klrint" (8087) whenever an input character is received from the hardware controller.

The parameters passed to "ttyinput" are a character and a reference to a "tty" structure.

8342: If the character is a "carriage return" and the terminal operates with a "carriage return" only (instead of a "carriage return" "line feed" pair) change the character to a "new line";

8344: If the terminal is not operating in "raw" mode and the character is a "quit" or "delete" (7958) then call "signal" (3949) to send a software interrupt to every process which has the terminal as its controlling terminal, flush all the queues associated with the terminal, and return;

8349: If the "raw" input queue has grown excessively large, flush all the queues for the terminal and return. (This may seem a trifle harsh at first sight but it will usually be what is required.);

8353: If the terminal has a limited character set, and the character is an upper case alphabetic, translate it into lower case;

8356: If the terminal is operating in "raw" mode, or the character was a "new line" or "eot" then ...

8357: "wakeup" any process waiting for input from the terminal, place a delimiter character (all ones) also in the "raw" queue and increment the delimiter count. Note this is one point where possible failure of "putc" (when there is no buffer space) is explicitly recognised. A failure occurring here would explain why the test on line 8316 may sometimes succeed.

8361: Finally, if the input character is to be echoed i.e. the terminal is running in full duplex mode, insert a copy of the character into the output queue, and and arrange to have it transmitted ("ttstart") back to the terminal.

Character Output

ttwrite (8550)

This procedure is called via "klwrite" (8067) when output is to be sent to the terminal.

8556: If the terminal is logically inactive, do nothing;

8558: Loop for each character to be transmitted ...

8560: While there are still an adequate number of characters queued for transmission to the terminal ...

8561: call "ttstart" just in case it is time to send another character to the terminal;

8562: Setting the "ASLEEP" flag here (also in "wflushtty" (8224)) is rather pointless since it is never interrogated and never

reset until the file is closed;

8563: Go to sleep. In the meanwhile the interrupt handler will be draining characters from the output queue and sending them down the line to the terminal;

8566: Call "ttyoutput" to insert the character in the output queue and arrange to have it transmitted;

8568: Call "ttstart" again, for luck.

ttstart (8505)

This procedure is called whenever it seems reasonable to try and send the next character to the terminal. It often achieves nothing useful.

8514: See the comment on line 8499. This code is not relevant here;

8518: If the controller is not ready (i.e. bit 7 of the transmitter status register is not set) or the necessary delay following the previous character has not yet elapsed, do nothing;

8520: Remove a character from the output queue. If "c" is positive, the queue was not empty (as expected) ...

8521: If "c" is less than "0177" it is a character to be transmitted ...

8522: After setting the parity bit from the corresponding element of the array "partab", write "c" to the transmitter data buffer register to initiate the hardware operation;

8524: Otherwise ("c" > 0177) the character was inserted in the output queue to signal a delay. Call "timeout" (3845) to make an entry in the "callout" list. The result of this will be to initiate an execution of "ttrstrt" (8486) after "c & 0177" clock ticks . It will be seen that

"ttrstrt" calls "ttstart" again, and that the manipulation of the "TIMEOUT" flag (8524, 8491) will ensure that if another execution of "ttstart" is initiated in the interim, on behalf of the same terminal, it will (8518) return without doing anything.

ttrstrt (8486)

See the comment above for line 8524.

ttyoutput (8373)

This procedure has more comments in the source code and hence requires less explanation than some others. Note the use of recursion (8392) to generate a string of blanks in place of a tab character. Other recursive calls are on lines 8403 and 8413.

Terminals with a restricted character set

8400: "colp" points to a string of pairs of characters. If the character to be output matches the second character of any of these pairs, the character is replaced by a backslash followed by the first character of the pair.

8407: Lower case alphabetics are converted to upper case alphabetics by the addition of a constant.

Note. The conversion here should be compared with the handling of the reverse problem on input. Here we have an algorithm which clearly trades space (no table analogous to "maptab") for time (a serial search through the string on line 8400). A space conserving approach could be adopted in "canon" but the problem is rather more complicated there.

8414: Insert the character into the output queue. If perchance, "putc" fails for lack of buffer space, don't worry about inserting any subsequent delay, or updating the system's idea of the current printing column;

8423: Set "colp" to point to the "t_col" character of the "tty" structure, i.e. "*colp" has a value which is the ordinal number of the column which has just been printed;

8424: Set "ctype" to the element of "partab" corresponding to the output character "c";

8425: Clear "c";

8426: Mask out the significant bits of "ctype" and use the result as the "switch" index;

8428: (Case 0) The common situation! Increment "t_col";

8431: (Case 1) Non-printing characters. This group consists of the first, third and fourth octet of the ASCII character set, plus "so" (016), "si" (017) and "del" (0177). Don't increment "t_col";

8434: (Case 2) Backspace. Decrement "t_col" unless it is already zero;

8439: (Case 3) Newline. Obviously "t_col" should be set to zero. The main problem is to calculate the delay which should ensue before another character is sent.

For a Model 37 teletype, this depends on how far the print mechanism has progressed across the page. The value chosen is at least a tenth of a second (six clock ticks) and may be as much as ((132/16) + 3)/60 = 0.19 seconds.

For a VT05, the delay is 0.1 second. For a DECwriter it is zero because the terminal

incorporates buffer storage and has a double speed "catch up" print mode;

8451: (Case 4) Horizontal tab. Assign the value of bits 10, 11 of "t_flags" to "ctype";

8453: For the only non-trivial case recognised ("c" == 1 or Model 37 teletype), calculate the the number of positions to the next tab stop (via the obscure calculation of line 8454). If this turns out to be four columns or less, take it as zero;

8458: Round "*colp" (i.e. the value pointed to by "colp"!) to the next multiple of 8 less one;

8459: Increment "*colp" to be an exact multiple of eight;

8462: (Case 5) Vertical Motion. If bit 14 is set in "t_flags", make the delay as long as possible, i.e. 0177 or 127 clock ticks, i.e. just over two seconds;

8467: (Case 6) Carriage Return. Assign the value of bits 12, 13 of "t_flags" to "ctype";

8469: For the first class, allow a delay of five clock ticks;

8472: For the second class, allow a delay of ten clock ticks;

8475: Set the "*colp" (the last column printed) to zero.

====================

Before leaving the file "tty.c", there are two matters which deserve further examination.

A. The test for 'TTLOWAT' (Line 8074)

On line 8074 in "klxint", a test is made whether to restart any processes waiting to send output to the terminal. The test is successful if the number of characters is zero or if it is equal to "TTLOWAT".

If the number of characters is between these values, no "wakeup" is performed until the queue is completely empty, with the strong likelihood that there will then be a hiatus in the flow of output to the terminal. Since temporary interruptions to the flow of output are quite frequently observed in practice and represent a source of occasional irritation if nothing more, one may reasonably enquire "is there any way the character count can get from being greater than "TTLOWAT" to below it, without this being detected at line 8074?"

Quite clearly there is, since each call on "ttstart" can decrement the queue size, and only one such call is followed by the test. Thus if the call on "ttstart" from one of "ttrstrt" (8492) or "ttwrite" (8568) happens to cross the boundary, a delay will result. The probability that this will happen is small, but finite and hence the event is likely to be observed in any reasonably long output sequence.

There are two other situations in which "ttstart" is called which seem to be satisfactory. At "ttwrite" (8561) the queue is at its maximum extent; and at "ttyinput" (8363) there is a preceding call on "ttyoutput" which usually (but not invariably!) will have added a character to the output queue.

When the last special file for a terminal is closed, "klclose" (8055) is called and resets (8059) the "ISOPEN" and "CARR_ON" flags. However the "read enable" bit of the receiver control status register is not reset, so that incoming characters may still be received and will be stored away (8087) in the terminal's "raw" input queue by "klrint" (8078), and "ttyinput" (8333), which do not test the "CARR_ON" flag, to see if the terminal is logically connected.

These characters may accumulate for a long time and clog up the character buffer storage. Only when the "raw" input queue reaches 256 characters ("TTYHOG", 8349) will the contents of this queue be thrown away. It does seem therefore, that a statement to disable reader interrupts should be included in "klclose" before line 8058.

-oOo-

well, that's all, folks ...

Now that you, oh long-suffering, exhausted reader have reached this point, you will have no trouble in disposing of the last remaining file, "mem.c" (Sheet 90). And on this note, we end this discussion of the UNIX Operating System Source Code.

Of course there are lots more device drivers for your patient examination, and in truth the whole UNIX Time-sharing System Source Code has hardly been scratched. So this is not really

T H E   E N D

CHAPTER TWENTY-SIX

Suggested Exercises

Any operating system design involves many subjective and ad hoc judgements on the part of system's designers. At many places in the UNIX source code, you will find yourself wondering "Why did they do it that way?", "What would happen if I changed this?"

The following exercises express some of these questions. Some can be answered from an examination of the source code alone after a study in more depth; others require some experimental probing and measurement, for which read-only access to the file "/dev/kmem" via terminal will prove invaluable; and still others really require the construction and testing of experimental versions of the operating system.

Section One

1.1 Devise changes to "malloc" (2528) to implement the Best Fit algorithm.

1.2 Rewrite the procedure "mfree" (2556) to render its function more easily discernible by the reader.

1.3 Investigate the adequacy of the sizes of the arrays "coremap" and "swapmap" (0203, 0204). How should "CMAPSIZ" and "SMAPSIZ" change when "NPROC" is increased?

1.4 Prove that "malloc" and "mfree" jointly solve the memory allocation problem correctly.

1.5 By monitoring the contents of "coremap", estimate the efficiency with which main memory is utilised. Estimate also the cost of compacting "in use areas" of main memory from time to time to reduce memory fragmentation.
Hence decide whether it would be worthwhile to extend the present memory allocation scheme to include memory compaction.

1.6 In setting the first six kernel page description registers, UNIX does not make use of all the hardware protection features that are available e.g. some pages which contain only pure text could be made read-only. Devise changes to the code to maximise the use of the available hardware protection.

1.7 Compile the program
```
char *init "/etc/init";
main ( ) {
execl (init, init, 0);
while (1);
}
```
and compare the result with the contents of the array "icode" (1516).

1.8 Investigate the size required for kernel mode stack areas. Hence show that the 367 word area which is provided is adequate.

1.9 If main memory consists of several independent memory modules and one of these, not the last, is down, "main" will not include memory modules beyond the one which is down, in the list of available space in "coremap". Devise some simple changes to "main" to handle this situation. What other parts of the system would also need revision?

1.10 Rewrite the routines "estabur" (1650) and "sureg" (1739) so that they will work as efficiently as possible on the PDP11/40. How often are these routines used in practice? Would it really be worthwhile trying to implement your improved versions?

1.11 Investigate the overheads involved in initiating a new process. Perform a series of measurements for a set of different sized programs under different conditions.

1.12 Evaluate the following scheme which is intended by Ken Thompson as the basis for a revised scheduling algorithm:
A number "p" is kept for each process, stored as "p_cpu". "p" is incremented by one every clock tick that the process is found to be executing. "p" therefore accumulates the CPU usage. Every second, each value of "p" is replaced by four fifths of its value rounded to the nearest integer. This means that "p" has values which are bounded by zero and the solution of the equation $\{ k = 0.8*(k + HZ) \}$ i.e. $4*HZ$. Hence if HZ is 50 or 60, and "p" is integerised, "p" can be stored in one byte.

1.13 The "proc" table is always searched via a direct linear search. As the table size is increased, the search overheads also increase. Survey the alternatives for improving the search mechanism, when "NPROC" is say 300.

2.1 Explain in detail how the system reacts to a floating point trap which occurs when the processor is in kernel mode.

2.2 When a process dies, a "zombie" record is written to disk, and is subsequently read back by the parent. Devise a scheme for passing back the necessary information to the parent which will avoid the overhead of the two i/o operations.

2.3 Document "backup" (1012).

2.4 It is relatively easy using the "shell" to set up a set of asynchronous processes which will flood your terminal with useless output. Trying to stop these processes individually can be a problem, since their identifying numbers may not be known. Use of the command "kill 0" is usually an act of sheer desperation. Devise an alternative scheme, e.g. based on the use of messages such as "kill -99", which will be effective, but more selective.

2.5 Design a form of coroutine jump which will cause control to pass more efficiently between a program which is being traced, and its parent.

Section Three

3.1 Rewrite the procedure "sched" to avoid the use of "goto" statements.

3.2 Modify "sched" so that the text segment and data segment for a program will possibly be allocated in separate main memory areas if a single large area is not immediately available.

3.3 If the system crashes and must be "rebooted" the contents of the buffers which were not written out at the time

of the crash are lost. However if a core dump is taken, the contents of the buffers can be obtained and hence the contents of the disk can be brought completely up to date. Outline a detailed plan for carrying out this scheme. How effective do you think it would be?

3.4 Explain why the buffer areas declared on line 4720 are 514, and not 512, characters long.

3.5 Explain how deadlock situations may arise if there are too few "large" buffers available. What measures can you suggest to alleviate the problem, assuming that increasing the number of buffers is not possible.

Section Four

4.1 Devise a scheme for labelling file system volumes and checking these labels when the volumes are mounted.

4.2 Discuss the problems of supporting ANSI standard labelled tapes under UNIX, and propose a solution.

4.3 Design a scheme for providing index sequential access to files.

4.4 The emergence of the "sticky bit" (see "CHMOD(I)" in the UPM) confirms that there are some residual advantages in allocating all the space for a file contiguously. Discuss the merits of making "contiguous files" more generally available.

4.5 Devise a technique to measure the efficiency of pipes. Apply the technique and report your results.

4.6 Devise modifications to "pipe.c" which will make pipes more efficient according to the following scheme:

whenever the "read" pointer is greater than 512, rotate the non-null block numbers in the "inode" and decrease both the "read" and "write" pointers by 512.

Section Five

5.1 By monitoring the number of free buffers or otherwise, determine whether the number of character buffers provided at your installation is adequate.

5.2 Perform measurements and/or experiments to determine whether the character buffer blocks would be more efficiently utilised if they consisted of four or eight characters, rather than six, per block.

5.3 Redesign the line printer driver to handle overprinting and backspacing more efficiently in the sense of minimising the number of print cycles.

5.4 Document "mmread" (0916) and "mmwrite" (9042).

General

6.1 The easiest way to vary the main memory space used by the operating system is to vary "NBUF". If this is forbidden, propose the best way to:

(a) reduce the space required by 500 words;

(b) utilise an additional 500 words.

6.2 Discuss the merits of "C" as a systems programming language. What features are missing? or superfluous?

-oOo-

Procedure Index

APPRECIATIONS

Greg Rose

These two volumes first appeared as line printer listings, distributed a chapter at a time to the students of "6.602A - Computer Systems I", at the University of New South Wales, in 1976. The course was taught by Associate Professor John Lions. I was one of the students. It is twenty years ago, as I write this introduction, that John Lions was busy writing the *Commentary*, reformatting source code, and teaching the course.

In late 1974 and early 1975, the University of New South Wales was in the process of moving from an IBM 360/50 to a CDC Cyber/72 in its Computer Services Unit. The Cyber allowed Remote Batch Terminals, little areas with a card reader and a line printer, for job submission. One no longer had to go to the central site. Instead of expensive CDC machines to perform this function, DEC PDP-11s of various configurations were purchased. A bigger machine, a PDP-11/40 with three 2.5 megabyte disk drives and (later) 104 kilobytes of memory, was installed in the School of Electrical Engineering.

In June 1974, Ritchie and Thompson's paper appeared in the *Communications of the ACM*, describing the "UNIX Timesharing System." Since it ran on PDP-11s, and was available essentially for free, one of the lecturers wrote off for it. Niklaus Wirth's Pascal language was coming into vogue at the same time, and was available for the CDC Cyber. Ironically, John Lions wrote off to get Pascal, but it was maintained and taught by Ken Robinson; it was Ken who wrote off to get UNIX, which was then taken over, academically speaking, by John Lions!

This PDP-11 became the focus of UNIX development in Australia for a number of years, as John Lions and a bunch of staff and students fought to develop and use the machine for teaching and remote job submission. Battles around which operating system this machine should run caused a strike by academics and the resignation of a director of the central Computer Services Unit, and contributed to the promotion of the Department of Computer Science within the University hierarchy.

UNIX meant a lot to the University of New South Wales, as it did to other universities around the world. Up until that time, academics, researchers and students could study compilers, databases, and so on, but it was almost impossible to do anything "hands on" with operating systems. Real computers with real operating systems were locked up in machine rooms and committed to processing twenty four hours a day. UNIX changed that. The whole documentation, plus John's source code and commentary, "could easily fit into a student's briefcase". A few years later, John quipped that this was "fixed in 4BSD."

UNIX was available, and amenable, to study and experimentation by students. Enhancements from institutions around the world began to be exchanged, and contributed in no small way to the growth of UNIX. These two volumes made it far easier to get started with this kind of experimentation, and contributed greatly to the success of UNIX during the late 1970s and early 1980s.

One measure of the success of the *Commentary* and *Source Code* books was the number of illicit photocopies floating around. I was visiting a minicomputer company in 1987, and found a copy of the *Commentary* on a bookshelf. It had, based on the names written on the title page, been copied from a copy at least four times. It was nearly illegible, and yet was dog-eared from use.

John Lions had a number of reasons for writing *A Commentary on the UNIX Operating System*, and organising the course, the way he did. Many of these are listed in the original introduction. Not the least of these reasons was one which has rarely been expressed in print. He felt that all of the other courses making up the Computer Science degree program at the time, with the exception of the hardware course, involved teaching the students to write and debug programs. No other course required the students to be able to READ programs. The other courses usually involved the students with small (that is, manageable by students) programs, whereas the UNIX kernel was clearly a fairly large program. With biting sarcasm, John expressed this by saying "the only other big programs they see were written by them; at least this one is written well." In later years, teaching students to read and review code became accepted practice.

Looking back at the volumes now, I find these goals to be as relevant as ever. The UNIX Version 6 kernel is a well structured, concise program, and to this day I haven't found another program which demonstrates engineering tradeoffs so well. The insight and elegance is exposed, made accessible by the simplicity, juxtaposed with the compromises and inefficient code which simply didn't need to be optimised. Part of John Lions' achievement was recognising this, and working it into his books.

It is a pleasure and an honour to be asked to write this introduction for the new edition of John Lions' volumes. Rightly, that task should have been undertaken by John himself. Unfortunately, John is not well enough to do this. I hope I have expressed some of his feelings here. I owe him a great debt for his friendship and guidance through the twenty two years I have known him and been his student.

Greg Rose
Sydney, February 1996

Greg Rose studied at the University of New South Wales, then founded two software companies, one of which even survived the experience. After a sabbatical at IBM's T. J. Watson Research Center, and passing through the Australian Computing and Communications Institute, and Sterling Software, Greg has joined Qualcomm. Greg is a past president of Australian UNIX Systems User Group Inc., and a Director of USENIX.

Mike O'Dell

I still vividly remember reading about John Lions' booklets the first time. I was standing in the CS department office at the University of Oklahoma, going through my mailbox, and the latest version of *UNIX NEWS* had arrived. I stopped looking at the rest of the incoming mail to look at it. I was standing up against a bank of file cabinets, using the top as a reading stand, and in the middle of the first page was an article announcing that somebody down in Australia had written a *Commentary on the UNIX Operating System*. Even better, they were distributing it for a price even a graduate student could afford. The biggest problem was finding an up-to-date exchange rate table so I could translate the Australian price into US dollars (being utterly naive about the importance of sending native currency in such matters). I then dashed around and sent a check off straight away and then mostly forgot about it.

A month or so later, a package arrived from the University of New South Wales and the secretary saved it for me. She was very curious about a package from half-way around the world bearing an elaborate coat-of-arms. At first, I was also puzzled, but I opened it up and out came two thin but very colorfully-bound volumes: *A Commentary on the UNIX Operating System*, in red, and the *UNIX Operating System Source Code Level Six*, in orange, both prepared by one John Lions.

Several days later, I reappeared in the CS Dept. office and my professor, also the department chair, wondered where I'd been since I usually lived at the office as at least as much as at home.

I was beaming. "I've been reading this," holding out the books, "and now I know a lot more about how it really works!" Of course, "it" was UNIX Version 6. That was 1977, almost 20 years ago.

I looked back at my original copies not long ago and marvelled at how much things have changed, not all for the better. The C language back then was a much more graceful language. It lay on the page with a grace and beauty later bespoilt by the nattering legalisms of casts and politically-correct type definitions. The modern C language, for all its improved utility and portability, seems to have become mostly points and sharp edges, where the old language was flowing soft curves, molding itself around the concepts with a marvelous economy.

So too with the rest of the system. Yes, I enjoy the modern tty handler, able to squeeze ergonomically-useful behavior from the ugliest of terminals, and the networking subsystem which whizzes my keystrokes across an ISDN line to the machine I'm using to write this with better performance than I got on a local 9600 baud terminal. And most importantly, I *really* enjoy a filesystem which doesn't eat itself in a fit of pique when provoked by an unclean shutdown.

But that system in the books—it really is all there. Yes, the seats are better padded now, and the gearbox is synchromesh, but the real soul of the system was all there, and John Lions' marvelous exegesis revealed the inner beauty that Ken and Dennis set down. His commentary was spare but incisive, mirroring the shape of the code, filling in the curiosity just as the questions formed in my mind. A guided tour of a wonderfully curious museum display by someone who knew the deep meaning of the show in a most wondrous way, and always with a quick wit and gleam in his eye.

Quite a few years later, I was invited to attend the UKUUG meeting in Cambridge (the real one). En route, I stayed with a good friend who was having several other meeting guests at his house the weekend before the meeting. After arriving in London and being whisked down to Farnborough, I walked into the house and was greeted by the other guests, some of whom I knew well. Then I was introduced to John Lions. Slightly slackjawed, the only question I could form was "The John Lions?" He smiled sheepishly and said "You probably mean the books, don't you. Yes, I am." All I could think to do was thank him for launching me on a career and adventure richer than I ever could have imagined. I spent the rest of that weekend getting the "Cook's tour" of London architecture from John. He had been a student at Cambridge and visited London many times. We revisited many of his old haunts all over London. The quality of his gentle pedagogy was still a marvel.

Two years ago, I had the immense pleasure of presenting John the USENIX Lifetime Achievement Award, for launching the careers of a generation of UNIX hackers, many of whom played crucial roles at the companies which made a commercial and intellectual success of the code in the thin little orange book. His words in the thin little red companion helped provide the deep understanding that shaped people's thinking in fundamental ways.

John, every student has mentors who shaped their thinking and careers in fundamental ways, and while I never sat an hour in a classroom with you, please know that my debt of gratitude to you for those little books is simply eternal.

Mike O'Dell

Mike O'Dell went from Oklahoma to Lawrence Berkeley Labs, where he shared an office with Debbie Scherrer. After roaming from Berkeley to Washington, D.C. to Colorado Springs, he returned to the D.C. area. He was the founding editor of *Computing Systems* and Vice President of the USENIX Association. He is Vice President and Chief Scientist at UUNET Technologies.

Berny Goodheart

I first met John Lions in person when I migrated to Australia from England in 1989. Since then I have had the greatest pleasure of his friendship. In principle, however, I met John in the late 1970s when a friend (mentioning no names) furnished me with an early generation photocopy of his booklets. I still have those faded and very much used drum-rolled copies to this day. In some respects they have more sentimental value to me than a copy of the original booklets which John recently gave me. Like many students of that era studying computer science, John's booklets became a necessary part of my UNIX documentation which in itself was only a three-quarter inch thick bound document reproduced under licence from the Western Electric Company.

In July 1995, Associate Professor John Lions retired from the University of New South Wales after 23 years of service. During that time he made considerable contributions both in the school of Computer Science and previously in Electrical Engineering. In Australia, John has occupied a significant role in the profession. He was Editor of *The Australian Computer Journal* for many years and was responsible for installing the first UNIX system in Australia. In 1975, he founded the Australian UNIX User Group (AUUG) and in 1976 he wrote these booklets.

It is important to understand the significance of John's work at that time: for students studying computer science in the 1970s, complex issues such as process scheduling, security, synchronization, file systems and other concepts were beyond normal comprehension and were extremely difficult to teach—there simply wasn't anything available with enough accessibility for students to use as a case study. Instead, a student's discipline in computer science was earned by punching holes in cards, collecting fan-fold paper printouts, and so on. Basically, a computer operating system in that era was considered to be a huge chunk of inaccessible proprietary code. UNIX changed all this of course, but it wasn't until John's booklets that university students could really benefit from having a UNIX source licence on campus. Here at last was an operating system that could be used for case study. Unfortunately, the booklets had a limited distribution and were never formally published, but there were few university students around the world studying computer science who didn't have a photocopy of them.

The significance of John's work today is more for nostalgic purposes than for a practical one—besides, you are not expected to understand it! Modern UNIX systems and their look-alikes are much larger, radically different and more complex than the 10,000 lines of elegantly written code seen in the Edition 6 kernel, which John describes here. Furthermore, you would be hard pushed to find a working PDP11/40 let alone an RK05 with the Edition 6 distribution on it to boot. Nevertheless, what you have in your hands is the first ever and only public release of the UNIX system source code from Bell Laboratories. An operating system as John once described as being practical in size for a program which is to be understood and maintained by a single individual—a far cry from what can be said of modern day UNIX systems. Paradoxically, it has taken 20 years to publish this first ever UNIX book!

If the UNIX system's prominence came from its widespread use in universities, then John's booklets can be directly attributed to its success. It goes without saying then that we can thank John for his contribution to the success of the UNIX system and to the evolution of the computer system technology that we are currently witnessing.

Berny M. Goodheart

Berny Goodheart is the author of *UNIX curses Explained* and the co-author of *The Magic Garden Explained* and its *Solutions Manual*. He works for Tandem Computers in Sydney.

Peter Collinson

Computing has changed significantly in the twenty years since I started working with UNIX. I would like to give you some impression of why *A Commentary on the UNIX Operating System* was so important to those of us responsible for pioneering the use of the system.

I started with UNIX V6, as it became known later, about a year or so before the Lions book was made available. I was a lecturer in Computer Science at the University of Kent, Canterbury, UK. After a very short period of running UNIX experimentally on our PDP-11/40, we switched to full time use. I became responsible for providing a 'service'.

The UNIX distribution came on two RK05 packs, we had no tape drive. One RK05 contained the binaries, the kernel source and manual pages, and the other the source for the entire system. Just to put things in context, an RK05 pack held a little under 2.5 Megabytes. At the start, we had to remove the second disk pack to give users working space on the machine. Much later we obtained an old RP02, which was huge, holding 20 Megabytes.

The system was mostly documented by the source. If you wanted to change something, then you found the source, changed the code and installed the new version. The source was mostly in C, and was reasonably comprehensible. C was documented, very tersely, by the C reference manual. I mostly learned C by reading the code and changing the sources. This was a brilliant way to learn, you would find some example of how to do things and modify it for your own use. I miss this when grappling with new systems today. Of course, in extremis, it was necessary to resort to looking at the assembler that the compiler generated.

However, when you installed a new version of something and it didn't work, then you had to fix it. You alone were responsible. There was no one to ask using email, no Usenet news to broadcast a request for help, and no help desk to call. You existed in isolation. It was necessary to understand each change that you made, so you could get it right.

Several things helped. First, the code was nearly always very well written. Programs were modular, so it was hopefully not necessary to understand all of a program to make a change. Programs nearly always used the C pre-processor to define constants, so there were very few hard code magic numeric constants that defied explanation. Programs were small, they did one thing well and this made them more comprehensible. However, on the whole, if you didn't understand things, then you didn't meddle with the code.

The UNIX kernel fitted into this scheme. It was mostly in C, with only a small amount of assembler glue tying it to the hardware. It was very modular with clean interfaces between each section. Many people started hacking the kernel by writing device drivers, and I was no different.

There was some documentation on how to write a device driver. Dennis Ritchie had written a paper 'The UNIX I/O System' that explains how device drivers worked, you can still find this in the 4.4BSD Programmer's Supplementary documents manual published by USENIX and O'Reilly & Associates Inc.

Device drivers were required for several reasons. First, there was a need to make-do-and-mend. To add a printer onto our system, we connected it via a serial interface attaching the busy signal line on the printer to the interrupt line that was usually used to tell the interface that the phone had rung. This was my first device driver, or more accurately, I created it from bits of other drivers.

Second, there was a need to add drivers for new hardware that came along. I wrote a driver for an early floppy disk drive that appeared. Later I wrote a driver for the Cambridge Ring network that was being used to wire systems together on the campus.

Finally, there were several deficiencies in the system that we didn't really like. For example, the terminal interface was arcane. When you deleted a character, it didn't disappear from the screen, the delete character echoed a '#.' Changing this required a fundamental change to the terminal device driver. I also spent a lot of time squeezing performance from the system. I put some work into the RP02 driver, attempting to minimise seek time by starting the filesystem in the centre of the disk.

Device drivers had begun to appear courtesy of the UNIX user groups that had sprung up. Useable software emerged that was passed from hand to hand, usually on RK05 packs. The new terminal driver was a good example, it was originally written by folks at the Boston Children's museum and was worked on independently by three people in the UK, Emrys Jones in Swansea, Jim McKie in Glasgow and myself in Canterbury. We all had to understand the code, make sure it worked and install it into our systems. We all had to take the rap when things fell over. We didn't collaborate until much later when a single unified working version was generated and disseminated by UKUUG, the UK UNIX systems User group.

The start of Usenix and the UKUUG meant that there was a venue for people to ask for help, or more usually, offer it. The newsletter of Usenix, then called *UNIX News*, informed members of the existence of John Lions' *Commentary* in 1977. Later in the year, the UKUUG newsletter also carried the same information. We ordered three copies of the book from Australia.

A Commentary on the UNIX Operating System gave me the chance to verify what I already had deduced from the source. It closely documented the parts of the system that I did not understand. I think that when the books arrived I mostly needed to know how processes were managed, how fork/exec worked, process scheduling and the like. The book explained the famous comment: /* You are not expected to understand this */ By documenting the source as it was released from Bell Labs, John made his book accessible to all. His aim was to create a teaching document. The book did require you to apply your brain to the code, to read through the code line-by-line and comprehend what was happening. This meant that the book engaged you, it was not just documentation. It tried to make you understand what was going on in the system. As a result, the book is filled with questions that point the way to comprehension. The book also indicates deficiencies in the code, places where there was a better way of doing things. There were also challenges: try to write this code in a better way.

A Commentary on the UNIX Operating System provided me with the confidence to install other fundamental system changes that had come into the UK on a tape from John's group in Australia. Some of these were originated by Ken Thompson and fixed things like races in the pipe device driver. It was still necessary to follow the rules about understanding what the new code did. If it broke the system, then I got to fix it. John's book was an important part of my life for some time.

John's book didn't flood the world, at least not officially. Bell Labs took over distribution after a short time. At some point, we got a note from AT&T offering the book and saying that an academic site was permitted to have a single copy. By then, we had several. Many people who were around at the time talk of only seeing a photocopy of the book. There are jokes about the book being the most copied book of all time.

John's book gave many people the information that they wanted to know, it made learning about UNIX considerably easier. What's more, the information that you gleaned was correct. I am sure that the generation of UNIX gurus that the book nurtured now look back with a great deal of grateful thanks and respect for the man who wrote it.

Peter Collinson
Canterbury, Kent, UK
March 1996

Peter Collinson was one of the earliest British UNIX users and was instrumental in bringing *News* to the UK.

Peter Reintjes

I first heard about John Lions' *Commentary* in 1977, shortly after the 6th Edition of UNIX had been brought up on a PDP-11/45 at the University of North Carolina. The system was still largely a mystery to us and so we desperately wanted to believe the rumor that someone at the University of New South Wales had written an extensive analysis of UNIX. We soon came into possession of what looked like a fifth-generation photocopy and someone who shall remain nameless spent all night in the copier room spawning a sixth, an act expressly forbidden by a carefully worded disclaimer on the first page.

Four remarkable things were happening at the same time. One, we had discovered the first piece of software that would inspire rather than annoy us; two, we had acquired what amounted to a literary criticism of that computer software; three, we were making the single most significant advancement of our education in computer science by actually reading an entire operating system; and four, we were breaking the law.

We had been taught previously that an operating system was something only to be undertaken by an army of programmers. Once written, it would not admit analysis, composed as it was of millions of lines of assembly language instructions. Happily, Ken Thompson and Dennis Ritchie proved this wrong, producing a kernel for the Sixth Edition of UNIX in less than 10,000 lines of code that would not merely admit, but invite, analysis.

A novice reading this book might get the impression that UNIX is complex and has many flaws, but it must be stressed that it is the only real operating system that could even be subjected to this sort of analysis. UNIX is easily the most comprehensible operating system to walk the face of a disk, and with all its faults, it simply outclasses the systems which preceded it and arguably, those which have followed. And while it may have been superceded by more capable versions of UNIX, the Sixth Edition remains unparalleled in terms of capability provided per line-of-code.

A generation of UNIX kernel hackers learned from this book, circulated in *samizdat* editions after AT&T and Western Electric enforced restrictions on the distribution of this material and its use in teaching courses. I used the word "hackers" in the older sense of those who program incessantly and creatively rather than those who illegally break into computer systems, but the fact remains that we were breaking the law by possessing and circulating this particular collection of writing by Thompson, Ritchie, and Lions. Although we liked to complain about this and imagine ourselves as some sort of electronic freedom fighters, this was not really censorship of any kind. Western Electric was simply trying to protect the trade secret status of the UNIX System source code, something that the success of UNIX would make increasingly difficult.

Eventually, because Lions' *A Commentary on the UNIX Operating System* was such a valuable book, Western Electric relented and allowed each customer with a UNIX source license to have one copy — strictly forbidding the making of any more. But even with that concession, one still had to know about the existence of the book and submit a formal request to Western Electric, and of course, include the flap from the boxtop to prove that you owned an actual UNIX Source Code license.

The value of this book to those of us learning about UNIX and the intrigue surrounding its distribution have given this book a mythic status. Because we couldn't legally discuss the book in the University's operating systems class, several of us would meet at night in an empty classroom to discuss the book. It was the only time in my life that I was an active member of an underground.

Although this commentary does not represent a state-of-the-art UNIX implementation, it offers students of computer science, among which I still number myself after twenty years of programming, a chance to read production code written by excellent practitioners. It is first and foremost an opportunity to peer over the shoulders of Ken Thompson and Dennis Ritchie and see them at work. And it must be stressed that this was production code; the Sixth Edition of UNIX was used for many applications in addition to computer science research. Textbook examples of code may be elegant, but they often ignore difficult aspects of real world programming, such as error- and interrupt-handling.

In addition to thanking Dennis Ritchie for providing the high-level language for Ken Thompson to express himself, and to John Lions for translating it all into an even higher-level language, we also owe thanks to the management of AT&T Bell Laboratories for making it all possible. History is full of examples of how the most basic advancements can go unrewarded. The biggest problem with UNIX was that after the transistor and the laser, Bell Laboratories had again produced something of such immense value that it essentially belonged to the world. I have always been grateful to AT&T for not enforcing the basic patents on the transistor, and for being as generous as they were with UNIX Source Code distributions. And I have always felt guilty for having my copy of John Lions' *Commentary*, which was as important to my education and my career as the UNIX System itself. I now look forward to the prospect of purchasing a legitimate copy of this book.

Peter Reintjes
IBM T. J. Watson Research Center
February, 1995

Peter Reintjes currently works on multimedia Internet applications for NetSpeak Corporation. During his first ten years as a computer scientist he ported several flavors of UNIX to various machines and developed VLSI CAD applications for workstations for the Microelectronics Center of North Carolina. He was then actively involved in the development of logic programming applications in Prolog for Quintus Corporation and deductive database applications at IBM's T. J. Watson Research Center.

ABOUT THE AUTHOR

John Lions was born in 1937 in Sydney, Australia. He attended Sydney Boys High School and, in 1959, received his B.Sc with honours in Applied Mathematics at the University of Sydney. From there, he won a scholarship to the University of Cambridge in England where he worked with the EDSAC II, and in 1963 he completed a Ph.D in Control Engineering. Following this he took up employment as a consultant at KCS Ltd in Toronto, Canada, and in 1967 he took up a university appointment as Director of the Computer Centre and Associate Professor at Dalhousie University, Nova Scotia. In 1970, he went to Los Angeles where he worked on the B5000 for Burroughs as a systems designer. He returned to Australia in 1972 to take up a senior lecturer's post at the University of New South Wales.

In May 1974, John read Ritchie and Thompson's empirical paper, "The UNIX Time-Sharing System" in the *Communications of the ACM*, and became interested enough to encourage his colleagues in the Department of Computer Science to apply for a license. Several people on campus became interested in their new UNIX computer system since it offered better performance and more connectivity than the incumbent IBM 360/50 or their Control Data Cyber 72-26 system. It was even possible to run the line printer at its rated speed! The interest that it gathered led John to found the Australian UNIX systems Users Group.

John's continuing interest in the UNIX system led him to use the operating system for his classes. In 1976 he prepared a booklet for his students called "UNIX Operating System Source Code, Level Six," which contained almost the entire source code for Edition 6 UNIX that ran on the PDP 11/40—only a few device drivers were left out. The following year he completed a set of explanatory notes that was intended to introduce his students to the code. These notes eventually became known as *A Commentary on the UNIX Operating System*.

John wrote to Mel Ferentz, Lou Katz and others from USENIX (then the academic UNIX users association) and offered to make copies of his notes available to others. After some negotiation with Western Electric over the patent licensing, he distributed the notes to other UNIX licensees on request. A steady stream of orders from overseas followed—at one stage he received a bulk order for 200 copies from Bell Laboratories.

One night in 1978 John received a telephone call from Doug McIlroy at Bell Laboratories saying that they would like to assume responsibility for distributing the notes. John was happy to agree since the novelty of printing, packaging and shipping them on his own was beginning to wear off—he had shipped approximately 600 copies!

In mid 1978, John visited Bell Laboratories at Murray Hill, New Jersey after being invited by Berkley Tague to spend a sabbatical year there as a member of the technical team. Soon after, he was appointed Associate Professor in the Department of Computer Science. John returned to Bell Laboratories in 1983 and while spending his third and final sabbatical there in 1989 he prepared yet another set of notes similar to his UNIX commentary but this time based on Plan 9. The documents had restricted circulation within Bell Laboratories and were called "Plan 9: Volume 1: Kernel Source Code" and "Plan 9: Volume 2: Summaries & Commentary." In the years that followed John continued his academic interests, focusing more on computer networking.

John is a member of the Association for Computer Machinery and a Fellow member of the Australian Computer Society. Between 1982 and 1987 John was Editor of the *Australian Computer Journal* and is a Life member of the Australian UNIX Systems User Group.

In July, 1995 after 23 years of service, John Lions retired from the University of New South Wales due to his failing medical condition.

This biography of John Lions was prepared by Berny Goodheart with the help of John's wife, Marianne Lions, and several of his university students.

Other Books by Peer-to-Peer Communications

Building the ARPANET

Peter Salus (ed.)
ISBN# 1-57398-016-1
425 pages (estimated), due Summer 2005

Part I: Design

In 1966 the US Defense Department's ARPA office wanted a "heterogeneous" network that could connect diverse brands of machines, This historic research effort created the landmark ARPANET, the direct predecessor of today's Internet. Included in this volume are:

- The earliest handwritten RFCs (some never before available)

- Elmer Shapiro's SRI feasibility study which became the blueprint for the ARPANET

- The classic 1968 paper "The Computer as a Communication Device" (J.C.R. Licklider and Robert Taylor).

- Retrospective essays by key researchers and an introduction by series editor Peter Salus.

Part II: Construction

Based on the SRI study (see above!), ARPA awarded Bolt Beranek & Newman (BBN) the contract to build the ARPANET. Here, for the first time in print, are:

- The four 1969 BBN technical reports that paint a comprehensive technical picture of the year-long ARPANET development project that successfully linked four sites running heterogeneous machines on the same network

- A retrospective essay by Dave Walden, ARPANET team member and former VP of BBN, plus an introduction by Peter Salus.

Operating System Source Code Secrets

In 1989 Bill Jolitz (the chief developer of one of the early releases of Berkeley UNIX) and his wife Lynne began the 386BSD project, writing their own version of UNIX from scratch to run on IBM PCs. Their ambitious project captured the imagination of the computing world; Dr. Dobb's Journal ran an unprecedented 17-part serialization over a 2-year period.

The fruits of almost twenty years of 386BSD work (the operating system is still evolving) will eventually be published as a 5-book series *Operating System Source Code Secrets*. Its approximately 2500 pages will explore and explain the difficult implementation problems and underlying theoretical issues that all operating systems must balance.

Individual books in the series are:

Volume 1: The Basic Kernel
ISBN: 1-57398-026-9, 530 pages, Hardcover
Named a "Book of the Year" by *Unix Review* Magazine (1996)

Future Volumes:

Volume 2: The Virtual Memory System
ISBN: 1-57398-027-7

Volume 3: Sockets Operating System
ISBN: 1-57398-003-X

Volume 4: TCP/IP Networking Protocol
ISBN: 1-57398-007-2

Volume 5: 386BSD: From the Inside Out
ISBN: 1-57398-032-3

For current price and availability of these works please visit our website: http://www.peerllc.com

Lightning Source UK Ltd.
Milton Keynes UK
UKHW051212090720
366271UK00008B/1215

9 781573 9801